2004

Academic Library Trends and Statistics

for Carnegie Classification:
Master's Colleges and Institutions
Baccalaureate Colleges

compiled by
Library Research Center
The Graduate School of Library and Information Science
University of Illinois at Urbana-Champaign

Project Coordinator
Hugh A. Thompson
Association of College and Research Libraries

Association of College and Research Libraries
A division of the American Library Association
Chicago 2005

ISBN 0-8389-8353-7

Printed in the United States of America.

Association of College and Research Libraries
A division of the American Library Association
50 East Huron Street
Chicago, IL 60611

TABLE OF CONTENTS

INTRODUCTION

The publication of the *2004 Academic Library Trends and Statistics* marks the seventh year of ACRL's effort to provide timely data on academic library management on an annual basis. The ultimate goal is to represent libraries from all institutions of higher learning in the United States and Canada. With 1,119 institutions reporting out of a sample of 2,729, the total represents 41% of all institutions.

As was done previously, the survey collected data on a range of library operations, including collections, expenditures for operations, expenditures for computers and electronic resources, personnel and public services, and demographic information such as Ph.D.s granted and faculty and enrollment statistics. In addition, ratios such as support staff as a percent of total staff, serial expenditures as a percent of total library materials expenditures, and others, are provided. These data are intended to provide useful comparisons among peer groups as well as to facilitate benchmarking across various time frames. This year the survey also continued its examination of "trends": new activities or other developments of interest that might affect library operations and management.

The use of electronic resources by academic libraries has increased significantly during the last ten years. This trend has impacts ranging from expenditures to information delivery modes to use of space, among others. To quantify these impacts, the 2004 survey trends section adapted questions from the ARL supplementary form, which had originally been part of the E-metrics project. Principal areas of investigation in the trends section include electronic resources, network resources and services, and digitization activities.

ACRL feels that the data from the 2004 survey continues to meet a need among academic libraries for information on operations that can inform management decisions through comparison to other organizations, through benchmarking, and through awareness of current trends. We solicit your suggestions for ways this survey may be improved and for additional trends about which current data would be useful.

ACRL would like to acknowledge the contributions of Martha Kyrillidou from the Association of Research Libraries. The Association of Research Libraries publishes a separate publication entitled ARL Statistics. The ACRL publication on Academic Library Statistics would not have been possible without the generous support of the Association of Research Libraries (ARL) and its member libraries. ARL has supported the production of the ACRL/ALA publication on Academic Library Statistics by providing permission to utilize the ARL Statistics survey instruments and by providing full-access to the ARL Statistics data that are included in this compilation. For more information about the ARL Statistics and Measurement Program, please see: <http://www.arl.org/stats/>.

Hugh Thompson
Publications Manager
ACRL

The fiscal year 2004 Academic Library Trends and Statistics publication was prepared by the Association of College and Research Libraries (ACRL) and the Library Research Center (LRC) at the University of Illinois. Data was compiled from a web-based survey conducted December 12, 2004 through February 25, 2005.

Study Population
We defined the survey population as libraries at all accredited colleges and universities found in the United States (including Puerto Rico) and Canada. This population is defined in a similar manner to that of ACRL studies dating back to fiscal year 1999. The contact list originated as a commercially purchased list of college and university libraries. This list has been maintained and modified in previous years by the Center for Survey Research (CSR) at the University of Virginia. For the 2004 survey, the respondent population included 2,729 college and university libraries.

Questionnaire
As in previous years, ACRL has collaborated with the Association of Research Libraries (ARL) in this survey. The survey questionnaire and instructions were developed from the ARL Statistics survey. This was necessary to allow for the incorporation of data provided from ARL member libraries into the ACRL data set.

The 2004 ACRL survey gathered core information on collections, expenditures, personnel, instruction, public services, circulation, and interlibrary services. Additionally each year, ACRL selects a different area to gather information, referred to in the survey as the "trends" section. This year the survey collected data on Trends in E-metrics.

To simplify the data collection process, data was gathered by means of a web-based questionnaire. However, reporting libraries were given the option of completing and submitting a paper survey. The 2004 survey was administered by the LRC.

Survey Administration
The Library Research Center managed the development of the online form, the necessary web-hosting, data collection, analysis, and assisted in developing the final report. The web questionnaire was developed using commercial survey software. Each institution was assigned a unique respondent key, which served as both a unique identifier and a password for access to the web questionnaire.

All respondents, excluding ARL member libraries, were directed to an information website before entering the online survey. This website included the official invitation from ACRL Executive Director Mary Ellen Davis, survey instructions, instructions on the use of the online questionnaire, a frequently-asked-questions page, a link to the summary reports of previous surveys, and a link to begin the survey. The survey questionnaire itself was designed with a simple user interface to allow for navigation within the questionnaire and to save partial data. The questionnaire utilized "session" files so that respondents could save and resume the survey.

ARL member libraries were invited to a separate questionnaire, as they had already provided most of the requested data in the ARL Statistics survey. These institutions were directed to a questionnaire that consisted solely of the "trends" section. In the survey form, ARL member libraries were asked if they would give permission for the use of their ARL Statistics data in the ACRL Academic Library Trends and Statistics survey. Their trends information was then incorporated with their data from the ARL Statistics survey. We thank ARL for its cooperation in sharing this data.

The contact e-mail list was checked using e-mail verifying software to isolate invalid e-mail addresses. Those institutions with valid e-mail addresses were sent e-mail invitations during the week of December 12, 2004. Institutions for which we had no valid e-mail address were sent a paper invitation via U.S. mail the following week. Multiple reminders were sent to both groups. Institutions for which we had valid e-mail addresses were sent reminder e-mails on January 13th, February 14th and February 21st. Paper reminders were sent to those institutions for which we did not have valid e-mail invitations on January 28th and February 11th.

For the fiscal year 2004 survey a total of 1,119 institutions responded. The following tables show the final disposition from the ACRL 2004 survey broken down by country as well as by invitation medium.

Table 1. Final Disposition – Overall			
	Population (N)	Completed Returns (N)	Response Rate(%)
United States	2,568	1,073	41.8
Canada	161	46	28.6
Combined	2,729	1,119	41.0

Table 2. Final Disposition – E-mail Invitations			
	Population (N)	Completed Returns (N)	Response Rate (%)
United States	2,229	1,014	45.5
Canada	136	46	33.8
Combined	2,365	1,060	45.0

Table 3. Final Disposition – U.S. Mail Invitations			
	Population (N)	Completed Returns (N)	Response Rate (%)
United States	339	59	17.4
Canada	25	0	0
Combined	364	59	16.2

Coding Procedure

In order to present a clean data set, the LRC made an effort to locate and correct errors in the data. However, given the abbreviated time frame of this year's survey, we were unable to contact institutions which provided obvious data errors to determine the correct figure. In such cases, data was removed and replaced with the symbol "U/A" (data unavailable).

Institutions were assigned to one of four Carnegie Classifications based on the information provided by the Carnegie Foundation through a spreadsheet available on their website (cc2000-public.xls).

Canadian libraries were given the option of reporting expenditures in Canadian dollars. Expenditures indicated as reported in Canadian dollars were converted into U.S. dollars. The exchange rate used (0.813618, Canadian to U.S.) is consistent with that used by ARL to allow for accurate comparison between ARL and non-ARL member libraries.

Institutions were given the option of providing a footnote for each question. Footnotes were published as is, with the exclusion of minor editorial changes and the removal of notes that did not provide information useful to the interpretation of an institution's data. Respondents also had the opportunity to communicate with ACRL and the LRC through the "notes to the editor." This field was reserved for general comments not pertaining to specific data and is not published.

Library Research Center Acknowledgments

Prof. Leigh Estabrook, Director of the Library Research Center, and Edward Lakner, Assistant Director, gave valuable oversight throughout the project. Project Coordinators Diane LaBarbera, and Katy Mullaly gave additional assistance in the planning and execution of data collection and cleaning. Garret Gengler provided invaluable support in the maintenance of the survey software as well as help in managing the data set and mailing lists. Andrew Eldridge acted as the primary contact with ACRL and responding institutions, updated the online survey questionnaire and website, and oversaw data collection and cleaning. Lauren Drogos put an enormous effort into cleaning the final data. Navadeep Khanal worked on preparing the summaries and analyzing the variables. Charity Clevinger and Katy Mulally helped as contact people for respondents with questions. Our greatest appreciation goes to the thousands of library personnel who took the time to respond to this project. Questions may be directed to the Library Research Center, Graduate School of Library and Information Science, University of Illinois at Urbana Champaign, 501 E. Daniel, Champaign, IL 61820. The LRC may be reached by telephone at (217) 333-1980, or on the World Wide Web at: http://lrc.lis.uiuc.edu.

2004

ACRL LIBRARY DATA TABLES

Key to Notes and Symbols

B – Includes branch campuses

b – Bibliographic count

G– Government documents not included in serials count

L– Includes law library

M– Includes medical library

f – Figures include fringe benefits in expenditures for salaries and wages.

* – Includes both graduate and undergraduate students

ACRL LIBRARY DATA TABLES 2004

SUMMARY DATA: COLLECTIONS

ALL INSTITUTIONS REPORTING

(Survey Question #)	Volumes in Library	Volumes Added (Gross)	Volumes Added (Net)	Mono-graphs Purchased	Current Serials Purchased	Current Serials Not Purchased	Current Serials Total	Microform Units
	1	2	3	4	5	6	7	8
High	11,389,504	280,572	275,196	225,204	254,670	55,714	254,670	9,848,258
Mean	529,931	12,104	9,143	6,410	4,528	1,220	6,149	651,451
Median	155,822	3,544	2,164	2,251	710	28	929	72,414
Low	1,272	0	-136,025	0	0	0	0	0
Total	586,633,777	13,096,516	9,884,015	6,396,810	4,528,149	1,117,373	6,671,647	695,749,798
Libraries Reporting	1,107	1,082	1,081	998	1,000	916	1,085	1,068

ACRL LIBRARY DATA TABLES 2004

SUMMARY DATA: COLLECTIONS

ALL INSTITUTIONS REPORTING

Government Documents	Computer Files	Archives and Manus.	Carto-graphic Materials	Graphic Materials	Audio Materials	Film and Video	
9	10	11	12	13	14	15	(Survey Question #)
2,662,166	320,740	228,271	1,474,640	18,888,461	359,025	132,217	High
73,143	2,221	3,547	27,292	108,609	8,282	4,475	Mean
0	100	211	32	112	1,757	2,170	Median
0	0	0	0	0	0	0	Low
69,924,260	2,199,249	3,284,628	25,408,714	99,051,488	8,555,309	4,779,013	Total
956	990	926	931	912	1,033	1,068	Libraries Reporting

ACRL LIBRARY DATA TABLES 2004

SUMMARY DATA: COLLECTIONS

INSTITUTIONS GRANTING BACHELOR OF ARTS DEGREES (Carnegie Code B)

	Volumes in Library	Volumes Added (Gross)	Volumes Added (Net)	Mono-graphs Purchased	Current Serials Purchased	Current Serials Not Purchased	Current Serials Total	Microform Units
(Survey Question #)	1	2	3	4	5	6	7	8
High	981,074	50,289	52,988	27,341	24,085	20,478	26,396	1,251,615
Mean	185,599	5,483	4,472	2,923	2,189	543	2,827	89,976
Median	122,881	2,720	2,068	1,947	522	24	598	25,202
Low	1,272	1	-4,480	0	29	0	38	0
Total	34,521,387	981,472	818,453	482,338	361,146	84,147	506,083	15,835,856
Libraries Reporting	186	179	183	165	165	155	179	176

ACRL LIBRARY DATA TABLES 2004

SUMMARY DATA: COLLECTIONS

INSTITUTIONS GRANTING BACHELOR OF ARTS DEGREES (Carnegie Code B)

Government Documents	Computer Files	Archives and Manus.	Carto-graphic Materials	Graphic Materials	Audio Materials	Film and Video	
9	10	11	12	13	14	15	(Survey Question #)
455,024	23,305	9,267	81,070	163,122	25,252	60,395	High
28,819	603	794	1,666	10,823	3,250	3,007	Mean
0	54	134	8	39	2,044	1,708	Median
0	0	0	0	0	0	50	Low
4,524,626	100,179	115,114	246,617	1,504,338	552,499	532,300	Total
157	166	145	148	139	170	177	Libraries Reporting

ACRL LIBRARY DATA TABLES 2004

SUMMARY DATA: COLLECTIONS

NSTITUTIONS GRANTING MASTER OF ARTS AND PROFESSIONAL DEGREES (Carnegie Code M)

(Survey Question #)	Volumes in Library	Volumes Added (Gross)	Volumes Added (Net)	Mono-graphs Purchased	Current Serials Purchased	Current Serials Not Purchased	Current Serials Total	Microform Units
	1	2	3	4	5	6	7	8
High	1,470,843	65,708	42,695	27,496	24,293	33,051	33,677	3,187,530
Mean	271,546	5,985	3,646	3,427	3,254	537	3,753	412,218
Median	186,652	3,819	2,276	2,239	943	29	1,136	205,758
Low	3,029	0	-27,768	0	0	0	3	0
Total	99,929,046	2,172,717	1,312,628	1,151,502	1,096,593	162,261	1,362,219	148,398,424
Libraries Reporting	368	363	360	336	337	302	363	360

ACRL LIBRARY DATA TABLES 2004

SUMMARY DATA: COLLECTIONS

NSTITUTIONS GRANTING MASTER OF ARTS AND PROFESSIONAL DEGREES (Carnegie Code M)

Government Documents	Computer Files	Archives and Manus.	Carto-graphic Materials	Graphic Materials	Audio Materials	Film and Video	
9	10	11	12	13	14	15	(Survey Question #)
1,799,969	320,740	50,237	260,390	701,901	74,802	32,893	High
49,902	1,886	1,174	5,140	9,970	5,037	3,354	Mean
0	81	314	12	97	2,202	2,108	Median
0	0	0	0	0	0	0	Low
16,068,498	614,985	356,968	1,567,549	3,000,838	1,752,787	1,207,352	Total
322	326	304	305	301	348	360	Libraries Reporting

ACRL Library Data Tables 2004
COLLECTIONS

INSTITUTIONS GRANTING BACHELOR OF ARTS DEGREES (Carnegie Code B)

Lib. No.	Survey Question # Institution	Notes	Volumes in Library 1	Volumes added (Gross) 2	Volumes added (Net) 3	Monographs Purchased 4	Serials Purchased 5	Serials Received (not purchased) 6	Total Serials Received 7	Microfo Units 8
1	AB C Art & Design	bf	2,389	2,389	2,389	-1	67	-1	67	748
2	Adrian C		148,066	2,359	2,047	2,238	623	17	640	47,950
3	Albion C	G	368,060	6,890	1,057	2,585	2,035	56	2,091	61,293
4	Amherst C	Gf	-1	-1	-1	-1	-1	-1	-1	-1
5	Aquinas C TN	G	46,414	2,253	1,972	1,579	284 [1]	-1	284 [1]	162,805
6	Atlanta C Art	bG	21,887	483	2,871	483	185	0	185	0
7	Atlanta Christian C	bf	45,588	1,892	1,233	631	205	26	231	6,522
8	Augustana C RI	G	262,227	2,361	1,430	1,953	785	-1	785	91,883
9	Barber-Scotia C		49,137	2,166	2,068	23 [1]	184	12	196	97,901
10	Bard C	b	250,449	6,047	5,949	4,942	3,000	50	3,050	1,200
11	Barton C	b	169,752	12,510	12,426	-1	384	49	433	301,132
12	Bates C	bG	588,211	27,862	-2,088	-1	-1	-1	26,396 [1]	298,706
13	Benedict C	G	118,304	2,932	2,932	2,229	229 [1]	51 [1]	280	163,615
14	Berry C	b	231,916	5,916	5,432	3,567	-1	-1	1,792	53,992
15	Bethany C Bethany	b	122,107	428	428	1,175	91	0	91	160,200
16	Bethany C Lindsborg		149,119	1,420	1,420	1,420	193	0	193	51,442
17	Bethel C KS		140,408	1,870	1,660	-1	19,422	6,393	25,815	14,001
18	Blackburn C	bG	60,464	878	-1,122	854	79	0	79	10,845
19	Bluefield C	bf	42,747	625	497	625	215	4	219	0
20	Boise Bible C		-1	-1	-1	-1	-1	-1	-1	-1
21	Bowdoin C		981,074	18,236	15,819	9,737	5,687	-1	-1	110,537
22	Bridgewater C	b	190,196	3,104	2,690	2,428	650	38	688	415,706
23	Bryan C	bf	106,045	11,082	9,290	11,037	10,189	0	10,189	13,026
24	C Holy Cross		601,730	8,870	8,169	5,756	2,231	5	2,236	15,913
25	C Visual Arts	b	7,075	447	398	124	29	9	38	0
26	C Wooster		673,789	31,401	30,150	5,487	1,771	-1	1,771	213,380
27	Campion C	G	51,950	650	650	600	141	12	153	7,000
28	Carroll C-Helena	b	85,000	-1	-1	1,115	300	0	300	11,580
29	Cazenovia C	b	72,235	1,947	1,947	1,947	430	15	445	14,144
30	Centennial C	bf	64,499	2,244	-541	2,244	510	0	510	-1
31	Central Bible C	b	117,166	2,463	2,364	2,230	232	84	316	38,981
32	Central C		226,961	5,275	3,473	3,005	1,150	0	1,150	55,972
33	Central Christian C Bible	b	71,767	27,382	27,378	-1	110	73	183	4,929
34	Centre C	G	218,543	3,033	3,033	3,033	721	60	781	52,659
35	Christian Heritage C		70,309	2,675	2,450	1,216	225	5	230	0
36	Clear Creek Bible		39,125	201	178	157	143	123	266	3,091
37	Cmty Hosp C Health		14,381	797	212	675	113	10	123	947
38	Colby C	bG	476,203	28,603	28,603	10,326	7,976	0 [1]	7,976	35,000
39	Colby Sawyer C	b	89,604	1,996	1,900	1,996 [1]	514	0	514	203,532
40	Columbia Union C	bG	139,706	1,320	1,051	1,320	347	25	372	-1

Key to Notes on Page 1   1 -- See Footnotes   -1 -- Unavailable   -2 -- Not Applicable

ACRL Library Data Tables 2004
COLLECTIONS

INSTITUTIONS GRANTING BACHELOR OF ARTS DEGREES (Carnegie Code B)

Gov't Documents	Computer Files	Manuscripts and Archives	Cartographic	Graphic	Audio	Film and Video	Survey Question #
9	10	11	12	13	14	15	Institution
-1	-1	-1	-1	124,845 [1]	-1	604	AB C Art & Design
0	12	-1	0	0	660	1,295	Adrian C
83,838	201	1,117	3,220	24	335	4,595	Albion C
-1	-1	-1	-1	-1	-1	-1	Amherst C
0	133	110	-1	-1	280	1,491	Aquinas C TN
0	63	0	0	98,000 [1]	0	505	Atlanta C Art
0	5	87	336	0	1,626	251	Atlanta Christian C
0	-1	-1	40,000	-1	214	2,048	Augustana C RI
0	2	0 [1]	0 [1]	0 [1]	0 [1]	143 [1]	Barber-Scotia C
0	325	350	0	0	2,045	920	Bard C
0	573	0	4,971	200	805	2,203	Barton C
95,581	1,852	4,266	1,610	-1	23,581	8,075	Bates C
26,900	2,102	1,007	61	2,816	1,288	2,196 [1]	Benedict C
82,479	595	402	0	0	190	2,950	Berry C
0	0	6,795	1	0	198	1,234	Bethany C Bethany
0	0	-1	-1	-1	-1	1,044	Bethany C Lindsborg
0	5	5,454	-1	158,249	5,583	621	Bethel C KS
0	0	231	0	0	170	1,011	Blackburn C
0	0	0	0	0	734	2,079	Bluefield C
-1	-1	-1	-1	-1	-1	-1	Boise Bible C
455,024	1,294	4,481	-1	-1	-1	21,922 [1]	Bowdoin C
49,732	307	1,657	7,634	163,122	6,578	1,903	Bridgewater C
0	2	0	0	0	0	1,230	Bryan C
-1	402	3,600	-1	-1	23,746	2,907	C Holy Cross
0	0	0	0	32,394	0	216	C Visual Arts
-1	1,723	293	7,238	304	5,440	6,989	C Wooster
0	34	90	100	0	345	740	Campion C
0	0	-1	0	0	3,100	900	Carroll C-Helena
0	0	300	0	0	1,856	2,184	Cazenovia C
-1	-1	750	-1	-1	-1	2,800	Centennial C
0	3	350	3	1,218	3,403	754	Central Bible C
0	700	720	313	355	5,231	5,686	Central C
0	213	134	251	289	3,535	1,757	Central Christian C Bible
30,534	298	550	0	0	3,482	50	Centre C
0	84	0	0	27	319	402	Christian Heritage C
0	42	26	12	156	2,850	2,226	Clear Creek Bible
0	222	0	0	0	46	865	Cmty Hosp C Health
0 [1]	0 [1]	1,090	0 [1]	0 [1]	8,800	8,869	Colby C
0	105	1,386	224	0	240	1,635	Colby Sawyer C
0	7	34	9	-1	-1	-1	Columbia Union C

Key to Notes on Page 1   1 -- See Footnotes   -1 -- Unavailable   -2 -- Not Applicable

ACRL Library Data Tables 2004
COLLECTIONS

INSTITUTIONS GRANTING BACHELOR OF ARTS DEGREES (Carnegie Code B)

Lib. No.	Institution	Notes	Volumes in Library 1	Volumes added (Gross) 2	Volumes added (Net) 3	Monographs Purchased 4	Serials Purchased 5	Serials Received (not purchased) 6	Total Serials Received 7	Microfo Units 8
41	Concordia C-MN	b	320,733	8,745	7,305	7,142 [1]	8,468	17,470	25,938	44,048
42	Concordia C-NY	b	70,719	943	-144 [1]	-1	322	92	414	-1
43	Cornish C Arts		14,294	1	1,839	1	137	0	137	0
44	Crichton C	b	49,510	919	845	681	220	77	297	75,929
45	Crown C-MN	G	97,386 [1]	2,657	130	2,500 [1]	15,000	0	15,000	70,000
46	Culver Stockton C	b	158,829	7,094	7,094	7,094 [1]	225	47	272	5,253
47	CUNY City C		182,751	2,204	-1,139	2,112	2,030	20,478	22,508	13,804
48	CUNY York C	b	178,294	2,573	2,207	1,220	662	0	662	146,404
49	Dakota Wesleyan U	b	74,244	4,365	2,343	3,919	627	14	641	65,047
50	Dana C	bG	127,472	5,224	5,197	4,375	6,675	0	6,675	15,284
51	Davidson C	bG	611,926	10,528	9,094	8,179	-1	-1	2,688	491,420
52	Dean C	bL	44,204	1,039	945	714	169	0	169	18,271
53	Defiance C	b	107,454	2,036	1,783	729	322	9	331	7,378
54	Denison U		346,258	6,291	5,462	-1	-1	-1	-1	-1
55	DeVry Inst Tech GA	b	351,207	29,434	29,434	27,341	2,160	0	2,160	1
56	Dickinson ST U		102,097	3,787 [1]	3,561	3,673 [1]	2,103 [1]	35	2,138	8,491
57	Divine Word C		95,465	1,020	850	672	280	105	385	1,032
58	East Texas Baptist U	Bb	121,411	335	143	300	262	0	262	10,000
59	Eckerd C		137,096	2,976	336	2,449	1,283	7	1,290	14,414
60	Emmanuel C GA	b	46,735	1,171	405	1,140	76	58	134	6,055
61	Eugene Bible C		-1	-1	-1	-1	-1	-1	-1	-1
62	Evangel U		94,329	2,682	2,462	-1	-1	-1	-1	-1
63	F&M C		472,980	11,261	8,482	10,914	2,746	135	2,881	505,770
64	Ferrum C	bf	114,370	2,066	-698	2,002	10,618	0	10,618	7,733
65	Finlandia U	bG	43,139	1,817	1,464	-1	725	104	829	1,867
66	FL Christian C	b	41,398	2,415	2,403	515	232	20	252	18,750
67	Flagler C	bG	85,654	-1	-1	1,833	464	24	488	69,158
68	Fort Lewis C	b	166,350	1,593	346	688	438	22	460	345,266
69	G Adolphus C	b	288,685	4,794	1,442	4,157	2,137	20	2,157	210,453
70	Green Mountain C	bf	78,778	3,422	3,278	1,269	249	24	273	42,631
71	Grinnell C		522,445	17,562	17,500	7,488	-1	-1	5,147	399,532
72	Guilford C	bG	208,528	3,152	14,190 [1]	2,272	1,419	5,641 [1]	7,060	20,913
73	H Inst Int Desgn	b	20,118	595	446	505	89	11	100	0
74	H LaGrange C	G	92,959	1,938	1,174	759	6,053	5,302	11,355	21,376
75	Hamilton C		598,077	11,487	9,819	6,943	4,620	-1	2,290	428,016
76	Hampshire C		136,326	6,767	3,907	3,493	8,219	9,137	17,356	5,429
77	Hanover C	bG	233,416	-1 [1]	10,634 [1]	3,144	1,762	52	1,814	52,049
78	Haskell Indian Nations U	bf	1,272	1,342	52,988	0	-1	-1	173	13,716
79	Haverford C	Bb	565,998	9,858	8,919	6,164	4,616	202	4,818	4,844
80	Hendrix C	b	220,978	4,798	4,798	3,276	774	2	776	183,633

Key to Notes on Page 1   1 -- See Footnotes   -1 -- Unavailable   -2 -- Not Applicable

ACRL Library Data Tables 2004
COLLECTIONS

INSTITUTIONS GRANTING BACHELOR OF ARTS DEGREES (Carnegie Code B)

Gov't Documents	Computer Files	Manuscripts and Archives	Cartographic	Graphic	Audio	Film and Video	
9	10	11	12	13	14	15	Survey Question # Institution
0	126	2,051	5	75	4,636	1,904	Concordia C-MN
0	13	-1	0	0	4,277	1,226	Concordia C-NY
0	47	0	35	58,000 [1]	3,679 [1]	1,028 [1]	Cornish C Arts
0	11	0	0	65	778	1,238	Crichton C
0	0	115	0	0	64	1,036	Crown C-MN
0	0	1,808	0	-1	936	3,290	Culver Stockton C
0	1	300	74	-1	3,094	2,817	CUNY City C
0	0	0	0	0	0	314	CUNY York C
0	54	816	113	17,000	2,209	1,708	Dakota Wesleyan U
7,115	85	2,453	1,621	35	2,805	1,929	Dana C
-1	1,737	754	-1	-1	-1	11,854	Davidson C
0	0	0	0	0	255	934	Dean C
0	23	179	0	0	2,682	769	Defiance C
-1	-1	-1	-1	-1	-1	-1	Denison U
-1	23,305	0	28	-1	1,502	15,534	DeVry Inst Tech GA
0 [1]	126	40	1,190	984	2,053	2,745	Dickinson ST U
0	0	0	533	0	376	1,091	Divine Word C
0	0	600	0	0	2,059 [1]	1,100	East Texas Baptist U
0	278	67	293	0	519	882	Eckerd C
-1	34	-1	-1	-1	2,073	1,091	Emmanuel C GA
-1	-1	-1	-1	-1	-1	-1	Eugene Bible C
-1	-1	-1	-1	-1	-1	-1	Evangel U
228,595	657	3,125	-1	-1	8,475	4,580	F&M C
0	127	43	0	0	78	2,012	Ferrum C
0	85	0	331	3,381	2,060	497	Finlandia U
0	411	40	150	129	1,119	1,119	FL Christian C
-2	53	-2	0	17	563	2,936	Flagler C
0	227	0	404	-1	47	164	Fort Lewis C
101,741	1,244	742	81,070	-1	13,058	5,354	G Adolphus C
0	0	34	0	1,095	905	319	Green Mountain C
162,157	8,140	1,825	3,124	-1	25,252	4,200	Grinnell C
0	261	928	956	6,354	1,307	2,190	Guilford C
0	0	0	0	0	0	385	H Inst Int Desgn
0	282	60	2	603	2,373	2,979	H LaGrange C
0	-1	-1	-1	-1	-1	60,395 [1]	Hamilton C
0	8	858	106	28,905	6,629	3,495	Hampshire C
307,707 [1]	1,191	-1	-1	-1	3,090	4,714	Hanover C
0	2	0	0	0	50	315	Haskell Indian Nations U
207,403	3,081	9,267	1,328	12,869	8,394	4,608	Haverford C
30,542	0	392	0	0	602	1,194	Hendrix C

Key to Notes on Page 1   1 -- See Footnotes   -1 -- Unavailable   -2 -- Not Applicable

INSTITUTIONS GRANTING BACHELOR OF ARTS DEGREES (Carnegie Code B)

Lib. No.	Survey Question # Institution	Notes	Volumes in Library 1	Volumes added (Gross) 2	Volumes added (Net) 3	Monographs Purchased 4	Serials Purchased 5	Serials Received (not purchased) 6	Total Serials Received 7	Microfo Units 8
81	Hiram C	bG	218,391	4,769	4,656	2,061	564	332	896	115,990
82	Hobart &William Smith Cs	G	380,419	4,704	4,657	3,658	-1	-1	2,911	77,510
83	Hope C		355,998	6,849	6,258	4,552	2,955	0	2,955	383,999
84	Houghton C	Bb	242,866	-1	4,566	2,660	7,598	12	7,610	39,550
85	Howard Payne U	G	121,256	2,975	2,431	1,649	560	38	598	271,542
86	Illinois C	bGf	163,810	2,905	2,905	2,492	634	0	634	7,957
87	Jamestown C	b	110,969	3,540	3,118	2,066	626	4	630	9,380
88	Johnson C Smith U	b	96,839	2,910	2,708	2,217	279	11	290	173,636
89	Judson C	b	103,433	2,101	14	2,101	450	22	472	20,015
90	Kent ST U Salem	b	22,028	645	594	124	71	31	102	2,415
91	Kent ST U Trumbull		79,474	750	550	426	341	18	359	-1
92	Kenyon C	b	430,058	8,946	8,518	7,334	8,574	0	8,574	141,663
93	Kettering C Med	bG	24,043	1,204	-4,480	1,200	260	2	262	1,308
94	Keuka C	b	106,464	2,211	2,133	1,811	401	12	413	104,021
95	Knox C	G	308,614	4,613	3,816	1,947	877	38	916	98,696
96	Kwantlen UC		140,643	-1	4,138	8,458 [1]	-1	17	-1	983
97	Lambuth U	bGf	161,002	37,695	37,317	4,525	235	26	261	203,130
98	Lawrence U		389,262	6,893	6,233	5,605	-1	-1	1,734	104,081
99	Lemoyne-Owen C	Gf	91,712	1,829	1,579	1,598	399	50	449	2,093
100	Lester B Pearson C Pacifi		19,210	250	210	-1	74	2	76	-1
101	LIFE Bible C	b	40,022 [1]	3,220	1,146	1,267	-1	-1	1,954 [1]	513
102	Lyndon State C		101,357	2,987	2,050	-1	-1	-1	557 [1]	-1
103	Lyon C		145,480	2,300	2,300	2,300	646	0	646	2,928
104	Macon ST C	BbG	88,322	1,073	28	1,073	313	6	319	77,070
105	Marlboro C		64,384	2,557	146	2,557	134	0	134 [1]	5,699
106	Mars Hill C	b	84,801	2,436	456	627	13,144	0	13,144	198,955
107	Martin Luther C	bG	158,187	1,303	494	1,016	878	149	1,027	316,114
108	Mayville ST U		92,645	834	-15	618	402	95	497	14,022
109	McKendree C	bG	96,265	3,735	3,301	2,737	344	201	545	42,145
110	McPherson C		96,202	1,665	1,517	903	266	64	330	60,765
111	Methodist C	G	109,022	2,539	2,371	987	616 [1]	54	670	69,236
112	Midland Lutheran C		107,000	3,700	1,900	2,400	11,000	120	11,120	3,500
113	Milwaukee Inst Art Design	b	25,272	533	533	365	112	18	130	0
114	MO Baptist C		63,627	2,339	2,329	900	271	52	323	6,052
115	MO Western ST C	bG	214,228	3,484	2,870	2,462	1,130	15	1,145	110,722
116	Monmouth C	bGf	185,771	5,694	3,896	1,893	1,196 [1]	55 [1]	1,251	245,635
117	Mount Royal C	bG	169,686	6,146	2,871	6,146	1,056	175	1,231	3,942
118	Mount Union C		242,758	3,740	-157	3,740	907	34	941	52,412
119	Muhlenberg C	bG	302,744	5,831	1,130	2,593	817	48	865	332,735
120	NC Wesleyan C	BbG	93,265	1,943	1,915	1,740	430	50	480	34,227

Key to Notes on Page 1   1 -- See Footnotes   -1 -- Unavailable   -2 -- Not Applicable

ACRL Library Data Tables 2004
COLLECTIONS

INSTITUTIONS GRANTING BACHELOR OF ARTS DEGREES (Carnegie Code B)

Gov't Documents	Computer Files	Manuscripts and Archives	Cartographic	Graphic	Audio	Film and Video	
9	10	11	12	13	14	15	Survey Question # Institution
278,721	127	-1	-1	-1	6,642	2,137	Hiram C
0	335	-1	5,654	1,600	2,672	8,057	Hobart &William Smith Cs
2,067	269	4,800 [1]	305	1,507	6,412	4,429	Hope C
-1	30	-1	23	61	6,662	2,961	Houghton C
0	126	44	468	230	1,879	472	Howard Payne U
0	149	-1	0	0	2,912	950	Illinois C
0	25	530	150	174	2,813	1,981	Jamestown C
0	0	1,400	0	0	1,630	1,276	Johnson C Smith U
0	0	20	0	15,000	12,200	503	Judson C
0	5	0	65	62	533	221	Kent ST U Salem
-1	-1	-1	-1	-1	-1	-1	Kent ST U Trumbull
369,001	14,731	-1	5,849	-1	8,338	9,198	Kenyon C
0	0	0	0	0	282	1,047	Kettering C Med
0	123	500	0	95,000	5,011	1,486	Keuka C
0	215	-1	-1	-1	5,042	2,131	Knox C
-1	-1	292	1,654	-1	2,439	6,367	Kwantlen UC
11,989 [1]	862 [1]	4,308	-1	-1	952	482	Lambuth U
339,835	394	-1	-1	65,000	14,281	5,717	Lawrence U
0	0	6	0	250 [1]	2,690	385	Lemoyne-Owen C
-1	6	-1	-1	-1	-1	-1	Lester B Pearson C Pacific
0	10	100	0	0	956	607	LIFE Bible C
-1	-1	42	-1	-1	2,270	2,270	Lyndon State C
0	117	0	0	0	3,010	3,734	Lyon C
0	26	0	212	0	2,780	1,340	Macon ST C
0	0	155	0	0	536 [1]	2,073 [1]	Marlboro C
0	39	240	0	407	3,853	978	Mars Hill C
0	429	300	-1	8,607	4,140	3,559	Martin Luther C
0	81	71	2	12,109	5,209	1,019	Mayville ST U
6,443	674	130	205	401	1,355	3,576	McKendree C
0	-1	-1	-1 [1]	-1	-1	-1	McPherson C
0	334	-1	509	7,808	3,285	1,793	Methodist C
2,200	300	200	0	0	2,800	1,700	Midland Lutheran C
0	79	0	0	53,662 [1]	9	616	Milwaukee Inst Art Design
0	0	0	0	0	0	153	MO Baptist C
0	636	445	41	161	10,160	5,469	MO Western ST C
87,396	1,219	-1	1,394	0	3,136	2,573	Monmouth C
-1	-1	0	-1	-1	2,571	8,527	Mount Royal C
408,002	-1	-1	0	0	2,268	5,519	Mount Union C
0	202	725	1,052 [1]	3,089	5,032	5,727	Muhlenberg C
0	113	82	665	0	579	1,582	NC Wesleyan C

Key to Notes on Page 1   1 -- See Footnotes   -1 -- Unavailable   -2 -- Not Applicable

ACRL Library Data Tables 2004
COLLECTIONS
INSTITUTIONS GRANTING BACHELOR OF ARTS DEGREES (Carnegie Code B)

Lib. No.	Survey Question # Institution	Notes	Volumes in Library 1	Volumes added (Gross) 2	Volumes added (Net) 3	Monographs Purchased 4	Serials Purchased 5	Serials Received (not purchased) 6	Total Serials Received 7	Microfo Units 8
121	New C U South FL	bG	258,799	5,406	1,752	1,052	1,852	98	1,950	533,984
122	OH Dominican C	bG	105,722	5,434	-3,884	-1	-1	-1	6,258	9,816
123	OH Wesleyan U	b	424,186	21,475	19,838	5,902	7,753	-1	7,753	114,705
124	OK Panhandle ST U	b	111,170	2,761	-435	1,773	281	10	291	9,356
125	Paier C Art		12,595	201	197	101	57	9	66 [1]	0
126	Peace C	b	51,483	1,331	1,209	1,331	4,197 [1]	1	4,198	28,000
127	Potomac C	G	7,321	671	498	671	43	30	73	0
128	Presbyterian C	bG	128,813	3,161	3,114	3,091	6,137	6,712	12,849	13,376
129	Principia C	bG	166,593 [1]	2,703	2,123	2,118	18,766	2	18,768	29,129
130	Randolph-Macon C	bf	182,368	2,720	2,156	2,815	1,455	0	1,455	209,300
131	Randolph-Macon WC	bG	197,375	1,820	-482	1,720	642	10	652	190,000
132	Reformed Bible C		54,828	705	84	709	178	65	243	4,913
133	Reinhardt C	Bb	49,503	3,865	2,063	2,889	315	0	315	1,161
134	Ricks C		532,450	14,407	9,518	14,407	-1	-1	874	122,074
135	Ringling Sch Art & Design		46,802	3,479	2,565	-1	340	4	344	0
136	Rochester C	b	45,413	2,398	2,398	795	170	32	202	21,868
137	Rocky Mountain C	bGf	98,728	1,303	826	500	250	25	275	1,266
138	Rogers ST U	bG	65,382	3,590	3,567	3,138	551	3	554	134,628
139	SE C Assemblies God	bG	-1	-1	-1	-1	-1	-1	-1	-1
140	Shawnee ST U	Gf	137,862	11,888	2,166	1,099	-1	-1	13,949	85,459
141	Shepherd C	G	164,206	2,356	1,428	1,339	7,024	38	7,062	200,474
142	Siena C	G	326,332	7,431	4,531	4,640	-1	-1	5,259	27,586
143	Simpson C IA	bG	157,713	4,677	2,580	3,142	623	26	649	12,492
144	Skidmore C	b	395,380	11,837	10,124	6,912	2,976	6	2,982	65,601
145	Southwest U	f	333,384	11,014	10,384	11,014	2,824	-1	2,824	60,491
146	Spartan Aero-Flight Schl	B	7,736	518	385	-1	-1	-1	-1	-1
147	St Andrews Presby C	bG	133,304	689	-511	-1	10,223	4,110	14,332	14,659
148	St Gregory's U	b	80,621	2,171	1,721	321 [1]	-1	-1	-1	3,315
149	St John Vianney C Sem		54,991	929	919	538	154	7	161	300
150	St Olaf C	b	697,516	37,979	21,135	11,214	2,149	-1	2,149	11,317
151	St. Mary's C Maryland		157,077	2,610	-44	-1	1,940 [1]	43	1,983	44,816
152	Sterling C-VT		8,420	478	465	297	24,085	15	24,100	0
153	Stillman C		116,875	579	579	0	228	6	234	6,368
154	Susquehanna U	bG	246,894	7,171	4,051	5,108	523	71	594	123,134
155	SW Baptist Theo Sem		818,639	12,433	5,691	586	6,648	223	6,871	223
156	Swarthmore C	G	756,983	16,760	9,306	7,520	6,183	1,628 [1]	7,811	277,906
157	Sweet Briar C	bG	255,175 [1]	3,086	-3,425	1,326	567	182	749	450,838
158	Talladega C	bf	127,158	690	690	4	100	300	300	180
159	Taylor U-Ft Wayne	b	189,307	3,468	3,168	3,050	595	30	625	10,915
160	Teikyo Post U	bL	104,635	1,656	1,656	1,656	432	35	467	75,158

Key to Notes on Page 1   1 -- See Footnotes   -1 -- Unavailable   -2 -- Not Applicable

ACRL Library Data Tables 2004
COLLECTIONS

INSTITUTIONS GRANTING BACHELOR OF ARTS DEGREES (Carnegie Code B)

Gov't Documents	Computer Files	Manuscripts and Archives	Cartographic	Graphic	Audio	Film and Video	
9	10	11	12	13	14	15	Survey Question # Institution
0	116	1,487	148	0	2,553	1,986	New C U South FL
-1	178	-1	-1	-1	309	3,872	OH Dominican C
126,890	-1	-1	1,222	39	7,992	3,477	OH Wesleyan U
0	10	262	0	1,375	444	2,454	OK Panhandle ST U
0	0	0	0	54,191	1	143	Paier C Art
0	0	90	2	0	878	1,735	Peace C
0	0	0	0	0	0	56	Potomac C
0	11	294	0	0	7,306	14,181	Presbyterian C
4,936	692	-1	679	-1	3,743	474	Principia C
0	0	6,050	0	0	280	5,116	Randolph-Macon C
0	60	3,000	50	100	200	2,500	Randolph-Macon WC
-2	16	-2	-2	2,802	2,974	381	Reformed Bible C
0	6	0	0	10,207	2,769	2,186	Reinhardt C
0	1,392	1,418	15,274	8,292	13,464	10,464	Ricks C
0	395	-1	0	118,982	749	3,778	Ringling Sch Art & Design
0	38	0	135	0	568	689	Rochester C
0	0	0	6,000	0	359	652	Rocky Mountain C
0	30	0	485	104	1,464	4,781	Rogers ST U
-1	-1	-1	-1	-1	-1	-1	SE C Assemblies God
0	592	31	1,353	14,413	1,757	2,713	Shawnee ST U
138,622	0	0	0	0	3,536	2,715	Shepherd C
-1	28	202	62	5,390	2,043	3,940	Siena C
0	167	850	-1	0	2,898	2,259	Simpson C IA
-1	0	411	1	129,306	5,977	5,153	Skidmore C
-1	395	-1	-1	-1	2,539	5,745	Southwest U
-1	-1	-1	-1	-1	-1	-1	Spartan Aero-Flight Schl
0	28	-1	814	-1	843	54	St Andrews Presby C
0	42	0	-1	-1	182	232	St Gregory's U
0	48	0	260	2,580	1,080	702	St John Vianney C Sem
378,067	-1	-1	970	-1	11,664	7,039	St Olaf C
0	397	800	137	5,397	6,472	1,527	St. Mary's C Maryland
-1	13	0	60	0	35	425	Sterling C-VT
0	160	325	3	882	420	1,380	Stillman C
0	356	694	134	7,082	3,319	3,567	Susquehanna U
-1	-1	2,468	-1	-1	433	586	SW Baptist Theo Sem
118,402	1,224	0	21,078	0	14,648	6,138	Swarthmore C
0	28	1,435	197	5	4,483	5,881	Sweet Briar C
80	29	25	316	1,900	107	330	Talladega C
0	-1	-2	350	-2	4,998	3,332	Taylor U-Ft Wayne
0	0	0	0	0	209	1,119	Teikyo Post U

Key to Notes on Page 1   1 -- See Footnotes   -1 -- Unavailable   -2 -- Not Applicable

INSTITUTIONS GRANTING BACHELOR OF ARTS DEGREES (Carnegie Code B)

Lib. No.	Institution / Survey Question #	Notes	Volumes in Library 1	Volumes added (Gross) 2	Volumes added (Net) 3	Monographs Purchased 4	Serials Purchased 5	Serials Received (not purchased) 6	Total Serials Received 7	Microform Units 8
161	TN Wesleyan C		123,654	-1	3,654	880	825	-1	825	9,525
162	Tri ST U		73,859 [1]	675	-1,248	645	359	71	430	48,098
163	Trinity Christian C	b	77,700 [1]	-1	-1	2,084	-1	-1	437	34,690
164	Trinity Wstrn U	bf	201,880	10,981	9,741	6,968	17,406	0	17,406	352,156
165	Truett McConnell C	b	31,133	2,090	1,937	1,210	203	0	203	38,800
166	TX Lutheran U	bG	170,801	3,740	3,740	1,513	-1	-1	603	118,592
167	U Maine-Machias	G	82,369	1,205	1,083	1,067	249	84	333	4,789
168	U ME Fort Kent	b	67,507	1,660	1,557	801	276	59	335	6,267
169	U Ozarks	G	91,540	1,712	1,397	-1	390	58	448	9,862
170	U VA C Wise	G	143,745	1,409	-698	631	509	77	586	22,818
171	Union C-NE	b	167,960	9,578	9,362	-1	487	89	576	1,785
172	US C Guard Acad	b	153,547	1,501	1,501	1,501	522	0	522	50,000
173	US Merchant Marine Acad	bG	182,895 [1]	4,580	786	-1	508	458	966	17,978
174	US Mil Acad	f	438,104	8,748	8,116	7,536	-1	-1	902	-1
175	US Naval Acad		662,575 [1]	17,945	15,684	8,474	2,709	-1	-1	188,825
176	UT Valley ST C	Bb	165,203	9,695	9,227	3,982	573	3	576	10
177	VA Wesleyan C	b	121,373	1,927	1,595	875	405	13	418	15,844
178	Vassar C	G	878,177	21,162	17,194	8,971 [1]	5,294	1,159	6,453	706,348
179	VMI	b	253,859	3,209	3,063	1,839	712	17	729	20,064
180	Wabash C	G	281,949	5,225	4,671	4,671	6,735	0	6,735	12,195
181	Warner Sthrn C	Gf	83,260	2,064	1,914	1,957	173	50	223	7,447
182	Warren Wilson C	b	98,573	3,766	1,561	3,710 [1]	256	50	306	33,194
183	Wells C	b	258,191	1,344	1,344	526	380	12	392	16,587
184	Western ST C	bf	442,045	3,128	2,112	1,029	390	1	391	1,251,615
185	Westmont C	b	111,320	2,401	229	-1	346	70	416	19,175
186	Whitman C	b	374,131	12,647	12,522	-1	2,859	84	2,943	206,000
187	Wiley C	bG	76,555	2,450	822	0	305	50	355	40,000
188	Winston-Salem ST U	b	209,170	7,053	6,595	7,053	1,016	0	1,016	271,064
189	Wofford C	bG	195,861	3,692	-1,458	1 [1]	532	1	532	37,005
190	York C		106,695 [1]	50,289 [1]	50,283 [1]	428	274	64	338	21,075

ACRL Library Data Tables 2004
COLLECTIONS

INSTITUTIONS GRANTING BACHELOR OF ARTS DEGREES (Carnegie Code B)

Gov't Documents	Computer Files	Manuscripts and Archives	Cartographic	Graphic	Audio	Film and Video	
9	10	11	12	13	14	15	Survey Question # Institution
-1	16	846	-1	-1	2,511	1,039	TN Wesleyan C
0	107	-1	31	537	381	440	Tri ST U
0	95	0	0	163	198	814	Trinity Christian C
0	0	150	0	0	449	3,460	Trinity Wstrn U
0	27	0	0	18	251	1,506	Truett McConnell C
0 [1]	1,079	0	436	476	2,872	1,464	TX Lutheran U
0	34	0	49	971	168	504	U Maine-Machias
0	143	0	1,187	-1	4,033	1,176	U ME Fort Kent
46,397	0	0	0	0	3,435	817	U Ozarks
0	526	512	0	0	1,572	1,634	U VA C Wise
0	31	538	-1	610	582	1,379	Union C-NE
0	0	0	0	0	0	2,388	US C Guard Acad
-1	2,698	1,002	4,001	908	814	1,217	US Merchant Marine Acad
-1	-1	-1	-1	-1	-1	-1	US Mil Acad
0	-1	-1	-1	-1	-1	-1	US Naval Acad
0	830	31	2,969	363	1,735	11,477	UT Valley ST C
0	0	-1	0	0	2,875	611	VA Wesleyan C
0	1,707	3,348	11,668	144,000	13,197	9,148	Vassar C
176,995	86	6,272	-1	-1	1,922	3,424	VMI
159,234	0	-1	0	0	8,886	2,088	Wabash C
0	84	0	3	12,904	3,329	711	Warner Sthrn C
0 [1]	9,823 [1]	0 [1]	0 [1]	0 [1]	80	2,588	Warren Wilson C
-1	1,752	555	-1	-1	58	803	Wells C
0	0	888	0	0	23,932	3,405	Western ST C
0	25	-1	0	0	9,105	987	Westmont C
-1	-1	3,500	-1	-1	-2	6,548	Whitman C
0	7	8	27	270	323	540	Wiley C
0	14	30	0	0	1,540	854	Winston-Salem ST U
1	1	855	915	1	85	3,437	Wofford C
0	74	570	7	3,431	2,452	218	York C

Key to Notes on Page 1   1 -- See Footnotes   -1 -- Unavailable   -2 -- Not Applicable

INSTITUTIONS GRANTING MASTER OF ARTS AND PROFESSIONAL DEGREES (Carnegie Code M)

Lib. No.	Institution	Notes	Volumes in Library 1	Volumes added (Gross) 2	Volumes added (Net) 3	Monographs Purchased 4	Serials Purchased 5	Serials Received (not purchased) 6	Total Serials Received 7	Microform Units 8
	Survey Question #									
1	Abilene Christian U	bG	499,551	10,221	8,578	3,055	1,386	1,113	2,499	1,187,119
2	Agnes Scott C	G	220,041	2,491	2,282	2,241	-1	-1	2,044	32,920
3	Albany C Pharmacy		17,339	427	352	-1	4,023	6	4,027	29,512
4	Albany Law Schl Union U	GL	275,008	6,755	5,375	2,709	2,903	300	3,203	1,759,878
5	Alcorn ST U	bG	220,393	10,543	10,357	2,155	906	140	1,046	577,874
6	Amer Intl C	b	-1	-1	-1	-1	-1	-1	-1	-1
7	Amer U Puerto Rico	Bb	82,796	1,999	1,693	1,999	106	41	147	0
8	Anderson U		205,026	4,061	1,345	3,309	-1	-1	-1	252,730
9	Angelo ST U		488,210	7,932	7,065	3,753	1,629	0	1,629	949,295
10	Aquinas C MI	b	94,822	2,326	-882	1,326	649	21	670	222,009
11	Ark Tech U	G	153,815	1,522	1,413	1,028	1,054	40	1,094	880,000
12	Armstrong Atlantic ST U	bG	223,033	6,742	1,309	3,982	1,175	0	1,175	681,900
13	Assemblies God Theo Se	f	89,853	1,425	1,419	1,261	317	106	423	72,694
14	Assumption C	bG	199,585	4,073	3,910	1,593	3	0	3	19,825
15	Athenaeum of Ohio		103,334	2,026	1,931	1,826	332	30	362	1,336
16	Auburn U Montgomery	b	328,134	9,803	9,494	6,020	1,707	494	2,201	2,474,246
17	Augusta ST U	bG	433,988	5,592	2,309	2,928	7,236	26,081	33,317	1,261,469
18	Augustana C SF	bG	261,426	2,962	-4,853	700	960	33	993	16,739
19	Austin C	b	215,972	3,276	3,073	2,708	2,733	0	2,733	113,834
20	Austin Presb Theo Sem	f	155,822	2,503	-1,912	2,503	581	-1	581	11,297
21	Averett C	b	111,885	2,303	-617	1,781 [1]	11,739	38	11,777	63,125
22	Babson C	bG	126,211	1,139	-1	-1	626	33,051	33,677	346,993
23	Baker C System	Bb	193,744	12,502	3,157	9,354	-1	-1	1,843	138,416
24	Baker U	G	100,399	3,870	2,653	2,370	540	88	620	208,903
25	Baptist Bible C and Sem	bf	61,114	903	495	110	11,487	0	11,487	20,225
26	Bayamon Central U	bf	45,300	500	300	5	5,000 [1]	0	5,000	0
27	Bellevue U	bf	81,008	2,375	2,074	1,725	177	16	193	15,237
28	Bennington C	b	114,468	1,838	-2,004	1,299	-1	-1	14,183	6,112
29	Bethel C IN	bf	106,573	2,497	2,497	2,188	450	0	450	4,422
30	Birmingham Southern C	bG	282,943	6,659	6,048	3,911	1,215	23	1,238 [1]	47,205
31	Bluffton C	b	167,908	3,337	2,229	-1	-1	-1	-1	137,950
32	BowlGrn SU Fireld	b	42,815	2,354	1,534	408	200	41	241	2,663
33	Bradley U	b	435,366	6,364	5,503	3,198	14,488 [1]	9,000 [1]	23,448	816,601
34	Brescia U	bG	83,380	1,616	-2,198	878	11,942	9	11,951	342,840
35	Brooks Institute	B	32,144	862	829	862	198	9	207	0
36	Bryn Athyn C	b	104,212	1,572	1,499	-1	172	88	260	3,284
37	Buena Vista U		136,596	2,914	2,914	1,682	-1	-1	642	41,377
38	Butler U	b	288,803	4,648	-18,464	3,308	2,239	29	2,268	94,225
39	C Atlantic	b	39,590	1,095	481	800	397 [1]	11	408	-1
40	C Mt St Joseph	b	97,576	1,189	-1,915	900	425	0	425	380,391

Key to Notes on Page 1   1 -- See Footnotes   -1 -- Unavailable   -2 -- Not Applicable

INSTITUTIONS GRANTING MASTER OF ARTS AND PROFESSIONAL DEGREES (Carnegie Code M)

Gov't Documents	Computer Files	Manuscripts and Archives	Cartographic	Graphic	Audio	Film and Video	Survey Question #
9	10	11	12	13	14	15	Institution
0	33,494	1,675	23,469	23,737	35,071	6,405	Abilene Christian U
0	91	-1	-1	3,073	12,388	3,117	Agnes Scott C
0	27	108	0	0	15	427	Albany C Pharmacy
0	66	0	0	0	206	259	Albany Law Schl Union U
0	720	2,045	555	7,762	3,748	5,087	Alcorn ST U
-1	-1	-1	-1	-1	-1	-1	Amer Intl C
38	50	0	0	0	3	23	Amer U Puerto Rico
37,599	52	-1	0	0	304	96	Anderson U
437	690	6,500	500	16,477	6,453	7,718	Angelo ST U
0	146	69	25	48	3,749	5,928	Aquinas C MI
105,557	421	-1	161	0	4,952	2,023	Ark Tech U
0	210	0	0	250	1,367	5,740	Armstrong Atlantic ST U
-1	62	-1	-1	-1	4,326	701	Assemblies God Theo Sem
0	30	180	0	0	237	1,986	Assumption C
0	42	31	0	0	2,212	220	Athenaeum of Ohio
501,113	2,052	810	0	16,577	4,509	3,985	Auburn U Montgomery
271,149	1,529	460	22,588	0	0	0	Augusta ST U
0	1,730	4,000	156	63	5,508	2,337	Augustana C SF
0	-1	2,100	2,187	-1 [1]	1,682	6,237	Austin C
0	68	0	0	0	6,558	398	Austin Presb Theo Sem
0	41	898	22	1 [1]	19	108	Averett C
0	247	3,750	0	0	2,712	2,699	Babson C
0	3	187	7	688	28	1,887	Baker C System
38,875	1,037	-1	901	21	2,692	781	Baker U
2,437	10	24	235	3,685	1,709	1,392	Baptist Bible C and Sem
30	50	200	0 [1]	0	0	0	Bayamon Central U
0	221	0	0	0	50	4,462	Bellevue U
0	0	500	0	26,060	165	1,972	Bennington C
0	0	705	0	0	252	707	Bethel C IN
50,506	1,404	0 [1]	927	6,984 [1]	22,062	5,246	Birmingham Southern C
-1	488	-1	-1	-1	-1	944	Bluffton C
0	42	63 [1]	130	355	338	1,449	BowlGrn SU Fireld
102,629 [1]	-1	835	52	62	7,637	2,270	Bradley U
0	1	-1	0	0	943	688	Brescia U
0	371	0	0	0	0	1,360	Brooks Institute
0	13	1,875	11	-1	514	190	Bryn Athyn C
-1	12	-1	-1	369	1,336	3,289	Buena Vista U
56,416	17	778	72	0	11,639	2,638	Butler U
-2	25 [1]	-1	235	-1	1,443	1,085	C Atlantic
0	0	0	0	0	1,791	1,623	C Mt St Joseph

Key to Notes on Page 1   1 -- See Footnotes   -1 -- Unavailable   -2 -- Not Applicable

ACRL Library Data Tables 2004
COLLECTIONS

INSTITUTIONS GRANTING MASTER OF ARTS AND PROFESSIONAL DEGREES (Carnegie Code M)

Lib. No.	Survey Question # Institution	Notes	Volumes in Library 1	Volumes added (Gross) 2	Volumes added (Net) 3	Monographs Purchased 4	Serials Purchased 5	Serials Received (not purchased) 6	Total Serials Received 7	Microf. Units 8
41	C Mt St Vincent	bG	100,969	808	-1,838	767	11,051	0	11,051	10,111
42	C Our Lady Elms	bG	166,599	1,026	-975	240	773	50	823	134,53
43	C.R. Drew U Med & Sci	bM	43,810	1,952	1,503	837	1,331	3	1,334	
44	CA C Arts & Crafts	b	60,190 [1]	4,404 [1]	2,770	1,441	273	9	281	
45	CA St Polytechnic U-Pomol	G	755,671	13,998	-460	4,590	5,193	173	5,366	1,828,68
46	CA St U - Sacramento	bG	1,306,088	30,585	28,693	27,496	3,448	313	3,761	2,373,50
47	CA ST U Dominguez Hills	b	424,025	3,606	3,523	3,606	1	1	1,967	741,42
48	CA ST U Fresno		1,035,842	17,972	10,151	-1	3,696	0	3,696	1,212,06
49	CA ST U Fullerton	Bb	1,188,529	28,886	20,704	26,644	3,690 [1]	0 [1]	3,690	26,279
50	CA ST U Hayward	B	925,649	6,675	1,311	4,442	1,652	0	1,652	872,98
51	CA ST U Long Beach	G	1,470,843	13,853	-6,351 [1]	6,290	2,871	174	3,045	1,502,71
52	CA ST U Northridge	bG	1,301,603	27,252	27,252	21,224	18,654	-1 [1]	18,654	3,187,53
53	CA ST U S Bernadino	f	789,907	16,175	15,867	13,694	1,407	51	1,458	68,56
54	CA ST U San Marcos	bG	233,445	13,953	11,232	5,336	843 [1]	1,200 [1]	2,043 [1]	941,48
55	CA ST U Stanislaus	B	359,626	6,945	5,799	5,501	1,605	106	1,711	1,300,67
56	CA West Sch Law	GL	167,895	6,647	4,018	1,507 [1]	-1	-1	3,955	802,35
57	Calvin C		709,433	14,629	14,547	11,572	2,750	0	2,750	800,470
58	Cameron U	Gf	262,215	2,255	-622	2,255	1,425	26	1,451	548,99
59	Canisius C	G	336,449	6,425	4,878	4,239	2,796	0	2,796	598,06
60	Carlow C		125,869	1,558	1,495	1,057	349	16	365	11,63
61	Carroll C-Waukesha		150,000	2,767	0	2,767	1,705	0	1,705	27,21
62	Cedar Crest C		139,662	1,536	987	868	1,208	37	1,245	16,00
63	Cedarville U	G	162,195	7,911	4,277	5,580	802	106	908	22,00
64	Centenary C	b	72,606	669	208	0 [1]	88	88	88	22,72
65	Centenary C LA	bf	203,784	5,926	5,773	1,010	369	10	379	340,70
66	Central Baptist C	bf	54,243	1,389	1,316	1,212	252	67	319	27,26
67	Central CT ST U		675,260	14,012	9,655	8,742	2,243	275	2,518	554,64
68	Central MO ST U		891,790	19,731	13,100	7,106	3,488	60	3,548 [1]	1,664,625
69	Charleston Sthrn U		221,729	3,006	12,422	1,309	1,029	11	1,037	215,900
70	Chicago ST U	b	417,094	4,419	1,479	3,081	1,478	206	1,684	26,75
71	Chris Newport U		200,704	598	-618	877	9,077	85	9,162	815,892
72	Christendom C	Bb	80,520	4,334	4,334	719	221	31	252	-1
73	Christian Brothers U	b	83,169	1,003	702	1,003	516	0	516	60,810
74	Clarion U PA	Bb	437,068	5,060	-2,299	5,060	18,887	0	18,887	1,603,492
75	Clarke C-IA		128,598	1,526	1,450	975	848	36	884	11,792
76	Clarkson C-NE	f	17,110 [1]	-1	-1	241	214	0	214	-1
77	Colorado C	bG	499,596	14,140	12,142	14,140	2,567	0	2,567	125,603
78	Columbia C MO		62,889	1,644	624	1,294	10,680	26	10,706	12,860
79	Columbia C SC		145,800	1,820	1,468	1,447	360	27	387	11,809
80	Columbia Intl U	bf	106,203	2,233	1,781	657	1,338	0	690	51,267

Key to Notes on Page 1   1 -- See Footnotes   -1 -- Unavailable   -2 -- Not Applicable

ACRL Library Data Tables 2004
COLLECTIONS

INSTITUTIONS GRANTING MASTER OF ARTS AND PROFESSIONAL DEGREES (Carnegie Code M)

Gov't Documents	Computer Files	Manuscripts and Archives	Cartographic	Graphic	Audio	Film and Video	
9	10	11	12	13	14	15	Survey Question # Institution
0	0	0	0	0	0	382	C Mt St Vincent
0	1,124	115	2,046	8,258	962	1,451	C Our Lady Elms
0	0	12	0	0	1,321	1,439	C.R. Drew U Med & Sci
0	74	108	20	-1	173	1,379	CA C Arts & Crafts
0	100	1,128	13,018	76	5,622	5,566	A St Polytechnic U-Pomona
0	2,430	5,332 [1]	22,313	118,448	6,575	13,824	CA St U - Sacramento
46,100	1	2,000	150	1,104	5,439	5,095	CA ST U Dominguez Hills
282,043	8,744	918	162,215	2,793	74,802	4,747	CA ST U Fresno
0	3,650	977	9,955	22,516	21,810	5,715	CA ST U Fullerton
66,423	1,056	0	248	0	24,633	5,359	CA ST U Hayward
0	-1	12,489	36,047	13,884	16,132	15,840	CA ST U Long Beach
1,799,969	843	3,950	-1 [1]	59,780	10,735	8,335	CA ST U Northridge
11,707	218	826	16,097	416	10,704	5,103	CA ST U S Bernadino
0	1,194	491	735	19,415	2,909	5,619	CA ST U San Marcos
114,644	208	2,569	9,875	1,268	1,855	2,191	CA ST U Stanislaus
0	182	4,088	-1	-1	1,198	762	CA West Sch Law
157,998	0	0	0	0	23,487	2,307	Calvin C
0	75	0	0	0	5,000	715	Cameron U
0	679	817	417	0	5,027	3,416	Canisius C
0	15	572	133	2,493	1,613	474	Carlow C
0	24	217	36	0	838	413	Carroll C-Waukesha
-1	83	365	-1	9,158	4,421	2,323	Cedar Crest C
0	666	649	0	7,039	4,897	3,169	Cedarville U
0	0	-1 [1]	0	0 [1]	-1	5,235 [1]	Centenary C
0	0	2,500	0	400	6,347	2,111	Centenary C LA
0	0	0	1	1,423	1,204	1,176	Central Baptist C
-1	-1	-1	-1	-1	-1	7,659 [1]	Central CT ST U
0	525	2,950	40,147	4,128	5,377	10,967	Central MO ST U
0	902	599	434	4,630	1,465	2,253	Charleston Sthrn U
114,440	-1 [1]	438	1,681	-1 [1]	8,463	1,497	Chicago ST U
0	320,740	0	-1	-1	-1	9,132 [1]	Chris Newport U
0	45	-1	0	0	789	725	Christendom C
0	0 [1]	0	0	0	0 [1]	732	Christian Brothers U
0	0	16,164	0	0	0	23,743	Clarion U PA
0	0	52	0	0	551	979	Clarke C-IA
0	38	0	0	0	13	660	Clarkson C-NE
308,204	1,456	2,917	2,920	41,251	20	7,473	Colorado C
0	195	0	0	416	42	1,086	Columbia C MO
0	30	231	1	3,132	12,575	10,522	Columbia C SC
0	0	263	452	10,144	4,003	1,808	Columbia Intl U

Key to Notes on Page 1   1 -- See Footnotes   -1 -- Unavailable   -2 -- Not Applicable

INSTITUTIONS GRANTING MASTER OF ARTS AND PROFESSIONAL DEGREES (Carnegie Code M)

Lib. No.	Survey Question # Institution	Notes	Volumes in Library 1	Volumes added (Gross) 2	Volumes added (Net) 3	Monographs Purchased 4	Serials Purchased 5	Serials Received (not purchased) 6	Total Serials Received 7	Microfo Unit 8
81	Columbus ST U	BG	376,242	4,510	3,424	1,595	1,394	223	1,617	456,91
82	Concordia U Irvine	b	85,432	907	-5,035	907	251	32	283	53,17
83	Concordia U RiverF	b	227,530	-1	7,808	821	389	-1	389	4,33
84	Concordia U St Paul		136,216	2,784	2,350	-1	355	42	397	10,26
85	Cooper Union	b	103,430	1,660	-1 [1]	633	2,016	3,130	5,146	19,38
86	Cornerstone U	bG	124,816	3,753	-2,074	3,570	1,163	0	1,163	289,06
87	Creighton U	b	407,943	9,143	7,534	6,503	2,176	-1	2,176	924,58
88	Cumberland U		35,228	-1	450	350	391	6	397	1,05
89	CUNY BMB C		456,132	7,193	6,978	-1	-1	-1	4,548	2,066,10
90	CUNY C Stn Island	f	229,345	4,903	4,229	-1	820	0	820	46
91	CUNY City C	bGM	1,444,400	28,611	26,170	-1	22,027	7,963	29,990	887,47
92	CUNY HH Lehman C	bG	571,956	6,148	4,113	6,148	2,279	533	2,812	713,48
93	CUNY John Jay C Crim J	G	240,025	5,458	4,549	3,149	-1	-1	7,043	205,15
94	CUNY Queens C	bG	790,233	10,399	9,689	-1	4,400	250	465	937,60
95	Curtis Inst Music	G	72,773	1,074	-1,071	1,074	72	0	72	3,96
96	Daniel Webster C	b	28,971	2,002	-3,667	2,131	183	20	203	60,06
97	DeSales U		144,467	3,705	3,520	3,390	8,991 [1]	0	8,891	462,80
98	DN Myers C		15,556	248	248	248	141	0	141	63
99	Dominican C San Rafael	b	92,536	4,544	4,424	2,628	572 [1]	25	597	3,50
100	Dominican U	b	202,069	3,323	1,831	3,037	814	22	836	4,96
101	Drake U	b	482,196	9,949	8,076	5,817	1,865	-1	15,363 [1]	920,66
102	Drury C	b	176,304	5,527	-13,804	1,438 [1]	948	45	993	19,23
103	E R Aero U		105,307	3,164	2,154	3,466	835	835	835	255,81
104	Earlham C	Gf	403,639	5,010	3,341	5,010	2,330	0	2,330	249,50
105	Eastern IL U	bG	870,733	65,708	42,695	9,938	3,677	59	3,736	1,379,77
106	Eastern U	Bb	187,142	3,646	2,270	2,500	625	20	645	825,87
107	Eastern WA U	Bb	878,475	20,421	12,877	6,454	6,392	-1	6,392	1,438,907
108	Eastrn NM U Main	BbG	270,935	5,134	-308	4,886	15,264	1,317	16,481	458,292
109	Edinboro U PA	b	501,283	6,764	6,197	3,817	1,744	51	1,795	1,401,951
110	Elizabethtown C	b	194,688	2,948	2,586	2,236	898	72	970	19,814
111	Elmhurst C	b	218,107	4,044	3,760	2,163 [1]	-1	-1	1,091	53,894
112	Elon U	b	240,058	15,376	13,758	11,993	2,097	-1	2,097	898,440
113	Emmanuel C MA	b	97,627	835	783	736	394	0	394	2,128
114	Emory & Henry C	bGf	182,553	1,975	1,263	1,675 [1]	387	52	439	42,359
115	Evergreen ST C	bGf	475,189	5,203	3,354	-1	2,731	49	2,780	492,853
116	Fisk U	bG	209,389	2,046	2,046	170	844	1,722	2,566	114,998
117	Fitchburg ST C	G	242,762	1,854	-5	382	2,158	-1 [1]	2,158	480,301
118	FL Southern C	bG	166,755	3,757	-2,022	3,757	672	14	686	459,886
119	Fort Hays ST U	b	654,004	3,571	326	3,181	1,464	0 [1]	1,464	442,096
120	Francis Marion U	G	332,092	3,077	2,691	1,387	2,033	47	2,080	546,844

Key to Notes on Page 1   1 -- See Footnotes   -1 -- Unavailable   -2 -- Not Applicable

ACRL Library Data Tables 2004
COLLECTIONS

INSTITUTIONS GRANTING MASTER OF ARTS AND PROFESSIONAL DEGREES (Carnegie Code M)

Gov't Documents	Computer Files	Manuscripts and Archives	Cartographic	Graphic	Audio	Film and Video	
9	10	11	12	13	14	15	Survey Question # Institution
0	929	1,971	1,093	4,967	7,539	1,409	Columbus ST U
0	15	0	0	0	2,525	1,167	Concordia U Irvine
-1	1	-1	4	-1	7,988	3,682	Concordia U RiverF
-1	-1	-1	-1	-1	-1	6,847 [1]	Concordia U St Paul
0	562	467	2,600	64,169	96	1,068	Cooper Union
0	118	-1	-1	52	2,286	1,782	Cornerstone U
41,269	699	1,898	6	97	2,515	4,310	Creighton U
0	30	-1	269	0	78	1,327	Cumberland U
-1	48	1,198	0	0	0	1,114	CUNY BMB C
0	-1	-1	-1	4,500	5,013	20,595	CUNY C Stn Island
0	10,241	1,869	-1	145,050	18,371	19,929	CUNY City C
-1	86	-1	-1	-1	3,190	5,391	CUNY HH Lehman C
0	-1	415	-1	-1	-1	-1	UNY John Jay C Crim Just
219,225	3,002	1,074	258	69,933	32,303	2,003	CUNY Queens C
0	15	246 [1]	0	0	24,192	1,350	Curtis Inst Music
0	2 [1]	15	0	5,040 [1]	157	1,577	Daniel Webster C
0	15	205	12	1,134 [1]	3,031 [1]	3,370	DeSales U
0	1	14	12	0	6	11	DN Myers C
0	0	0	0	0	45	110 [1]	Dominican C San Rafael
-1	66	-1	34	2	2,948	2,901	Dominican U
104,941	1,000	350	0	0	744	1,216	Drake U
0	119	1,218	0	58,140	237	3,294	Drury C
24,950	750	0	100	100	0	5,150	E R Aero U
0	-1	1,800	17,653	30,268	-1	-1	Earlham C
140,049	2,578	2,489	26,752	10,880	14,762	10,815	Eastern IL U
-1	548	45 [1]	-1	-1	14,855	3,239	Eastern U
10,573	-1	2,011	0	2,176	27,324	7,383	Eastern WA U
493,100	1,615	1,183	3,218	10,204	17,626	6,192	Eastrn NM U Main
0	642	420	674	16,248	9,413	2,533	Edinboro U PA
0	214	255	-1	629	5,839	2,128	Elizabethtown C
0	22,401	255	0	40,127	3,051	2,981	Elmhurst C
74,428	300	-1	3	35	4,849	11,233	Elon U
0	0	138	0	0	0	597	Emmanuel C MA
160,213	0	23	1,860	0	322	4,255	Emory & Henry C
0	744	2,157	6,341	68,742	13,526	2,705	Evergreen ST C
20,398	83	725	7	-1	3,508	372	Fisk U
-1	5	2,818	-1	2,519 [1]	1,823	20	Fitchburg ST C
0	407	130	0	0	9,751	3,847	FL Southern C
0	0	0	0	0	0	0 [1]	Fort Hays ST U
46,661	21	909	0 [1]	0 [1]	0 [1]	0 [1]	Francis Marion U

Key to Notes on Page 1   1 -- See Footnotes   -1 -- Unavailable   -2 -- Not Applicable

INSTITUTIONS GRANTING MASTER OF ARTS AND PROFESSIONAL DEGREES (Carnegie Code M)

Lib. No.	Institution	Notes	Volumes in Library 1	Volumes added (Gross) 2	Volumes added (Net) 3	Monographs Purchased 4	Serials Purchased 5	Serials Received (not purchased) 6	Total Serials Received 7	Microf Uni 8
121	Franklin Inst Boston	b	4,435	15	15	15	50	0	50	
122	Franklin U		9,304	1,527	1,527	1,527	188	-1	188	
123	Free Will Baptist Bible C	bG	63,890	2,457	2,407	2,100	177	211	388	71,23
124	Frostburg ST U	bG	330,314	4,584	3,070	920	2,345	39	2,384	320,31
125	Furman U	G	422,200	24,858	20,059	9,346	3,348	495	3,843	851,00
126	GA SWstrn ST U	b	179,491	3,547	2,634	430	516 [1]	109 [1]	625	234,73
127	Gardner-Webb U	BbG	230,531	3,814	2,642	1,600 [1]	13,000	25	13,025	644,76
128	Geneva C	G	163,734	3,503	-6,263	2,879	734	123	857	223,04
129	Georgetown C		160,862	4,554	4,236	2,587	541	0	541	189,41
130	Goucher C	b	309,792	5,089	924	4,570	1,600	15	1,615	24,90
131	Governors ST U	bG	242,545	4,542	3,005	2,387	1,897	226	2,123	794,80
132	Greenville C		125,782	1,780	-5,643	553	370	128	498	15,88
133	Grove City C	b	136,558	6,244	-1,713	4,233	0	0	410	22,48
134	Harding U Main	bG	205,857	3,380	-15,418 [1]	2,777	988	203	1,191	254,07
135	Hebrew C		90,609	1,864	1,864	1,864	185	0	185 [1]	98
136	Heidelberg C	Bbf	148,349	1,900	857	1,722	475	16	491	264,09
137	Hillsdale Free Will Baptist C		23,904	626	493	93	123	109	232	4,70
138	Holy Apostles C & Sem	bGf	58,871	329	-16	98	220	6	226	22
139	Hood C	G	208,563	2,506	1,278	1,933	18,703 [1]	4,623 [1]	23,326	583,03
140	Humboldt ST U	G	597,921 [1]	9,929	6,335	6,664	1,423	705	2,128	608,10
141	IN Inst of Tech	bf	32,004	49	4	45	125	25	150	
142	IN U Kokomo	G	193,019	5,168	4,599	-1	976	76	1,052	472,43
143	IN U S Bend	b	300,476	7,796	5,835	4,086	1,719	0	1,719	1,145,68
144	IN U-Purdue U Ft Wayne	G	352,023	9,049	5,728	3,886 [1]	20,950 [1]	374 [1]	21,324	542,09
145	IN Wesleyan U	B	133,396	9,982	8,854	-1	659	-1	659	295,71
146	Intl Fine Arts C		19,373	671	700	671	195	10	205	
147	Jacksonville ST U	bG	674,818	16,064	14,936	-1	14,376 [1]	0	14,376	1,406,03
148	Johnson Bible C		104,808	3,014 [1]	2,460	-2	-2	-2	461	16,93
149	Kean U		286,100	6,100	6,100	6,000	16,000	0	16,000	193,00
150	Keene State C	b	301,741	5,711	3,596	8,247	903	0	903	757,56
151	Kent ST U Stark	b	75,259	2,141	1,683	1,426	253	18	271	-1
152	Kentucky Christian C	f	102,889	1,038 [1]	-272	808	378	7	385	8,20
153	Kentucky ST U	G	309,222	4,438	1,613	606	1	1	874	323,86
154	Kettering U	b	128,501	7,813	2,485	1,452	-1	-1	547	35,00
155	King's C PA		168,793	3,918	1,436	3,585	791	-1	974	562,74
156	LaGrange C	Bb	114,366	5,327 [1]	2,692 [1]	-1	-1 [1]	-1	-1	120,00
157	Lakeland C-AB		64,371	589	431	589	593	0	593	36,00
158	Lakeview C Nursing	b	3,029	439	431	50	41	8	49	0
159	Lancaster Bible C		132,599	5,611	-1	2,152	-1	-1	8,675	30,24
160	Lander U	G	178,389	3,398	2,593	1,263	879	136	1,015	154,61

Key to Notes on Page 1   1 -- See Footnotes   -1 -- Unavailable   -2 -- Not Applicable

ACRL Library Data Tables 2004
COLLECTIONS

INSTITUTIONS GRANTING MASTER OF ARTS AND PROFESSIONAL DEGREES (Carnegie Code M)

Gov't Documents	Computer Files	Manuscripts and Archives	Cartographic	Graphic	Audio	Film and Video	
9	10	11	12	13	14	15	Survey Question # Institution
0	0	0	0	0	0	44	Franklin Inst Boston
0	149	1	0	0	100	82	Franklin U
0	23	175	2	18	3,314	501	Free Will Baptist Bible C
0	53	250	30,387	10,129	5,831	2,854	Frostburg ST U
0	1,235	2,350	55,000	0	4,701	2,770	Furman U
153,977	31,112 [1]	-1	1,621 [1]	-1	9,356 [1]	-1 [1]	GA SWstrn ST U
15,000	468	115	100	773	2,655	2,072	Gardner-Webb U
0	0	91	202	996	10,193	2,380	Geneva C
0	3	300	0	-1	-1	-1	Georgetown C
0	-1	60	-1	-1	1,005	2,940	Goucher C
230,506	446	3,000	2,086	11,934	3,798	8,402	Governors ST U
-1	62	-1	-1	-1	1,771	2,148	Greenville C
0	365	0	0	0	18	965	Grove City C
38,614	721	6	634	223	6,751	1,170	Harding U Main
792	23	252	125	150	496	297	Hebrew C
142,246	151	24	141	35	7,841	472	Heidelberg C
0	28	-1	1	-1	120	344	Hillsdale Free Will Baptist C
0	16	15	0	4	115	149	Holy Apostles C & Sem
0	1,751	821	0	52	1,115	4,198	Hood C
400,419	1,179	9,792	26,486	5,885	14,318	6,007	Humboldt ST U
0	0	0	0	0	2	30	IN Inst of Tech
0	1,293	246	1,247	633	1,465	4,203	IN U Kokomo
155,308	3,229	1,370	4,933	18,475	2,750	17,686	IN U S Bend
8,235	627	-1	4,143	1,592	5,123	1,039	IN U-Purdue U Ft Wayne
-1	149	233	15	135	2,959	6,615	IN Wesleyan U
0	0	0	0	0	25	2,600	Intl Fine Arts C
0	-1	-1	-1	-1	33,319	2,317	Jacksonville ST U
0	5	95	0	1,985	9,887	1,076	Johnson Bible C
0	0	-1	-1	-1	-1	-1	Kean U
0	18	310	0	0	1,568	5,062	Keene State C
0	31	-1	-1	0	279	2,769	Kent ST U Stark
0	0	0	0	0	2,808 [1]	1,660 [1]	Kentucky Christian C
129,133	1,274	1 [1]	715	342	1,925	1,528	Kentucky ST U
0	400	4,500	0	0	125	125	Kettering U
0	22	0	0	0	436	2,157	King's C PA
-1	-1	180 [1]	1	-1	-1	2,505 [1]	LaGrange C
0	0	0	0	0	1,420	835	Lakeland C-AB
0	20	0	0	0	15	459	Lakeview C Nursing
0	16	0	0	909	2,844	854	Lancaster Bible C
3,134	759	-1	157	40	2,428	849	Lander U

Key to Notes on Page 1   1 -- See Footnotes   -1 -- Unavailable   -2 -- Not Applicable

INSTITUTIONS GRANTING MASTER OF ARTS AND PROFESSIONAL DEGREES (Carnegie Code M)

Lib. No. Institution	Notes	Volumes in Library 1	Volumes added (Gross) 2	Volumes added (Net) 3	Monographs Purchased 4	Serials Purchased 5	Serials Received (not purchased) 6	Total Serials Received 7	Microf. Unit 8
161 Langston U	BG	81,404	2,836	1,774	526	907	44	985	847,77
162 Laurentian U JN	bG	867,254	-1 [1]	-1 [1]	3,895	12	3,437	3,449	403,55
163 Le Moyne C	G	260,535	5,245	2,885	10,241	16,720	9	16,729	612,16
164 Lebanon Valley C	b	155,666	3,960	3,643	3,520	800	-1	800	14,01
165 Lewis U		149,849	3,852	3,540	2,750	857	15	872	165,51
166 Lewis&Clark C	G	291,432	11,531	10,273	7,126 [1]	-1	-1	2,543	461,09
167 Lincoln U-MO	b	196,489	6,120	5,741	5,587	397	3	400	91,58
168 Lindsey Wilson C	bG	49,996	2,301 [1]	2,141	1,552 [1]	13,145 [1]	23	13,145	420,200
169 Lipscomb U		209,085	2,723	2,404	-1	879	-1	879	397,74
170 Lock Haven U PA	BbG	429,941	7,127	-2,580	3,279	849	116	965	741,69
171 Longwood C	G	325,290 [1]	9,337	5,954	5,793	4,112	996	5,108	720,20
172 Lourdes C		59,682	1,262	1,181	573	446	3	449	10,18
173 Loyola Marymount U	b	398,758	16,092	11,603	15,416	18,509	0	18,509	142,73
174 Loyola U New Orleans	G	356,644	8,355	7,835	6,977	1,263	43	1,306	356,94
175 Lubbock Christian U	b	115,731	2,771	2,175	0	548	0	548	98,79
176 Luth Theo Sem Philly	bf	190,429	1,286	491	969	442	30	472	26,11
177 Lynchburg C		192,907	4,776	425	4,071	634	0	634	438,01
178 Malone C		179,979 [1]	5,152	3,685	2,828	969	416	1,385	652,63
179 Manchester C		178,464	1,718	1,602	1,385	590	27	617	23,07
180 Manhattan C		219,346	5,792	4,218	4,184	-1	-1	1,519	661,71
181 Marist C	G	181,126	5,326	4,779	-1	16,495	7	16,502	12,13
182 Mary Baldwin C	b	150,039	2,041	1,939	1,653	15,866	34	15,900	65,67
183 Mary Washington C	BbG	366,938	11,397	6,022	7,421	5,782	-1	5,782	631,70
184 Marymount U	G	194,887	5,057	2,012	4,723	1,398	-1	1,398	336,57
185 Maryville U St Louis	b	189,078	1,860	1,485	868 [1]	4,920	35	4,955	521,96
186 McNeese ST U		408,504	8,319	5,856	7,351	14,650 [1]	44	14,694	1,611,213
187 Medical C Wisconsin	BbGM	264,956	9,470	8,935	2,813	1,984	3,500 [1]	5,484	1,100
188 Merrimack C	b	115,925	2,498	-129	2,031	528	0	528	11,624
189 MidAmer Nazarene U		85,293	683	124	0	225	0	225	340,02
190 Millikin U	bG	211,539	1,632	-606	804	460	51	511	21,534
191 Millsaps C	G	190,982	3,043	2,661	1,247	9,214	85	9,299	79,24
192 Minnesota ST U-Mankato	bG	773,185	6,492	3,218	6,492	2,544 [1]	2,206	4,750	260,39
193 Minot ST U	G	175,470	1,988	1,815	1,988	752	-1	752	709,857
194 Monterey Inst Intl St	f	91,158	1,720	1,720	1,700	575	20	595	23
195 Moravian C		255,800	6,084	-1,837	4,124	1,166	50	1,216	12,000
196 Morehead ST U	G	506,116	26,599	17,913	5,031	2,556	272	2,828	835,491
197 Morningside C	bG	113,169	1,310	-1,692 [1]	433	528	0	528	295,215
198 MS Valley ST U	BG	114,291	2,350	2,050	10	400	36	436	341,455
199 Mt Holyoke C		717,393	13,661	11,443	10,000	3,364	200	3,564	23,088
200 Mt Marty C		76,571	686	-870	-1	385	17	402	12,068

Key to Notes on Page 1   1 -- See Footnotes   -1 -- Unavailable   -2 -- Not Applicable

ACRL Library Data Tables 2004
COLLECTIONS

INSTITUTIONS GRANTING MASTER OF ARTS AND PROFESSIONAL DEGREES (Carnegie Code M)

Gov't Documents	Computer Files	Manuscripts and Archives	Cartographic	Graphic	Audio	Film and Video	
9	10	11	12	13	14	15	Survey Question # Institution
17,163	1,294	221	598	3,425	534	714	Langston U
-1 [1]	416	1,234	120	0	333	325	Laurentian U JN
0	241	1,866	0	3,359	3,913	5,491	Le Moyne C
-1	-1	-1	-1	-1	5,059	4,831	Lebanon Valley C
217,143	23	0	0	0	138	3,480	Lewis U
-1	-1	-1	360	0	9,170	4,650	Lewis&Clark C
-1	-1	1,055	-1	-1	1,863	5,135	Lincoln U-MO
3,853 [1]	494 [1]	126 [1]	795 [1]	96 [1]	266 [1]	2,044 [1]	Lindsey Wilson C
-1	0	60	-1	-1	0	2	Lipscomb U
0	0	0	1,895	0	5,308	972	Lock Haven U PA
0	102	666	4	12	6,609	11,661	Longwood C
0	1	0	275 [1]	362	39	1,446 [1]	Lourdes C
0	304	2,645	384	20,942	6,657	13,405	Loyola Marymount U
-1	-1	-1	-1	-1	8,189	5,066	Loyola U New Orleans
0	0	0	0	36	440	58	Lubbock Christian U
0	55	3,726	0	0	3,834	1,492	Luth Theo Sem Philly
0	-1	-1	-1	0	2,331	2,648	Lynchburg C
0	1,433	560	2,904	0	6,112	2,105	Malone C
0	119	-1	0	0	5,053	498	Manchester C
-1	-1	4,000	-1	-1	94	1,057	Manhattan C
0	0	1,857	0	-1	46	4,955	Marist C
0	45	1,060	55	5	3,376	3,155	Mary Baldwin C
0	-1	-1	-1	-1	-1	1,206	Mary Washington C
-1	-1	-1	-1	-1	-1 [1]	-1 [1]	Marymount U
58,735	0	320	546	2,887	8,949	2,042	Maryville U St Louis
-1	491	0 [1]	-1	-1	52	1,074	McNeese ST U
0 [1]	147 [1]	210	0	0	0	100	Medical C Wisconsin
0	17	0	0	0	2	1,972	Merrimack C
0	227	0	0	2,146	4,504	2,775	MidAmer Nazarene U
0	0	142 [1]	115	245	9,037	2,388	Millikin U
0	9	577	-1	-1	8,409 [1]	-1	Millsaps C
0	847	1,800	260,390	25,046	10,091	7,207	Minnesota ST U-Mankato
182,146	579	101	121,559	-1	9,964	3,019	Minot ST U
0	1	1	0	0	0	0	Monterey Inst Intl St
0	-1	422	0	0	549	2,920	Moravian C
20,158	1,430	2,800	1,722	2,864	7,808	10,832	Morehead ST U
0	0	430	0	0	3,756	1,845	Morningside C
950	1,450	529	0	307	2,507	944	MS Valley ST U
0	0	9,000	182	484	1,683	4,104	Mt Holyoke C
0	0	-1	2	1,392	5,898	1,265	Mt Marty C

Key to Notes on Page 1   1 -- See Footnotes   -1 -- Unavailable   -2 -- Not Applicable

ACRL Library Data Tables 2004
COLLECTIONS

INSTITUTIONS GRANTING MASTER OF ARTS AND PROFESSIONAL DEGREES (Carnegie Code M)

Lib. No. / Institution	Notes	Volumes in Library 1	Volumes added (Gross) 2	Volumes added (Net) 3	Monographs Purchased 4	Serials Purchased 5	Serials Received (not purchased) 6	Total Serials Received 7	Microf Unit 8
201 Mt Mary C-WI	bf	85,144	1,698	751	1,362	285	0	285	-
202 MT ST U Northern	bG	143,571	3,342	-4,180	1,606	286	48	334	1,042,82
203 Mt St Vincent U	Gf	231,141	2,878	2,705	2,160	4,634	26	4,660	791,26
204 MT Tech U Montana	bG	165,898	6,535	6,094	342	22,085	2,866	23,951	108,40
205 Murray ST U-KY	L	508,253	6,507	5,269	2,436	1,898	1	1,898	203,80
206 Muskingum C		203,710	1,192	801	1,000 [1]	622	20	642	160,00
207 Natl C Naturopathic Med	bM	12,020	120	20	105	130	10	140	85
208 Natl Defense U	bGf	278,710 [1]	12,210	7,944	5,815	1,284	220	1,504	500,00
209 NC Sch Arts		114,875	1,955	1,930	1,542	5,495 [1]	0	5,495	25,35
210 NEastrn IL U	B	713,076	12,579	4,663	-1	20,564	-1	20,564	869,24
211 Nipissing U	B	178,058	7,053	4,406	6,703	12,896	2,526	13,350	324,47
212 NJ City U		253,818	3,893	3,865	1,379	901	28	929	14,65
213 NM Highlands U	B	415,582	5,911	1,138	1,736	740	0	740	92
214 North Central C		150,777	2,108	1,596	1,517	560	43	603	212,62
215 Northern KY U	b	296,436	4,730	2,230	3,087	1,886	0	1,886	1,499,37
216 Northern ST U	bGf	192,742	-1	5,368	2,553	-1	-1	150	390,16
217 Northwest C	b	125,124	497	299	1,121	468	22	490	76
218 Norwich U	G	305,264	3,723	1,534	2,045	11,945	99	12,044	89,88
219 Notre Dame C OH		93,464	858	133	171	174	102	276	16,59
220 Notre Dame Sem	b	84,613	775	184	375	160	25	185	2,779
221 NW MO ST U	bG	326,919	11,240	9,761	4,500	-1 [1]	-1	10,914 [1]	827,74
222 NY Inst Tech Islip		44,957	1,707	1,496	1,498	192	17	209	80,57
223 NY Inst Tech Main	M	127,845	3,204	1,099	3,204	2,136	30	2,166	692,91
224 Oberlin C	B	1,330,222	27,679	25,747	17,174	20,793	-1	20,793	345,64
225 OH U Lancaster	b	97,038	2,782	2,445	2,400	236	12	248	391,07
226 Olivet Nazarene U	G	202,303	3,923	3,663	2,059	731	158	889	324,37
227 Otterbein C	G	202,733 [1]	5,128	3,281	2,574	7,976	-1 [1]	7,976	393,84
228 Pace U Law		648,947	6,236	2,116	3,537	243	0	243	47,27
229 Pacific Lutheran U	f	340,842	11,273	-7,964 [1]	-1	3,370	-1	3,370	235,93
230 Pacific Union C		141,729	4,639	4,581	3,209	676	136	812	17,19
231 Palm Beach Atl C	b	113,498	6,973	6,762	3,268	4,976	11	4,987	253,19
232 Pfeiffer U	Bb	121,594	2,104	2,027	1,883	-1	-1	396	33,14
233 Philadelphia U	b	109,235	2,642	-1,534	2,309	976	35	1,011	125,00
234 Plymouth ST C	G	324,370 [1]	9,752 [1]	8,605 [1]	7,996 [1]	1,356 [1]	-1	1,356 [1]	657,49
235 Pont C Josephinum		138,764	2,729	2,442	1,512	2,355	4	2,359	1,87
236 Pope John Ntl Sem	bf	55,727	1,089	1,064	1,061	233	0	227	0
237 Prescott C	Bb	25,054	1,817	1,568	477	241	11	252	101
238 Providence C	b	314,695	6,985	-1	5,900 [1]	-1	-1	1,775	12,019
239 Purchase C SUNY		279,003	4,615	3,323	2,801	14,149	1,508	15,657	253,222
240 Purdue U Calumet	G	271,607	8,286	3,315	5,234	1,063	165	1,228	764,621

Key to Notes on Page 1   1 -- See Footnotes   -1 -- Unavailable   -2 -- Not Applicable

ACRL Library Data Tables 2004
COLLECTIONS

INSTITUTIONS GRANTING MASTER OF ARTS AND PROFESSIONAL DEGREES (Carnegie Code M)

Gov't Documents	Computer Files	Manuscripts and Archives	Cartographic	Graphic	Audio	Film and Video	
9	10	11	12	13	14	15	Survey Question # Institution
-1	-1	-1	-1	-1	3,600	6,629	Mt Mary C-WI
-2	-2	513	4,772	-11	299	378	MT ST U Northern
6,835	142	-1	-1	-1	417	624	Mt St Vincent U
56,790 [1]	3,162	-1 [1]	7,622 [1]	-1	0	46	MT Tech U Montana
217,369	2,030	1,594	11,726	7,523	5,159	6,151	Murray ST U-KY
167,741	-1	-1	-1	-1	122	112	Muskingum C
0	12	3	0	0	400	450	Natl C Naturopathic Med
0	0	7,162	42,000	5,000	1,500	3,000	Natl Defense U
0	0	875	0	5,000	47,500	4,000	NC Sch Arts
0	1,959	1,018	4,670	38,124	2,186	3,963	NEastrn IL U
8,765	178	30	-1	-1	1,761	3,226	Nipissing U
1,509	0	0	0	0	0	3,180	NJ City U
0	0	0	0	0	0	0	NM Highlands U
0	-1	644	-1	-1	2,308	1,653	North Central C
210,318	789	-1	307	5,044	1,881	1,532	Northern KY U
35,770	12,322	700	-1	-1	960	2,580	Northern ST U
0	0	0	572	14,616	3,103	1,715	Northwest C
0	223	-1	254	0	540	2,150	Norwich U
0	2,385	0	473	7,405	2,191	487	Notre Dame C OH
0	4	-1 [1]	0	0	155	590	Notre Dame Sem
0 [1]	69	304	75	232	1,574	3,676	NW MO ST U
0 [1]	335	3	442	3,785	245	346	NY Inst Tech Islip
-1	271	6	1,121	37,946	0	1,607	NY Inst Tech Main
477,924	1,334	7,527 [1]	-1	-1	63,195	19,361	Oberlin C
0	0	837	3	20	1,753	1,153	OH U Lancaster
74,360	81	575	11,101	0	5,748	1,988	Olivet Nazarene U
54,863	960	1,800 [1]	2,500	1,469	5,387	6,141	Otterbein C
0	0	0	0	0	25	1,922	Pace U Law
-1	270	-1	12,210 [1]	-1	-1	-1	Pacific Lutheran U
0	118	42	955	30,019	5,922	3,299	Pacific Union C
0	34	403	0	1	99 [1]	256	Palm Beach Atl C
0	1	-1	5	149	2,521	371	Pfeiffer U
0	250	87	0	48,260	60	2,370	Philadelphia U
0	81	0	262	1,501	7,917	3,381	Plymouth ST C
0	12	0	0	2,252	2,435	829	Pont C Josephinum
0	52	0	10	0	7,593 [1]	539	Pope John Ntl Sem
0	0	125	0	9	255	1,666	Prescott C
248,594	0	-1	-1	0	0	0	Providence C
0	239	58	431	87,567	14,295	1,999	Purchase C SUNY
0	0	342	0	0	0	998	Purdue U Calumet

Key to Notes on Page 1   1 -- See Footnotes   -1 -- Unavailable   -2 -- Not Applicable

ACRL Library Data Tables 2004
COLLECTIONS

INSTITUTIONS GRANTING MASTER OF ARTS AND PROFESSIONAL DEGREES (Carnegie Code M)

Lib. No.	Institution	Notes	Volumes in Library 1	Volumes added (Gross) 2	Volumes added (Net) 3	Monographs Purchased 4	Serials Purchased 5	Serials Received (not purchased) 6	Total Serials Received 7	Microfo Unit 8
241	Purdue U North Central	G	86,212	3,174	1,890	1,941	397	0	397	2,88
242	Quincy U	b	194,145	3,874	1,330	1,751	492	32	524	188,59
243	R.Wesleyan C	G	123,434	3,063	2,402	2,867	1,057 [1]	29	1,086	171,16
244	Radford U	G	396,040	20,009	19,341	4,136	3,375	1,088	4,463	1,485,93
245	Ramapo C NJ	bf	156,590	6,577	6,002	-1 [1]	567	-1	567	20,25
246	Recnstrctnst Rabbinical C	b	45,570	590	590	590	128	5	133	
247	RI Sch Design		122,692	3,496	3,213	2,916 [1]	420	0	420	1,85
248	Rivier C	b	90,494	4,811	-2,811	4,311	588	0	588	130,00
249	Rockhurst U	bG	306,200	4,950	3,950	3,000	800	50	850	234,10
250	Roger Williams U	G	202,528	9,317	7,949	8,725	1,511	530	2,041	138,57
251	Roosevelt U	Bb	186,096	6,507	5,468	3,833	20,719 [1]	0	1,129	170,62
252	Rosemont C	b	161,374	2,100	1,643	2,093	529	10	539	25,02
253	Salem Teiko U	G	106,427	1,243	889	0	0 [1]	11	11	279,14
254	Salisbury ST U		254,151	5,347	983	3,912	-1	-1	1,271	747,87
255	San Jose ST U	bG	1,193,024	24,658	22,599	13,062	2,454	412	2,866	1,674,25
256	Savannah ST U	bf	150,430	816	540	945	743	5	748	585,12
257	Schreiner C		77,432	1,307	1,057	897	225	15	240	55,06
258	SE LA U	Bf	382,877	6,779	5,983	6,916	-1	-1	2,468	765,22
259	SE MO ST U		427,233	11,126	6,862	6,171	24,108	-1	24,108	1,285,23
260	SE Oklahoma St U	b	291,141	7,162	3,112	1,722	661	286	947	586,11
261	Seton Hill C		106,027	2,109	1,965	1,498	396	119	515	5,13
262	SF Consrv Music		54,047	1,684	721	879	-1	-1	77	
263	Shaw U		154,368	1,194	1,064	1,194	138 [1]	440	578	-
264	Shorter C	Bb	136,400	3,627	1,875	1,129	596	48	644	7,33
265	Silver Lake C	f	60,309	1,332	-201 [1]	680	199	78	277	2,15
266	Sisseton-Wahpeton CC	bG	14,215	0	0	200	115	47	162	
267	Southrn C Opt	M	21,983	278	208	-1	131	53	184	51
268	Southrn IL U Edward		799,302	9,115	7,491	6,091	11,686	487	12,173	1,660,67
269	Southrn OR U	G	356,855	9,807	7,518	5,026	2,306	166	2,472	797,06
270	Spring Hill C	bf	172,973	3,840	3,529	2,074	570	10	580	479,11
271	St Ambrose U		141,610	3,819	3,170	2,607	1,180	40	1,220	6,72
272	St C.Borromeo Sem	bf	125,212	3,387	3,062	6,444	3,331 [1]	20	3,351	2,18
273	St Cloud ST U	b	897,973	12,038	10,511	6,393	3,954	38	3,992	1,839,50
274	St Francis C PA	G	117,918	1,484	464	473	330	0	330	8,05
275	St Francis-Xavier U	bf	646,321	4,771	1,825	3,445	6,380	15	6,395	305,06
276	St John Fisher C	bGf	177,574	5,948	1,011	5,875	983 [1]	0	983	206,35
277	St Joseph C Suffolk	b	110,144	3,179	2,175	3,087	323 [1]	0	323	3,75
278	St Joseph's C IN	bG	157,021	1,322	90	1,322	409	-1	409	69,13
279	St Joseph's C NY	bf	110,550	1,550	1,550	1,550	220	5	225	3,99
280	St Joseph's Sem	b	87,125	969	0	523	285	0	285	9,66

Key to Notes on Page 1   1 -- See Footnotes   -1 -- Unavailable   -2 -- Not Applicable

COLLECTIONS

INSTITUTIONS GRANTING MASTER OF ARTS AND PROFESSIONAL DEGREES (Carnegie Code M)

Gov't Documents	Computer Files	Manuscripts and Archives	Cartographic	Graphic	Audio	Film and Video	
9	10	11	12	13	14	15	Survey Question # Institution
0	0	0	0	0	0	259	Purdue U North Central
0	4	2,500	12	0	5,167	2,194	Quincy U
0	8	25	0	0	3,447	448	R.Wesleyan C
0	203	420	81	971	6,433	7,995	Radford U
-1	-1	-1	-1	-1	461	2,602	Ramapo C NJ
0	5	0	0	0	0	0	Recnstrctnst Rabbinical C
0	267	1,571	1	701,901	986	2,710	RI Sch Design
0	246	0	0	0	1,404	142	Rivier C
0	10	0	0	0	950	3,000	Rockhurst U
0	723	516	409	64,225	2,291	2,696	Roger Williams U
0	0	-1	0	0	11,805	0	Roosevelt U
0	0	50,237	0	0	988	1,870	Rosemont C
0	0	-1	-1	-1	-1	-1	Salem Teiko U
241,604	654	-1	-1	3,551	822	94	Salisbury ST U
329,963	1,054	2,797	10,370	3,001	21,936	10,172	San Jose ST U
0	0	738 [1]	0	540	1,077	2,645	Savannah ST U
0	29,495 [1]	-1	-1	-1	104	1,257	Schreiner C
212,462	1,653	0	531	36,808	5,883	5,978	SE LA U
314,187	3,250	317	2,277	759	1,744	11,363	SE MO ST U
75,969	970	441	1,408	508	3,680	3,453	SE Oklahoma St U
0	141	0	0	0	3,863	6,478	Seton Hill C
0	0	12	0	0	15,272	1,427	SF Consrv Music
0	-1	980	1 [1]	0	0	33	Shaw U
0	52	0	52	382	9,718	1,652	Shorter C
0	11	0	124	4,867 [1]	7,130	1,411	Silver Lake C
780 [1]	0	0	6 [1]	0	300 [1]	347	Sisseton-Wahpeton CC
0	78	0	0	13,030	951	283	Southrn C Opt
649,399	952	8,162	3,108	4,642	38,010	5,968	Southrn IL U Edward
250,551	170	0	9,947	3,970	767	7,012	Southrn OR U
180,201	161	565	290	0	123	131	Spring Hill C
0	-1	1,084	26	-1	-1	3,351	St Ambrose U
0	81	0	2	50	9,081	7,231	St C.Borromeo Sem
0	298	1,803	1,572	607	5,484	16,726	St Cloud ST U
0	415	1,194	0	421	218	2,681	St Francis C PA
-1	-1	2,334	0	0	6,365	1,377	St Francis-Xavier U
0	0	50	210	12,000	11,500	5,600	St John Fisher C
0	0	56	0	0	32 [1]	1,299 [1]	St Joseph C Suffolk
99,933	290	-1	-1	14,193	7,493	896	St Joseph's C IN
0	0	15 [1]	0	0	481	550	St Joseph's C NY
0	0	0	0	0	0	0	St Joseph's Sem

Key to Notes on Page 1   1 -- See Footnotes   -1 -- Unavailable   -2 -- Not Applicable

INSTITUTIONS GRANTING MASTER OF ARTS AND PROFESSIONAL DEGREES (Carnegie Code M)

Lib. No.	Institution	Notes	Volumes in Library 1	Volumes added (Gross) 2	Volumes added (Net) 3	Monographs Purchased 4	Serials Purchased 5	Serials Received (not purchased) 6	Total Serials Received 7	Microf. Unit 8
281	St Mary's U MN	G	168,923	2,858	2,140	2,181	708	-1	708	-
282	St Meinrad Theo	b	170,542	1,142	1,127	914 [1]	-1	-1	329	10,46
283	St Michael's C	b	220,288	6,135	5,143	3,900 [1]	1,429	50	1,479	128,50
284	St Norbert C		209,475	2,695	2,371	1,795	652	0	652	29,92
285	St Patrick's Sem	f	102,439	2,061	2,025	1,429	319	35	354	2,17
286	St Peter's Abbey & C	bGf	51,800	934	934	87	28	47	75	
287	ST U W GA		391,330	9,681	7,081	9,681	2,264	-1	2,264	1,132,93
288	St Vincent Sem		62,936	1,796	880	1,310	380	0	380	79
289	St. John's C		105,945	7,000	5,927	1,538	112	5	117	41
290	Stetson U	B	378,988	7,576	5,381	4,125 [1]	14,505 [1]	375	14,880	408,12
291	Sthrn Polytech ST U	G	120,764	2,182	-1,578	1,202	1,124	12	1,136	57,57
292	Stonehill C	bG	215,581	14,417 [1]	10,981	2,306	2,224	1,873	4,097 [1]	360,23
293	Sul Ross ST U	bf	250,356	2,866	1,201	2,866	1,592	0	1,592	573,09
294	SUNY Brockport		642,650 [1]	15,741	9,116	-1	1,960	-1	1,960	2,055,86
295	SUNY Buffalo		655,096	5,968	3,910	2,804	2,674	0	2,674	1,007,63
296	SUNY C Potsdam	G	409,026	3,663	271	1,966	640	293	933	770,00
297	SUNY IT Utica	G	195,491	1,084	28	552	617	30	647	65,71
298	SUNY Oneonta	G	552,389	6,477	5,242	4,009	18,876	174	19,050	1,166,99
299	SUNY Oswego	G	475,507	8,383	2,605	5,228	2,910	158	3,068	2,066,96
300	SW MO ST U	B	835,338	13,002	10,924	5,454	3,639	-1	3,639	1,043,62
301	SWstrn Adventist U	b	110,261	-1	-1	-1	-1	-1	439	7,03
302	SWstrn OK ST U	bf	-1	-1	-1	-1	-1	-1	-1	-
303	Tabor C	b	81,384 [1]	1,651	1,384	1,497	132	14	146	
304	Tiffin U	b	33,688	1,600	1,600	1,600	250	1	251	34,72
305	TM Cooley Law Sch	BbGL	232,834	16,320	14,123	1,359 [1]	887	0	887	1,259,29
306	Trinity Luth Sem		137,972	1,813	1,761	1,284	318	108	426	3,28
307	Trinity U	b	917,781	14,128	12,225	8,462	24,293	15	24,308	1,358,70
308	Trinity U		216,567	1,248	887	-1	223	10	233	6,88
309	Troy ST U	Bb	443,415	16,823	13,681	4,077	1,397	0	1,397	1,578,14
310	Troy ST U Dothan	bG	103,223	1,935	1,285	-1	403	12	415	290,05
311	Truman ST U	b	455,971	8,488	6,696	-1	3,631	-1	3,631	1,531,45
312	TX Chiro C	bM	16,346	721	324	700	131	28	159	
313	U Arts	bG	126,799	3,460	2,314	2,464 [1]	551	1	552	46
314	U C Cape	bG	231,208	3,732	3,632	2,247	-1	-1	21,555	17,767
315	U Charleston	b	120,044	1,633	1,265	1,633	298	2	300	229,551
316	U DC	b	561,627	3,909	-1	-1	630	-1	-1	607,224
317	U Del Turabo		112,090	2,544	2,421	2,544	134	29	163	26,884
318	U Findlay	bG	143,945	12,888	11,893	-1	817	62	879	111,645
319	U Hawaii-Hilo	bG	225,868	3,027	2,643	3,988	20,711	3,232	23,943	486,027
320	U HI-Kauai CC	b	57,739	3,541	3,202	203	175	21	196	6,709

Key to Notes on Page 1   1 -- See Footnotes   -1 -- Unavailable   -2 -- Not Applicable

ACRL Library Data Tables 2004
COLLECTIONS

INSTITUTIONS GRANTING MASTER OF ARTS AND PROFESSIONAL DEGREES (Carnegie Code M)

Gov't Documents	Computer Files	Manuscripts and Archives	Cartographic	Graphic	Audio	Film and Video	
9	10	11	12	13	14	15	Survey Question # Institution
0	0	-1	180	64	5,201	2,617	St Mary's U MN
0	49	26	-1	976	4,157	756	St Meinrad Theo
0	459	100	492	87	1,840	4,488	St Michael's C
-1	-1	345	860	-1	3,290	3,292	St Norbert C
0	4	8	0	0	1,390	730	St Patrick's Sem
0	40	0	0	800	35	45	St Peter's Abbey & C
201,779	-1	348	20,744	7,125	1,098	1,807	ST U W GA
0	37	400	0	0	927	531	St Vincent Sem
20	15	745	0	0	836	540	St. John's C
231,596	2,860	950	1,418	2,252	12,515 [1]	2,681	Stetson U
0	9	114	2,650	0	0	52	Sthrn Polytech ST U
44,143	682	3,940	583	0	2,783	3,306	Stonehill C
0	4,582	0	683	2,117	622	5,535	Sul Ross ST U
141,106	-1	353	1,940	210	5,785	7,375	SUNY Brockport
0	674	9,681	538	4,382	8,909	7,413	SUNY Buffalo
57,637	1,771	720	6,785	2,436	14,140	1,430	SUNY C Potsdam
61,717	532	206	0	8,238	2,541	723	SUNY IT Utica
26,997	1,109	597	28,200	15,238	9,603	2,351	SUNY Oneonta
150,767	66	669	4,450	15,177	7,404	5,154	SUNY Oswego
923,651	-1	2,814	176,905	-1	7,328	32,893	SW MO ST U
-1	-1	715	-1	-1	-1	1,741	SWstrn Adventist U
-1	-1	-1	-1	-1	-1	-1	SWstrn OK ST U
0	4	2,304 [1]	0	9	1,127	807	Tabor C
-2	15	30	-2	-2	-2	564	Tiffin U
0	63	147	0	0	1,946	1,194	TM Cooley Law Sch
0	57	336	0	0	4,714	1,408	Trinity Luth Sem
449,146	1,828	1,098	6,070	28,586	27,815	8,169	Trinity U
0	0	-1	-1	10,000	2,000	1,589	Trinity U
0	80	389	1,112	770	5,938	8,096	Troy ST U
0	0	268	-1	-1	90	1,599	Troy ST U Dothan
36,945	-1	1,000	596	13,876	10,670	14,142	Truman ST U
0	56	46	0	264	118	962	TX Chiro C
0	283	200	9	311,206	20,503	1,904	U Arts
-1	-1	4,921	588	-1	630	2,682	U C Cape
-1	-1	177	219	-1	2,936	598	U Charleston
-1	-1	-1	-1	-1	-1	20,009 [1]	U DC
-1	468	-1	73	231	406	2,155	U Del Turabo
33,757	721	563	1,594	966	525	4,758	U Findlay
357,956	-1	-1	-1	-1	2,936	6,188	U Hawaii-Hilo
0	100	0	312	1,648	1,890	1,360	U HI-Kauai CC

Key to Notes on Page 1   1 -- See Footnotes   -1 -- Unavailable   -2 -- Not Applicable

INSTITUTIONS GRANTING MASTER OF ARTS AND PROFESSIONAL DEGREES (Carnegie Code M)

Lib. No.	Institution	Notes	Volumes in Library 1	Volumes added (Gross) 2	Volumes added (Net) 3	Monographs Purchased 4	Serials Purchased 5	Serials Received (not purchased) 6	Total Serials Received 7	Microf Uni 8
321	U Houston	b	461,281 [1]	17,965	16,529	4,944	965	84	1,049	1,955,95
322	U Mary	bGf	65,842	2,572	-2,810 [1]	2,197	584	0	584	1,04
323	U MI Dearborn		346,079	6,801	6,271	4,765	650	-2	650	550,63
324	U Mobile	bG	69,544	2,085	1,916	1,876	483	38	521	154,95
325	U NE Kearney	b	501,785	23,120	18,822	3,400	1,514	69	1,583	1,004,49
326	U Portland	bG	340,837	7,539	-758	7,342	2,451	0	2,451	547,38
327	U Richmond		788,203	17,795	15,814	12,219	20,542	289	20,831	394,92
328	U Rio Grande	bGf	91,791	576	517	518	380	3,248	3,628	439,92
329	U Scranton	b	357,821	8,717	8,355	5,531	1,714 [1]	20	1,734	525,88
330	U Sthn IN	bG	300,450	8,401	4,028	4,007	6,965	7,769	14,734	579,37
331	U Tampa	bG	254,016	3,587	376	5,018	-1	-1	7,524	51,27
332	U TN Chatt	bG	503,848	11,924	7,754	3,992	11,782	49	11,831	1,307,49
333	U TN Martin	BbG	350,400	3,788	1,482	2,030	1,724 [1]	7	1,731	703,69
334	U TX Tyler	BG	-1	-1	-1	-1	-1	-1	-1	-
335	U West AL		149,298	1,833	1,833	1,833	257	0	257	473,47
336	U WI E Claire	b	760,132	14,268	-4,143	7,247	2,206	40	2,246	136,69
337	U WI La Crosse	G	671,993	10,285	6,460	7,003	3,213	41	1,750	1,240,98
338	U WI Platteville	bG	272,065	4,359	2,742	2,527	2,122	0	2,122	1,015,08
339	U Winnipeg	bG	452,727	11,750	10,085	7,180	1,206	-1	1,206	143,07
340	UNC Asheville	b	387,513	8,847	2,402	4,658	3,871	58	3,929	857,21
341	UNC Pembroke	bGf	325,499	26,849	10,017	3,982	1,102	98	1,200	694,58
342	Union C-NY		583,517	13,659	12,009	9,903	-1	-1	3,728	642,40
343	Valparaiso U		314,914	5,529	-27,768	4,707	20,518	0	20,518	980,77
344	Villa Julie C	bG	76,421	3,891	3,487	3,085	717	1	718	167,73
345	W.Carey College	Bb	98,139	3,394	2,039	880	387	85	472	15,56
346	W.Mitchell C Law	GL	186,161	6,575	4,055	1,107 [1]	4,119	389	4,508	865,16
347	Walla Walla C	b	175,522	12,088	10,757	2,923 [1]	943	203	1,146	18,00
348	Walsh C Acct Bus Admin	B	-1	-1	-1	-1	-1	-1	-1	-
349	Wartburg Theo Sem	bf	89,942	1,548	1,536	812	225	31	256	-
350	Washburn U Topeka	bG	338,842	9,509	1,869	4,803	1,436	297	1,733	584,13
351	Washington C	Gf	246,710	3,475	2,758	22,624	-1	-1	15,678	252,80
352	Washington Theo Union	bf	87,130	2,179	2,179	2,017	438	37	475	55
353	Wayland Bap U		119,105	2,092	1,772	1,819	695	0	695	276,69
354	Wayne ST C	bG	-1	13,007	-1	-1	652	-1	-1	625,34
355	Webber Intl U	b	14,649	423	-10,997	423	39	10	49	0
356	Wesley C	bf	102,584	1,742	1,742	196	232	10	242	178,07
357	West Chester U PA		616,789	11,628	8,420	10,668	5,373	735	6,108	879,548
358	West TX A & M U	bG	514,585	7,496	6,999	702	6,396	10,577 [1]	16,973	1,266,671
359	West VA Wesleyan C		135,160	3,019	890	2,140	-1 [1]	-1	-1	37,693
360	Western MD C	b	201,180	4,269	3,894	3,632	1,929	65	1,994	1,434,443

Key to Notes on Page 1   1 -- See Footnotes   -1 -- Unavailable   -2 -- Not Applicable

ACRL Library Data Tables 2004
COLLECTIONS

INSTITUTIONS GRANTING MASTER OF ARTS AND PROFESSIONAL DEGREES (Carnegie Code M)

Gov't Documents	Computer Files	Manuscripts and Archives	Cartographic	Graphic	Audio	Film and Video	
9	10	11	12	13	14	15	Survey Question # Institution
70,777	1,854	3,600	1	1	1	869	U Houston
0	0	0	0	25	120	5,462	U Mary
-2	534	-2	122	11	1,895	2,721	U MI Dearborn
0	55	0	400	0	2,011	1,266	U Mobile
89,105	321	677	162	42,380	5,118	27,815	U NE Kearney
0	42	0	0	2,224	7,662	4,336	U Portland
0	3,495	2,352	2,592	0	17,535	9,338	U Richmond
29,396	45	0	0	0	1,368	967	U Rio Grande
0	2,151	2,000	0	2,251	4,735	6,913	U Scranton
40,555	664	2,667	5,293	17,212	3,143	2,234	U Sthn IN
0	1,035	660	1,109	3,001	2,160	2,900	U Tampa
0	292	1,344	0	85	11,855	7,582	U TN Chatt
134,002	595	1,190	-1	217	7,380 [1]	4,777 [1]	U TN Martin
-1	-1	-1	-1	-1	-1	-1	U TX Tyler
0	63	2,000	0	0	0	3,072	U West AL
0	858	2,852	75,121	6,889	4,078	5,033	U WI E Claire
202,424	1,894	869	28,559	167,117	1,772	2,485	U WI La Crosse
90,182	3,087	3,252	19,533	2,216	5,916	3,106	U WI Platteville
0	0	102	0	0	225	4,140	U Winnipeg
0	2,230	617	800	32,205	6,286	4,887	UNC Asheville
0	0	110	0	0	295	2,000	UNC Pembroke
232,926	-1	4,071	-1	-1	8,167	3,986	Union C-NY
0	2,015	1,200	76,206	16	2,593	1,952	Valparaiso U
0	87	130	-1	-1	144	2,337	Villa Julie C
0	37	0	0	1,375	333	456	W.Carey College
1,914	359	84	0	0	779	666	W.Mitchell C Law
-2	3,131	369	-1	-1	-1	3,431	Walla Walla C
-1	-1	-1	-1	-1	-1	-1	Walsh C Acct Bus Admin
0	73	-1	-2	-2	-1	529	Wartburg Theo Sem
0	558	444	4,635	9,824	1,009	1,928	Washburn U Topeka
0	762	555	1,794	0	2,117	1,681	Washington C
0	23	0	0	0	62	196	Washington Theo Union
0	68	-1	0	5,702	3,517	2,182	Wayland Bap U
-1	-1	-1	-1	-1	-1	13,029 [1]	Wayne ST C
0	0	45	0	110	7	91	Webber Intl U
0	0	0	0	0	0	940	Wesley C
138,150	1,391	782	3,321	20,430	42,916	6,702	West Chester U PA
561,172	3,179	182	3,839	22	558	975	West TX A & M U
-1 [1]	577	15	62	212	1,334	4,669	West VA Wesleyan C
212,528	0	2,500	45	34	8,576	3,165	Western MD C

Key to Notes on Page 1   1 -- See Footnotes   -1 -- Unavailable   -2 -- Not Applicable

INSTITUTIONS GRANTING MASTER OF ARTS AND PROFESSIONAL DEGREES (Carnegie Code M)

Lib. No.	Institution	Notes	Volumes in Library 1	Volumes added (Gross) 2	Volumes added (Net) 3	Monographs Purchased 4	Serials Purchased 5	Serials Received (not purchased) 6	Total Serials Received 7	Microf Unit 8
361	Western OR U	bG	210,792	8,501	7,676	971 [1]	1,152	345	1,497	704,96
362	Western Sem	b	56,085	1,011	192	540	-1	-1	657	-
363	Western WA U	G	1,377,949	20,137	17,242	6,233 [1]	4,130 [1]	386	4,516	1,964,99
364	Westfield ST C	b	158,795	2,116	-5,652	1,582	14,463	4,828	19,291	481,02
365	Westminster C-UT	G	137,870	11,008 [1]	2,787	9,183 [1]	727	3,667	4,394	248,79
366	Wheeling Jesuit U	b	153,590	1,898	1,065	1,439	473	39	512	127,77
367	Whitworth C	G	175,543	3,405	3,055	-1	1,231	18	1,249	66,43
368	Wilkes U	G	358,269	12,439	8,359	-1	-1	-1	1,836	337,28
369	William Woods U	bL	143,677	11,914 [1]	11,857	11,119 [1]	15,756	40	15,796	11,07
370	Williams C		918,554	20,019	15,371	16,273	1,686	0	1,686	492,04
371	Wstrn IL U	Bb	1,249,506	26,270	26,111	7,754	20,452	-1	20,452	55,57
372	Wstrn Theo Sem	f	117,065	796	771	774	442	-1	442	4,62
373	Xavier U LA	b	214,489	7,037	6,745	5,174	18,038 [1]	8	18,046	785,99

ACRL Library Data Tables 2004
COLLECTIONS

INSTITUTIONS GRANTING MASTER OF ARTS AND PROFESSIONAL DEGREES (Carnegie Code M)

Gov't Documents	Computer Files	Manuscripts and Archives	Cartographic	Graphic	Audio	Film and Video	Survey Question #
9	10	11	12	13	14	15	Institution
134	56	516	3,031	208	243	1,982	Western OR U
0	0	50	0	6,638	3,216	535	Western Sem
-1	2,052	-1	-1	-1	23,944	8,873	Western WA U
0	125	300	10	35	1,032	2,690	Westfield ST C
0	32	1,100	1	31	2,293	4,341	Westminster C-UT
-1	-1	10	0	0	0	0	Wheeling Jesuit U
0	3	464	-1	-1	3,211	0	Whitworth C
-1	695	-1	0	0	5,056	5,627	Wilkes U
0	485	-1	2	47	13,871	4,226	William Woods U
426,811	475	4,466	-1	-1	29,342	8,734	Williams C
-1	1,127	-1	-1	-1	11,613	5,825	Wstrn IL U
-1	23	1,767	-1	-1	642	318	Wstrn Theo Sem
23,685	0	1,528	0	0	3,955	2,231	Xavier U LA

Key to Notes on Page 1   1 -- See Footnotes   -1 -- Unavailable   -2 -- Not Applicable

ACRL LIBRARY DATA TABLES 2004

SUMMARY DATA: EXPENDITURES

ALL INSTITUTIONS REPORTING

(Survey Question #)	Monographs	Current Serials	Other Library Materials	Misc. Materials	Total Library Materials	Contract Binding
	16	17	18	19	20	21
High	10,257,593	12,966,684	9,618,918	1,434,336	27,485,613	961,035
Mean	299,362	737,109	92,837	55,735	1,183,764	23,847
Median	84,875	119,131	15,485	4,502	269,242	4,123
Low	0	0	0	0	2,317	0
Total	329,896,919	807,871,925	94,322,684	57,407,114	1,295,038,354	25,278,104
Libraries Reporting	1,102	1,096	1,016	1,030	1,094	1,060

ACRL LIBRARY DATA TABLES 2004

SUMMARY DATA: EXPENDITURES

ALL INSTITUTIONS REPORTING

Salaries & Wages Professional Staff*	Salaries & Wages Support Staff*	Salaries & Wages Student Assistants	Total Salaries & Wages*	Other Operating Expend.	Total Library Expend.	
22	23	24	25	26	27	(Survey Question #)
15,701,492	11,844,788	4,964,100	27,787,061	9,283,152	65,212,582	High
779,872	604,987	126,111	1,478,023	358,977	3,008,684	Mean
299,383	185,024	37,117	513,638	82,075	888,017	Median
0	0	0	0	0	0	Low
813,406,393	624,951,618	132,669,182	1,593,308,512	377,643,993	3,222,300,512	Total
1,043	1,033	1,052	1,078	1,052	1,071	Libraries Reporting

ACRL LIBRARY DATA TABLES 2004

SUMMARY DATA: EXPENDITURES

INSTITUTIONS GRANTING BACHELOR OF ARTS DEGREES (Carnegie Code B)

	Monographs	Current Serials	Other Library Materials	Misc. Materials	Total Library Materials	Contract Binding
(Survey Question #)	16	17	18	19	20	21
High	597,403	1,450,680	256,975	256,400	2,057,800	64,396
Mean	107,434	184,167	22,968	16,864	323,310	6,502
Median	61,147	67,479	10,123	1,100	168,217	1,498
Low	0	1,080	0	0	4,180	0
Total	19,982,693	33,702,649	3,973,425	3,018,662	60,459,048	1,170,333
Libraries Reporting	186	183	173	179	187	180

ACRL LIBRARY DATA TABLES 2004

SUMMARY DATA: EXPENDITURES

INSTITUTIONS GRANTING BACHELOR OF ARTS DEGREES (Carnegie Code B)

Salaries & Wages Professional Staff*	Salaries & Wages Support Staff*	Salaries & Wages Student Assistants	Total Salaries & Wages*	Other Operating Expend.	Total Library Expend.	
22	23	24	25	26	27	(Survey Question #)
1,655,750	1,070,578	673,000	2,500,000	1,825,511	7,092,374	High
255,116	153,651	50,315	464,516	95,031	880,278	Mean
169,360	86,509	25,000	285,058	37,226	482,212	Median
25,500	0	0	35,750	0	63,100	Low
45,155,492	26,735,319	9,207,646	84,541,824	16,535,312	157,569,811	Total
177	174	183	182	174	179	Libraries Reporting

ACRL LIBRARY DATA TABLES 2004

SUMMARY DATA: EXPENDITURES

INSTITUTIONS GRANTING MASTER OF ARTS AND PROFESSIONAL DEGREES (Carnegie Code M)

(Survey Question #)	Monographs	Current Serials	Other Library Materials	Misc. Materials	Total Library Materials	Contract Binding
	16	17	18	19	20	21
High	1,000,082	1,499,799	584,617	807,956	2,490,706	158,575
Mean	131,967	271,128	40,851	35,373	476,397	9,532
Median	85,361	161,310	18,800	2,916	314,820	5,180
Low	0	829	0	0	5,360	0
Total	49,091,845	100,859,587	14,093,597	12,133,098	174,837,674	3,412,517
Libraries Reporting	372	372	345	343	367	358

ACRL LIBRARY DATA TABLES 2004

SUMMARY DATA: EXPENDITURES

INSTITUTIONS GRANTING MASTER OF ARTS AND PROFESSIONAL DEGREES (Carnegie Code M)

Salaries & Wages Professional Staff*	Salaries & Wages Support Staff*	Salaries & Wages Student Assistants	Total Salaries & Wages*	Other Operating Expend.	Total Library Expend.	
22	23	24	25	26	27	(Survey Question #)
2,516,004	2,336,008	789,959	5,397,615	2,049,605	8,017,589	High
427,707	292,587	70,740	762,451	165,703	1,363,948	Mean
300,513	164,418	46,049	496,068	88,898	911,938	Median
0	0	0	0	0	0	Low
147,131,352	98,894,324	24,971,282	276,007,329	58,327,359	493,749,148	Total
344	338	353	362	352	362	Libraries Reporting

ACRL Library Data Tables 2004
EXPENDITURES

INSTITUTIONS GRANTING BACHELOR OF ARTS DEGREES (Carnegie Code B)

Lib. No.	Institution	Notes	Monographs 16	Current Serials 17	Other Library Materials 18	Misc. Materials 19	Total Library Materials 20	Contract Binding 21
	Survey Question #							
1	AB C Art & Design	bf	42,000	14,000	5,000	19,000	80,000	-1
2	Adrian C		80,500	119,693	16,626	52,577[1]	269,396	5,871
3	Albion C	G	96,642	347,504	8,504	0	452,650	12,025
4	Amherst C	Gf	597,403	1,192,359	61,741	0	1,851,503	64,396
5	Aquinas C TN	G	85,400	86,000	8,600	0	180,000	0
6	Atlanta C Art	bG	20,956	19,360	9,295	2,600	52,211	3,440
7	Atlanta Christian C	bf	5,050	27,864	189	0	32,103	0
8	Augustana C RI	G	131,382	148,603	15,466	46,982	342,433	85
9	Barber-Scotia C		101,000	21,000	28,000	200	150,000	0
10	Bard C	b	209,630	198,200	0	0	407,830	18,300
11	Barton C	b	53,053	54,840	3,297	112	111,302	1,726
12	Bates C	bG	468,213	1,004,956	42,569	-1	1,515,738	20,543
13	Benedict C	G	102,747	41,827	47,273	16,937	208,784	0
14	Berry C	b	209,300	362,626	19,500	0	591,426	3,255
15	Bethany C Bethany	b	33,053	111,509	10,682	0	155,244	1,432
16	Bethany C Lindsborg		32,968	14,484	0	41,883	89,335	2,200
17	Bethel C KS		34,746	41,567	-1[1]	0	76,313	0
18	Blackburn C	bG	36,021	8,993	7,597	0	52,611	0
19	Bluefield C	bf	31,000	1,800	2,500	0	35,300	0
20	Boise Bible C		4,172	2,033	0	0	6,205	0
21	Bowdoin C		447,847	1,277,171	90,229	0	1,815,247	60,995
22	Bridgewater C	b	97,870	106,891	18,209	33,531	256,501	6,659
23	Bryan C	bf	20,136	12,867	516	31,113	64,632	0
24	C Holy Cross		276,570	790,737	-1[1]	32,736	1,100,043	30,510
25	C Visual Arts	b	2,420	1,080	680	0	4,180	0
26	C Wooster		214,421	678,764	51,718	0	944,903	17,876
27	Campion C	G	43,000	34,000	-1[1]	3,500	80,500	2,000
28	Carroll C-Helena	b	48,710	76,225	8,813[1]	19,858[1]	104,895	0
29	Cazenovia C	b	85,025	66,923	13,566	4,968	170,482	8,798
30	Centennial C	bf	130,500	82,500	-1	150,000	363,000	0
31	Central Bible C	b	47,828	8,001	1,347	127	57,303	1,913
32	Central C		103,398	173,944	37,886	0	315,228	7,331
33	Central Christian C Bible	b	104,681	3,144	5,853	0	113,678	1,299
34	Centre C	G	130,916	208,257	-1	0	339,170	8,675
35	Christian Heritage C		31,342	21,205	0	1,570	54,117	0
36	Clear Creek Bible		3,603	9,842	2,393	0	15,838	0
37	Cmty Hosp C Health		35,572	23,850	8,207	659	8,866	-1
38	Colby C	bG	453,979	1,030,397	82,373	0[1]	1,566,749	21,207
39	Colby Sawyer C	b	55,900	67,300	12,300	0	135,500	0
40	Columbia Union C	bG	71,453	81,946	1,861	2,000	157,260	11,931

Key to Notes on Page 1   1 -- See Footnotes   -1 -- Unavailable   -2 -- Not Applicable

ACRL Library Data Tables 2004
EXPENDITURES

INSTITUTIONS GRANTING BACHELOR OF ARTS DEGREES (Carnegie Code B)

Salaries & Wages Prof. Staff* 22	Salaries & Wages Suppt. Staff* 23	Salaries & Wages Stud. Ass'ts* 24	Total Salaries & Wages* 25	Other Operating Expenditures 26	Total Library Expenditures 27	Survey Question #
						Institution
80,712	226,310	3,317	310,339	26,997	417,336	AB C Art & Design
134,080	69,158	33,470	236,708	7,718	519,693	Adrian C
330,179	194,493	76,681	601,353	164,812	1,230,840	Albion C
986,313	892,031	153,267	2,031,611	362,023	4,309,533	Amherst C
95,000	35,000	14,500	144,500	56,500	381,000	Aquinas C TN
146,951 [1]	0	14,360	161,311	38,575	199,886	Atlanta C Art
50,000	15,000	25,000	90,000	12,000	102,000	Atlanta Christian C
342,140	192,118	84,090	618,348	31,724	992,590	Augustana C RI
90,000	48,000	1,200	139,200	20,000 [1]	191,400	Barber-Scotia C
440,000	212,600	53,025	705,625	98,288	1,230,043	Bard C
178,294	35,604	13,914	227,812	31,349	372,189	Barton C
572,627	465,777	116,002	1,154,406	278,143	2,968,830	Bates C
-1	-1	7,866	369,191	72,814	650,789	Benedict C
-1 [1]	-1	95,000	567,551	442,684	1,604,916	Berry C
124,365	11,939	17,386	153,590	43,125	353,491	Bethany C Bethany
29,700	26,000	19,828	75,528	0	167,063	Bethany C Lindsborg
112,109	26,670	22,721	161,500	128,962	290,462	Bethel C KS
55,166	25,401	9,838	-1	0	-1	Blackburn C
94,143	24,936	2,700	121,779	3,500	125,279	Bluefield C
35,999	-1	-1	-1	-1	-1	Boise Bible C
1,046,133	483,143	235,648	1,764,924	370,104	4,011,270	Bowdoin C
226,959	90,152	25,428	342,539	23,080	628,779	Bridgewater C
96,000	71,186	16,268	179,454	26,760	270,846	Bryan C
722,743	466,516	146,396	1,335,655	74,933	2,541,141	C Holy Cross
70,243	8,125	11,744	90,112	8,301	102,593	C Visual Arts
268,308	426,416	195,439	890,163	-1	1,852,942	C Wooster
70,400 [1]	37,000	13,000 [1]	120,400	0	202,900	Campion C
-1 [1]	-1 [1]	19,312	188,874	17,741	206,614	Carroll C-Helena
164,637	13,853	11,239	189,729	0	369,009	Cazenovia C
435,888	909,845	24,750	1,370,483	154,953	1,888,436	Centennial C
59,720	32,181	14,865	106,766	5,939	213,182	Central Bible C
205,734	142,518	64,684	412,936	176,613	912,108	Central C
25,824	6,140	8,811	40,775	4,564	160,316	Central Christian C Bible
216,660	85,595	28,572	330,827	134,574	813,245	Centre C
112,600	24,600	11,845	149,045	18,002	221,164	Christian Heritage C
37,142	16,000	23,642	76,184	10,910	102,932	Clear Creek Bible
45,531	75,074	13,520	134,125	0	134,125	Cmty Hosp C Health
530,260	407,840	191,338	1,129,438	0 [1]	1,129,438	Colby C
117,569	165,991	10,864	294,424	0	294,424	Colby Sawyer C
168,842	96,141	54,292	319,275	82,977	571,463	Columbia Union C

Key to Notes on Page 1   1 -- See Footnotes   -1 -- Unavailable   -2 -- Not Applicable

ACRL Library Data Tables 2004
EXPENDITURES

INSTITUTIONS GRANTING BACHELOR OF ARTS DEGREES (Carnegie Code B)

Lib. No.	Institution	Notes	Monographs 16	Current Serials 17	Other Library Materials 18	Misc. Materials 19	Total Library Materials 20	Contract Binding 21
	Survey Question #							
41	Concordia C-MN	b	205,544	226,807	14,716	77,938[1]	525,004	9,620
42	Concordia C-NY	b	46,558	46,988	17,929	14,352	125,827	756
43	Cornish C Arts		1[1]	-1[1]	-1[1]	-1	38,185	862
44	Crichton C	b	29,171	22,035	21,579	40,951	113,736	4,514
45	Crown C-MN	G	25,462	16,313	10,123[1]	35,327[1]	87,225	0
46	Culver Stockton C	b	27,996	42,759	6,723	42,261[1]	119,739	4,229
47	CUNY City C		114,863	129,901[1]	6,371	5,269[1]	256,404	1,235
48	CUNY York C	b	55,000	165,688	45,639	0	266,327	0
49	Dakota Wesleyan U	b	36,375	46,060	2,775	6,000	91,210	0
50	Dana C	bG	14,315	32,294	10,651	0	57,259	893
51	Davidson C	bG	296,160	918,817	168,217	0	168,217	27,599
52	Dean C	bL	22,735	13,169	8,935	6,209	51,048	0
53	Defiance C	b	36,768	60,000	750	15,760	113,278	4,000
54	Denison U		342,785	416,085	68,686	141,510	969,066	18,681
55	DeVry Inst Tech GA	b	394,545	-1	-1	-1	394,545	-1
56	Dickinson ST U		70,281[1]	104,349[1]	18,719	40,833	234,182	65
57	Divine Word C		21,630	16,154	2,472	397	40,653	1,757
58	East Texas Baptist U	Bb	20,000[1]	67,000[1]	60,000[1]	3,500	150,500	0[1]
59	Eckerd C		133,498	412,017	29,986	0	575,501	100
60	Emmanuel C GA	b	37,195	5,802	5,626	2,618	48,885	523
61	Eugene Bible C		-1	-1	-1	-1	-1	-1
62	Evangel U		47,116	133,928	0[1]	0	181,044	1,907
63	F&M C		485,086	671,122	64,505	256,400	1,477,113	44,325
64	Ferrum C	bf	44,063	37,209	12,224	0	93,496	5,555
65	Finlandia U	bG	6,208	27,119	3,736	0	37,063	199
66	FL Christian C	b	14,981[1]	11,617	3,709	0	30,307[1]	0
67	Flagler C	bG	87,043	74,073	23,493	-2	184,609	764
68	Fort Lewis C	b	73,142	123,890	4,778	370	202,180	6,700
69	G Adolphus C	b	127,934	293,687	33,675	59,547	514,843	1,467
70	Green Mountain C	bf	27,800	30,000	1,800	0	596,000	0
71	Grinnell C		345,661	917,522	48,815	0	1,311,998	22,222
72	Guilford C	bG	78,806	225,998	117,869	15,320[1]	437,993	4,536
73	H Inst Int Desgn	b	15,144	6,789	2,767	4,478	28,178	492
74	H LaGrange C	G	37,073	31,807	6,337	0	75,217	484
75	Hamilton C		394,460	1,022,360	88,231	0	1,497,051	42,878
76	Hampshire C		70,715	117,975	22,230	0	210,920	13,075
77	Hanover C	bG	96,025	354,407	33,203	0	483,635	6,970
78	Haskell Indian Nations U	bf	46,745	17,889	515	7,144	72,293	0
79	Haverford C	Bb	307,331	770,439	33,347	0	1,111,117	23,339
80	Hendrix C	b	99,606	148,675	77,500	15,595	341,376	6,990

Key to Notes on Page 1   1 -- See Footnotes   -1 -- Unavailable   -2 -- Not Applicable

ACRL Library Data Tables 2004
EXPENDITURES

INSTITUTIONS GRANTING BACHELOR OF ARTS DEGREES (Carnegie Code B)

Salaries & Wages Prof. Staff* 22	Salaries & Wages Suppt. Staff* 23	Salaries & Wages Stud. Ass'ts* 24	Total Salaries & Wages* 25	Other Operating Expenditures 26	Total Library Expenditures 27	Survey Question #
						Institution
384,511	227,809	108,428	720,748	36,070	1,291,442	Concordia C-MN
102,564	0	21,611	124,175	9,288	260,046	Concordia C-NY
95,889	12,116	28,068	136,073	140,577	315,697	Cornish C Arts
-1 [1]	-1	10,366	108,008 [1]	10,987	237,425	Crichton C
135,326 [1]	-1 [1]	20,863	199,751 [1]	111,560 [1]	320,258	Crown C-MN
72,677	40,822	25,161	138,660	11,745	274,373	Culver Stockton C
751,149 [1]	310,447	120,000 [1]	1,181,596	34,305 [1]	1,473,539	CUNY City C
431,632	183,880	77,000	688,512	0	954,839	CUNY York C
77,000	68,000	13,420	158,420	38,980	288,610	Dakota Wesleyan U
71,500	29,225	14,300	115,025	7,385	180,562	Dana C
658,117	280,565	109,608	1,048,290	290,221	2,749,304	Davidson C
73,579	25,737	1,120	100,436	22,287	173,771	Dean C
139,900	17,800	35,000	192,700	77,040	387,018	Defiance C
464,798	396,580	121,640	983,018	538,933	2,509,698	Denison U
1,312,000	429,000	673,000	2,414,000	114,000	2,922,545	DeVry Inst Tech GA
144,223	17,510	50,000	211,733	83,970	529,950	Dickinson ST U
74,597	20,708	0	95,305	14,702	152,417	Divine Word C
160,000	77,383	35,844	273,227	37,060 [1]	460,787	East Texas Baptist U
214,100	124,800	37,008	375,908	209,897	1,161,406	Eckerd C
40,000 [1]	55,000 [1]	3,000 [1]	98,000	29,960	147,399	Emmanuel C GA
-1	-1	-1	-1	-1	-1	Eugene Bible C
157,191	141,849	-1	-1	-1	-1	Evangel U
523,448	341,969	88,796	954,213	56,286	2,531,937	F&M C
218,490	53,180	39,903	311,573	76,802	486,586	Ferrum C
-1	-1 [1]	20,044	120,025	13,478	170,765	Finlandia U
43,834	21,821	12,724	78,379	24,651	133,337	FL Christian C
192,229	60,320	20,800	273,349	109,710	568,432	Flagler C
335,208	260,273	67,714	663,195	14,271	399,084	Fort Lewis C
331,562	261,640	136,688	729,890	402,021	1,648,221	G Adolphus C
80,900	-1	-1	-1	-1	-1	Green Mountain C
544,825	454,842	140,490	1,140,157	174,251	2,648,628	Grinnell C
235,995	88,770	58,093	382,858	75,000	900,387	Guilford C
86,925	62,336	31,200	180,461	-1	210,131	H Inst Int Desgn
69,903	85,242	17,550	172,695	69,517 [1]	317,913 [1]	H LaGrange C
692,603	552,226	134,674	1,379,503	405,531	3,324,963	Hamilton C
1,028,879	466,209	124,188	1,619,276	918,672	2,788,019	Hampshire C
203,058	185,024	47,702	435,784	120,595 [1]	1,046,984	Hanover C
157,328	127,370	18,550	283,248	6,125	289,323	Haskell Indian Nations U
775,160	332,212	202,335	1,309,707	703,222	3,147,385	Haverford C
240,883	117,814	18,700	377,397	0	725,763	Hendrix C

Key to Notes on Page 1   1 -- See Footnotes   -1 -- Unavailable   -2 -- Not Applicable

47

ACRL Library Data Tables 2004
EXPENDITURES

INSTITUTIONS GRANTING BACHELOR OF ARTS DEGREES (Carnegie Code B)

Lib. No.	Institution	Notes	Monographs 16	Current Serials 17	Other Library Materials 18	Misc. Materials 19	Total Library Materials 20	Contract Binding 21
		Survey Question #						
81	Hiram C	bG	109,556	181,290	6,296	0	297,142	4,107
82	Hobart &William Smith Cs	G	85,014	493,406	22,134	0	600,554	20,351
83	Hope C		212,021	540,511	31,554	0	784,086	10,687
84	Houghton C	Bb	195,611	-1	-1	2,784	198,395	0 [1]
85	Howard Payne U	G	49,448	108,807 [1]	2,658	78,486	239,399	1,300
86	Illinois C	bGf	101,922	96,331	0	0	198,253	0
87	Jamestown C	b	35,741	37,556	3,357	0	76,654	0
88	Johnson C Smith U	b	79,040	76,589	12,757	1,601	169,987	2,700
89	Judson C	b	80,060	39,107	1,761	43,522 [1]	177,234	0
90	Kent ST U Salem	b	8,084	7,074	0	0	15,158	0
91	Kent ST U Trumbull		35,549	53,728	-1	10,754	100,029	-1
92	Kenyon C	b	302,293	532,514	50,895	0	885,702	21,461
93	Kettering C Med	bG	73,784	44,686	12,038	9,048	139,556	1,206
94	Keuka C	b	40,120	65,000	8,702	41,341	155,163	2,620
95	Knox C	G	61,458	208,098	3,998	14,882	291,251	9,822
96	Kwantlen UC		359,852	212,499	52,604	0	624,954	2,571
97	Lambuth U	bGf	29,921	27,839	13,272	24,756	95,788	426
98	Lawrence U		237,394	421,765	23,618	23,652	706,429	19,428
99	Lemoyne-Owen C	Gf	48,702	25,622	12,737	17,899	104,959	0
100	Lester B Pearson C Pacific		-1	-1	-1	-1	-1	-1
101	LIFE Bible C	b	27,318	23,904	2,138	3,198	56,558	968
102	Lyndon State C		58,089	68,634	701	7,371	76,706	-1
103	Lyon C		34,500	118,000	3,500	43,500	199,500	1,000
104	Macon ST C	BbG	92,063	36,477	9,623	0	138,163	3,940
105	Marlboro C		34,806 [1]	19,704 [1]	3,500 [1]	17,424 [1]	75,434	1,224
106	Mars Hill C	b	22,280	54,029	10,947	0	87,256	0
107	Martin Luther C	bG	28,671	28,954	4,157	0	61,782	539
108	Mayville ST U		24,528	43,174	15,506	0	83,208	413
109	McKendree C	bG	51,708	31,440	19,980	51,222	154,350	1,240
110	McPherson C		-1	-1	-1	-1	-1	-1
111	Methodist C	G	54,109 [1]	72,712	2,352 [1]	32,766	161,939	3,939
112	Midland Lutheran C		47,000	32,000	8,000	5,800	92,800	0
113	Milwaukee Inst Art Design	b	12,108	5,364	2,523	26,903	46,898	606
114	MO Baptist C		65,515	29,713	2,416	8,325	105,969	4,288
115	MO Western ST C	bG	88,382	233,836	28,782	0	351,000	7,300
116	Monmouth C	bGf	46,744	164,595	15,998 [1]	9,800 [1]	237,167	7,230
117	Mount Royal C	bG	298,500	238,000	79,500	0	616,000	9,500
118	Mount Union C		152,471	160,846	214,108	0	527,425	11,687
119	Muhlenberg C	bG	164,700	196,000	22,115	164,200	547,015	9,800
120	NC Wesleyan C	BbG	41,756	60,000	8,662	27,636	137,454	1,496

Key to Notes on Page 1   1 -- See Footnotes   -1 -- Unavailable   -2 -- Not Applicable

ACRL Library Data Tables 2004
EXPENDITURES

INSTITUTIONS GRANTING BACHELOR OF ARTS DEGREES (Carnegie Code B)

Salaries & Wages Prof. Staff* 22	Salaries & Wages Suppt. Staff* 23	Salaries & Wages Stud. Ass'ts* 24	Total Salaries & Wages* 25	Other Operating Expenditures 26	Total Library Expenditures 27	Survey Question #
						Institution
169,360	106,140	68,536	344,036	102,274	747,559	Hiram C
315,923	347,353	59,659	722,935	243,579	1,587,419	Hobart &William Smith Cs
480,955	285,890	148,390	915,235	160,396	1,870,404	Hope C
-1	-1	27,155	419,186 [1]	102,219	719,800	Houghton C
107,435	106,041	28,037	241,513	0	482,212	Howard Payne U
173,022	54,391	17,190	244,603	2,466	445,322	Illinois C
-1	-1	5,000	154,133	67,395	298,182	Jamestown C
443,448	101,916	6,000	551,364	78,428	802,479	Johnson C Smith U
188,470	42,481	61,069	292,020	19,967 [1]	477,536	Judson C
49,460	23,820	8,004	81,284	0	96,442	Kent ST U Salem
119,060	75,329	29,288	223,676	123,692	447,396	Kent ST U Trumbull
583,442	209,861	77,695	870,998	25,339	1,803,500	Kenyon C
139,686	28,724	0 [1]	168,410 [1]	14,592	323,764	Kettering C Med
139,516	42,260	25,895	207,670	34,190	409,643	Keuka C
234,144	180,321	105,938	520,403	75,862	897,338	Knox C
756,033 [1]	1,102,263	21,260	1,879,555	-1	-1	Kwantlen UC
117,900 [1]	83,397 [1]	8,509	209,806 [1]	9,464	315,484 [1]	Lambuth U
333,405	257,022	70,829	661,256	125,425	1,512,538	Lawrence U
106,672	27,782	5,880	140,254	19,049	264,262	Lemoyne-Owen C
-1	-1	-1	-1	-1	-1	Lester B Pearson C Pacific
48,000	49,446	18,563	116,009	8,878	182,413 [1]	LIFE Bible C
207,472	-1	28,802	236,274	-1	-1	Lyndon State C
124,000	39,000	27,000	190,000	58,000	448,500	Lyon C
192,148	91,828	30,000	313,976	0	456,079	Macon ST C
112,590 [1]	20,156 [1]	5,272	138,018	4,827 [1]	219,503	Marlboro C
180,000	57,000	0	237,000	16,970	341,226	Mars Hill C
74,806	54,149	29,796	158,751	43,405	264,477	Martin Luther C
105,420	1,597	21,900	128,917	27,554	240,092	Mayville ST U
192,507	24,720	17,240	234,467	32,245	422,302	McKendree C
-1	-1	-1	-1	-1	-1	McPherson C
143,423	145,695	5,668	294,786	36,114	496,778	Methodist C
112,000	58,000	15,000	185,000	-1	-1	Midland Lutheran C
88,661	223	18,290	107,174	2,768	157,446	Milwaukee Inst Art Design
75,090	65,196	10,000	150,286	0	260,543	MO Baptist C
343,830	116,132	55,600	515,562	97,180	971,042	MO Western ST C
140,008	103,963	37,303	281,274	171,460	697,131	Monmouth C
770,000	1,438,000	114,000	2,322,000	62,500	3,010,000	Mount Royal C
255,029	127,681	72,135	454,845	92,510	1,086,467	Mount Union C
406,683	197,823	89,400	693,906	123,200	1,373,921	Muhlenberg C
116,575	71,875	29,322	217,772	12,116	386,905	NC Wesleyan C

Key to Notes on Page 1   1 -- See Footnotes   -1 -- Unavailable   -2 -- Not Applicable

49

ACRL Library Data Tables 2004
EXPENDITURES

INSTITUTIONS GRANTING BACHELOR OF ARTS DEGREES (Carnegie Code B)

Lib. No.	Institution	Notes	Monographs 16	Current Serials 17	Other Library Materials 18	Misc. Materials 19	Total Library Materials 20	Contract Binding 21
121	New C U South FL	bG	59,223	267,335	7,673	67,193	401,424	21,443
122	OH Dominican C	bG	84,320	209,786	-1	4,438	298,544	1,400
123	OH Wesleyan U	b	293,870	413,917	14,758	-1	722,545	9,277
124	OK Panhandle ST U	b	25,114	30,584	8,970	5,000	69,668	1,212
125	Paier C Art		4,200	4,780	0	3,185	12,165	0
126	Peace C	b	60,288	27,788	16,538	3,763	108,377	1,111
127	Potomac C	G	41,200	6,530	2,800	0	50,530	0
128	Presbyterian C	bG	83,647	233,223	54,550	0	371,420	7,706
129	Principia C	bG	73,682	41,149	3,877	83,574	202,282	1,392
130	Randolph-Macon C	bf	74,645	174,879	23,456	0	272,980	4,500
131	Randolph-Macon WC	bG	95,000	99,957	40,921	1,000	236,678	1,000
132	Reformed Bible C		18,445	11,332	10,614	0	40,391	164
133	Reinhardt C	Bb	82,577	52,296	0	0	134,873	1,500
134	Ricks C		-1 [1]	-1 [1]	-1 [1]	-1 [1]	616,426 [1]	9,522
135	Ringling Sch Art & Design		63,825	22,805	34,455	0	121,085	4,126
136	Rochester C	b	31,084	16,562	9,462	0	57,108	0
137	Rocky Mountain C	bGf	17,933	23,996	1,000	0	42,929	0
138	Rogers ST U	bG	180,378	84,263	27,102	103,429 [1]	395,172	954
139	SE C Assemblies God	bG	113,000	117,200	24,000	0	254,200	5,000
140	Shawnee ST U	Gf	65,740	111,339	61,896	0	238,974	152
141	Shepherd C	G	121,499	161,831	29,617	0	312,947	2,127
142	Siena C	G	178,265	356,127	11,806 [1]	31,534 [1]	577,732	19,247
143	Simpson C IA	bG	85,063	108,089	6,195	17,982	217,329	798
144	Skidmore C	b	236,854	720,524	35,968	87,436	1,080,782	14,363
145	Southwest U	f	572,181	425,514	29,869	-1	1,027,564	7,172
146	Spartan Aero-Flight Schl	B	15,453	9,631	3,666	10,000	38,750	0
147	St Andrews Presby C	bG	14,469	28,089	15,705	0	58,263	785
148	St Gregory's U	b	3,420	29,673	741	0	33,834	0
149	St John Vianney C Sem		19,723	10,951	892	5,974	37,540	910
150	St Olaf C	b	372,650	428,339	118,750	0	919,739	19,140
151	St. Mary's C Maryland		86,638	457,755	-1	0	544,393	1,841
152	Sterling C-VT		8,480	18,690	1,190	0	28,360	0
153	Stillman C		0	23,422	0	0	23,422	0
154	Susquehanna U	bG	276,022	154,279	47,140	0	477,441	1,212
155	SW Baptist Theo Sem		123,715	67,479	3,177	938	195,309	-1
156	Swarthmore C	G	347,758	1,173,197	46,905	59,437	1,627,297	29,105
157	Sweet Briar C	bG	60,835	199,128	12,875	0	272,838	2,043
158	Talladega C	bf	10,000	3,000	3,500	15,000	22,500	22,500
159	Taylor U-Ft Wayne	b	48,411	52,093	7,522	-1	108,026	5,522
160	Teikyo Post U	bL	115,000	90,650	0	15,000	220,650	0

Key to Notes on Page 1   1 -- See Footnotes   -1 -- Unavailable   -2 -- Not Applicable

ACRL Library Data Tables 2004
EXPENDITURES

INSTITUTIONS GRANTING BACHELOR OF ARTS DEGREES (Carnegie Code B)

Salaries & Wages Prof. Staff* 22	Salaries & Wages Suppt. Staff* 23	Salaries & Wages Stud. Ass'ts* 24	Total Salaries & Wages* 25	Other Operating Expenditures 26	Total Library Expenditures 27	Survey Question #
						Institution
341,162	336,128	24,573	701,863	0	1,103,287	New C U South FL
166,517	111,017	43,429	320,963	95,373	716,280	OH Dominican C
441,181	271,131	125,958	838,270	525,876	2,095,968	OH Wesleyan U
98,855	31,767	33,500	164,122	65,620	300,622	OK Panhandle ST U
33,000	0	5,400	38,400	12,535	63,100	Paier C Art
136,629	0	13,127	149,756	2,002	293,795	Peace C
-1	0	0	41,000	1,250	92,780	Potomac C
181,725	109,048	15,520	306,293	64,384	749,803	Presbyterian C
146,981	93,199	46,687	286,867	115,542 [1]	606,083	Principia C
242,211	186,064	25,000	453,275	29,002	701,753	Randolph-Macon C
175,579	179,106	30,048	384,733	50,750	673,361	Randolph-Macon WC
90,521	0	8,188	98,709	28,931	168,195	Reformed Bible C
130,470	47,468	0	177,938	41,311	354,122	Reinhardt C
725,860	268,047	450,397	1,444,304	3,119	2,073,371	Ricks C
179,801	179,176	20,557	379,534	56,909	561,654	Ringling Sch Art & Design
48,000	40,000	14,821	102,821	20,796	180,726	Rochester C
67,435	16,000	18,381	101,816	37,392	182,937	Rocky Mountain C
209,390	67,445	21,376	298,211	83,998	778,335	Rogers ST U
123,000	124,996	6,267	254,263	14,950	528,413	SE C Assemblies God
282,702	217,191	80,907	580,800	430,625	1,250,550	Shawnee ST U
258,753	275,156	19,801	533,710	151,885	1,000,669	Shepherd C
452,539	168,269	70,862	691,670	63,803	1,352,452	Siena C
150,096	101,422	49,641	301,159	82,399	601,685	Simpson C IA
709,783	208,318	74,376	992,477	45,421	2,133,043	Skidmore C
499,700	293,680	91,038	884,418	210,510	2,129,664 [1]	Southwest U
79,491	13,987	45,000	138,478	0	138,478	Spartan Aero-Flight Schl
112,993	50,289	8,705	171,987	21,085	252,120	St Andrews Presby C
67,622	0	-1	67,622 [1]	-1	101,456	St Gregory's U
41,733	54,881 [1]	0	96,614	-1	135,064	St John Vianney C Sem
401,388	514,300	162,482	1,078,170	0	2,017,049	St Olaf C
314,591	362,803	24,890	665,109	-1	702,284	St. Mary's C Maryland
25,500	7,750	2,500	35,750	1,737 [1]	65,847	Sterling C-VT
149,918	61,971	36,582	248,471	54,833	347,134	Stillman C
443,926	117,689	73,201	634,816	0	1,270,844	Susquehanna U
420,456	122,118	300,514	843,088	-1	1,715,272	SW Baptist Theo Sem
928,602	394,797	117,554	1,440,953	297,678	3,395,033	Swarthmore C
279,611	157,945	66,769	504,325	16,615	795,821	Sweet Briar C
170,705	0	0	170,705	26,500	290,705	Talladega C
271,170	78,442	72,846	422,458	-1	536,006	Taylor U-Ft Wayne
79,693	64,687	4,000	148,380	0	369,030	Teikyo Post U

Key to Notes on Page 1   1 -- See Footnotes   -1 -- Unavailable   -2 -- Not Applicable

ACRL Library Data Tables 2004
EXPENDITURES

INSTITUTIONS GRANTING BACHELOR OF ARTS DEGREES (Carnegie Code B)

Lib. No.	Institution	Notes	Monographs 16	Current Serials 17	Other Library Materials 18	Misc. Materials 19	Total Library Materials 20	Contract Binding 21
	Survey Question #							
161	TN Wesleyan C		35,026	46,473	1,424	28,028	110,951	368
162	Tri ST U		19,378	57,277	3,911	1,100[1]	81,666	1,549
163	Trinity Christian C	b	67,035	49,204	4,878	22,981	144,098	1,232
164	Trinity Wstrn U	bf	198,200	81,800	70,000	0	350,000	12,000
165	Truett McConnell C	b	13,154	16,626	13,559	9,076	52,915	0
166	TX Lutheran U	bG	71,521	83,673	5,031	39,229	199,454	9,336
167	U Maine-Machias	G	42,359	40,084	2,562	0	85,005	0
168	U ME Fort Kent	b	9,750	31,551	5,642	21,505	68,448	0
169	U Ozarks	G	44,344	59,897	14,408	0	118,649	13,252
170	U VA C Wise	G	30,800	94,150	27,906	11,282	164,138	3,081
171	Union C-NE	b	50,701[1]	81,180	-1	22,206	154,087	4,309
172	US C Guard Acad	b	61,500	257,500	0	37,000	356,000	8,000
173	US Merchant Marine Acad	bG	33,956	70,000	48,815	21,200	173,971	-1
174	US Mil Acad	f	371,684	706,977	15,045	96,482	1,190,188	28,000
175	US Naval Acad		415,000	1,450,680	34,794	0	1,878,474	32,500
176	UT Valley ST C	Bb	169,443[1]	96,357	20,778	0	286,578	24,921
177	VA Wesleyan C	b	41,135	62,522	2,512	30,196	136,365	2,416
178	Vassar C	G	456,708	1,349,642	251,450	0	2,057,800	31,098
179	VMI	b	116,802	197,283	17,073	0	331,158	5,820
180	Wabash C	G	150,257	371,860	33,642	9,343	565,102	9,343
181	Warner Sthrn C	Gf	15,725	21,821	3,814	0	41,360	1,878
182	Warren Wilson C	b	99,165	26,871	12,055	76,293	214,384	1,100
183	Wells C	b	13,991	76,424	1,144	72,380	163,939	3,635
184	Western ST C	bf	33,163	68,823	869	0	102,855	120
185	Westmont C	b	38,767	58,430	0	0	97,197	570
186	Whitman C	b	395,000	490,000	45,000	0	930,000	18,000
187	Wiley C	bG	58,095	34,567	1,109	5,449	99,266	0
188	Winston-Salem ST U	b	309,677	131,506	256,975	0	698,158	1,166
189	Wofford C	bG	107,483	134,672	-1	120,476	362,631	35,023
190	York C		15,140[1]	33,158	46	4,626[1]	52,970	0

Key to Notes on Page 1   1 -- See Footnotes   -1 -- Unavailable   -2 -- Not Applicable

ACRL Library Data Tables 2004
EXPENDITURES

INSTITUTIONS GRANTING BACHELOR OF ARTS DEGREES (Carnegie Code B)

Salaries & Wages Prof. Staff* 22	Salaries & Wages Suppt. Staff* 23	Salaries & Wages Stud. Ass'ts* 24	Total Salaries & Wages* 25	Other Operating Expenditures 26	Total Library Expenditures 27	Survey Question #
						Institution
90,719	46,676	15,067	152,462	1,753	154,215	TN Wesleyan C
94,416	50,256	6,692	151,364	41,853	276,432	Tri ST U
127,453	20,918	24,101	172,472	27,789	345,561	Trinity Christian C
266,500	266,100	34,800	567,400	0	929,400	Trinity Wstrn U
41,278	35,636	1,401	78,315	8,794	139,524	Truett McConnell C
230,082 [1]	87,423 [1]	23,500	341,005	54,700	604,495	TX Lutheran U
45,738	58,606	7,668	112,012	2,486	114,498	U Maine-Machias
64,335	56,899	25,600	146,835	21,505	215,281	U ME Fort Kent
-1	-1	11,789	-1	19,334	-1	U Ozarks
208,504	202,819	4,861	416,184	54,355	637,758	U VA C Wise
138,710	44,153	41,986	224,849	95,027	478,272	Union C-NE
331,188	184,532	0	515,720	0	879,720	US C Guard Acad
287,368	129,069	0	416,437	13,901	604,309	US Merchant Marine Acad
1,655,750	844,250	0	2,500,000	1,825,511	4,325,511	US Mil Acad
-1	-1	0	2,219,000	227,520	4,357,494 [1]	US Naval Acad
554,228	265,401	158,719	978,348	132,513	1,422,360	UT Valley ST C
162,358	92,634	15,509	270,501	43,449	452,731	VA Wesleyan C
1,084,371	951,691	307,215	2,343,277	316,922	7,092,374	Vassar C
246,205	250,507	1,853 [1]	498,565	138,854	974,397	VMI
210,780	133,103	41,621	385,504	201,228	1,161,177	Wabash C
212,874	28,328	21,191	262,393	73,713	336,106	Warner Sthrn C
262,114 [1]	0 [1]	63,967	328,081	51,490	595,055	Warren Wilson C
161,318	47,879	33,505	242,702	8,037	418,313	Wells C
262,554	88,728	9,509	360,791	0	464,097	Western ST C
293,802	73,322	64,318	431,112	260,777	692,219	Westmont C
325,013	175,007	91,091	591,111	38,500	1,644,411	Whitman C
111,499	40,911	27,686	180,096	11,890	191,096	Wiley C
229,677	361,673	12,652	604,002	117,926	212,931	Winston-Salem ST U
338,255	114,422	25,510	478,187	240,510	1,116,351	Wofford C
59,979	47,586	13,848	121,413	2,775	177,158	York C

ACRL Library Data Tables 2004
EXPENDITURES

INSTITUTIONS GRANTING MASTER OF ARTS AND PROFESSIONAL DEGREES (Carnegie Code M)

Lib. No.	Institution	Notes	Monographs 16	Current Serials 17	Other Library Materials 18	Misc. Materials 19	Total Library Materials 20	Contract Binding 21
	Survey Question #		16	17	18	19	20	21
1	Abilene Christian U	bG	167,468	290,177	29,494	0	487,139	17,845
2	Agnes Scott C	G	85,320	248,371	28,598	0	362,289	2,746
3	Albany C Pharmacy		11,695	65,308	75	347	77,425	2,808
4	Albany Law Schl Union U	GL	85,044	1,222,248	80,881	0	1,388,173	13,292
5	Alcorn ST U	bG	165,426	247,802	20,209	89,950	523,387	0
6	Amer Intl C	b	67,451	110,313	35,681	39,025	252,470	2,585
7	Amer U Puerto Rico	Bb	118,181	35,490	20,863	0	174,534	3,000
8	Anderson U		86,501	94,278	72,740	0	253,519	4,603
9	Angelo ST U		249,485	575,716	24,816	500	850,517	15,004
10	Aquinas C MI	b	70,100	94,241	35,795	112,175	312,311	5,490
11	Ark Tech U	G	57,251	148,595	48,204	162,475	416,525	9,774
12	Armstrong Atlantic ST U	bG	88,805	292,292	87,226	0	468,323	15,000
13	Assemblies God Theo Sem	f	39,647	26,493	11,732	-1	77,872	-1
14	Assumption C	bG	139,087	306,428	3,500	0	449,015	15,000
15	Athenaeum of Ohio		45,157	22,554	704	0	68,415	3,877
16	Auburn U Montgomery	b	317,473	349,164	9,925	0 [1]	676,562	9,000
17	Augusta ST U	bG	92,502	228,632	8,845	0	329,979	13,822
18	Augustana C SF	bG	31,373	224,429	9,852	4,000	269,654	3,409
19	Austin C	b	154,280	208,436	82,386	57,667	502,769	6,589
20	Austin Presb Theo Sem	f	85,130	36,951	16,919	-1	139,000	4,194
21	Averett C	b	65,027	121,036	22,464	0	208,527	3,560
22	Babson C	bG	31,526	162,290	444,191	0	638,637	220
23	Baker C System	Bb	409,500	197,500	505	0	607,505	3,200
24	Baker U	G	60,635	132,354	-1 [1]	297	193,286	6,400
25	Baptist Bible C and Sem	bf	9,622	29,053	1,116	0	39,791	6,256
26	Bayamon Central U	bf	300	70,000	0	500,000	570,300	0
27	Bellevue U	bf	100,969	150,425	25,072	0	276,466	2,259
28	Bennington C	b	41,250	57,000	6,750	46,045	151,045	3,000
29	Bethel C IN	bf	52,492	75,739	12,006	0	140,237	18,000
30	Birmingham Southern C	bG	171,319	223,296	30,823 [1]	0	425,438	25,922
31	Bluffton C	b	68,864	47,836 [1]	5,450 [1]	76,880 [1]	199,030	1,324
32	BowlGrn SU Fireld	b	23,016	18,426	5,464	5,281	52,187	0
33	Bradley U	b	193,921	854,208 [1]	32,868	0	1,080,997	14,026
34	Brescia U	bG	32,260	28,740	2,749	0	63,749	444
35	Brooks Institute	B	33,285	14,401	10,154	0	57,840	1,505
36	Bryn Athyn C	b	19,014	23,996	9,708	0	52,718	900
37	Buena Vista U		100,907	132,359	13,824	-1	247,090	8,628
38	Butler U	b	140,640	715,579	42,510	25,041 [1]	932,770	26,120
39	C Atlantic	b	29,915 [1]	65,697 [1]	58,448 [1]	0	154,060	595
40	C Mt St Joseph	b	57,245	88,106	21,404	10,562	177,317	2,689

Key to Notes on Page 1   1 -- See Footnotes   -1 -- Unavailable   -2 -- Not Applicable

ACRL Library Data Tables 2004
EXPENDITURES

INSTITUTIONS GRANTING MASTER OF ARTS AND PROFESSIONAL DEGREES (Carnegie Code M)

Salaries & Wages Prof. Staff* 22	Salaries & Wages Suppt. Staff* 23	Salaries & Wages Stud. Ass'ts* 24	Total Salaries & Wages* 25	Other Operating Expenditures 26	Total Library Expenditures 27	Survey Question #
						Institution
448,664	174,131	155,563	778,358	352,822	1,636,164	Abilene Christian U
233,649	144,920	43,105	431,674	145,978	943,687	Agnes Scott C
111,986	36,412	6,973	155,371	1,760	258,020	Albany C Pharmacy
487,995	245,054	76,000	809,049	63,438	2,273,952	Albany Law Schl Union U
299,383	305,334	34,034	638,751	149,034	1,311,172	Alcorn ST U
142,012	49,950	29,578	221,540	0	476,595	Amer Intl C
138,113	314,969	34,739	487,821	59,666	725,021	Amer U Puerto Rico
280,658	77,257	82,980	440,895	82,735	781,752	Anderson U
414,044	278,647	92,836	785,527	147,552	1,798,600	Angelo ST U
243,249	106,578	63,679	413,506	85,739	817,046	Aquinas C MI
301,026	220,446	51,231	572,703	126,131	1,125,133	Ark Tech U
624,760	80,221	50,000	754,981	119,250	1,357,554	Armstrong Atlantic ST U
90,533	62,202	15,120	167,855	49,882	295,609	Assemblies God Theo Sem
312,791	135,748	59,205	507,744	108,918	1,080,677	Assumption C
81,281	31,109	9,761	122,151	49,727	244,170	Athenaeum of Ohio
355,550	404,387	112,528	872,465	905,486	1,777,951	Auburn U Montgomery
590,848	259,051	27,085	876,984	434,776	1,655,561	Augusta ST U
238,425	141,316	64,402	444,143	109,969	827,175	Augustana C SF
233,544	150,046	67,128	450,718	20,578	980,654	Austin C
253,176	67,277	16,978	337,431	62,306	560,358	Austin Presb Theo Sem
166,985	110,295	15,926	293,206	32,096	537,389	Averett C
826,923	77,942	137,989	1,042,754	64,985	1,746,596	Babson C
931,450	45,839	173,202	1,150,491	361,874	2,123,970	Baker C System
149,636	67,577	27,060	246,943	47,826	494,453	Baker U
31,385	72,195	21,068	114,648	125,274	285,969	Baptist Bible C and Sem
300,000 [1]	200,000	0	50,000	200,000	700,000	Bayamon Central U
204,923	146,208	36,137	387,268	62,599	728,592	Bellevue U
-1	-1	31,500	269,636	36,800	460,481	Bennington C
137,942	68,312	27,720	233,974	6,764 [1]	398,975	Bethel C IN
303,479	147,975	30,603	482,057	79,997	1,013,414	Birmingham Southern C
187,067	43,720	48,554	279,341	13,732	493,426	Bluffton C
94,455	69,438	14,248	178,141	5,493	235,821	BowlGrn SU Fireld
465,907	485,082	162,798	1,113,787	174,819	2,383,629	Bradley U
133,739	-1	10,927	148,666	27,136	239,551	Brescia U
67,920	51,571	7,106	126,597	-2	185,942	Brooks Institute
123,315	86,320	18,432	228,067	0	291,393	Bryn Athyn C
164,778	101,118	30,861	296,757	330,626	883,101	Buena Vista U
514,388	316,762	91,930	923,080	162,559	2,044,529	Butler U
107,500	33,387	32,000 [1]	172,887	15,000	342,542	C Atlantic
180,551	83,277	23,400	287,228	20,294	487,728	C Mt St Joseph

Key to Notes on Page 1   1 -- See Footnotes   -1 -- Unavailable   -2 -- Not Applicable

INSTITUTIONS GRANTING MASTER OF ARTS AND PROFESSIONAL DEGREES (Carnegie Code M)

Lib. No.	Institution	Notes	Monographs 16	Current Serials 17	Other Library Materials 18	Misc. Materials 19	Total Library Materials 20	Contract Binding 21
	Survey Question #							
41	C Mt St Vincent	bG	45,956	67,881	5,163	0	119,000	0
42	C Our Lady Elms	bG	32,097	145,729	-1	0	177,826	5,000
43	C.R. Drew U Med & Sci	bM	75,000	317,000	5,000	0	397,000	18,122
44	CA C Arts & Crafts	b	47,842	20,929	11,575	22,510	102,856	3,175
45	CA St Polytechnic U-Pomona	G	226,678	653,196	470,546 [1]	0	1,350,420	18,319
46	CA St U - Sacramento	bG	739,894	974,771	145,952	4,114	1,864,731	38,000
47	CA ST U Dominguez Hills	b	196,788	234,617	11,369	279,153 [1]	721,927	10,000
48	CA ST U Fresno		791,238	777,686	134,372	47,626	1,750,922	44,626
49	CA ST U Fullerton	Bb	725,219	454,322	62,796	1,422	1,243,759	23,836 [1]
50	CA ST U Hayward	B	167,588	755,639	49,532	0	972,759	12,542
51	CA ST U Long Beach	G	266,206	1,335,989	77,171	807,956 [1]	2,487,322	39,814
52	CA ST U Northridge	bG	633,928	896,356 [1]	584,617	5,000 [1]	2,119,901	104,999
53	CA ST U S Bernadino	f	153,691	658,091	15,475	2,901	830,158	19,806
54	CA ST U San Marcos	bG	294,648 [1]	270,071 [1]	195,944	13,847 [1]	774,510 [1]	89,247
55	CA ST U Stanislaus	B	272,499	473,680	-1	0	746,179	6,410
56	CA West Sch Law	GL	106,740	763,788	46,345	141,240	1,056,113	13,245
57	Calvin C		464,831	645,044	95,062	0	1,204,937	47,958
58	Cameron U	Gf	100,806	185,368	67,829	0	354,003	11,191
59	Canisius C	G	207,794	501,547	9,817	0 [1]	719,158	12,604
60	Carlow C		45,596	47,290	4,894	0	97,780	3,593
61	Carroll C-Waukesha		95,000	138,770	4,789	2,000	240,559	7,000
62	Cedar Crest C		60,319	127,486	30,898	4,804 [1]	223,505	3,985
63	Cedarville U	G	201,082	125,969	26,330	106,794	460,178	8,923
64	Centenary C	b	12,565	9,187	33,774	34,123	89,648	0
65	Centenary C LA	bf	48,280	110,991	58,003	4,323	221,597	0
66	Central Baptist C	bf	40,021	19,768	4,212	0	64,001	487
67	Central CT ST U		341,755	900,239	15,774	227,827	1,485,595	25,000
68	Central MO ST U		221,388	861,289	159,024	0 [1]	1,241,701	23,639
69	Charleston Sthrn U		94,141	158,622	13,775	2,550	269,088	2,170
70	Chicago ST U	b	112,386	275,411	8,904	22,156	418,859	28,500
71	Chris Newport U		44,810	642,197	27,735	106,517 [1]	821,259	10,098
72	Christendom C	Bb	18,059	21,118	1,113	5,664	45,954	234
73	Christian Brothers U	b	55,000	104,475	7,000	2,639	169,114	2,500
74	Clarion U PA	Bb	195,681	230,891	22,449	0	449,021	9,634
75	Clarke C-IA		53,043	101,931	40,994	2,539	198,507	2,427
76	Clarkson C-NE	f	11,066	58,266	0	0	69,332	0
77	Colorado C	bG	478,507	817,253	20,119	0	1,315,879	16,870
78	Columbia C MO		33,593	76,080	16,020	15,552	-1	-1
79	Columbia C SC		79,445	41,508 [1]	9,900	9,940	140,793	2,039
80	Columbia Intl U	bf	20,959	25,682	43,003	93,299	182,943	8,624

Key to Notes on Page 1   1 -- See Footnotes   -1 -- Unavailable   -2 -- Not Applicable

ACRL Library Data Tables 2004
EXPENDITURES

INSTITUTIONS GRANTING MASTER OF ARTS AND PROFESSIONAL DEGREES (Carnegie Code M)

Salaries & Wages Prof. Staff* 22	Salaries & Wages Suppt. Staff* 23	Salaries & Wages Stud. Ass'ts* 24	Total Salaries & Wages* 25	Other Operating Expenditures 26	Total Library Expenditures 27	Survey Question #
						Institution
-1	-1	17,039	337,347	62,903	519,280	C Mt St Vincent
200,607	69,742	27,358	297,707	59,846	540,379	C Our Lady Elms
247,484	201,540	0	449,024	12,750	876,896	C.R. Drew U Med & Sci
157,900	194,722	36,231	388,903	62,360	557,294	CA C Arts & Crafts
1,174,396	1,489,421	179,206	2,843,023	237,837 [1]	4,449,599	CA St Polytechnic U-Pomona
2,383,188	2,014,913	634,251	5,032,352	477,118	7,883,686	CA St U - Sacramento
916,434	674,840	113,718	1,704,992	80,323	2,517,242	CA ST U Dominguez Hills
1,917,630	1,819,764	527,552	4,264,946	272,276	6,332,770	CA ST U Fresno
1,838,320	1,480,495	546,147	3,864,962	194,185	4,059,147	CA ST U Fullerton
1,135,646	760,425	199,348	2,095,419	215,102	3,295,822	CA ST U Hayward
2,516,004	1,326,984	452,294	4,295,282	234,769	7,057,187	CA ST U Long Beach
2,251,830 [1]	2,184,824	663,928	5,069,929	629,389	7,126,099	CA ST U Northridge
954,002	1,212,600	201,044	2,367,646	1,022,251	4,239,861	CA ST U S Bernadino
847,622	829,739	178,966	1,856,327	311,510	3,031,594	CA ST U San Marcos
596,272	618,069	148,510	1,362,851	129,533	2,244,973	CA ST U Stanislaus
-1	-1	-1	-1 [1]	123,043	1,194,401 [1]	CA West Sch Law
383,584	233,554	144,453	761,591	126,292	2,140,778	Calvin C
268,183	125,556	51,000	444,739	55,671	865,604	Cameron U
438,059	202,402	83,951	724,412	144,354	1,600,528	Canisius C
187,121	38,428	32,270	257,819	14,754	373,946	Carlow C
318,946	101,379	70,460	490,785	103,250	841,594	Carroll C-Waukesha
249,582	88,509	60,642	398,733	104,609	730,893	Cedar Crest C
423,375	399,210	85,634	908,219	183,792	1,561,112	Cedarville U
109,580	88,195	0	197,775	-1 [1]	287,423	Centenary C
118,228	139,714	24,954	282,896	42,241 [1]	546,734	Centenary C LA
82,089	1,680	10,939	94,708	4,178	163,374	Central Baptist C
1,139,659	1,013,232	78,279	2,231,170	90,917	3,832,682	Central CT ST U
803,660	839,668	182,125	1,825,453	239,607	3,330,400	Central MO ST U
285,595	141,788	50,473	477,856	69,923	819,037	Charleston Sthrn U
1,482,454	1,001,558	70,000	2,554,012	126,275	3,124,647	Chicago ST U
269,700	234,680	70,899	575,279	1,194,931 [1]	2,601,567	Chris Newport U
79,000 [1]	83,000 [1]	50,000 [1]	212,000	-1	258,188	Christendom C
161,300	63,000	19,918	244,218	8,000	418,693	Christian Brothers U
625,579	425,192	123,761	1,174,532	95,155	1,728,342	Clarion U PA
215,974	20,467	40,960	277,401	57,657	535,992	Clarke C-IA
148,502	0	8,520	157,022	0	157,022	Clarkson C-NE
521,817	361,185	89,002	972,004	347,755	2,652,508	Colorado C
-1	-1	-1	-1	-1	-1	Columbia C MO
214,565	88,696	39,463	342,724	35,137	520,693	Columbia C SC
140,992	70,440	52,159	263,591	118,263	381,854	Columbia Intl U

Key to Notes on Page 1   1 -- See Footnotes   -1 -- Unavailable   -2 -- Not Applicable

ACRL Library Data Tables 2004
EXPENDITURES

INSTITUTIONS GRANTING MASTER OF ARTS AND PROFESSIONAL DEGREES (Carnegie Code M)

Lib. No.	Institution	Notes	Monographs 16	Current Serials 17	Other Library Materials 18	Misc. Materials 19	Total Library Materials 20	Contract Binding 21
81	Columbus ST U	BG	59,391	121,561	39,950	1,450	222,352	3,638
82	Concordia U Irvine	b	23,920	10,063	11,764	2,916	48,663	0
83	Concordia U RiverF	b	45,000	38,050	8,000	-1	91,050	6,500
84	Concordia U St Paul		31,200	48,946	10,097	126,893	217,135	720
85	Cooper Union	b	40,986	58,927	54,021	67,102 [1]	221,036	5,141
86	Cornerstone U	bG	146,838	139,273	-1	-1	286,111	5,175
87	Creighton U	b	220,961	705,777	39,759	120,535	1,087,032	14,369
88	Cumberland U		20,000	49,500	1,000	15,200	85,700	0
89	CUNY BMB C		118,987	845,987	27,037	29,714	1,021,725	11,827
90	CUNY C Stn Island	f	82,234	128,860	33,711	1,768	246,573	0
91	CUNY City C	bGM	194,694	1,122,810	4,282	1,200	1,322,986	20,699
92	CUNY HH Lehman C	bG	144,846	321,041 [1]	16,915 [1]	162,896 [1]	645,698	14,891
93	CUNY John Jay C Crim Just	G	123,874	495,652	-1	18,554	638,080	12,144
94	CUNY Queens C	bG	146,568	762,776	-1	18,632	927,976	22,610
95	Curtis Inst Music	G	38,964	5,741	6,152	0	50,857	6,529
96	Daniel Webster C	b	29,154 [1]	30,744	1,762	0	62,098	438 [1]
97	DeSales U		78,719	114,533	20,800	23,700	237,752	5,400
98	DN Myers C		11,946	25,203	56	0	37,205	0
99	Dominican C San Rafael	b	107,530	99,054	0	51,128	257,712	6,888
100	Dominican U	b	128,850	129,068	20,000	-1	277,918	4,300
101	Drake U	b	217,702	727,732	28,235	0	973,669	21,842
102	Drury C	b	143,056	204,631	22,094	0	369,781	8,872
103	E R Aero U		169,257	325,000	36,500	0	530,757	6,000
104	Earlham C	Gf	136,962	241,301	-1	141,793	520,056	11,220
105	Eastern IL U	bG	401,550	651,538	119,453	239,120	1,392,751	59,840
106	Eastern U	Bb	110,000 [1]	71,000	15,000	92,000 [1]	288,000	5,000
107	Eastern WA U	Bb	222,554	832,725	-1	-1	1,055,279	9,986
108	Eastrn NM U Main	BbG	96,445	365,820	17,412	1,000	480,677	0 [1]
109	Edinboro U PA	b	173,170	290,759	219,415	42,754	726,098	15,976
110	Elizabethtown C	b	149,236	262,679	543	0	412,458	4,381
111	Elmhurst C	b	141,319	183,308	7,636	1,650	333,913	6,152
112	Elon U	b	469,265	371,984	127,856	0	969,105	17,825
113	Emmanuel C MA	b	35,495	66,067	7,900 [1]	95,000 [1]	204,462	4,789
114	Emory & Henry C	bGf	51,085	41,983	-1	45,000 [1]	138,068	0
115	Evergreen ST C	bGf	216,237	246,526	14,887	0	477,650	1,069
116	Fisk U	bG	20,000	17,560	0	0	37,560	306
117	Fitchburg ST C	G	13,130	230,137 [1]	55,506 [1]	37 [1]	298,810	829
118	FL Southern C	bG	108,430	209,026	20,291	-1	337,747	10,097
119	Fort Hays ST U	b	141,291	357,399	108,622	0	607,312	13,000
120	Francis Marion U	G	22,891	483,978	35,272	65,658 [1]	607,797	10,952

Key to Notes on Page 1   1 -- See Footnotes   -1 -- Unavailable   -2 -- Not Applicable

ACRL Library Data Tables 2004
EXPENDITURES

INSTITUTIONS GRANTING MASTER OF ARTS AND PROFESSIONAL DEGREES (Carnegie Code M)

Salaries & Wages Prof. Staff* 22	Salaries & Wages Suppt. Staff* 23	Salaries & Wages Stud. Ass'ts* 24	Total Salaries & Wages* 25	Other Operating Expenditures 26	Total Library Expenditures 27	Survey Question #
						Institution
684,966	183,850	58,490	927,206	81,750	1,239,146	Columbus ST U
-1	-1	-1	-1	0	-1	Concordia U Irvine
113,538	37,685	66,307	217,530	43,488	358,568	Concordia U RiverF
175,244	-1	41,707	216,951	-1	434,806	Concordia U St Paul
285,278	121,543	9,808	416,629	6,799	649,804	Cooper Union
121,121	91,102	78,362	290,585	111,729	693,600	Cornerstone U
466,544	241,160	108,709	816,413	111,099	2,125,896	Creighton U
102,442	0	-1	102,442	-1	188,142	Cumberland U
1,813,666	778,620	39,801	2,632,087	113,856	3,779,495	CUNY BMB C
886,549	1,031,300	8,000	1,925,849	3,121	2,175,543	CUNY C Stn Island
1,552,987	570,742	279,879	2,403,608	293,219	4,040,512	CUNY City C
784,811 [1]	520,154	78,927 [1]	1,383,892	-1	2,044,481	CUNY HH Lehman C
949,250	258,903	92,362	1,300,515	36,224	1,986,963	CUNY John Jay C Crim Just
1,410,516	915,126	94,467	2,420,109	160,406	3,531,101	CUNY Queens C
166,615	101,114	16,868	284,597	-1	341,983	Curtis Inst Music
183,995	53,840	13,412	251,247	0	313,783	Daniel Webster C
-1	-1	50,000	340,000 [1]	47,160 [1]	630,312	DeSales U
63,000	15,000	9,051	87,051	0	124,256	DN Myers C
162,965	233,169	55,670	451,804	88,104	804,508	Dominican C San Rafael
361,962	212,337	171,000	745,299	257,454	1,002,753	Dominican U
374,077	480,834	116,674	971,585	168,170	2,135,266	Drake U
342,215	127,502	80,850	550,567	443,238	993,895	Drury C
0 [1]	0 [1]	119,000	1,185,202	387,153	1,691,355	E R Aero U
398,119	149,716	108,695	656,530	125,666	1,313,472	Earlham C
1,188,481	1,045,334	167,970	2,401,785	200,166	4,054,542	Eastern IL U
-1	-1	-1	-1	-1	700,734	Eastern U
700,921	1,069,729	178,552	1,949,202	949,118	3,963,584	Eastern WA U
410,233	221,813	127,922	759,968	104,127	1,411,114	Eastrn NM U Main
737,490	367,162	51,810	1,156,462	137,389	2,035,925	Edinboro U PA
199,091	121,199	29,604	349,894	80,075	429,969	Elizabethtown C
280,632	269,888	32,863	583,383	4,591	928,039	Elmhurst C
444,338	268,401	63,046	775,785	599,046	2,361,761	Elon U
233,953	62,090	50,011	346,954	41,371	596,676	Emmanuel C MA
216,497	216,220	16,616	449,333	95,775 [1]	683,176	Emory & Henry C
481,962	1,271,453	172,758	1,926,173	1,000,790	3,405,682	Evergreen ST C
-1	-1	4,764	281,553	46,641	328,194	Fisk U
284,834 [1]	174,877 [1]	34,036 [1]	493,757	102,307 [1]	895,703	Fitchburg ST C
201,520	82,297	24,606	308,473	182,253	838,570	FL Southern C
382,769	248,269	176,457	807,495	710,000	1,517,495	Fort Hays ST U
421,571	389,184	38,326	849,081	96,728	1,564,558	Francis Marion U

Key to Notes on Page 1   1 -- See Footnotes   -1 -- Unavailable   -2 -- Not Applicable

INSTITUTIONS GRANTING MASTER OF ARTS AND PROFESSIONAL DEGREES (Carnegie Code M)

Lib. No.	Institution	Notes	Monographs 16	Current Serials 17	Other Library Materials 18	Misc. Materials 19	Total Library Materials 20	Contract Binding 21
	Survey Question #							
121	Franklin Inst Boston	b	3,934	7,708	0	0	11,642	0
122	Franklin U		75,000	13,925	7,000	513	96,438	0
123	Free Will Baptist Bible C	bG	44,054	14,985	4,294	4,000	67,333	0
124	Frostburg ST U	bG	68,216	146,600	14,931	578	229,746	8,332
125	Furman U	G	325,042	831,512	19,844	0	1,176,398	21,469
126	GA SWstrn ST U	b	46,854	73,222	60,556	2,650	183,282	3,719
127	Gardner-Webb U	BbG	104,613	156,802 [1]	9,157	0	270,572	830
128	Geneva C	G	77,795	108,853	14,169	0	200,817	16,106
129	Georgetown C		80,000	75,743	19,983	49,666	225,392	700
130	Goucher C	b	180,551	176,285	1,066	147,916	505,818	9,145
131	Governors ST U	bG	52,591	260,891	7,184	490	321,156	8,016
132	Greenville C		26,047	59,956	1,104	-1	87,107	3,640
133	Grove City C	b	165,000	119,000	49,000	223,000	533,000	25,000
134	Harding U Main	bG	118,602	134,794	48,213	0	301,609	5,280
135	Hebrew C		46,105	11,167	4,028	15,500	76,800	0
136	Heidelberg C	Bbf	48,500	62,770	20,000	15,624	146,894	4,000
137	Hillsdale Free Will Baptist C		3,500	7,576	5,294	0	16,370	0
138	Holy Apostles C & Sem	bGf	4,562	18,063 [1]	-1 [1]	674	23,299	-1
139	Hood C	G	65,235	173,950	1,583 [1]	0	240,768	2,958
140	Humboldt ST U	G	248,882	263,893	375,723	0	888,498	2,900
141	IN Inst of Tech	bf	4,000	23,000	58,000	6,000	91,000	1,000
142	IN U Kokomo	G	47,573	214,860	54,493	-1	316,926	2,589
143	IN U S Bend	b	167,615	484,109	-1	7,700	659,424	13,316
144	IN U-Purdue U Ft Wayne	G	170,669	298,779	31,953	228,089	729,490	10,277
145	IN Wesleyan U	B	236,110	257,118	34,114	-1	527,342	24,763
146	Intl Fine Arts C		35,000	8,000	10,000	0	53,000	0
147	Jacksonville ST U	bG	352,869	403,564	9,848	0	766,281	10,878
148	Johnson Bible C		64,941	22,947	13,771	192	101,851	1,518
149	Kean U		300,000	500,000	40,000	0	840,000	5,000
150	Keene State C	b	281,101	262,993	76,703	0	620,797	8,637
151	Kent ST U Stark	b	79,704	41,000	19,479	6,707	146,890	5,391
152	Kentucky Christian C	f	30,861	49,137	2,994	0	82,992	5,313
153	Kentucky ST U	G	70,069	222,048	15,232	0	307,349	0
154	Kettering U	b	80,814	232,800	31,865	13,500	358,979	1,600
155	King's C PA		154,654	176,496	35,004	80,622	446,776	5,007
156	LaGrange C	Bb	109,964	71,793	14,768	67,000	263,525	4,953
157	Lakeland C-AB		31,847	80,041	12,530	0	124,418	0
158	Lakeview C Nursing	b	2,000	10,925	0	0	12,925	5,000
159	Lancaster Bible C		74,250	24,790	4,768	27,974 [1]	131,782	0 [1]
160	Lander U	G	40,879	100,272	28,905	23,459	193,025	2,584

Key to Notes on Page 1   1 -- See Footnotes   -1 -- Unavailable   -2 -- Not Applicable

ACRL Library Data Tables 2004
EXPENDITURES

INSTITUTIONS GRANTING MASTER OF ARTS AND PROFESSIONAL DEGREES (Carnegie Code M)

Salaries & Wages Prof. Staff* 22	Salaries & Wages Suppt. Staff* 23	Salaries & Wages Stud. Ass'ts* 24	Total Salaries & Wages* 25	Other Operating Expenditures 26	Total Library Expenditures 27	Survey Question #
						Institution
58,410	0	1,776	60,186	1,991	73,819	Franklin Inst Boston
347,752	-1	24,500	375,252	42,492	514,182	Franklin U
68,992 [1]	-1	12,107	81,099	6,628	155,060	Free Will Baptist Bible C
-1	-1	13,773	828,720	386,041	1,452,839	Frostburg ST U
614,607	360,960	87,614	1,063,181	242,188	2,503,236	Furman U
182,851 [1]	98,963	12,000 [1]	293,814	32,474	513,289	GA SWstrn ST U
221,729	159,326	30,000	411,055	83,750	766,207	Gardner-Webb U
281,053	44,855	81,251	407,159	206,503	830,585	Geneva C
141,158	140,608	52,151	307,907	134,900	668,909	Georgetown C
417,308	155,867	49,645	622,820	89,442	1,227,225	Goucher C
390,377	685,315	51,870	1,127,562	239,466	1,367,028	Governors ST U
123,412	23,000	47,632	194,044	17,574	302,365	Greenville C
0	0	0	0	0	0	Grove City C
272,755	123,359	64,184	460,298	201,101	968,288	Harding U Main
403,587	0	0	403,587 [1]	55,540	535,927	Hebrew C
112,270	114,680	47,021	273,971	55,917	480,782	Heidelberg C
69,758	0	10,639	80,397	13,631	110,398	Hillsdale Free Will Baptist C
-1	-1	-1	-1	-1	-1	Holy Apostles C & Sem
217,815	89,524	33,384	340,723	112,241	696,690	Hood C
1,167,091	820,681	145,815	2,133,587	76,947 [1]	3,101,932	Humboldt ST U
36,000	54,000	10,000	100,000	2,000	193,000	IN Inst of Tech
231,886	78,055	71,855	301,672	34,844	736,155	IN U Kokomo
639,942	144,519	166,391	950,852	86,664	1,037,516	IN U S Bend
625,578	291,788	68,356	985,722	296,707	2,022,196	IN U-Purdue U Ft Wayne
405,660	168,912	91,676	666,248	131,230	1,349,583	IN Wesleyan U
40,000	0	24,000	64,000	1,600	80,000	Intl Fine Arts C
884,340	406,963	22,445	1,313,748	1,962,162	2,275,910	Jacksonville ST U
71,806	48,199 [1]	28,006	148,011	37,086	288,466	Johnson Bible C
673,000	580,000	16,000	1,269,000	255,000	1,524,000	Kean U
601,254	309,799	43,152	954,205	272,211	1,855,850	Keene State C
256,514	85,944	33,050	375,508	7,304	535,093	Kent ST U Stark
84,753	17,226	42,500	144,479	12,564	245,348	Kentucky Christian C
474,084	264,605	10,100	748,789	38,795	1,094,933	Kentucky ST U
260,351	173,000	4,000	437,351	131,745	927,675	Kettering U
324,497	167,539	22,099	514,135	46,318	1,012,236	King's C PA
197,617	53,009	-1	272,658	-1	-1	LaGrange C
98,907	15,320	17,612	131,838	24,941	281,195	Lakeland C-AB
21,424	0	5,280	26,704	2,442	47,071	Lakeview C Nursing
134,900	11,533	46,049	192,482	34,173	358,437	Lancaster Bible C
271,573	150,218	35,188	435,572	65,564	696,745	Lander U

Key to Notes on Page 1   1 -- See Footnotes   -1 -- Unavailable   -2 -- Not Applicable

61

ACRL Library Data Tables 2004
EXPENDITURES

INSTITUTIONS GRANTING MASTER OF ARTS AND PROFESSIONAL DEGREES (Carnegie Code M)

Lib. No.	Institution	Notes	Monographs 16	Current Serials 17	Other Library Materials 18	Misc. Materials 19	Total Library Materials 20	Contract Binding 21
		Survey Question #						
161	Langston U	BG	22,922	161,075	56,782	20,689	261,468	2,794
162	Laurentian U JN	bG	239,534	1,080,650	-1 [1]	61,766 [1]	1,381,950	12,482
163	Le Moyne C	G	142,332	430,057	31,406	7,588 [1]	611,383	13,194
164	Lebanon Valley C	b	175,420	325,430	95,160	45,160	641,170	9,000
165	Lewis U		143,500	215,650	35,000	99,350	493,500	6,000
166	Lewis&Clark C	G	302,078 [1]	675,200	12,390	1,426 [1]	991,094	10,606
167	Lincoln U-MO	b	33,541	68,640	1,022	30,620	133,823	2,013
168	Lindsey Wilson C	bG	48,114 [1]	57,494 [1]	12,004 [1]	17,892 [1]	135,504	159
169	Lipscomb U		107,512	178,633	-1	0	286,145	11,738
170	Lock Haven U PA	BbG	63,311	219,176	38,872	0	321,359	13,400
171	Longwood C	G	191,331	335,198	0	0	526,529	15,617
172	Lourdes C		27,119	42,950	4,368	40,118	114,555	0
173	Loyola Marymount U	b	925,596	1,487,381	77,729	0	2,490,706	26,179
174	Loyola U New Orleans	G	332,954	380,515	-1	59,934	970,725	25,095
175	Lubbock Christian U	b	-1 [1]	-1 [1]	-1 [1]	-1 [1]	-1 [1]	0
176	Luth Theo Sem Philly	bf	38,815	12,040	5,698	0	56,553	8,477
177	Lynchburg C		57,778	124,043	12,438	67,481	261,740	4,848
178	Malone C		83,858	171,710	66,346	113,238	435,152	12,025
179	Manchester C		39,609	67,797	3,850	0	111,256	3,300
180	Manhattan C		246,710	325,712	15,765	-1	588,187	9,931
181	Marist C	G	135,241	388,172	16,057	5,215	544,685	0
182	Mary Baldwin C	b	60,867	72,228	6,383	19,386	158,864	4,300
183	Mary Washington C	BbG	297,758	128,564	-1 [1]	0	426,322	0
184	Marymount U	G	195,613	301,212	35,792	-1	532,616	14,994
185	Maryville U St Louis	b	33,730	196,382	9,430	1,826 [1]	241,368	752
186	McNeese ST U		266,430	431,731	-1	22,841 [1]	721,002	8,237
187	Medical C Wisconsin	BbGM	68,083	1,128,422	254,037	0	1,450,542	15,000
188	Merrimack C	b	120,292	129,349	42,717	100,994	393,352	5,759
189	MidAmer Nazarene U		35,000	70,000	0	53,575	-1	158,575
190	Millikin U	bG	35,244	113,200	12,382 [1]	61,646 [1]	222,472	2,186
191	Millsaps C	G	52,017	150,071	-1 [1]	59,690	261,778	5,457
192	Minnesota ST U-Mankato	bG	278,151	1,141,576	43,961	-1	1,463,688	20,000
193	Minot ST U	G	31,224	262,549	14,915	0	308,688	0
194	Monterey Inst Intl St	f	58,000	150,000	0	0	208,000	100
195	Moravian C		145,135	235,655	18,800	72,355	471,945	13,220
196	Morehead ST U	G	290,134	668,306	59,595	31,485	1,049,520	16,136
197	Morningside C	bG	33,848	67,930	33,971	131	135,880	0
198	MS Valley ST U	BG	450	96,550	74,500	131,785	303,285	5,200
199	Mt Holyoke C		395,480	918,451	23,532	0	1,337,463	37,355
200	Mt Marty C		16,810	36,355	10,629	0	-1	-1

Key to Notes on Page 1   1 -- See Footnotes   -1 -- Unavailable   -2 -- Not Applicable

ACRL Library Data Tables 2004
EXPENDITURES

INSTITUTIONS GRANTING MASTER OF ARTS AND PROFESSIONAL DEGREES (Carnegie Code M)

Salaries & Wages Prof. Staff* 22	Salaries & Wages Suppt. Staff* 23	Salaries & Wages Stud. Ass'ts* 24	Total Salaries & Wages* 25	Other Operating Expenditures 26	Total Library Expenditures 27	Survey Question #
						Institution
370,035	89,707	45,229	504,917	37,988	545,753	Langston U
674,794	969,648	52,268	1,696,710	148,631	3,178,007	Laurentian U JN
500,252	75,145	127,207	702,604	96,741	1,423,922	Le Moyne C
213,000	79,000	58,740	350,740	695	1,001,605	Lebanon Valley C
304,574	158,175	93,683	556,432	0	1,055,932	Lewis U
490,653	238,257	100,272	829,182	174,678	2,004,560	Lewis&Clark C
278,715	123,686	25,986	428,387	38,132	602,355	Lincoln U-MO
120,947	55,091	16,864	192,952	37,150 [1]	365,962	Lindsey Wilson C
312,843	75,456	24,230	412,529	70,574	780,986	Lipscomb U
580,656	259,942	89,253	929,851	96,500	1,360,110	Lock Haven U PA
305,328	491,716	45,638	842,682	254,703	1,639,531	Longwood C
62,223	24,500	1,800	88,523	7,028	210,106	Lourdes C
963,391	711,897	255,125	1,930,413	548,077	4,995,375	Loyola Marymount U
707,677	536,582	79,499	1,323,758	1,385,565	2,709,323	Loyola U New Orleans
145,199	53,904	16,296 [1]	215,398	245,592 [1]	460,990	Lubbock Christian U
101,211	101,032	7,146	209,389	13,340	287,759	Luth Theo Sem Philly
-1	-1	54,135	376,701	54,841	698,130	Lynchburg C
205,956	105,739	33,843	345,538	72,419	865,134	Malone C
158,155	55,204	27,079	240,438	180,118	535,112	Manchester C
696,860	338,080	42,633	1,077,573	-1	1,675,691	Manhattan C
467,600	200,075	76,019	743,694	133,079	1,421,458	Marist C
189,050	67,910	51,735	308,695	31,722	503,581	Mary Baldwin C
560,527	362,022	41,697	966,343	478,323	1,900,988 [1]	Mary Washington C
476,890 [1]	890,799 [1]	14,552 [1]	1,382,241 [1]	398,121 [1]	2,327,973 [1]	Marymount U
272,835	223,805	30,492	527,132	68,814	838,066	Maryville U St Louis
636,176	269,849	107,752	1,013,777	160,475 [1]	1,903,491	McNeese ST U
658,300	457,450	0	1,115,750	147,964	2,729,256	Medical C Wisconsin
271,691	158,296	77,473	507,460	92,238	998,809	Merrimack C
110,000	105,000	20,000	225,000	0	423,388	MidAmer Nazarene U
158,927	136,774	36,478	332,179	124,975 [1]	681,812	Millikin U
219,576	83,390	35,487	338,453	46,332	652,020	Millsaps C
1,192,075	771,828	169,380	2,133,283	454,931	4,071,902	Minnesota ST U-Mankato
-1	-1	34,484	537,440	167,413	1,013,541	Minot ST U
300,000	150,000	80,000	530,000	0	738,000	Monterey Inst Intl St
184,130	109,590	65,000	358,720	-1	954,910	Moravian C
630,666	557,430	117,559	1,305,655	113,213	2,468,389	Morehead ST U
112,060	39,010	8,660	159,730	99,181	394,791	Morningside C
222,964	219,481	3,600	366,045	126,097	880,627	MS Valley ST U
775,498	621,674	88,253	1,485,425	40,000	2,900,243	Mt Holyoke C
-1	-1	-1	-1	-1	-1	Mt Marty C

Key to Notes on Page 1   1 -- See Footnotes   -1 -- Unavailable   -2 -- Not Applicable

INSTITUTIONS GRANTING MASTER OF ARTS AND PROFESSIONAL DEGREES (Carnegie Code M)

Lib. No.	Institution	Notes	Monographs 16	Current Serials 17	Other Library Materials 18	Misc. Materials 19	Total Library Materials 20	Contract Binding 21
		Survey Question #						
201	Mt Mary C-WI	bf	56,000	72,500	9,200	47,900	185,000	3,700
202	MT ST U Northern	bG	28,353	50,349	4,988	0	83,690	0
203	Mt St Vincent U	Gf	100,754	374,777	-1	0	475,531	10,315
204	MT Tech U Montana	bG	31,282	147,820	1,200	11,769	192,071	3,500
205	Murray ST U-KY	L	156,085	942,337	40,251	23,594	1,141,953	20,583
206	Muskingum C		42,000	31,000	6,000	0	79,000	1,400
207	Natl C Naturopathic Med	bM	14,400	48,400	3,500	0	66,300	0
208	Natl Defense U	bGf	250,000	1,000,000	30,000	100,000	1,380,000	6,000
209	NC Sch Arts		46,000	65,000 [1]	55,275 [1]	0	166,275	8,000
210	NEastrn IL U	B	198,757	944,252	24,067	6,518	1,173,594	15,004
211	Nipissing U	B	206,426	305,203	44,300	11,261	567,190	3,090
212	NJ City U		150,000	130,000	10,000	0	290,000	0
213	NM Highlands U	B	90,268	282,839	25,164	0	398,271	1,386
214	North Central C		60,695	214,297	6,583	32,975	314,820	2,374
215	Northern KY U	b	180,871	705,152	-1	-1	886,023	10,882
216	Northern ST U	bGf	84,328	40,009	36,252	105,423	266,012	4,531
217	Northwest C	b	29,834	45,184	6,444	36,831	118,293	0
218	Norwich U	G	175,352	116,843	14,490	14,000	320,685	5,648
219	Notre Dame C OH		7,737	27,389	683	62,549 [1]	-1	-1
220	Notre Dame Sem	b	15,654	16,793	807	3,119	36,373	3,772
221	NW MO ST U	bG	234,151	289,939	18,727	0	542,817	12,288
222	NY Inst Tech Islip		0 [1]	40,585 [1]	0 [1]	0	40,585	1,800
223	NY Inst Tech Main	M	132,042	358,399	-1	199,450	689,891	10,751
224	Oberlin C	B	941,643	1,009,923	100,260	-1	2,051,826	90,000
225	OH U Lancaster	b	60,000	55,000	15,500	600	131,100	600
226	Olivet Nazarene U	G	95,075	100,762	111,545	0	307,382	2,724
227	Otterbein C	G	70,317	99,027	25,609	115,932	310,885	7,973
228	Pace U Law		222,344	66,664	24,423	57,219	370,650	3,833
229	Pacific Lutheran U	f	259,426	602,675	80,038	34,850	976,989	0 [1]
230	Pacific Union C		180,099	99,061	6,111	0	285,271	6,595
231	Palm Beach Atl C	b	87,891	27,753	18,478 [1]	91,868 [1]	225,990	659
232	Pfeiffer U	Bb	61,851	52,038	11,955	0	125,844	3,541
233	Philadelphia U	b	107,000	134,575	34,000	30,535	306,110	9,800
234	Plymouth ST C	G	308,330 [1]	250,935 [1]	-1 [1]	0	559,265	3,604
235	Pont C Josephinum		45,725	34,827	2,198	0	82,750	3,684
236	Pope John Ntl Sem	bf	21,824	15,962	2,199	0	39,985	2,316
237	Prescott C	Bb	16,904	29,677	2,727	9,419	58,727	592
238	Providence C	b	263,415	446,395	29,601	332,925	1,072,336	13,562
239	Purchase C SUNY		65,204	304,286	15,091	20,285	404,866	9,559
240	Purdue U Calumet	G	197,658	300,170	10,499	93,650	601,978	11,657

Key to Notes on Page 1   1 -- See Footnotes   -1 -- Unavailable   -2 -- Not Applicable

ACRL Library Data Tables 2004
EXPENDITURES

INSTITUTIONS GRANTING MASTER OF ARTS AND PROFESSIONAL DEGREES (Carnegie Code M)

Salaries & Wages Prof. Staff* 22	Salaries & Wages Suppt. Staff* 23	Salaries & Wages Stud. Ass'ts* 24	Total Salaries & Wages* 25	Other Operating Expenditures 26	Total Library Expenditures 27	Survey Question #
						Institution
-1	-1	14,750	271,060	15,000	475,360	Mt Mary C-WI
95,409	86,050	33,782	215,241	29,203	328,134	MT ST U Northern
230,666	445,075	15,445	691,186	72,737	1,249,769	Mt St Vincent U
97,947	132,014	27,000	256,961	35,769	488,301	MT Tech U Montana
453,674	445,259	125,839	1,024,772	137,253	2,324,561	Murray ST U-KY
235,450	23,077	42,276	300,803	2,000	302,803	Muskingum C
75,000	55,000	25,000	155,000	19,500	240,800	Natl C Naturopathic Med
1,400,000 [1]	400,000	0	1,800,000	300,000 [1]	3,486,000	Natl Defense U
223,958	226,721	23,125	473,804	208,221	856,300	NC Sch Arts
1,210,565	1,006,324	81,075	2,297,964	308,899	3,795,461	NEastrn IL U
286,425	434,727	4,804	725,956	72,645	1,368,881	Nipissing U
1,059,010	450,819	128,000	1,636,829	-1	1,636,829	NJ City U
368,388	114,250	48,000	530,638	370,603	1,300,898	NM Highlands U
321,671	193,299	65,492	580,462	70,012	967,668	North Central C
925,979	705,233	162,275	1,794,487	606,441	2,400,928	Northern KY U
276,324	169,471	13,236	459,031	86,706	816,280	Northern ST U
199,533	101,854	55,306	354,693	162,346	635,332	Northwest C
252,941	202,008	51,249	506,198	238,556	1,071,087	Norwich U
-1	-1	-1	-1	-1	-1	Notre Dame C OH
40,695	-1	3,500	36,373	10,510 [1]	94,850	Notre Dame Sem
377,884 [1]	398,167 [1]	46,369	822,420 [1]	99,898	1,477,423	NW MO ST U
220,575	47,513	1,558	269,646	55,470	317,531	NY Inst Tech Islip
675,615 [1]	369,014 [1]	-1 [1]	1,044,629	202,631	1,947,902	NY Inst Tech Main
1,057,353	1,228,310	375,775	2,661,438	331,289	5,134,553	Oberlin C
97,206	70,907	25,086	193,199	11,800	336,699	OH U Lancaster
225,870	140,882	94,802	461,554	300,625	1,072,285	Olivet Nazarene U
302,866	124,601	53,404	480,871	65,567	865,296 [1]	Otterbein C
1,931,396	545,653	89,810	2,566,859	139,272	3,080,614	Pace U Law
504,232	414,124	214,193	1,132,549 [1]	374,215	2,483,753	Pacific Lutheran U
305,666	80,051	53,928	439,645	126,505	858,016	Pacific Union C
211,606	76,675	60,876	349,157	35,505	611,311	Palm Beach Atl C
164,143	25,387	9,392	198,922	10,939	339,246	Pfeiffer U
304,974	204,920	77,948	587,842	131,817	1,035,569	Philadelphia U
445,411	370,915	44,982	861,308	130,832	1,555,009	Plymouth ST C
-1	-1	-1	-1	-1	-1	Pont C Josephinum
94,035	0	0	94,035	11,957	148,292	Pope John Ntl Sem
90,656	92,419	9,100	192,175	10,874	262,368	Prescott C
799,966 [1]	376,454 [1]	48,519	1,224,939	481,014	2,791,851	Providence C
318,884	583,739	48,700	951,323	58,939	1,424,687	Purchase C SUNY
379,310	280,403	36,908	696,621	177,431	1,487,687	Purdue U Calumet

Key to Notes on Page 1   1 -- See Footnotes   -1 -- Unavailable   -2 -- Not Applicable

ACRL Library Data Tables 2004
EXPENDITURES

INSTITUTIONS GRANTING MASTER OF ARTS AND PROFESSIONAL DEGREES (Carnegie Code M)

Lib. No.	Institution	Notes	Monographs 16	Current Serials 17	Other Library Materials 18	Misc. Materials 19	Total Library Materials 20	Contract Binding 21
241	Purdue U North Central	G	57,625	57,520	1,648	33,937 [1]	150,731	2,787
242	Quincy U	b	48,305	60,920	2,580	0	111,805	4,120
243	R.Wesleyan C	G	116,371	191,382 [1]	3,525	0	311,278	2,063
244	Radford U	G	198,770	657,327	75,076	7,043	938,216	35,848
245	Ramapo C NJ	bf	235,588	349,063	34,426	35,872	619,077	3,073
246	Recnstrctnst Rabbinical C	b	20,305	7,772	12,784	3,178	44,039	0
247	RI Sch Design		126,444	33,761	36,333	0	196,538	8,638
248	Rivier C	b	173,040	65,603	16,260	0	254,903	3,850
249	Rockhurst U	bG	110,500	135,500	39,000	30,400	315,000	0
250	Roger Williams U	G	262,500	312,000	216,850	17,180	808,530	9,180
251	Roosevelt U	Bb	231,520	347,673	90,343	0	669,536	16,124
252	Rosemont C	b	32,000	60,000	8,200	17,890	118,090	1,000
253	Salem Teiko U	G	0	9,174	0	0	9,174	0
254	Salisbury ST U		82,017	358,335	33,353	49,326	523,031	12,525
255	San Jose ST U	bG	532,862	631,784	34,546	718,556	1,917,748	26,097
256	Savannah ST U	bf	26,638	201,266	42,285	23,047	293,236	0
257	Schreiner C		16,639	43,166	1,083	11,227	72,114	-1
258	SE LA U	Bf	348,410	570,501	99,524	317	1,018,750	7,698
259	SE MO ST U		261,604	1,023,319	53,189	1,952 [1]	1,340,064	16,989
260	SE Oklahoma St U	b	80,399	105,113	20,705	55,412	261,628	6,000
261	Seton Hill C		62,000	63,744	0	0	125,744	5,910
262	SF Consrv Music		17,000	5,800	13,000 [1]	6,200	42,000	4,000
263	Shaw U		85,402	35,808	2,153	8,992 [1]	132,355	5,321
264	Shorter C	Bb	84,531	60,773	4,354	16,400	166,058	0
265	Silver Lake C	f	20,225	13,560	6,845	12,200 [1]	52,830	0
266	Sisseton-Wahpeton CC	bG	1,637 [1]	7,762	5,439 [1]	2,162 [1]	17,549	0
267	Southrn C Opt	M	11,873	32,218	227	0	44,318	3,464
268	Southrn IL U Edward		249,847	744,044	336,250	67,884	1,398,025	24,962
269	Southrn OR U	G	174,774	180,555	102,593	26,196	484,118	20,527
270	Spring Hill C	bf	75,000	108,000	14,500	20,400	217,900	4,500
271	St Ambrose U		112,397	192,678	30,192	60,623	395,890	8,962
272	St C.Borromeo Sem	bf	41,032	47,828	4,116	925	96,338	9,677
273	St Cloud ST U	b	346,486	713,023	45,125	49,857	1,154,491	4,811
274	St Francis C PA	G	27,728	84,254	166,105	0	278,087	2,303
275	St Francis-Xavier U	bf	238,790	676,486	-1	-1	915,276	0
276	St John Fisher C	bGf	211,000	243,150	20,000 [1]	159,582 [1]	633,732	6,900
277	St Joseph C Suffolk	b	58,377	84,750 [1]	6,242	12,696	162,065	2,049
278	St Joseph's C IN	bG	27,078	52,568	665	0	80,311	2,515
279	St Joseph's C NY	bf	24,144	38,238	854	45,205 [1]	108,441	2,768
280	St Joseph's Sem	b	24,820	32,661	2,632	9,239	69,352	3,759

Key to Notes on Page 1   1 -- See Footnotes   -1 -- Unavailable   -2 -- Not Applicable

ACRL Library Data Tables 2004
EXPENDITURES

INSTITUTIONS GRANTING MASTER OF ARTS AND PROFESSIONAL DEGREES (Carnegie Code M)

Salaries & Wages Prof. Staff* 22	Salaries & Wages Suppt. Staff* 23	Salaries & Wages Stud. Ass'ts* 24	Total Salaries & Wages* 25	Other Operating Expenditures 26	Total Library Expenditures 27	Survey Question #
						Institution
134,857	63,128	-1	197,985	9,650	361,153	Purdue U North Central
112,516	334,129	31,003	177,648	59,894	237,542	Quincy U
202,029	98,667	33,743	334,439	63,228	711,008	R.Wesleyan C
599,381	486,656	167,508	1,253,545	492,187	2,719,796	Radford U
650,907	633,074	58,000	1,341,981	-1	1,341,981	Ramapo C NJ
89,916	7,942	4,200	102,058	0	146,097	Recnstrctnst Rabbinical C
432,239	377,446	75,932	885,617	87,354	1,178,147	RI Sch Design
317,648	42,312	40,191	400,151	35,263	694,167	Rivier C
196,048	132,274	25,000	353,322	45,400	713,722	Rockhurst U
782,066	362,809	21,000	1,165,875	69,270	2,043,675	Roger Williams U
597,730	450,036	24,500	1,072,266	105,940	1,863,866	Roosevelt U
177,170	73,443	0	250,613	0	369,703	Rosemont C
-1 [1]	-1	-1	81,936	-1	-1	Salem Teiko U
526,435	302,714	74,599	903,748	383,827	1,823,131	Salisbury ST U
2,271,648	2,336,008	789,959	5,397,615	676,129	8,017,589	San Jose ST U
389,904	53,573	10,657	454,134	45,829	793,199	Savannah ST U
176,408	92,085	3,000	271,493	107,930	451,537	Schreiner C
1,044,802	647,368	302,574	1,994,744	366,765	3,387,957	SE LA U
968,487	383,101	140,074	1,491,662	281,664	3,130,379	SE MO ST U
195,510	81,354	74,949	351,812	76,968	696,407	SE Oklahoma St U
-1	-1	-1	-1	-1	-1	Seton Hill C
66,500	34,000	45,500	146,000	6,800	198,801	SF Consrv Music
355,940	-1	16,143	372,083	0	372,083	Shaw U
186,868	4,600	14,300	205,768	43,750	475,571	Shorter C
102,438	9,620	7,475	119,533	6,155	178,518	Silver Lake C
24,521	15,000	0	39,521	0	57,069	Sisseton-Wahpeton CC
102,600	25,906	28,069	156,575	96,466	253,041	Southrn C Opt
1,199,901	1,049,963	247,441	2,497,305	494,206	4,414,501	Southrn IL U Edward
555,554	267,910	81,582	905,046	572,617 [1]	1,982,308	Southrn OR U
209,876	132,431	7,231	349,538	0	571,938	Spring Hill C
276,395	185,546	68,982	530,923	123,826	1,059,601	St Ambrose U
71,965	155,941	7,920	235,826	56,294	398,135	St C.Borromeo Sem
863,873	844,032	225,478	1,933,383	129,825	3,222,510	St Cloud ST U
355,195	132,509	10,675	498,379	77,584	856,353	St Francis C PA
682,682	502,371	32,999	1,218,052	175,027	2,308,355	St Francis-Xavier U
-1	-1	45,560	582,617 [1]	101,118	-1	St John Fisher C
368,386	142,292	10,659	521,337	80,749	896,200	St Joseph C Suffolk
152,342	65,035	15,893	233,270	90,480	406,576	St Joseph's C IN
135,577	206,195	345	342,117	126,132	553,246	St Joseph's C NY
66,543	46,224	0	112,767	28,499	141,266	St Joseph's Sem

Key to Notes on Page 1   1 -- See Footnotes   -1 -- Unavailable   -2 -- Not Applicable

ACRL Library Data Tables 2004
EXPENDITURES

INSTITUTIONS GRANTING MASTER OF ARTS AND PROFESSIONAL DEGREES (Carnegie Code M)

Lib. No.	Institution	Notes	Monographs 16	Current Serials 17	Other Library Materials 18	Misc. Materials 19	Total Library Materials 20	Contract Binding 21
281	St Mary's U MN	G	70,911	131,914	3,581	1,643	208,049	2,479
282	St Meinrad Theo	b	37,928	22,857	3,574	-1	64,359	3,750
283	St Michael's C	b	114,929	299,056	46,678	13,631 [1]	474,294	13,291
284	St Norbert C		106,390	161,544	29,059	0	267,934	3,322
285	St Patrick's Sem	f	42,038	24,231	348	0	66,617	2,304
286	St Peter's Abbey & C	bGf	4,594	1,113	1,492	0	7,199	0
287	ST U W GA		159,185	331,843	5,482	36,224 [1]	532,734	-1
288	St Vincent Sem		47,457	25,741	3,275	0	76,473	4,395
289	St. John's C		40,000	19,700	1,000	29,500	90,200	4,000
290	Stetson U	B	199,959	239,273	115,408 [1]	13,667	568,308	10,422
291	Sthrn Polytech ST U	G	45,000	181,444	1,345	0	235,117	7,328
292	Stonehill C	bG	88,286	368,478	43,706	0	501,170	3,138
293	Sul Ross ST U	bf	168,248	254,043	-1 [1]	46,023 [1]	468,314	3,562
294	SUNY Brockport		213,047	482,238	41,780	137,435	874,500	20,434
295	SUNY Buffalo		114,200	395,517	44,447 [1]	82,329 [1]	636,493	14,083
296	SUNY C Potsdam	G	100,651	201,469	17,449	143,242 [1]	462,811	12,256
297	SUNY IT Utica	G	54,089	207,346	82,405	45,600	389,440	-2
298	SUNY Oneonta	G	196,773	355,725	30,205	0	582,703	10,539
299	SUNY Oswego	G	140,138	320,325	15,893	0	476,356	9,020
300	SW MO ST U	B	294,520	1,452,079	56,169	0	1,802,768	66,824
301	SWstrn Adventist U	b	82,724	71,629	4,927	38,020	197,300	4,172
302	SWstrn OK ST U	bf	140,000	490,000	-1	-1	630,000	-1
303	Tabor C	b	27,311 [1]	16,718	-1	6,871	50,900	1,645
304	Tiffin U	b	15,018	56,571	20,526	0	92,115	-2
305	TM Cooley Law Sch	BbGL	133,935	912,973	96,800	126,811 [1]	1,270,519	8,889
306	Trinity Luth Sem		43,143	26,135	5,189	0	74,467	1,364
307	Trinity U	b	388,817	676,042	342,041	-1	1,406,900	32,500
308	Trinity U		31,924	47,586	3,542	84,115	167,167	267
309	Troy ST U	Bb	182,449	502,064	117,896	81,420	848,130	15,000
310	Troy ST U Dothan	bG	41,714	74,820	35,000	-1	151,534	-1
311	Truman ST U	b	148,065	827,829	146,230	171,354	1,293,478	26,830
312	TX Chiro C	bM	23,360	43,450	8,547	0	75,360	3,070
313	U Arts	bG	69,551	73,778	10,729	0	154,058	13,091
314	U C Cape	bG	125,000	228,175	-1	85,075	438,250	7,271
315	U Charleston	b	24,211	48,495	873	15,145	88,724	5,730
316	U DC	b	131,166	270,796	5,453	59,894	467,309	4,000
317	U Del Turabo		368,526	106,793	5,800	3,800	484,919	1,500
318	U Findlay	bG	71,678	114,948	10,648	133,479	330,753	8,209
319	U Hawaii-Hilo	bG	104,090	227,884	22,047	0	354,021	1,155
320	U HI-Kauai CC	b	11,961	13,800	17,377	0	43,135	300

Key to Notes on Page 1   1 -- See Footnotes   -1 -- Unavailable   -2 -- Not Applicable

ACRL Library Data Tables 2004
EXPENDITURES

INSTITUTIONS GRANTING MASTER OF ARTS AND PROFESSIONAL DEGREES (Carnegie Code M)

Salaries & Wages Prof. Staff* 22	Salaries & Wages Suppt. Staff* 23	Salaries & Wages Stud. Ass'ts* 24	Total Salaries & Wages* 25	Other Operating Expenditures 26	Total Library Expenditures 27	Survey Question #
						Institution
206,311	83,427	20,993	310,731	59,819	581,077	St Mary's U MN
-1	134,738	3,866	138,604	16,489	223,202	St Meinrad Theo
431,109	288,166	73,537	792,812	61,864	1,342,261	St Michael's C
230,098	217,648	27,620	475,366	141,395	888,017	St Norbert C
145,101	27,768	22,068	194,937	33,660	297,518	St Patrick's Sem
-1	-1	2,463	37,265	2,548	49,873	St Peter's Abbey & C
769,576	380,225	57,271	1,207,072	171,343	1,911,149	ST U W GA
88,886	-1	1,034	89,920	49,343	220,131	St Vincent Sem
155,594	48,356	56,783	260,733	0	354,933	St. John's C
471,668 [1]	329,354 [1]	64,041	865,063 [1]	147,917	1,591,710 [1]	Stetson U
291,872	73,629	28,000	393,501	50,000	443,501	Sthrn Polytech ST U
449,613	190,461	67,131	707,205	121,075	1,332,588 [1]	Stonehill C
309,704 [1]	202,078 [1]	73,759 [1]	575,541	80,369 [1]	1,127,786	Sul Ross ST U
835,151	404,033	140,370	1,379,554	966,027	2,345,581	SUNY Brockport
1,221,242	650,700	158,294	2,030,236	92,968 [1]	2,773,780	SUNY Buffalo
558,550	328,959	75,043	962,552	35,993	1,473,612	SUNY C Potsdam
321,111	162,887	21,845	505,843	0	895,283	SUNY IT Utica
625,945	481,798	73,576	1,181,319	771,730	1,953,049	SUNY Oneonta
782,897	508,030	79,361	1,370,288	233,661	2,089,325	SUNY Oswego
1,224,725	894,316	378,252	2,315,179	378,252	4,599,023	SW MO ST U
99,142	24,107	74,842	198,091	17,987	417,550	SWstrn Adventist U
303,962	192,344	84,800	581,106	99,000	1,370,706	SWstrn OK ST U
30,900	16,842	10,840	58,582	32,618	91,200	Tabor C
88,780	3,465	20,277	112,522	13,331	217,968	Tiffin U
816,324	453,924	46,484	1,316,732	582,036	3,178,176	TM Cooley Law Sch
92,077	82,646	18,504	193,227	6,506	275,564	Trinity Luth Sem
426,808	671,474	110,252	1,208,534	479,286	3,127,220	Trinity U
-1	-1	24,465	-1	17,267	209,166	Trinity U
416,547	165,132	44,070	625,749	107,250	1,596,129	Troy ST U
167,085	74,735	19,745	261,565	111,611	524,710	Troy ST U Dothan
629,633	307,105	146,821	1,083,559	90,202	2,494,069	Truman ST U
123,300	79,160	32,300	234,760	139,515	374,275	TX Chiro C
-1	-1	33,317	512,258	38,040	717,447	U Arts
-1	-1	8,072	581,370	26,761	1,053,652	U C Cape
73,148	51,949	2,031	127,128	24,906	246,488	U Charleston
697,520	764,281	-1	1,461,801	375,240	2,308,350	U DC
225,488	221,666	-1	447,154	138,607	1,072,260	U Del Turabo
142,456	121,895	62,987	327,338	77,228	743,528	U Findlay
313,883	370,902	136,516	821,301	125,919	1,302,396	U Hawaii-Hilo
186,000	105,000	8,020	299,020	0	342,458	U HI-Kauai CC

Key to Notes on Page 1   1 -- See Footnotes   -1 -- Unavailable   -2 -- Not Applicable

69

ACRL Library Data Tables 2004
EXPENDITURES

INSTITUTIONS GRANTING MASTER OF ARTS AND PROFESSIONAL DEGREES (Carnegie Code M)

Lib. No.	Institution	Notes	Monographs 16	Current Serials 17	Other Library Materials 18	Misc. Materials 19	Total Library Materials 20	Contract Binding 21
321	U Houston	b	176,572	333,834	130,999	0	641,405	14,492
322	U Mary	bGf	61,679	73,700	28,465	-1	163,844	-1
323	U MI Dearborn		225,727	153,500	20,680	0	399,907	5,309
324	U Mobile	bG	102,965	86,268	0	0	189,233	1,881
325	U NE Kearney	b	145,250	320,299	58,232	4,030 [1]	527,871	43,436
326	U Portland	bG	292,360	395,500	28,871	-1	716,731	19,000
327	U Richmond		423,594	1,499,799 [1]	86,865	0	2,010,258	25,490
328	U Rio Grande	bGf	12,554	55,953	29,109	26,139	123,755	2,770
329	U Scranton	b	275,666	518,957	269,388	0	1,064,011	20,507
330	U Sthn IN	bG	117,169	377,230	23,575	15,696	582,531	3,052
331	U Tampa	bG	17,265	205,395	50,057	1,297	274,014	0
332	U TN Chatt	bG	138,593	741,270	140,921	47,804	1,068,588	18,952
333	U TN Martin	BbG	66,886	326,527 [1]	52,689	204,757	650,859	13,496
334	U TX Tyler	BG	12,263	323,126 [1]	18,455	0	353,844	581
335	U West AL		25,000	113,072	2,500	60,574	201,146	0
336	U WI E Claire	b	209,059	670,447	30,756	0	910,262	3,709
337	U WI La Crosse	G	283,502	440,331	76,929	142,185	942,947	10,324
338	U WI Platteville	bG	151,694	277,490	30,997	3,554	463,735	5,991
339	U Winnipeg	bG	375,640	399,522	28,191	25,000	828,353	11,387
340	UNC Asheville	b	187,402	524,250	76,010	34	787,696	7,932
341	UNC Pembroke	bGf	426,424	263,017	27,397	181,806	898,644	10,471
342	Union C-NY		457,893	1,090,594	143,844	0	1,692,331	33,967
343	Valparaiso U		56,181	322,142	19,178	0	409,621	12,494
344	Villa Julie C	bG	84,735 [1]	202,468	70,054	48,376	405,633	1,725
345	W.Carey College	Bb	59,630	56,850	178	42,483	159,141	5,185
346	W.Mitchell C Law	GL	189,460	370,706	534,374	12,421 [1]	1,106,961	15,749
347	Walla Walla C	b	171,790	307,384	27,981	1,541	508,696	3,689
348	Walsh C Acct Bus Admin	B	50,000	60,000	9,000	2,000	121,000	4,000
349	Wartburg Theo Sem	bf	36,950	26,670	5,246	0	68,866	1,222
350	Washburn U Topeka	bG	182,399	399,361	26,141	0	607,901	13,950
351	Washington C	Gf	181,168	248,268 [1]	20,044 [1]	-1	449,480	4,972
352	Washington Theo Union	bf	60,282	33,525	4,967	-1	98,774	4,414
353	Wayland Bap U		89,523	83,424	-1	-1	172,947	-1
354	Wayne ST C	bG	70,256	116,559	15,564	-1	202,379	-1
355	Webber Intl U	b	23,000	7,000	3,000	0	33,000	0
356	Wesley C	bf	2,597	30,712	15,882	0	49,191	0
357	West Chester U PA		261,584	695,106	362,762	0	1,319,451	42,020
358	West TX A & M U	bG	65,568	222,543	66,244	177,006	531,361	1,610
359	West VA Wesleyan C		53,912	181,747	14,859	-1	-1	-1
360	Western MD C	b	176,370	185,992	22,189	0	384,551	9,770

Key to Notes on Page 1   1 -- See Footnotes   -1 -- Unavailable   -2 -- Not Applicable

ACRL Library Data Tables 2004
EXPENDITURES

INSTITUTIONS GRANTING MASTER OF ARTS AND PROFESSIONAL DEGREES (Carnegie Code M)

Salaries & Wages Prof. Staff* 22	Salaries & Wages Suppt. Staff* 23	Salaries & Wages Stud. Ass'ts* 24	Total Salaries & Wages* 25	Other Operating Expenditures 26	Total Library Expenditures 27	Survey Question #
						Institution
716,687	411,115	126,589	1,254,391	160,267	2,070,555	U Houston
138,548	-1	-1	138,548	25,111	327,503	U Mary
1,034,403	98,507	145,742	1,278,652	2,049,605	3,328,257	U MI Dearborn
139,520	49,545	15,772	204,837	58,449	454,400	U Mobile
537,686	355,162	48,159	941,007	113,007	1,625,261	U NE Kearney
287,588	231,708	178,258	697,549	354,132	1,787,412	U Portland
1,014,266	612,000	183,373	1,809,639	369,609	2,179,249	U Richmond
249,798	92,352	18,509	360,659	23,912	511,096	U Rio Grande
853,615	240,475	96,903	1,190,993	260,750	2,536,261 [1]	U Scranton
418,451	343,643	39,065	801,159	185,925	1,572,667	U Sthn IN
268,847	217,454	72,200	558,301	55,800	888,115	U Tampa
572,210	339,074	58,162	976,446	176,549	2,877,264	U TN Chatt
405,122	350,008	76,845	831,975	34,676	1,531,006	U TN Martin
257,348	331,126	69,982	658,456	218,395	1,231,276	U TX Tyler
248,332	23,050	40,815	312,197	0	513,343	U West AL
654,637	581,520	125,828	1,361,985	494,563	2,781,542	U WI E Claire
597,496	447,486	116,616	1,161,595	137,596	2,252,462	U WI La Crosse
356,678	343,425	116,455	816,558	50,371	1,336,655	U WI Platteville
519,320	1,144,895	24,588	1,688,803	198,094	2,726,637	U Winnipeg
301,101	380,472	93,142	783,715	280,480	1,859,823	UNC Asheville
498,088	412,324	17,608	928,020	185,856	2,022,991	UNC Pembroke
800,933	371,473	87,078	1,259,484	895,922	3,881,704	Union C-NY
387,461	225,594	63,385	681,440	265,353	1,368,908	Valparaiso U
266,684	107,374	6,834	380,892	17,691	805,941	Villa Julie C
-1 [1]	-1 [1]	28,691	268,882 [1]	0	433,208	W.Carey College
536,434	214,466	48,478	799,378	142,812	2,064,900	W.Mitchell C Law
302,576	180,176	114,543	597,295	88,353	1,198,033	Walla Walla C
190,000	120,000	28,000	338,000	23,000 [1]	364,000	Walsh C Acct Bus Admin
52,896	71,194	24,089	148,179	22,549	240,816	Wartburg Theo Sem
530,085	257,829	75,098	863,012	170,223	1,655,086	Washburn U Topeka
-1	462,512 [1]	50,864	513,376	80,863	1,048,691	Washington C
54,373	102,691	-1	157,064	32,812	292,414	Washington Theo Union
166,036	43,176	27,222	243,073	143,738	559,758	Wayland Bap U
326,254	144,317	70,100	540,671	34,774	777,824	Wayne ST C
31,250	27,950	0	59,200	20,030	112,203	Webber Intl U
-1 [1]	-1	-1	188,429	56,751	294,371	Wesley C
918,664	795,477	105,255	1,819,396	832,473	4,013,339	West Chester U PA
463,148	265,746	60,141	789,035	53,387	1,375,393	West TX A & M U
-1	-1	-1	-1	-1	-1	West VA Wesleyan C
323,402	98,435	76,806	498,643	127,188	1,020,152	Western MD C

Key to Notes on Page 1   1 -- See Footnotes   -1 -- Unavailable   -2 -- Not Applicable

71

INSTITUTIONS GRANTING MASTER OF ARTS AND PROFESSIONAL DEGREES (Carnegie Code M)

Lib. No.	Institution	Notes	Monographs 16	Current Serials 17	Other Library Materials 18	Misc. Materials 19	Total Library Materials 20	Contract Binding 21
		Survey Question #						
361	Western OR U	bG	127,635	148,295	10,563	126,491	412,984	7,203
362	Western Sem	b	10,028	14,021	6,371	17,055	47,475	0
363	Western WA U	G	257,115	1,389,960	55,775	0	1,702,850	15,034
364	Westfield ST C	b	54,821	243,965	10,928	60,557	370,271	7,115
365	Westminster C-UT	G	136,561	65,603 [1]	111,609	0	313,773	7,050
366	Wheeling Jesuit U	b	45,000	823,000	6,700	68,350 [1]	202,350	2,000
367	Whitworth C	G	97,830	186,689	9,394 [1]	661	294,574	4,107
368	Wilkes U	G	218,868	518,112	45,142	0	782,122	16,456
369	William Woods U	bL	31,245	79,491	8,693	7,894 [1]	127,323	7,048
370	Williams C		1,000,082 [1]	1,319,634 [1]	45,959	0	2,365,625	41,828
371	Wstrn IL U	Bb	329,861	1,182,432	43,684	0	1,555,977	35,000
372	Wstrn Theo Sem	f	44,537	19,742	138	-1	64,417	3,596
373	Xavier U LA	b	176,633	341,953	50,622	89,837	659,045	2,474

ACRL Library Data Tables 2004
EXPENDITURES

INSTITUTIONS GRANTING MASTER OF ARTS AND PROFESSIONAL DEGREES (Carnegie Code M)

Salaries & Wages Prof. Staff* 22	Salaries & Wages Suppt. Staff* 23	Salaries & Wages Stud. Ass'ts* 24	Total Salaries & Wages* 25	Other Operating Expenditures 26	Total Library Expenditures 27	Survey Question #
						Institution
406,378	299,608	165,378	871,364	179,423	1,470,974	Western OR U
-1	-1	0	109,440	9,714	166,629	Western Sem
1,048,919	1,449,750	210,884	2,709,553	408,622	4,836,059	Western WA U
397,846	163,704	43,020	604,570	27,578	1,011,534	Westfield ST C
250,128	76,018	58,344	384,490	74,669	779,982	Westminster C-UT
128,250	56,760	20,200	205,210	129,139	538,699	Wheeling Jesuit U
284,132	137,014	57,853	478,999	87,381	865,061	Whitworth C
497,086	153,705	104,073	754,864	157,756	1,711,198	Wilkes U
115,500	56,022	5,659	173,181	33,019	340,571	William Woods U
1,025,033	536,136	234,289	1,795,458	272,973	4,681,501	Williams C
1,311,558	1,383,353	242,697	2,937,608	1,580,101	4,517,709	Wstrn IL U
133,956	85,116	23,442	242,514	17,880 [1]	328,407	Wstrn Theo Sem
448,437	516,413	0 [1]	964,850	0	1,626,369	Xavier U LA

ACRL LIBRARY DATA TABLES 2004

SUMMARY DATA: ELECTRONIC MATERIALS EXPENDITURES

ALL INSTITUTIONS REPORTING

| | Computer Files | Electronic Serials | Bibl. Util./Networks/Consortia | | Computer Hardware & Software | Doc. Delivery ILL |
| | | | Internal Library Sources | External Sources | | |
Survey Question #)	28	29	30a	30b	31	32
High	1,474,573	5,200,540	997,410	1,985,269	2,168,246	493,453
Mean	34,949	309,311	43,087	41,970	73,853	15,824
Median	25	48,579	17,190	0	13,986	1,596
Low	0	0	0	0	0	0
Total	31,908,023	315,187,610	42,009,930	30,638,373	72,818,590	15,064,387
Libraries Reporting	913	1,019	975	730	986	952

ACRL LIBRARY DATA TABLES 2004

SUMMARY DATA: ELECTRONIC MATERIALS EXPENDITURES

INSTITUTIONS GRANTING BACHELOR OF ARTS DEGREES (Carnegie Code B)

| (Survey Question #) | Computer Files 28 | Electronic Serials 29 | Bibl. Util./Networks/Consortia | | Computer Hardware & Software 31 | Doc. Delivery ILL 32 |
			Internal Library Sources 30a	External Sources 30b		
High	151,860	520,116	147,000	821,165	315,164	60,396
Mean	3,935	65,942	18,403	13,102	20,376	4,598
Median	0	25,296	10,822	0	6,100	1,018
Low	0	0	0	0	0	0
Total	633,483	11,276,009	2,999,649	1,690,127	3,260,080	721,838
Libraries Reporting	161	171	163	129	160	157

ACRL LIBRARY DATA TABLES 2004

SUMMARY DATA: ELECTRONIC MATERIALS EXPENDITURES

INSTITUTIONS GRANTING MASTER OF ARTS AND PROFESSIONAL DEGREES (Carnegie Code M)

(Survey Question #)	Computer Files 28	Electronic Serials 29	Bibl. Util./Networks/Consortia		Computer Hardware & Software 31	Doc. Delivery ILL 32
			Internal Library Sources 30a	External Sources 30b		
High	56,402	149,358	365,000	1,850,200	157,223	9,000
Mean	1,750	16,692	10,023	21,384	9,762	731
Median	0	8,209	3,140	0	3,312	126
Low	0	0	0	0	0	0
Total	367,424	3,822,477	2,185,050	3,613,856	2,098,734	150,627
Libraries Reporting	210	229	218	169	215	206

ACRL Library Data Tables 2004
ELECTRONIC MATERIALS EXPENDITURES
INSTITUTIONS GRANTING BACHELOR OF ARTS DEGREES (Carnegie Code B)

Lib. No.	Institution	Notes	Computer Files 28	Electronic Serials 29	Bibl. Util. / Networks / Consortia		Computer Hardware & Software 31	Doc. Delivery, ILL 32
					Internal Library Sources 30a	External Sources 30b		
	Survey Question #		28	29	30a	30b	31	32
1	AB C Art & Design	bf	-1	10,000	2,468 [1]	-1	-1	-1
2	Adrian C		0	49,048	0	-1	0	556
3	Albion C	G	1,720	121,810	29,751	-1	60,912	13,716
4	Amherst C	Gf	0	164,377	54,025	0	16,500	3,985
5	Aquinas C TN	G	12,400	30,000	19,000	0	3,500	0
6	Atlanta C Art	bG	0	0	9,125	0	1,250 [1]	0
7	Atlanta Christian C	bf	3,500	21,184	4,500	0	0	150
8	Augustana C RI	G	667	137,146	62,789	-1	12,488	5,882
9	Barber-Scotia C		2,000	7,000	5,000 [1]	3,358 [1]	7,274	2,000 [1]
10	Bard C	b	0	84,652	40,100	0	38,288	0
11	Barton C	b	0	20,584	5,081	0	20,421	112
12	Bates C	bG	10,000	204,155	109,377	-1	0 [1]	18,807
13	Benedict C	G	9,802	34,337	5,000	20,770 [1]	70,155 [1]	29 [1]
14	Berry C	b	7,495	143,070	27,330	0	3,678	3,713
15	Bethany C Bethany	b	0	32,867	23,474	0	1,187	202
16	Bethany C Lindsborg		0	0	1,550	4,457	12,000	504
17	Bethel C KS		0	1,225	3,459	-1	20,902	1,893
18	Blackburn C	bG	1,000	9,789	0	0	0	571
19	Bluefield C	bf	0	20,000	-1	20,000	0	1,500
20	Boise Bible C		-1	-1	-1	-1	-1	-1
21	Bowdoin C		-1	235,206	78,941	-1	93,345	42,496
22	Bridgewater C	b	428	26,872	25,471	3,500	0	3,078
23	Bryan C	bf	1,150	24,231	7,982	0	0	100
24	C Holy Cross		0	133,927	24,442	-1	-1 [1]	8,140
25	C Visual Arts	b	0	3,210	545	0	0	0
26	C Wooster		-1	6,064	26,965	0	3,300	17,656
27	Campion C	G	-1 [1]	-1	-1	-1	-1	-1
28	Carroll C-Helena	b	0	23,000	-1 [1]	-1 [1]	-1 [1]	64
29	Cazenovia C	b	0	19,850	25,233	0	24,000	850
30	Centennial C	bf	-1	-1	147,000	0	0	3,000
31	Central Bible C	b	317	7,628	0	16,090	0	0
32	Central C		897	18,859	17,190	0	53,668	1,499
33	Central Christian C Bible	b	0	0	293	-1	0	100
34	Centre C	G	0	81,228	12,634	0	17,928	6,814
35	Christian Heritage C		2,863	30,348	2,865	0	0	0
36	Clear Creek Bible		487	8,782	3,019	-1	4,757	0
37	Cmty Hosp C Health		0	0	0	0	0	-1
38	Colby C	bG	151,860	492,104	0 [1]	0 [1]	0 [1]	60,396
39	Colby Sawyer C	b	0	69,422	13,000	0	26,000	1,500
40	Columbia Union C	bG	-1	36,248	40,760	0	0	-1

Key to Notes on Page 1   1 -- See Footnotes   -1 -- Unavailable   -2 -- Not Applicable

77

ACRL Library Data Tables 2004
ELECTRONIC MATERIALS EXPENDITURES
INSTITUTIONS GRANTING BACHELOR OF ARTS DEGREES (Carnegie Code B)

Lib. No.	Institution	Notes	Computer Files 28	Electronic Serials 29	Bibl. Util. / Networks / Consortia Internal Library Sources 30a	External Sources 30b	Computer Hardware & Software 31	Doc. Delivery, ILL 32
	Survey Question #							
41	Concordia C-MN	b	0	76,986	10,822	59,684	9,089	4,109
42	Concordia C-NY	b	0	12,649	2,423	0	0	-1
43	Cornish C Arts		250	0	0	420	12,000 [1]	0
44	Crichton C	b	-1	29,507	0	6,348	3,542	282
45	Crown C-MN	G	0	10,038	0	0	0	686
46	Culver Stockton C	b	1,000	21,658	20,603 [1]	0	3,415	1,049
47	CUNY City C		0	103,947	5,269 [1]	84,516 [1]	8,857	866
48	CUNY York C	b	0	0	0	0	0	0
49	Dakota Wesleyan U	b	1,500	9,000	16,535	0	800	975
50	Dana C	bG	0	13,735	5,350	7,448	0	698
51	Davidson C	bG	10,030	289,940	22,558	0	111,712	30,732
52	Dean C	bL	0	6,209	-1	-1	0	0
53	Defiance C	b	0	0	8,300	12,300	22,800	850
54	Denison U		0	141,510	-1	120,664	0	419
55	DeVry Inst Tech GA	b	114,000	475,000	-1	-1	-1	-1
56	Dickinson ST U		6,572	28,741	49,532	-1	26,899	88
57	Divine Word C		0	795	1,597	0	0	0
58	East Texas Baptist U	Bb	5,000 [1]	70,000	-1	-1	-1	-1
59	Eckerd C		7,925	122,507	0	21,716	18,319	1,500
60	Emmanuel C GA	b	0	10,497	2,534	8,900	-1 [1]	-1 [1]
61	Eugene Bible C		-1	-1	-1	-1	-1	-1
62	Evangel U		-1	-1	-1	-1	-1	-1
63	F&M C		0	251,150	0	0	42,090	18,147
64	Ferrum C	bf	0	39,887	15,959	0	0	2,058
65	Finlandia U	bG	1,000	8,916	3,110	-1	-1	-1
66	FL Christian C	b	285	1,750	2,265	-1 [1]	1,789 [1]	271
67	Flagler C	bG	2,400	51,173	18,705	-2	10,627	2,788
68	Fort Lewis C	b	1,200	100,742	0	0	62,490	11,501
69	G Adolphus C	b	0	108,296	0	14,842 [1]	26,100	-1
70	Green Mountain C	bf	1,200	13,200	-1	-1	-1	-1
71	Grinnell C		-1	167,443	83,705	0	53,108	32,150
72	Guilford C	bG	1,948	95,619	53,086	0	0	5,550 [1]
73	H Inst Int Desgn	b	0	7,000	1,560	16,475	5,998	100
74	H LaGrange C	G	1,000	11,417	20,903	0 [1]	15,373	0
75	Hamilton C		8,870	268,540	69,225	0	37,000	37,076
76	Hampshire C		0	89,944	13,135	0	315,164	11,551
77	Hanover C	bG	2,912	104,267	16,062	-1	4,894	11,789
78	Haskell Indian Nations U	bf	0	5,000	19,480	-1	3,644	11,789
79	Haverford C	Bb	0	369,794	45,173	0	76,005	6,732
80	Hendrix C	b	0	31,000	15,000	0	0	2,650

Key to Notes on Page 1   1 -- See Footnotes   -1 -- Unavailable   -2 -- Not Applicable

78

ACRL Library Data Tables 2004
ELECTRONIC MATERIALS EXPENDITURES
INSTITUTIONS GRANTING BACHELOR OF ARTS DEGREES (Carnegie Code B)

Lib. No.	Institution	Notes	Computer Files 28	Electronic Serials 29	Bibl. Util. / Networks / Consortia Internal Library Sources 30a	External Sources 30b	Computer Hardware & Software 31	Doc. Delivery, ILL 32
81	Hiram C	bG	52,066	-1	20,126	0	46,679	257
82	Hobart &William Smith Cs	G	8,433	179,664	27,160	-1	57,346	26,959
83	Hope C		0	150,655	32,629	0	7,583	6,675
84	Houghton C	Bb	-1	-1	-1	-1	59,356	-1
85	Howard Payne U	G	2,500	60,173	60,738	-1 [1]	0 [1]	0
86	Illinois C	bGf	-1	15,537	7,788	0	18,861	0
87	Jamestown C	b	0	27,125	11,459	-1	0	2,293
88	Johnson C Smith U	b	0	26,616	1,100	16,840	14,000	2,000
89	Judson C	b	0	38,199	12,784 [1]	-1	3,704	1,099
90	Kent ST U Salem	b	0	1,731	0	0	0	0
91	Kent ST U Trumbull		-1	-1	-1	-1	-1	-1
92	Kenyon C	b	29,116	209,031	30,339	28,928	-1	6,912
93	Kettering C Med	bG	836	7,110	13,715	0	475	25
94	Keuka C	b	3,100	39,176	8,700	35,000	0	2,620
95	Knox C	G	158	48,579	5,037	-1	30,047	7,982
96	Kwantlen UC		18,600	-1	27,902	-1	-1	7,000
97	Lambuth U	bGf	28 [1]	8,702	14,951	0	55	426
98	Lawrence U		-1	103,327	38,691	0	24,415	6,654
99	Lemoyne-Owen C	Gf	0	0	7,700	0	0	0
100	Lester B Pearson C Pacific		-1	-1	-1	-1	-1	-1
101	LIFE Bible C	b	-1	7,568	3,434	-2	-2	0
102	Lyndon State C		-1	-1	-1	-1	-1	-1
103	Lyon C		0	42,000	23,000	0	26,000	500
104	Macon ST C	BbG	1,300	24,938	10,474	41,724	0	169
105	Marlboro C		0	11,383 [1]	5,054 [1]	0	10,311 [1]	2,256 [1]
106	Mars Hill C	b	0	25,346	14,500	0	0	140
107	Martin Luther C	bG	115	11,966	6,752	-1	1,543	1,465
108	Mayville ST U		0	6,507	17,159	0	0	-1 [1]
109	McKendree C	bG	255	51,222	15,989	-1	153	985
110	McPherson C		-1	-1	-1	-1	-1	-1
111	Methodist C	G	0	36,802	-1	0	21,410	1,437
112	Midland Lutheran C		7,500	3,500	20,000	3,000	4,000	700
113	Milwaukee Inst Art Design	b	0	-1	-1	-1	-1	-1
114	MO Baptist C		0	0	20,250	2,250	1,000	25
115	MO Western ST C	bG	3,938	33,132	22,439	8,000	0	485
116	Monmouth C	bGf	9,800 [1]	56,723	22,549	-1	-1	-1
117	Mount Royal C	bG	-1	166,000	-2	-2	0	1,300
118	Mount Union C		7,425	152,502	57,033	28,736	3,066	324
119	Muhlenberg C	bG	7,805	145,600	24,530	0	61,000	20,000
120	NC Wesleyan C	BbG	0	23,676	9,215	0	10,690	1,203

Key to Notes on Page 1   1 -- See Footnotes   -1 -- Unavailable   -2 -- Not Applicable

ELECTRONIC MATERIALS EXPENDITURES

INSTITUTIONS GRANTING BACHELOR OF ARTS DEGREES (Carnegie Code B)

Lib. No.	Institution	Notes	Computer Files 28	Electronic Serials 29	Bibl. Util. / Networks / Consortia		Computer Hardware & Software 31	Doc. Delivery, ILL 32
	Survey Question #				Internal Library Sources 30a	External Sources 30b		
121	New C U South FL	bG	0	65,621	13,786	0	11,050	3,085
122	OH Dominican C	bG	5,013	91,375	-1	3,500	46,500	940
123	OH Wesleyan U	b	-1	150,361	116,243	22,645	20,649	6,405
124	OK Panhandle ST U	b	2,800	10,977	4,120	30,000	13,040	765
125	Paier C Art		0	0	0	0	0	0
126	Peace C	b	0	21,690	2,000	2,000	6,774	1,196
127	Potomac C	G	0	15,720	0	0	0 [1]	0
128	Presbyterian C	bG	0	54,550	10,000	3,000	32,557	627
129	Principia C	bG	29,279	17,559	9,936	-1	26,676	-1
130	Randolph-Macon C	bf	0	42,836	15,063	0	0	3,591
131	Randolph-Macon WC	bG	2,957	30,000	26,460	6,972	8,676	5,705
132	Reformed Bible C		96	4,257	3,539	-1	2,080	1,422
133	Reinhardt C	Bb	0	22,428	2,277	0	0	1,334
134	Ricks C		0	0	-1 [1]	-1 [1]	75,716	0
135	Ringling Sch Art & Design		-1	12,953	7,575	0	13,352	1,263
136	Rochester C	b	500	20,038	0	2,988	234	432
137	Rocky Mountain C	bGf	0	0	9,500	12,000	0	0
138	Rogers ST U	bG	2,800	82,799	20,630	0	19,440	-1
139	SE C Assemblies God	bG	3,000	25,000	22,000	0	4,200	1,950
140	Shawnee ST U	Gf	357	28,459	33,034	50,850	37,146	100
141	Shepherd C	G	0	79,601	16,000	0	52,687	1,142
142	Siena C	G	3,430	115,552	31,534	0	6,597	14,025
143	Simpson C IA	bG	1,806	25,296	8,169	-1	40,680	2,964
144	Skidmore C	b	0	246,496	81,673	0	9,264 [1]	19,154
145	Southwest U	f	2,629	159,634	31,000	0	6,202	6,650
146	Spartan Aero-Flight Schl	B	595	846	126	846	2,369 [1]	0
147	St Andrews Presby C	bG	0	2,202	0	6,110	65	55
148	St Gregory's U	b	0	0	0	-1	-1	-1
149	St John Vianney C Sem		0	5,224	0	0	-1	-1
150	St Olaf C	b	0	-1	-1	0	-1	1,865
151	St. Mary's C Maryland		1,485	73,628	8,850 [1]	-1	38,956 [1]	5,689
152	Sterling C-VT		0	15,200	0	0	480 [1]	350
153	Stillman C		0	12,471	600	0	7,285	0
154	Susquehanna U	bG	0	1,835	0	0	125,000	13,500
155	SW Baptist Theo Sem		-1	-1	-1	-1	-1	-1
156	Swarthmore C	G	11,225	467,680	42,281 [1]	0	8,129	19,125
157	Sweet Briar C	bG	0	90,912	23,040	0	12,047	4,311
158	Talladega C	bf	26,000	500	71,000 [1]	0	71,000 [1]	-1
159	Taylor U-Ft Wayne	b	1,100	48,693	57,546	0	13,822	648
160	Teikyo Post U	bL	0	0	0 [1]	6,000 [1]	0 [1]	500

Key to Notes on Page 1   1 -- See Footnotes   -1 -- Unavailable   -2 -- Not Applicable

ELECTRONIC MATERIALS EXPENDITURES

INSTITUTIONS GRANTING BACHELOR OF ARTS DEGREES (Carnegie Code B)

Lib. No.	Institution	Notes	Computer Files 28	Electronic Serials 29	Bibl. Util. / Networks / Consortia Internal Library Sources 30a	External Sources 30b	Computer Hardware & Software 31	Doc. Delivery, ILL 32
	Survey Question #		28	29	30a	30b	31	32
161	TN Wesleyan C		-1	-1	26,091	-1	-1	-1
162	Tri ST U		1,140	31,116	27,102	-1 [1]	262	2,357 [1]
163	Trinity Christian C	b	1,723	21,258	12,489	-1	0	174
164	Trinity Wstrn U	bf	0	70,000	0	0	0	0
165	Truett McConnell C	b	0	15,812	6,084	0	8,794	0
166	TX Lutheran U	bG	0	16,279	14,720	-1	29,320	1,990
167	U Maine-Machias	G	3,000	4,675	0	-1	0	0
168	U ME Fort Kent	b	0	0	0	821,165	626	200
169	U Ozarks	G	0	-1	-1	-1	-1	-1
170	U VA C Wise	G	0	24,731	11,100	1,559	5,994	3,692
171	Union C-NE	b	848	35	11,772	-1	645	1,018 [1]
172	US C Guard Acad	b	-1	-1	-1	-1	-1	-1
173	US Merchant Marine Acad	bG	-1	18,654	21,200	-1	4,580	137
174	US Mil Acad	f	0	414,094	0	84,000	241,000	0
175	US Naval Acad		-1	510,000	-1	-1	-1	-1
176	UT Valley ST C	Bb	0	58,673	13,500	0	44,247	36
177	VA Wesleyan C	b	1,500	1,500	200	3,550	24,225	8,242
178	Vassar C	G	0	520,116	69,126	-1	-1	58,287
179	VMI	b	0	45,442	0 [1]	0	9,882	3,120
180	Wabash C	G	0	68,784	57,799	0	0	11,110
181	Warner Sthrn C	Gf	0	0	20,721	0	0	311
182	Warren Wilson C	b	0 [1]	38,998	17	0	0 [1]	1,000
183	Wells C	b	-1	-1	-1	-1	35,674	-1
184	Western ST C	bf	0	20,443	10,000	0	42,411	5,430
185	Westmont C	b	1,046	14,522	9,576	0	13,910	4,323
186	Whitman C	b	-1	108,586	72,000	0	148,000	12,609
187	Wiley C	bG	2,500	0	0	0	6,259	5
188	Winston-Salem ST U	b	0	0	0	7,200	107,660	1,652
189	Wofford C	bG	1	59,328	0	28,317	58,956	618
190	York C		0	0	3,713	11,459 [1]	0	913

Key to Notes on Page 1   1 -- See Footnotes   -1 -- Unavailable   -2 -- Not Applicable

ACRL Library Data Tables 2004

ELECTRONIC MATERIALS EXPENDITURES

INSTITUTIONS GRANTING MASTER OF ARTS AND PROFESSIONAL DEGREES (Carnegie Code M)

Lib. No.	Institution	Notes	Computer Files 28	Electronic Serials 29	Bibl. Util. / Networks / Consortia		Computer Hardware & Software 31	Doc. Delivery, ILL 32
	Survey Question #				Internal Library Sources 30a	External Sources 30b		
1	Abilene Christian U	bG	0	63,149	84,552	8,000	101,436	907
2	Agnes Scott C	G	2,000	151,605	17,359	0	29,496	6,683
3	Albany C Pharmacy		0	22,639	17,866	0	2,790	3,764
4	Albany Law Schl Union U	GL	0	437,049	27,256	-1	12,000	1,311
5	Alcorn ST U	bG	0	69,838	20,112	0	20,988	520
6	Amer Intl C	b	0	43,000	0	25,000	9,800	1,200
7	Amer U Puerto Rico	Bb	1,306	7,121	23,094	121,765	500	200
8	Anderson U		-1	-1	-1	-1	-1	-1
9	Angelo ST U		0	202,562	21,250	0	42,659	500
10	Aquinas C MI	b	4,546	103,152	13,587	0	2,729	1,044
11	Ark Tech U	G	0	12,500	22,276	0	0	15,000
12	Armstrong Atlantic ST U	bG	8,000	68,521	30,000	-1 [1]	20,000	-1
13	Assemblies God Theo Se	f	2,865	-1	31,706	-1	3,068	302
14	Assumption C	bG	0	68,842	8,196	0 [1]	63,807	0
15	Athenaeum of Ohio		0	3,449	2,355	2,706	90	0
16	Auburn U Montgomery	b	3,496	109,648	68,587	-1	-1	-1
17	Augusta ST U	bG	15,125	91,030	7,763	58,228	26,626	2,999
18	Augustana C SF	bG	4,800	89,152	45,358	-1	11,755	2,130
19	Austin C	b	10,850	59,002	18,250	-1	0	7,771
20	Austin Presb Theo Sem	f	0	0	0	17,427	0	0
21	Averett C	b	0	73,345	1,600 [1]	9,276 [1]	290 [1]	2,553 [1]
22	Babson C	bG	11,446	414,951	10,170	0	0	933
23	Baker C System	Bb	0	188,100	10,400	0	75,400	1,000
24	Baker U	G	1,655	58,369	28,502	-1 [1]	0	764
25	Baptist Bible C and Sem	bf	2,212	2,072	0	4,283	70	1,346
26	Bayamon Central U	bf	0 [1]	0	70,000	15,000	15,000	0
27	Bellevue U	bf	1,053	99,374	31,276	10,794	7,951	8,500
28	Bennington C	b	1,000	25,000	18,000	-1	3,200	400
29	Bethel C IN	bf	0	31,514	0	28,163	0	1,713
30	Birmingham Southern C	bG	995	87,157	62,982	0	0	515
31	Bluffton C	b	-1	53,358 [1]	39,352 [1]	-1	-1	-1
32	BowlGrn SU Fireld	b	0	0	0	0	2,464	0
33	Bradley U	b	0	221,729	44,142	-1	32,850	1,501
34	Brescia U	bG	1,600	24,808	1,818	-1	17,466	1,141
35	Brooks Institute	B	100	120	0	1,672	4,429	12
36	Bryn Athyn C	b	1,325	6,794	14,106	0	3,318	1,600
37	Buena Vista U		-1	82,635	-1	-1	5,727	2,559
38	Butler U	b	0	209,731	25,041	0	6,750	19,779
39	C Atlantic	b	37,712	42,976	5,000	-1	1,040	3,500
40	C Mt St Joseph	b	0	0	43,001	0	0	3,034

Key to Notes on Page 1   1 -- See Footnotes   -1 -- Unavailable   -2 -- Not Applicable

ACRL Library Data Tables 2004

ELECTRONIC MATERIALS EXPENDITURES

INSTITUTIONS GRANTING MASTER OF ARTS AND PROFESSIONAL DEGREES (Carnegie Code M)

Lib. No.	Institution	Notes	Computer Files 28	Electronic Serials 29	Bibl. Util. / Networks / Consortia Internal Library Sources 30a	External Sources 30b	Computer Hardware & Software 31	Doc. Delivery, ILL 32
	Survey Question #		28	29	30a	30b	31	32
41	C Mt St Vincent	bG	0	67,881	45,534	-1	0	0
42	C Our Lady Elms	bG	-1	11,122	57,119	-1	-1	1,600
43	C.R. Drew U Med & Sci	bM	0	146,525	3,024	0	3,215	4,565
44	CA C Arts & Crafts	b	2,000	9,064 [1]	5,085	0	41,022	20
45	CA St Polytechnic U-Pomo	G	7,078	297,497	331,525	0 [1]	122,974	47,886
46	CA St U - Sacramento	bG	1,113	469,602	82,233	0	129,566	2,845
47	CA ST U Dominguez Hills	b	22,500	204,518	52,897	0	35,247	0
48	CA ST U Fresno		241,630	2,021	0	0	103,316	2,021
49	CA ST U Fullerton	Bb	360,554	292,798	59,470	0 [1]	158,487	106,891
50	CA ST U Hayward	B	0	320,031	64,900	0	65,744	7,691
51	CA ST U Long Beach	G	0	330,891	0	-1	224,328	33,006
52	CA ST U Northridge	bG	475,418	194,191	73,826	-1	216,019	5,000
53	CA ST U S Bernadino	f	0	229,938	0	0	99,117	2,901
54	CA ST U San Marcos	bG	0	174,198	43,508	0	104,370	13,847
55	CA ST U Stanislaus	B	-1	149,916	48,412	-1	92,231	11,559
56	CA West Sch Law	GL	366	64,356	121,047	-1	17,863	780
57	Calvin C		13,941	152,774	35,688	0	0	5,356
58	Cameron U	Gf	-1	38,158	-1	26,443	1,189	5,298
59	Canisius C	G	40,694	159,563	17,376	-1 [1]	76,954	0
60	Carlow C		159	31,055	7,111	0	13,971	1,065
61	Carroll C-Waukesha		0	38,570	19,000	0	5,000	10,000
62	Cedar Crest C		7,264	45,917	14,131	-1	26,133	5,830
63	Cedarville U	G	-1	30,614	25,841	-1	66,578	-1
64	Centenary C	b	0	30,110	9,200	-1 [1]	28,355	805
65	Centenary C LA	bf	0	34,877	16,384 [1]	3,126	805	4,931
66	Central Baptist C	bf	0	0	0	5,149	1,500	2,954
67	Central CT ST U		0	227,827	27,590	80,000	-1	-1
68	Central MO ST U		43,891	246,332	91,844	0	65,136	3,775
69	Charleston Sthrn U		2,418	67,461	32,234	-1	12,058	1,974
70	Chicago ST U	b	-1 [1]	2,721,865	9,731	-1 [1]	3,471	-1 [1]
71	Chris Newport U		0	106,517	27,372	63,575	2,156	14,578
72	Christendom C	Bb	-1	-1	-1	-1	-1	-1
73	Christian Brothers U	b	0	36,545	10,000	0	8,000	1,050
74	Clarion U PA	Bb	0	0	0	83,609	23,480	6,650
75	Clarke C-IA		1,962	31,911	11,103	0	0	863
76	Clarkson C-NE	f	-1	3,868	5,400	1,175	-1	-1
77	Colorado C	bG	19,744	321,763	52,259	0	37,791	45,589
78	Columbia C MO		-1	-1	-1	-1	-1	-1
79	Columbia C SC		0	41,902	7,000	-1	22,857	-1
80	Columbia Intl U	bf	0	0	0	33,653	1,415	0

Key to Notes on Page 1   1 -- See Footnotes   -1 -- Unavailable   -2 -- Not Applicable

ELECTRONIC MATERIALS EXPENDITURES

INSTITUTIONS GRANTING MASTER OF ARTS AND PROFESSIONAL DEGREES (Carnegie Code M)

Lib. No.	Institution	Notes	Computer Files 28	Electronic Serials 29	Bibl. Util. / Networks / Consortia Internal Library Sources 30a	External Sources 30b	Computer Hardware & Software 31	Doc. Delivery, ILL 32
81	Columbus ST U	BG	1,450	19,313	21,806	64,194 [1]	6,000	1,816
82	Concordia U Irvine	b	0	33,054	14,794	0	0	0
83	Concordia U RiverF	b	32,400	-1	-1	-1	-1	-1
84	Concordia U St Paul		57,263	9,437	-1	51,879	0	0
85	Cooper Union	b	8,184	81,258	61,437	-1	3,187	893
86	Cornerstone U	bG	-1	-1	13,120	-1	59,877	1,288
87	Creighton U	b	8,000	209,061	36,217	80,000	49,248	16,873
88	Cumberland U		1,000	0	-1	1,000	0	200
89	CUNY BMB C		-1	488,777	-1	23,682	47,875	978
90	CUNY C Stn Island	f	-1	204,831	25,044	-1	-1	-1
91	CUNY City C	bGM	0	643,115	18,250	9,000	102,000	32,210
92	CUNY HH Lehman C	bG	5,966	146,424 [1]	3,696	-1	23,472	973
93	CUNY John Jay C Crim J	G	12,555	158,161	12,498	84,516	22,926	2,537
94	CUNY Queens C	bG	0	406,976	20,473	-1	94,869	1,463
95	Curtis Inst Music	G	0	0	17,865	0	14,914	15
96	Daniel Webster C	b	0	42,182 [1]	26,090	0	0	500
97	DeSales U		500	50,408	19,000	0 [1]	15,900	3,500
98	DN Myers C		0	10,835	0	0	13,288	650
99	Dominican C San Rafael	b	1,580	54,200	21,144	0	0	1,059
100	Dominican U	b	-1	75,000	30,000	-1	-1	3,000
101	Drake U	b	12,979	215,052	-1	0	-1	12,218
102	Drury C	b	4,834	62,838	23,001	0	1,093	0
103	E R Aero U		0	313,033	35,000	0	20,000	7,125
104	Earlham C	Gf	20,054	174,144	75,407	-1 [1]	56,600 [1]	3,608
105	Eastern IL U	bG	550	274,630	79,020	-1	47,715	2,174
106	Eastern U	Bb	-1	100,000	-1	25,000	30,000	-1
107	Eastern WA U	Bb	62,450	133,140	133,140	0	145,651	34,163
108	Eastrn NM U Main	BbG	0	62,384	0	118,000	0 [1]	776
109	Edinboro U PA	b	7,780	175,019	33,113	0	84,709	6,919
110	Elizabethtown C	b	-1	98,768	40,717	0	46,731	10,145
111	Elmhurst C	b	7,235	135,074	23,306	-1	0	0
112	Elon U	b	37,685	240,848	56,670	41,108	685	-1
113	Emmanuel C MA	b	-1	95,000	28,922	-2	0	0
114	Emory & Henry C	bGf	-1	45,000	0	0	0	-1
115	Evergreen ST C	bGf	0	156,008	106,171	0	135,948	487
116	Fisk U	bG	0	19,606	2,971	125	1,755	-1
117	Fitchburg ST C	G	0	68,504 [1]	25,500 [1]	-1 [1]	20,039 [1]	37
118	FL Southern C	bG	-1	97,225	35,694	-1	890	2,975
119	Fort Hays ST U	b	423	125,922	0	47,172	17,199	2,000
120	Francis Marion U	G	0	65,657	-1	-1	0	150

Key to Notes on Page 1   1 -- See Footnotes   -1 -- Unavailable   -2 -- Not Applicable

ACRL Library Data Tables 2004
ELECTRONIC MATERIALS EXPENDITURES
INSTITUTIONS GRANTING MASTER OF ARTS AND PROFESSIONAL DEGREES (Carnegie Code M)

Lib. No.	Institution	Notes	Computer Files 28	Electronic Serials 29	Bibl. Util. / Networks / Consortia Internal Library Sources 30a	Bibl. Util. / Networks / Consortia External Sources 30b	Computer Hardware & Software 31	Doc. Delivery, ILL 32
121	Franklin Inst Boston	b	0	4,374	1,546	0	0	0
122	Franklin U		0	0	0	125,000	0	513
123	Free Will Baptist Bible C	bG	0	45	-1	4,000	0 [1]	205
124	Frostburg ST U	bG	40	8,030	19,816	246,108	0	8,704
125	Furman U	G	0	213,781	80,000	0	73,172	16,997
126	GA SWstrn ST U	b	-1	-1	-1	-1	20,190	30 [1]
127	Gardner-Webb U	BbG	818	63,300 [1]	14,043	0	29,907	1,730
128	Geneva C	G	0	60,694	60,138	0	6,123	355
129	Georgetown C		5,506	32,160	12,500	0	7,460	2,490
130	Goucher C	b	0	24,440	16,213	0	0	4,749
131	Governors ST U	bG	2,275	95	29,630	-1	73,352	12,101
132	Greenville C		0	15,173	9,330	0	0	147
133	Grove City C	b	0	142,000	0	0	0	18,000
134	Harding U Main	bG	0	67,044	20,987	28,000	26,412	5,223
135	Hebrew C		773	4,143	14,240	0	495	131
136	Heidelberg C	Bbf	9,000	20,000	12,000	28,000	2,500	550
137	Hillsdale Free Will Baptist (		0	0	0	3,922	11,300	102
138	Holy Apostles C & Sem	bGf	0	0	7,995	0	3,279	0
139	Hood C	G	0	39,249	70,670	17,663	8,793	1,740
140	Humboldt ST U	G	319	317,378	25,233	0	81,104	30,507
141	IN Inst of Tech	bf	1,000	58,000	1,100	1,500	3,000	250
142	IN U Kokomo	G	54,493	43,412	678	0	0	0
143	IN U S Bend	b	218	144,370	11,871	-1	-1	18,245
144	IN U-Purdue U Ft Wayne	G	-1	225,821	15,289	2,103	49,211	19,246
145	IN Wesleyan U	B	11,892	131,465	25,379	36,079	-1	5,287
146	Intl Fine Arts C		0	8,000	0	7,500	0	10
147	Jacksonville ST U	bG	24,942	123,643	42,200	0	82,076	0
148	Johnson Bible C		0	8,213	125	-2	21,153	67
149	Kean U		0	-1	-1	-1	-1	-1
150	Keene State C	b	0	92,567	54,500	0	4,065	2,836
151	Kent ST U Stark	b	0	18,052	4,957	95,617	137	0
152	Kentucky Christian C	f	0	0 [1]	15,890 [1]	22,402 [1]	0	2,024 [1]
153	Kentucky ST U	G	34,161	11,512	-1	4,091	21,454	-1
154	Kettering U	b	2,657	50,000	0	34,000	1,600	5,000
155	King's C PA		-1	-1	14,853	0	0	3,100
156	LaGrange C	Bb	-1	-1	-1	-1	-1	626
157	Lakeland C-AB		0	34,821	15,958	0	0	2,659
158	Lakeview C Nursing	b	0	3,047	0	0	0	0
159	Lancaster Bible C		627	22,755	12,129	0	14,327	2
160	Lander U	G	0	27,517	0	-1	24,611	520

Key to Notes on Page 1   1 -- See Footnotes   -1 -- Unavailable   -2 -- Not Applicable

ACRL Library Data Tables 2004
ELECTRONIC MATERIALS EXPENDITURES
INSTITUTIONS GRANTING MASTER OF ARTS AND PROFESSIONAL DEGREES (Carnegie Code M)

| | | | Computer Files | Electronic Serials | Bibl. Util. / Networks / Consortia | | Computer Hardware & Software | Doc. Delivery, ILL |
| | | | | | Internal Library Sources | External Sources | | |
Lib. No.	Institution (Survey Question #)	Notes	28	29	30a	30b	31	32
161	Langston U	BG	13,381	7,308	21,981	0 [1]	0 [1]	2,288
162	Laurentian U JN	bG	-1 [1]	-1 [1]	-1 [1]	-1 [1]	-1 [1]	-1 [1]
163	Le Moyne C	G	19,520	214,447	26,598	0	34,769	11,093
164	Lebanon Valley C	b	-1	77,506	45,860	-1	5,800	6,600
165	Lewis U		0	17,300	157,000	5,800	27,950	257
166	Lewis&Clark C	G	-1	-1	41,484	0	21,735	15,889
167	Lincoln U-MO	b	-1	0	28,129	0	20,980	0
168	Lindsey Wilson C	bG	0	22,201	0	0	2,985 [1]	0
169	Lipscomb U		-1	-1	32,215	-1	20,698	-1
170	Lock Haven U PA	BbG	0	129,071	79,807	0	27,636	3,443
171	Longwood C	G	7,266	96,140	39,414 [1]	59,845	84,919	605
172	Lourdes C		0	2,622	40,118	11,755	0	0
173	Loyola Marymount U	b	-1	250,000	36,000	0	0	40,300
174	Loyola U New Orleans	G	-1	197,322	34,434	-1	50,756	24,500
175	Lubbock Christian U	b	0	17,367 [1]	0	250	4,050	0
176	Luth Theo Sem Philly	bf	0	4,200	-1	-1	-1	-1
177	Lynchburg C		-1	-1	35,092	0	-1	1,406
178	Malone C		2,600	114,427	45,627	23,618	0	941
179	Manchester C		1,100	32,171	45,700	0	6,200	1,523
180	Manhattan C		3,353	84,324	49,726	-1	10,609	13,391
181	Marist C	G	8,500 [1]	166,766	23,666	-1	4,192	1,028 [1]
182	Mary Baldwin C	b	63	39,444	5,000	-1	24,967	6,637
183	Mary Washington C	BbG	4,065	156,564	45,911	-1	22,393	16,960
184	Marymount U	G	-1	139,088	32,902	6,500	-1	1,340
185	Maryville U St Louis	b	0	62,641	24,322	-1	11,702	7,113
186	McNeese ST U		-1	57,287	74,908	-1	-1	-1
187	Medical C Wisconsin	BbGM	75,000	309,504	9,000	0	18,000	10,000
188	Merrimack C	b	3,300	94,242	49,854	53,556	1,999	-1 [1]
189	MidAmer Nazarene U		0	30,000	0	0	0	0
190	Millikin U	bG	61,646 [1]	-1	-1 [1]	0 [1]	0	-1 [1]
191	Millsaps C	G	0	47,403	12,039	0	22,125	8,218
192	Minnesota ST U-Mankato	bG	4,390	390,647	21,045	221,920 [1]	65,694	25,845 [1]
193	Minot ST U	G	6,948	56,241	37,551	-1	30,673	335
194	Monterey Inst Intl St	f	0	55,000	-1	300	100,000	20,000
195	Moravian C		-1	-1	-1	-1	72,355	5,500
196	Morehead ST U	G	18,011	124,575	48,950	0	30,580	2,929
197	Morningside C	bG	0	13,957	0	3,231	0	0
198	MS Valley ST U	BG	20,000	74,500	10,000	5,000	40,000	500
199	Mt Holyoke C		0	225,390	40,000	0	-1	15,000
200	Mt Marty C		-1	-1	-1	-1	-1	-1

Key to Notes on Page 1   1 -- See Footnotes   -1 -- Unavailable   -2 -- Not Applicable

ACRL Library Data Tables 2004
ELECTRONIC MATERIALS EXPENDITURES
INSTITUTIONS GRANTING MASTER OF ARTS AND PROFESSIONAL DEGREES (Carnegie Code M)

Lib. No.	Institution	Notes	Computer Files 28	Electronic Serials 29	Bibl. Util. / Networks / Consortia Internal Library Sources 30a	External Sources 30b	Computer Hardware & Software 31	Doc. Delivery, ILL 32
201	Mt Mary C-WI	bf	-1	25,000	49,000	0	3,000	1,000
202	MT ST U Northern	bG	-1	18,124	8,879	-1	14,467	5,155
203	Mt St Vincent U	Gf	-1	134,969	53,840	0	0	-1
204	MT Tech U Montana	bG	200	51,599	-1	-1	16,190	3,493
205	Murray ST U-KY	L	1	161,304	14,652	-1	104,616	12,694
206	Muskingum C		0	20,000[1]	0	17,775[1]	5,000	500
207	Natl C Naturopathic Med	bM	0	30,000	14,000	-1	3,000	1,000
208	Natl Defense U	bGf	0	700,000	40,000	0	0	1,200
209	NC Sch Arts		0	24,500	18,000	0	3,000	0
210	NEastrn IL U	B	700	257,707	53,550	-1	83,693	6,518
211	Nipissing U	B	0	255,299	0	0	6,100	6,841
212	NJ City U		0	0	0	0	0	0
213	NM Highlands U	B	4,500	61,556	30,195	0	17,998	8,926
214	North Central C		-1	32,975	0	16,689	2,011	-1
215	Northern KY U	b	-1	247,362	-1	-1	-1	2,200
216	Northern ST U	bGf	1,500	80,598	39,588	0	10,665	137
217	Northwest C	b	203	0	0	7,709	150	2,928
218	Norwich U	G	0	85,874	0	0	70,693	13,751
219	Notre Dame C OH		-1	-1	-1	-1	-1	-1
220	Notre Dame Sem	b	-1	-1	-1	1,000[1]	2,000	307
221	NW MO ST U	bG	-1[1]	144,397	22,636	-1	43,435	1,731
222	NY Inst Tech Islip		0[1]	0[1]	-1	-1	-1	-1
223	NY Inst Tech Main	M	3,738	87,530	60,412	-1	-1	3,165
224	Oberlin C	B	18,927	412,573	81,303	34,341	45,732	8,890
225	OH U Lancaster	b	0	0	13,000	0	10,000	0
226	Olivet Nazarene U	G	0	95,438	35,009	0	221,909	166
227	Otterbein C	G	646	115,286	43,345	84,505[1]	2,492	179[1]
228	Pace U Law		0	0	13,651[1]	0	61,755	-1
229	Pacific Lutheran U	f	-1	196,022	34,850	0	83,937	34,412
230	Pacific Union C		0	76,013	15,407	0	7,058	1,454
231	Palm Beach Atl C	b	91,868	0	5,774	0	19,070	2,000
232	Pfeiffer U	Bb	0	8,750	14,855	0	15,786	0
233	Philadelphia U	b	-1	107,300	29,675	-1	25,650	4,700
234	Plymouth ST C	G	0	56,910	30,446	0	56,464	4,560
235	Pont C Josephinum		-1	-1	-1	-1	-1	-1
236	Pope John Ntl Sem	bf	0	0	4,325	800	0	0
237	Prescott C	Bb	0	31,680	15,444	0	0[1]	400
238	Providence C	b	0	332,925	47,378	0	0[1]	919
239	Purchase C SUNY		2,973	150,939	17,601	0	39,268	2,684
240	Purdue U Calumet	G	0	69,340	49,497	0	35,482	32,683

Key to Notes on Page 1   1 -- See Footnotes   -1 -- Unavailable   -2 -- Not Applicable

ACRL Library Data Tables 2004

ELECTRONIC MATERIALS EXPENDITURES

INSTITUTIONS GRANTING MASTER OF ARTS AND PROFESSIONAL DEGREES (Carnegie Code M)

Lib. No.	Institution	Notes	Computer Files 28	Electronic Serials 29	Bibl. Util. / Networks / Consortia		Computer Hardware & Software 31	Doc. Delivery, ILL 32
					Internal Library Sources 30a	External Sources 30b		
Survey Question #			28	29	30a	30b	31	32
241	Purdue U North Central	G	0	33,937	11,389 [1]	0	1,428	95
242	Quincy U	b	0	34,620	25,469	0	7,620	0
243	R.Wesleyan C	G	0	68,005	14,328	0	27,575	2,575
244	Radford U	G	23,295	238,870	1,325	171,207	42,117	28,550
245	Ramapo C NJ	bf	-1	130,749	83,465	-1	2,695	171
246	Recnstrctnst Rabbinical C	b	500	0	5,000	-1	9,999	55
247	RI Sch Design		400	11,324	15,828	0	12,219	0 [1]
248	Rivier C	b	0	55,915	41,889	0	0	5,170
249	Rockhurst U	bG	0	103,000	30,000	0	600	5,800
250	Roger Williams U	G	0	175,000	32,028	0	26,532	1,530
251	Roosevelt U	Bb	0	122,652	29,604	-1	0 [1]	5,121
252	Rosemont C	b	0	22,136	0	15,909	33,905	2,500
253	Salem Teiko U	G	-1	-1	-1	-1	-1	-1
254	Salisbury ST U		65,050 [1]	218,990 [1]	12,574	20,000	67,968	198
255	San Jose ST U	bG	22,140	683,257	159,687	51,062	100,428	13,159
256	Savannah ST U	bf	0	41,260	18,737	38,992	18,500	0
257	Schreiner C		-1	11,227	14,034	-1	3,000	930
258	SE LA U	Bf	684	230,742	98,744	0	31,254	22,418
259	SE MO ST U		0	185,421	105,306	-1	42,821	1,658
260	SE Oklahoma St U	b	0	-1	-1	-1	23,000	4,275
261	Seton Hill C		-1	10,765	-1	-1	9,524	1,163
262	SF Consrv Music		0	0	5,000	1,600	13,180	-2
263	Shaw U		-1	47,190 [1]	0	71	32,860 [1]	-1
264	Shorter C	Bb	2,385	500	28,000	28,000	1,500	1,500
265	Silver Lake C	f	0	2,660	11,800	0	9,265	64
266	Sisseton-Wahpeton CC	bG	0	0	550 [1]	0 [1]	0	0 [1]
267	Southrn C Opt	M	0	0	0	0	0	143
268	Southrn IL U Edward		18,976	426,827	26,808	-1 [1]	50,756	46,046
269	Southrn OR U	G	-1	80,213	35,476	-2	54,884	2,550
270	Spring Hill C	bf	1,200	7,250	68,750	0 [1]	0 [1]	3,000
271	St Ambrose U		1,719	61,863	25,200	-1	41,377	6,302 [1]
272	St C.Borromeo Sem	bf	2,500	10,928	19,352	0	18,003	12,053
273	St Cloud ST U	b	14,386	222,647	45,698	0	40,884	0
274	St Francis C PA	G	3,253	116,934	16,115	0	40,964	5,213
275	St Francis-Xavier U	bf	-1	219,048	-1	0	35,558	3,463
276	St John Fisher C	bGf	-1	-1	-1	-1	-1	-1
277	St Joseph C Suffolk	b	0	56,470 [1]	-1	-1	66,145	0
278	St Joseph's C IN	bG	0	0	16,543	-1	480	578
279	St Joseph's C NY	bf	0	33,494	9,140	-1	10,707	0
280	St Joseph's Sem	b	0	0	0	7,639	23,883	170

Key to Notes on Page 1   1 -- See Footnotes   -1 -- Unavailable   -2 -- Not Applicable

88

ELECTRONIC MATERIALS EXPENDITURES

INSTITUTIONS GRANTING MASTER OF ARTS AND PROFESSIONAL DEGREES (Carnegie Code M)

Lib. No.	Institution	Notes	Computer Files 28	Electronic Serials 29	Bibl. Util. / Networks / Consortia Internal Library Sources 30a	External Sources 30b	Computer Hardware & Software 31	Doc. Delivery, ILL 32
	Survey Question #							
281	St Mary's U MN	G	0	16,245	38,922	-1	6,000	1,643
282	St Meinrad Theo	b	-1	-1	8,044	-1	56,406	551
283	St Michael's C	b	176	72,952	13,604	0	18,585	13,631
284	St Norbert C		-1	65,210 [1]	23,368	-1	140	3,083
285	St Patrick's Sem	f	0	0	12,066	0	1,500	345
286	St Peter's Abbey & C	bGf	0	0	1,050	0	0	-1
287	ST U W GA		50,897	64,416	27,482	-1	20,461	315
288	St Vincent Sem		10,264	0	0	0	10,574	0
289	St. John's C		0	3,000	52,000	0	0	0
290	Stetson U	B	0	126,811	29,936	-1 [1]	59,876	4,563
291	Sthrn Polytech ST U	G	0	25,000	3,300	37,055	-1	-1
292	Stonehill C	bG	0	71,477	39,000	0	41,044	850
293	Sul Ross ST U	bf	0	46,023	13,567	0	0	1,990
294	SUNY Brockport		-1	197,692	39,083	-1	29,799	12,722
295	SUNY Buffalo		0	300,466	55,680	-1	11,487	20,506
296	SUNY C Potsdam	G	0	79,583	20,921	27,145	14,175	1,418
297	SUNY IT Utica	G	-1 [1]	92,750	31,907 [1]	-1	18,746 [1]	2,802 [1]
298	SUNY Oneonta	G	0	94,498	70,086	-1	28,091	6,058
299	SUNY Oswego	G	0	113,728	55,255	0	40,683	24,742
300	SW MO ST U	B	-1	498,600	211,733	-1	52,113	2,815
301	SWstrn Adventist U	b	-1	20,020 [1]	0	18,000 [1]	-1	-1
302	SWstrn OK ST U	bf	-1	-1	-1	-1	-1	-1
303	Tabor C	b	145	13,800	0	0	0	2,704
304	Tiffin U	b	-2	-2	43,476	-2	193	3,593
305	TM Cooley Law Sch	BbGL	35	38,203	18,518	0	31,213	123
306	Trinity Luth Sem		102	4,235	9,849	0	6,394	0
307	Trinity U	b	9,163	342,041	104,576	0 [1]	0	14,962
308	Trinity U		0	21,750	0	63,000	12,440	-1
309	Troy ST U	Bb	0	111,573	43,131	1,856	8,140	571
310	Troy ST U Dothan	bG	0	0	5,951	-1	-1	0
311	Truman ST U	b	-1	179,566	0	96,441	36,687	23,523
312	TX Chiro C	bM	500	350	7,855	0	2,040	990
313	U Arts	bG	0	32,258	14,307	0	8,549	-1
314	U C Cape	bG	-1	-1	45,541	-1	-1	-1
315	U Charleston	b	-1	-1	-1	10,694	5,413	563
316	U DC	b	-1	72,945	335,897	15,000	63,378	-1
317	U Del Turabo		10,000	45,687	3,000	80,000	-1	-1
318	U Findlay	bG	1,272	133,479	37,468	-1	2,240	1,549
319	U Hawaii-Hilo	bG	5,000	77,438	0	0	10,076	4,000
320	U HI-Kauai CC	b	0	2,500	3,500	0	0	800

Key to Notes on Page 1   1 -- See Footnotes   -1 -- Unavailable   -2 -- Not Applicable

ELECTRONIC MATERIALS EXPENDITURES

INSTITUTIONS GRANTING MASTER OF ARTS AND PROFESSIONAL DEGREES (Carnegie Code M)

Lib. No.	Institution	Notes	Computer Files 28	Electronic Serials 29	Bibl. Util. / Networks / Consortia Internal Library Sources 30a	External Sources 30b	Computer Hardware & Software 31	Doc. Delivery, ILL 32
321	U Houston	b	10,000	369,640	39,855	0	43,854	1,591
322	U Mary	bGf	-1	16,872	20,019	-1	-1	-1
323	U MI Dearborn		-1	37,089	0 [1]	0	100,167 [1]	17,917
324	U Mobile	bG	0	31,828	0	4,497	18,648	2,609
325	U NE Kearney	b	0	153,679	65,000	50,000	40,591	43,171
326	U Portland	bG	-1	142,077	44,002	-1	0	17,330
327	U Richmond		0	551,708 [1]	48,241	0	0 [1]	14,530
328	U Rio Grande	bGf	11,400	14,739	9,179	0	5,904	733
329	U Scranton	b	990	201,927	43,450	0	53,088 [1]	3,100
330	U Sthn IN	bG	0	264,200	21,518	-1	34,964	3,629
331	U Tampa	bG	2,000	147,885	25,815	-1	30,169	2,691
332	U TN Chatt	bG	108,316	65,468	40,685	0	5,640	953
333	U TN Martin	BbG	-1	204,757	17,550 [1]	30,000 [1]	58,406 [1]	2,650
334	U TX Tyler	BG	0	133,273 [1]	32,034	359,403	82,499	8,845
335	U West AL		0	74,423	5,836	0	47,465	0
336	U WI E Claire	b	-1 [1]	145,300	43,976	79,528 [1]	148,313	11,023
337	U WI La Crosse	G	18,066	29,395	0	136,665	68,221	823
338	U WI Platteville	bG	149	32,442	0	0	64	46,222
339	U Winnipeg	bG	-1	459,091	1,788	-1	87,927	25,000
340	UNC Asheville	b	65,386	166,407	48,567	-1	82,475	2,026
341	UNC Pembroke	bGf	0	181,806	0	16,992	31,556	0
342	Union C-NY		14,500	306,919	53,198	0	293,130	5,594
343	Valparaiso U		0	376	92,736	16,245	737,636	14,259
344	Villa Julie C	bG	499	75,243	8,540	20,013	8,792 [1]	60 [1]
345	W.Carey College	Bb	16,673	24,697	21,102	0	0	0
346	W.Mitchell C Law	GL	24,250	118,719	12,000	-1	47,846	-1
347	Walla Walla C	b	-1	86,708	24,559	0	32,400	1,541
348	Walsh C Acct Bus Admin	B	3,000	12,000	22,000	0	7,000	3,000
349	Wartburg Theo Sem	bf	4,061	3,909	-1	-1	5,480	-1
350	Washburn U Topeka	bG	0	4,183	15,531	0	48,371	17,398
351	Washington C	Gf	17,000	80,128	47,600	-1	-1 [1]	2,476
352	Washington Theo Union	bf	0	-1	8,151	0	0	0
353	Wayland Bap U		-1	-1	-1	-1	16,306	-1
354	Wayne ST C	bG	-1	38,833	10,137	-1	42,500	7,968
355	Webber Intl U	b	0	19,000	2,200	0	0	0
356	Wesley C	bf	0	35,626	11,067	0	0	70
357	West Chester U PA		16,729	325,375	48,400	0	8,104	7,789
358	West TX A & M U	bG	0	177,006	70,790	0	7,223	198
359	West VA Wesleyan C		-1	-1	-1	-1	-1	-1
360	Western MD C	b	0	81,944	69,647	0	19,188	0

Key to Notes on Page 1   1 -- See Footnotes   -1 -- Unavailable   -2 -- Not Applicable

ACRL Library Data Tables 2004

ELECTRONIC MATERIALS EXPENDITURES

INSTITUTIONS GRANTING MASTER OF ARTS AND PROFESSIONAL DEGREES (Carnegie Code M)

Lib. No.	Institution	Notes	Computer Files 28	Electronic Serials 29	Bibl. Util. / Networks / Consortia Internal Library Sources 30a	External Sources 30b	Computer Hardware & Software 31	Doc. Delivery, ILL 32
	Survey Question #							
361	Western OR U	bG	54,000	165,171	70,220	16,967	18,995	9,772
362	Western Sem	b	0	6,681	0	10,374	0	0
363	Western WA U	G	-1	-1	37,590	-1	124,887	84,764
364	Westfield ST C	b	980	155,584	22,957	0	30,642	3,180
365	Westminster C-UT	G	10,157	14,539	36,919	-1	35,682	903
366	Wheeling Jesuit U	b	0	67,000	29,000	-1	6,500	300
367	Whitworth C	G	7,700	76,743	41,437	-1	8,687	8,410
368	Wilkes U	G	2,700	185,471	55,887	-1	11,838	13,725
369	William Woods U	bL	0	25,919	17,081	-1	1,181	2,295
370	Williams C		609	673,875	141,521	-1	46,181	17,915
371	Wstrn IL U	Bb	20,375	213,041	-1	81,413	39,493	-1
372	Wstrn Theo Sem	f	955	-1	6,803	-1	-1	-1
373	Xavier U LA	b	0	29,712 [1]	40,712	0	23,928	0

ACRL LIBRARY DATA TABLES 2004

SUMMARY DATA: PERSONNEL AND PUBLIC SERVICES

ALL INSTITUTIONS REPORTING

	Professional Staff (FTE)	Support Staff (FTE)	Student Assistants (FTE)	Total Staff (FTE)	No. of Staffed Service Points	No. of Weekly Public Service Hours
(Survey Question #)	33	34	35	36	37	38
High	239	365	241	673	92	168
Mean	14	20	12	46	5	86
Median	6	7	4	18	3	86
Low	1	0	0	1	0	1
Total	15,963	22,354	12,674	50,646	5,892	94,933
Libraries Reporting	1,115	1,108	1,099	1,106	1,101	1,104

ACRL LIBRARY DATA TABLES 2004

SUMMARY DATA: PERSONNEL AND PUBLIC SERVICES

ALL INSTITUTIONS REPORTING

Library Presentations to Groups	Participants in Group Presentations	Reference Transactions	Initial Circulation Transactions	Total Circulation Transactions	Items Loaned (ILL)	Items Borrowed (ILL)	
39	40	41	42	43	44	45	(Survey Question #)
3,579	3	368,996	1,709,170	5,357,960	116,240	82,458	High
199	2	17,961	63,970	90,989	5,518	4,768	Mean
100	2	5,200	18,939	23,088	1,339	1,218	Median
0	1	0	0	0	0	0	Low
217,033	2,204	18,554,059	54,950,194	93,809,755	5,969,959	5,149,407	Total
1,092	1,119	1,033	859	1,031	1,082	1,080	Libraries Reporting

ACRL LIBRARY DATA TABLES 2004

SUMMARY DATA: PERSONNEL AND PUBLIC SERVICES

INSTITUTIONS GRANTING BACHELOR OF ARTS DEGREES (Carnegie Code B)

	Professional Staff (FTE)	Support Staff (FTE)	Student Assistants (FTE)	Total Staff (FTE)	No. of Staffed Service Points	No. of Weekly Public Service Hours
(Survey Question #)	33	34	35	36	37	38
High	33	80	60	79	23	168
Mean	6	6	6	17	3	87
Median	4	4	4	11	2	85
Low	1	0	0	1	1	35
Total	1,044	1,150	1,075	3,171	541	16,111
Libraries Reporting	189	188	187	188	186	186

ACRL LIBRARY DATA TABLES 2004

SUMMARY DATA: PERSONNEL AND PUBLIC SERVICES

INSTITUTIONS GRANTING BACHELOR OF ARTS DEGREES (Carnegie Code B)

Library Presentations to Groups	Participants in Group Presentations	Reference Transactions	Initial Circulation Transactions	Total Circulation Transactions	Items Loaned (ILL)	Items Borrowed (ILL)	
39	40	41	42	43	44	45	(Survey Question #)
2,029	15,455	56,045	160,689	352,202	24,334	19,900	High
87	1,322	4,174	22,659	31,622	2,006	2,102	Mean
49	698	1,947	11,536	14,787	687	1,017	Median
0	0	0	0	0	0	0	Low
15,916	241,921	697,033	3,036,337	5,438,949	367,059	384,734	Total
184	183	167	134	172	183	183	Libraries Reporting

ACRL LIBRARY DATA TABLES 2004

SUMMARY DATA: PERSONNEL AND PUBLIC SERVICES

INSTITUTIONS GRANTING MASTER OF ARTS AND PROFESSIONAL DEGREES (Carnegie Code M)

(Survey Question #)	Professional Staff (FTE)	Support Staff (FTE)	Student Assistants (FTE)	Total Staff (FTE)	No. of Staffed Service Points	No. of Weekly Public Service Hours
	33	34	35	36	37	38
High	33	58	74	137	92	168
Mean	8	10	7	26	4	87
Median	6	7	5	19	3	87
Low	1	0	0	1	1	15
Total	3,070	3,747	2,744	9,404	1,527	32,170
Libraries Reporting	372	370	367	367	369	369

SUMMARY DATA: PERSONNEL AND PUBLIC SERVICES

INSTITUTIONS GRANTING MASTER OF ARTS AND PROFESSIONAL DEGREES (Carnegie Code M)

Library Presentations to Groups	Participants in Group Presentations	Reference Transactions	Initial Circulation Transactions	Total Circulation Transactions	Items Loaned (ILL)	Items Borrowed (ILL)	
39	40	41	42	43	44	45	(Survey Question #)
1,152	22,283	354,600	729,656	592,024	22,234	32,160	High
126	2,316	10,918	35,051	41,321	2,836	2,751	Mean
92	1,533	4,543	18,917	23,720	1,660	1,360	Median
0	0	0	0	0	0	0	Low
46,214	840,596	3,821,360	9,814,225	14,214,447	1,026,655	992,943	Total
366	363	350	280	344	362	361	Libraries Reporting

ACRL Library Data Tables 2004
PERSONNEL AND PUBLIC SERVICES
INSTITUTIONS GRANTING BACHELOR OF ARTS DEGREES (Carnegie Code B)

Lib. No.	Institution	Notes	Professional Staff (FTE) 33	Support Staff (FTE) 34	Student Assistants (FTE) 35	Total Staff (FTE) 36	No. of Staffed Service Points 37	Weekly Public Service Hours 38
1	AB C Art & Design	bf	1	5	1	6	2	60
2	Adrian C		3	2	3	8	2	87
3	Albion C	G	6	7	8	21	2	110
4	Amherst C	Gf	16	26	11	53	7	110
5	Aquinas C TN	G	3	2	2	6	2	60
6	Atlanta C Art	bG	2	3	3	8	3 1	61
7	Atlanta Christian C	bf	2	0	3	4	1	63
8	Augustana C RI	G	8	8	8	24	6	98
9	Barber-Scotia C		2	2	0	4	3	75
10	Bard C	b	9	10	60	79	5	106
11	Barton C	b	5	2	2	9	2	87
12	Bates C	bG	11	16	8	36	3	112
13	Benedict C	G	6	4	2	12	5 1	81
14	Berry C	b	7	7	9	23	4	90
15	Bethany C Bethany	b	4	1	2	7	2	79
16	Bethany C Lindsborg		1	2	3	6	2	81
17	Bethel C KS		3	2	2	7	2	90
18	Blackburn C	bG	2	1	4	7	1	77
19	Bluefield C	bf	3	2	3	8	3	78
20	Boise Bible C		1	1	1	2	1	70
21	Bowdoin C		18	15	16	49	8	109
22	Bridgewater C	b	6	4	4	14	3	88
23	Bryan C	bf	3	2	2	7	1	80
24	C Holy Cross		17	20	11	48	6	112
25	C Visual Arts	b	2	1	1	4	2	75
26	C Wooster		7	11	19	37	5 1	107
27	Campion C	G	1	1	1	3	1	66
28	Carroll C-Helena	b	3	3	5	11	2	92
29	Cazenovia C	b	5	2	2	9	3	69
30	Centennial C	bf	8	28	2	37	16	64
31	Central Bible C	b	3	2	3	7	2	80
32	Central C		5	5	6	15	4	92
33	Central Christian C Bible	b	1	1 1	1	3	1	77
34	Centre C	G	4	5	6	15	2	102
35	Christian Heritage C		2	1	2	5	1	74
36	Clear Creek Bible		1	1	3	5	1	64
37	Cmty Hosp C Health		1	3	4	5 1	1	66
38	Colby C	bG	9	14	17	39	4	119
39	Colby Sawyer C	b	4	6	2	11	2	97
40	Columbia Union C	bG	3	2	4	9	3	74

Key to Notes on Page 1   1 -- See Footnotes   -1 -- Unavailable   -2 -- Not Applicable

ACRL Library Data Tables 2004
PERSONNEL AND PUBLIC SERVICES

INSTITUTIONS GRANTING BACHELOR OF ARTS DEGREES (Carnegie Code B)

No. of Presentations to Groups 39	Participants in Group Presentations 40	No. of Reference Transactions 41	No. of Initial Circulations 42	Total Circulations 43	ILL Materials Provided 44	ILL Materials Received 45	Survey Question # Institution
16	350	-1	-1	35,481	16	36	AB C Art & Design
49	633	1,151	-1	10,550	716	2.586	Adrian C
65	1,300	1,356	26,347	33,144	5,781	5.093	Albion C
104	1,768	11,908	-1 [1]	134,862	6,845	3.921	Amherst C
28	435	1,500	-1	11,000	598	99	Aquinas C TN
14	300	-1 [1]	5,904 [1]	5,904	307	136	Atlanta C Art
4	117	412	2,680	3,350	47	72	Atlanta Christian C
116	2,533	4,356	-1	38,176	7,851	12.156	Augustana C RI
43	302	582	1,127	1,542	261	16	Barber-Scotia C
12	150	5,000	27,985	36,460	677	1.974	Bard C
60	1,158	129	9,922	9,922	494	297	Barton C
84	1,058	6,400	-1	109,093	15,958	10.658	Bates C
108	943	13,285	2,832	2,832 [1]	12	78	Benedict C
102	1,473	1,793	-1	24,917	1,934	3.763	Berry C
38	485	715	0 [1]	8,526	324	587	Bethany C Bethany
15	100	10,500	6,127	6,127	569	1.095	Bethany C Lindsborg
16	154	6,912	8,102	9,316	1,344	1.385	Bethel C KS
17	250	375	3,936	4,246	5,690	1.698	Blackburn C
65	425	60	4,135	4,087	283	179	Bluefield C
3	54	45 [1]	-1	-1	-1	-1	Boise Bible C
219	2,316	8,633	43,758	59,397	9,120	11.247	Bowdoin C
44	557	1,928	14,762	21,505	1,550	635	Bridgewater C
27	486	1,974	27,975	29,809	371	288	Bryan C
66	1,555	6,456	41,911	51,022	6,563	4.059	C Holy Cross
15	300	825	13,797	17,385	45	387	C Visual Arts
87	1,311	88	36,225	43,517	17,566	19.900	C Wooster
-1 [1]	-1	-1 [1]	-1	13,243	427	0	Campion C
160	1,200	-1 [1]	-1 [1]	-1 [1]	-1 [1]	-1 [1]	Carroll C-Helena
39	865	1,956	5,814	-1	886	799	Cazenovia C
257	5,140	21,515	-1	57,188	107	63	Centennial C
12	220	960	16,020	24,095	702	102	Central Bible C
278	3,561	1,200	24,209	47,523	1,963	2.054	Central C
6	100	-1	5,096	5,871	0	15	Central Christian C Bible
59	652	1,300	27,235	36,606	2,425	1.321	Centre C
47	637	1,101	4,948	4,948	122	81	Christian Heritage C
3	65	23	8,018	12,670	285	237	Clear Creek Bible
10	150	1,356	-1	2,363	198	91	Cmty Hosp C Health
82	1,640	3,240	51,510	63,639	4,445	5.985	Colby C
43	707	-1 [1]	4,090	5,170	662	1.599	Colby Sawyer C
36	429	3,520	-1	4,088	440	762	Columbia Union C

Key to Notes on Page 1   1 -- See Footnotes   -1 -- Unavailable   -2 -- Not Applicable

ACRL Library Data Tables 2004
PERSONNEL AND PUBLIC SERVICES
INSTITUTIONS GRANTING BACHELOR OF ARTS DEGREES (Carnegie Code B)

Lib. No.	Institution	Notes	Professional Staff (FTE) 33	Support Staff (FTE) 34	Student Assistants (FTE) 35	Total Staff (FTE) 36	No. of Staffed Service Points 37	Weekly Public Service Hours 38
41	Concordia C-MN	b	8	10	8	26	4	97
42	Concordia C-NY	b	4	0	3	7	2	76
43	Cornish C Arts		3	1	2	5	3 [1]	136 [1]
44	Crichton C	b	2	2	1	5	1	68
45	Crown C-MN	G	3	2	4	8	1	85
46	Culver Stockton C	b	2	3	2	7	2 [1]	80 [1]
47	CUNY City C		13	8	13	31	6	68
48	CUNY York C	b	8	6	4	18	5	67
49	Dakota Wesleyan U	b	2	2	2	6	1	73
50	Dana C	bG	2	2	2	6	2	78
51	Davidson C	bG	12	12	8	32	4	106
52	Dean C	bL	2	1	1	4	1	75
53	Defiance C	b	4	1	4	9	2	82
54	Denison U		9	14	9	32	1	111
55	DeVry Inst Tech GA	b	33	17	-1	50	23	92
56	Dickinson ST U		4	5	6	10	2	74
57	Divine Word C		2	1	1	3	2	60
58	East Texas Baptist U	Bb	4 [1]	4	20	28	2	81
59	Eckerd C		5	6	5	16	2	91
60	Emmanuel C GA	b	1	4	1	5	1	67
61	Eugene Bible C		1	1	1	-1	-1	-1
62	Evangel U		4	4	6	14	3	82
63	F&M C		10	16	8	34	8	118
64	Ferrum C	bf	4	3	3	10	3	94
65	Finlandia U	bG	2	1	3	6	1	77
66	FL Christian C	b	1	1	2	4	2	68
67	Flagler C	bG	6	3	4	13	2	93
68	Fort Lewis C	b	8	8	6	22	2	81
69	G Adolphus C	b	8 [1]	9 [1]	15 [1]	32 [1]	8	95
70	Green Mountain C	bf	2	2	4	8	2	83
71	Grinnell C		8	15	8	31	2	105
72	Guilford C	bG	5	4	6	15	3	105
73	H Inst Int Desgn	b	2	2	2	6	2	67
74	H LaGrange C	G	2	5	3	10	2	71
75	Hamilton C		13	24	9	46	4	118
76	Hampshire C		17	18	10	45	4	108
77	Hanover C	bG	4 [1]	6	5	14	3 [1]	104 [1]
78	Haskell Indian Nations U	bf	3	3	3	8	1	83
79	Haverford C	Bb	15	14	9	38	5	100
80	Hendrix C	b	5	5	7	26	2	90

Key to Notes on Page 1   1 -- See Footnotes   -1 -- Unavailable   -2 -- Not Applicable

ACRL Library Data Tables 2004
PERSONNEL AND PUBLIC SERVICES

INSTITUTIONS GRANTING BACHELOR OF ARTS DEGREES (Carnegie Code B)

No. of Presentations to Groups 39	Participants in Group Presentations 40	No. of Reference Transactions 41	No. of Initial Circulations 42	Total Circulations 43	ILL Materials Provided 44	ILL Materials Received 45	Survey Question # Institution
125	2,305	4,681	93,616	113,008	10,790	7.632	Concordia C-MN
9	135	-1	-1	4,974	776	162	Concordia C-NY
35 [1]	512 [1]	805 [1]	-1 [1]	7,606	0 [1]	0 [1]	Cornish C Arts
43	547	53	7,403	7,403 [1]	104	101	Crichton C
33	498	402	12,876 [1]	-1 [1]	463	301	Crown C-MN
10	173	-1	8,104	36,499	2,038	1.117	Culver Stockton C
305	7,625	800	18,094 [1]	18,094 [1]	183 [1]	354 [1]	CUNY City C
44	840	19,449	100,575 [1]	100,575 [1]	31	1.182	CUNY York C
33	496	2,340	10,288	11,795	1,007	1.203	Dakota Wesleyan U
78	783	1,336	6,948	8,824	630	285	Dana C
130	2,775	297	-1	92,561	8,609	13.859	Davidson C
45	675	-1	-1	4,082	2,922	1.215	Dean C
21	407	2,275	-1	9,779	2,740	1.594	Defiance C
157	2,826	143	28,422	41,421	24,334	17.601	Denison U
2,029	-1	56,045	140,724	172,635	2,148	2.058	DeVry Inst Tech GA
132	2,251	9,100	98,100	96,229 [1]	1,915	1.703	Dickinson ST U
18	77	3,952	2,543	2,543 [1]	100	44	Divine Word C
25	476	492	9,700	10,501	397	520	East Texas Baptist U
39	858	6,320	19,118	23,279	2,787	1.333	Eckerd C
-1	-1	-1	-1	7,041	116	71	Emmanuel C GA
-1	-1	-1	-1	-1	-1	-1	Eugene Bible C
32	640	0 [1]	15,625	7,833	1,072	224	Evangel U
93	1,410	9,222	54,618	55,968	9,208	7.667	F&M C
42	585	3,920	0 [1]	0 [1]	861	438	Ferrum C
53	572	4,490	4,097	4,097 [1]	6	219	Finlandia U
3	60	1,000	9,464 [1]	9,464 [1]	50	218	FL Christian C
71	1,388	4,180	10,511	12,644	594	1.402	Flagler C
44	832	6,059	50,601	61,917	4,551	4.978	Fort Lewis C
118	2,180	3,840	-1	-1	4,176	8.084	G Adolphus C
82	656	2,528	2,573	-1	267	523	Green Mountain C
105	1,260	103	48,021	-1	3,039	4.910	Grinnell C
50	423	3,927	33,394 [1]	53,014	1,282	515	Guilford C
117	1,840	2,520	22,492	24,762	76	9	H Inst Int Desgn
62	449	1,900	22,008 [1]	22,008	407	860	H LaGrange C
40	1,250	5,204	-1	32,281	5,885	6.379	Hamilton C
71	1,113	3,016	43,543	71,164	1,425	2.420	Hampshire C
31	401	124 [1]	-1	39,769	2,304	2.515	Hanover C
59	1,330	-1	-1	12,688	665	55	Haskell Indian Nations U
39	624	-1	-1	66,442	6,432	4.324	Haverford C
18	398	3,515	26,523	0	2,490	1.702	Hendrix C

Key to Notes on Page 1   1 -- See Footnotes   -1 -- Unavailable   -2 -- Not Applicable

ACRL Library Data Tables 2004
PERSONNEL AND PUBLIC SERVICES
INSTITUTIONS GRANTING BACHELOR OF ARTS DEGREES (Carnegie Code B)

Lib. No.	Institution	Notes	Professional Staff (FTE) 33	Support Staff (FTE) 34	Student Assistants (FTE) 35	Total Staff (FTE) 36	No. of Staffed Service Points 37	Weekly Public Service Hours 38
	Survey Question #							
81	Hiram C	bG	5	4	8	17	3	94
82	Hobart &William Smith Cs	G	7	13	6	26	3	113
83	Hope C		9	9	14	32	5	94
84	Houghton C	Bb	5	7	3	15	4	86
85	Howard Payne U	G	3	6	6	15	2	82
86	Illinois C	bGf	4	4	4	11	1	94
87	Jamestown C	b	2	4	1	7	3	77
88	Johnson C Smith U	b	11	3	2	16	3	84
89	Judson C	b	4	1	5	10	3	81
90	Kent ST U Salem	b	1	1	1	3	1	58
91	Kent ST U Trumbull		2	3	4	9	4	64
92	Kenyon C	b	13	9	6	29	6	118
93	Kettering C Med	bG	3	1	1	5	1	65
94	Keuka C	b	4	2	5	11	2	92
95	Knox C	G	6	7	10	23	5	104
96	Kwantlen UC		13	32	8	53	9	67
97	Lambuth U	bGf	3	3	2	8	3	82
98	Lawrence U		9	6	7	22	4	110
99	Lemoyne-Owen C	Gf	3	3	2	8	2	73
100	Lester B Pearson C Pacific		1	1	1	3	-1	-1
101	LIFE Bible C	b	1	2	2	5	1	82
102	Lyndon State C		8	-1	25	33	-1	-1
103	Lyon C		3	3	3	9	1	90
104	Macon ST C	BbG	5	5	6	16	4	78
105	Marlboro C		3 [1]	1 [1]	1	5	1	69
106	Mars Hill C	b	5	3	4	12	2	78
107	Martin Luther C	bG	2	3	2	7	2	92
108	Mayville ST U		4	1	4	8	2	69
109	McKendree C	bG	4	1	2	7	2	78
110	McPherson C		-1	-1	-1	-1	-1	-1
111	Methodist C	G	4	8	1 [1]	13	2	89
112	Midland Lutheran C		2	3	3	8	2	80
113	Milwaukee Inst Art Design	b	3 [1]	0	1 [1]	4 [1]	1	68
114	MO Baptist C		3	5	2	10	2	65
115	MO Western ST C	bG	8	7	9	24	4	88
116	Monmouth C	bGf	4	5	3	11	2	93
117	Mount Royal C	bG	10	36	5	51	3	78
118	Mount Union C		6	7	7	20	3	95
119	Muhlenberg C	bG	14	1	9	24	3	108
120	NC Wesleyan C	BbG	3	3	2	8	2 [1]	90

Key to Notes on Page 1   1 -- See Footnotes   -1 -- Unavailable   -2 -- Not Applicable

ACRL Library Data Tables 2004
PERSONNEL AND PUBLIC SERVICES

INSTITUTIONS GRANTING BACHELOR OF ARTS DEGREES (Carnegie Code B)

No. of Presentations to Groups 39	Participants in Group Presentations 40	No. of Reference Transactions 41	No. of Initial Circulations 42	Total Circulations 43	ILL Materials Provided 44	ILL Materials Received 45	Survey Question # Institution
42	566	1,018	23,237	27,641	530	361	Hiram C
74	1,056	7,616	-1	-1	4,007	3.339	Hobart &William Smith Cs
166	3,283	231	-1	54,898	5,128	4.799	Hope C
24	350	-1	26,472	33,183	919	1.750	Houghton C
38	628	290	9,721	76	1,373	1.560	Howard Payne U
120	515	51	-1	37,781	2,501	2.254	Illinois C
85	1,700	1,270	9,660	12,242	1,550	1.610	Jamestown C
110	1,151	675	3,154	3,422	240	232	Johnson C Smith U
40	980	140	17,934	22,613	6,053	4.641	Judson C
46	1,046	6,850	3,852	8,424	14	135	Kent ST U Salem
35	698	-1	4,555	5,209	1,230	910	Kent ST U Trumbull
57	682	4,524	-1	61,982	1,037	1.740	Kenyon C
51	623	6,350	-1 [1]	6,438	551	135	Kettering C Med
83	1,212	1,229	8,332	8,487	582	416	Keuka C
81	1,132	2,970	-1	21,406	2,331	2.605	Knox C
343	7,903	34,317	74,902	82,141	1,283	1.121	Kwantlen UC
30	946	946	4,020	5,811	159	159	Lambuth U
63	945	5,627	-1	32,143	3,118	1.930	Lawrence U
15	300	5,628	12,787	12,787	8	8	Lemoyne-Owen C
12	200	-1	-1	-1	-1	-1	Lester B Pearson C Pacific
29	565	1,423	-1	4,730	0	0	LIFE Bible C
68	1,306	5,579	-1	-1	-1	-1	Lyndon State C
12	240	119	-1	10,466	1,842	1.038	Lyon C
124	2,584	3,801	7,219	8,142	568	526	Macon ST C
10	69	1,809	16,011	16,011 [1]	466	1.017	Marlboro C
87	1,288	2,352	-1	5,813	358	211	Mars Hill C
16	317	122	33,735	51,332	641	676	Martin Luther C
66	979	2,088	9,863	10,638	1,094	1.577	Mayville ST U
87	1,275	3,423	13,025	14,797	1,861	2.228	McKendree C
-1	-1	-1	-1	-1	-1	-1	McPherson C
173	1,822	5,046	8,409	9,046	422	626	Methodist C
60	20	800	13,000	14,000	950	530	Midland Lutheran C
31	527	916	9,898	12,958	850	2.061	Milwaukee Inst Art Design
10	195	759	5,883	192	506	202	MO Baptist C
142	3,412	7,274	-1 [1]	42,366	2,856	4.316	MO Western ST C
85	1,800	2,388	8,926	12,434	416	2.234	Monmouth C
642	15,455	34,494	-1	171,587	287	774	Mount Royal C
52	2,046	10,912	16,788	19,249	1,473	731	Mount Union C
138	2,384	9,453	26,061	42,006	2,388	5.388	Muhlenberg C
67	828	105	4,687	-1	212	590	NC Wesleyan C

Key to Notes on Page 1   1 -- See Footnotes   -1 -- Unavailable   -2 -- Not Applicable

ACRL Library Data Tables 2004
PERSONNEL AND PUBLIC SERVICES
INSTITUTIONS GRANTING BACHELOR OF ARTS DEGREES (Carnegie Code B)

Lib. No.	Institution	Notes	Professional Staff (FTE) 33	Support Staff (FTE) 34	Student Assistants (FTE) 35	Total Staff (FTE) 36	No. of Staffed Service Points 37	Weekly Public Service Hours 38
121	New C U South FL	bG	7	13	2	22	3	109
122	OH Dominican C	bG	5	4	5	14	2	88
123	OH Wesleyan U	b	11	8	12	31	6	104
124	OK Panhandle ST U	b	3	2	4	9	2	69
125	Paier C Art		1	0	1 [1]	2	1	47
126	Peace C	b	3	0	2	5	1	85
127	Potomac C	G	1	0	0	1	1	35
128	Presbyterian C	bG	4	5	2	11	2	98
129	Principia C	bG	5	1	5	11	2	97
130	Randolph-Macon C	bf	5	8	3	16	3	100
131	Randolph-Macon WC	bG	5	4	3	13	2	102
132	Reformed Bible C		2	0	1	3	1	76
133	Reinhardt C	Bb	3	3	2	8	2	78
134	Ricks C		12	10	38	60	6	92
135	Ringling Sch Art & Design		3	7	2	12	3	88
136	Rochester C	b	2	2	2	6	1	69
137	Rocky Mountain C	bGf	2	1	5	8	1	79
138	Rogers ST U	bG	5	3	4	12	2	85
139	SE C Assemblies God	bG	4	5	5	13	2	91
140	Shawnee ST U	Gf	6	9	28	43	3	90
141	Shepherd C	G	6	11	2	19	2	88
142	Siena C	G	8	8	9	25	4	106
143	Simpson C IA	bG	4	4	5	13	2	93
144	Skidmore C	b	14	9	5	27	2 [1]	109
145	Southwest U	f	10	10	9	29	6	99
146	Spartan Aero-Flight Schl	B	2	1	2	5	2	76
147	St Andrews Presby C	bG	3	4	2	8	1	77
148	St Gregory's U	b	3	0	1	4	1	70 [1]
149	St John Vianney C Sem		2	1	0	3	1	52
150	St Olaf C	b	9	15	21	45	3	115
151	St. Mary's C Maryland		7 [1]	12	4	23	1	101
152	Sterling C-VT		1	1	1	3	1	168 [1]
153	Stillman C		2	3	20	25	1	71
154	Susquehanna U	bG	8	5	9	22	3	97
155	SW Baptist Theo Sem		12	8	40	60	12	40
156	Swarthmore C	G	18	12	8	38	7	104
157	Sweet Briar C	bG	5	7	12	24	2	105
158	Talladega C	bf	6	2	11	19	5	82 [1]
159	Taylor U-Ft Wayne	b	5	4	5	14	1	89
160	Teikyo Post U	bL	3	1	4	8	2	82

Key to Notes on Page 1   1 -- See Footnotes   -1 -- Unavailable   -2 -- Not Applicable

ACRL Library Data Tables 2004
PERSONNEL AND PUBLIC SERVICES

INSTITUTIONS GRANTING BACHELOR OF ARTS DEGREES (Carnegie Code B)

No. of Presentations to Groups 39	Participants in Group Presentations 40	No. of Reference Transactions 41	No. of Initial Circulations 42	Total Circulations 43	ILL Materials Provided 44	ILL Materials Received 45	Survey Question # Institution
42	646	6,353	21,722	58,681	2,334	11.761	New C U South FL
50	891	2,469	15,675	20,525	4,892	5.195	OH Dominican C
186	2,639	4,137	29,825	39,850	19,466	9.962	OH Wesleyan U
74	1,328	7,770	9,034	9,093	129	221	OK Panhandle ST U
2	90	946	1,840	1,867	0	0	Paier C Art
11	138	30	4,108	6,108	166	572	Peace C
121	2,200	8,000	2,103	2,103	0	0	Potomac C
39	958	1,711	10,773	14,777	540	367	Presbyterian C
80	1,133	1,278	-1	18,349	335	431	Principia C
40	578	1,040	11,949	13,480	1,377	2.807	Randolph-Macon C
60	400	-1 [1]	22,400	28,901	1,580	2.004	Randolph-Macon WC
18	345	45	-1	7,423	472	574	Reformed Bible C
44	698	1,774	3,325	3,325	0	423	Reinhardt C
290	7,250	10,107	148,270	178,410	1,567	5.512	Ricks C
49	901	1,057	43,599	54,857	411	109	Ringling Sch Art & Design
0 [1]	0 [1]	0 [1]	5,653	6,237	51	219	Rochester C
14	328	576	0 [1]	8,777 [1]	549	628	Rocky Mountain C
37	927	5,200	-1 [1]	21,805	687	957	Rogers ST U
50	1,168	1,976	35,993	35,993 [1]	2,910	1.068	SE C Assemblies God
281	2,736	290	16,699	21,230	3,836	6.655	Shawnee ST U
36	653	129	17,812	17,812	779	1.672	Shepherd C
202	4,184	7,523	33,147	40,516	3,464	4.056	Siena C
47	960	-1	15,687	17,283	1,841	1.790	Simpson C IA
98	1,781	4,674	-1	41,805	4,451	6.122	Skidmore C
42	430	3,960	40,436	53,025	3,168	2.779	Southwest U
72	1,730	260	13,729	15,003	76	18	Spartan Aero-Flight Schl
18	252	772	3,843	4,543	386	482	St Andrews Presby C
13	140	192 [1]	2,315	2,512	0	67	St Gregory's U
5	60	1,520	1,000	1,211	203	30	St John Vianney C Sem
403	10,075	11,050	85,845	112,156	4,774	6.640	St Olaf C
84	1,257	5,330	41,556	68,568 [1]	1,740	2.418	St. Mary's C Maryland
25	250	-1	-1	3,290	0	290	Sterling C-VT
710	7,742	340	46,241	47,186	0	4	Stillman C
152	1,428	6,172	0	352,202	2,333	5.204	Susquehanna U
64	1,849	-1	-1	-1	-1	-1	SW Baptist Theo Sem
87	1,305	5,200	-1	95,634	8,070	5.213	Swarthmore C
38	568	9,500	28,520	33,675	1,539	1.788	Sweet Briar C
-1	9,957	7,145	3,223	4,392	14	6	Talladega C
66	1,092	2,432	27,016	7,564	1,892	2.511	Taylor U-Ft Wayne
64	20	13,000	1,370	1,626	211	117	Teikyo Post U

Key to Notes on Page 1   1 -- See Footnotes   -1 -- Unavailable   -2 -- Not Applicable

ACRL Library Data Tables 2004
PERSONNEL AND PUBLIC SERVICES
INSTITUTIONS GRANTING BACHELOR OF ARTS DEGREES (Carnegie Code B)

Lib. No.	Institution	Notes	Professional Staff (FTE) 33	Support Staff (FTE) 34	Student Assistants (FTE) 35	Total Staff (FTE) 36	No. of Staffed Service Points 37	Weekly Public Service Hours 38
161	TN Wesleyan C		3	4	2	9	3	67
162	Tri ST U		3	3	1	7	2	69
163	Trinity Christian C	b	3	1	2	6	2	79
164	Trinity Wstrn U	bf	7	80	4	19	2	83
165	Truett McConnell C	b	2	2	1	4	1	68
166	TX Lutheran U	bG	5	4	3	12	2	84
167	U Maine-Machias	G	1	2	4	7	1	84
168	U ME Fort Kent	b	3	3	3	9	5	81
169	U Ozarks	G	2	2	2	6	1	88
170	U VA C Wise	G	5	8	3	16	2	78
171	Union C-NE	b	3	1	-1 [1]	4	1	69
172	US C Guard Acad	b	5	5	0	10	1	105
173	US Merchant Marine Acad	bG	4	4	0	8	1	90
174	US Mil Acad	f	21	20	0	41	4	103
175	US Naval Acad		20	20	0	40	3	104
176	UT Valley ST C	Bb	13	12	14	39	4	85
177	VA Wesleyan C	b	4	4	2	10	2	89
178	Vassar C	G	18	28	24	70	7	110
179	VMI	b	6	9	3	18	2	103
180	Wabash C	G	4	6	3	13	2	107
181	Warner Sthrn C	Gf	5	2	3	10	2	79
182	Warren Wilson C	b	6	2	6	13	3 [1]	81
183	Wells C	b	4	3	3	10	2	92
184	Western ST C	bf	4	3	5	12	3	88
185	Westmont C	b	7	4	5	16	3	94
186	Whitman C	b	7	8	15	30	5	168
187	Wiley C	bG	3	2	5	10	4	76
188	Winston-Salem ST U	b	10	8	16	34	4	85
189	Wofford C	bG	7	4	4	15	4	93
190	York C		1	5 [1]	3	8	3	84

Key to Notes on Page 1   1 -- See Footnotes   -1 -- Unavailable   -2 -- Not Applicable

ACRL Library Data Tables 2004
PERSONNEL AND PUBLIC SERVICES

INSTITUTIONS GRANTING BACHELOR OF ARTS DEGREES (Carnegie Code B)

No. of Presentations to Groups 39	Participants in Group Presentations 40	No. of Reference Transactions 41	No. of Initial Circulations 42	Total Circulations 43	ILL Materials Provided 44	ILL Materials Received 45	Survey Question # Institution
36	477	-1	-1	9,037	79	114	TN Wesleyan C
21	327	520	3,299	235	230	278	Tri ST U
36	702	2,184	11,122	13,878	1,804	1.364	Trinity Christian C
25	1,500	4,584	160,689	160,689	250	1.500	Trinity Wstrn U
33	503	1,077	1,978	1,978	0	0	Truett McConnell C
30	661	800	-1 [1]	8,334	555	724	TX Lutheran U
0	0	1,980 [1]	7,945	8,692	746	1.589	U Maine-Machias
48	696	884	7,924	19,071	1,087	2.301	U ME Fort Kent
-1	-1	-1	-1	-1	739	148	U Ozarks
97	1,507	665	7,362	10,580	661	1.030	U VA C Wise
35	458	876	-1	9,605	384	101	Union C-NE
35	617	2,804	30,000	30,000	455	554	US C Guard Acad
14	500	5,200	10,799	-1	50	250	US Merchant Marine Acad
113	2,034	23,413	-1	80,757	1,095	1.716	US Mil Acad
181	-1	11,902	58,460	90,617	4,562	1.696	US Naval Acad
310	6,510	23,764	80,812	109,203	442	2.201	UT Valley ST C
115	1,232	145	5,597	8,701	206	600	VA Wesleyan C
124	2,375	8,327	106,807	124,042	8,317	11.899	Vassar C
56	777	200	21,965	21,965	2,295	1.646	VMI
82	894	1,947	-1	-1	1,826	1.955	Wabash C
37	644	1,830	3,963	4,359	1	230	Warner Sthrn C
47	686	1,530	0 [1]	27,323	659	1.322	Warren Wilson C
25	285	1,560	-1	5,275	362	2.086	Wells C
57	1,500	375	-1	-1	3,381	2.124	Western ST C
23	451	1,282	8,217	10,515	507	1.618	Westmont C
63	504	82	49,635	58,968	4,430	4.126	Whitman C
32	398	563	267	275	2	9	Wiley C
150	2,904	2,152	12,324	17,250	800	119	Winston-Salem ST U
67	1,005	1,967	-1	14,994	483	766	Wofford C
6	110	1,275	5,887	5,887 [1]	140	335	York C

ACRL Library Data Tables 2004
PERSONNEL AND PUBLIC SERVICES

INSTITUTIONS GRANTING MASTER OF ARTS AND PROFESSIONAL DEGREES (Carnegie Code M)

Lib. No.	Institution	Notes	Professional Staff (FTE) 33	Support Staff (FTE) 34	Student Assistants (FTE) 35	Total Staff (FTE) 36	No. of Staffed Service Points 37	Weekly Public Service Hours 38
1	Abilene Christian U	bG	12	14	14	39	7	93
2	Agnes Scott C	G	5	6	4	15	3	92
3	Albany C Pharmacy		3	2	1	5	1	86
4	Albany Law Schl Union U	GL	8	9	3	19	2	104
5	Alcorn ST U	bG	9	17	3	29	6	87
6	Amer Intl C	b	4	3	7	14	2	82
7	Amer U Puerto Rico	Bb	8	13	8	29	6	77
8	Anderson U		6	3	7	16	3	91
9	Angelo ST U		10	13	8	31	5	95
10	Aquinas C MI	b	6	4	10	20	3	88
11	Ark Tech U	G	7	10	5	22	4	89
12	Armstrong Atlantic ST U	bG	11	9	7	27	4	73
13	Assemblies God Theo Sem	f	2	3	4	8	1	80
14	Assumption C	bG	8	4	7	19	2	90
15	Athenaeum of Ohio		2	1	2	5	1	68
16	Auburn U Montgomery	b	10	13	13	36	4	87
17	Augusta ST U	bG	9	21	3	33	4	86
18	Augustana C SF	bG	6	7	5	18	2	89
19	Austin C	b	6	6	13	25	4	99
20	Austin Presb Theo Sem	f	5	3	2	10	6	73
21	Averett C	b	4	5	2	11	2	90
22	Babson C	bG	17	2	9	28	2	102
23	Baker C System	Bb	28	1	19	48	18	76
24	Baker U	G	4	3	2	9	84	83
25	Baptist Bible C and Sem	bf	1	5	2	8	2	77
26	Bayamon Central U	bf	12	20	20	52	6	48
27	Bellevue U	bf	5	9	2	15	3	77
28	Bennington C	b	4	5	3	12	1	98
29	Bethel C IN	bf	4	2	5	11	2	79
30	Birmingham Southern C	bG	6 1	6	6	18	2	91
31	Bluffton C	b	5	2	4	11	2	83
32	BowlGrn SU Fireld	b	2	2	2	6	2	63
33	Bradley U	b	11	21	14	46	6	96
34	Brescia U	bG	2	2	2	6	1	75
35	Brooks Institute	B	2	3	2	7	2	135
36	Bryn Athyn C	b	3	4	1	8	2	68
37	Buena Vista U		4	4	3	11	2	100
38	Butler U	b	13	14	9	35	3	100
39	C Atlantic	b	3	2	4	9	2	15 1
40	C Mt St Joseph	b	6	2	12	20	2	87

Key to Notes on Page 1   1 -- See Footnotes   -1 -- Unavailable   -2 -- Not Applicable

ACRL Library Data Tables 2004
PERSONNEL AND PUBLIC SERVICES

INSTITUTIONS GRANTING MASTER OF ARTS AND PROFESSIONAL DEGREES (Carnegie Code M)

No. of Presentations to Groups 39	Participants in Group Presentations 40	No. of Reference Transactions 41	No. of Initial Circulations 42	Total Circulations 43	ILL Materials Provided 44	ILL Materials Received 45	Survey Question # Institution
98	2,713	33,485	43,204	46,768	1,890	1,654	Abilene Christian U
33	567	102	23,823	30,858	1,931	1,742	Agnes Scott C
16	970	5,980	4,242	8,485	633	1,359	Albany C Pharmacy
22	280	16,800	7,854	8,500	587	368	Albany Law Schl Union U
390	8,381	2,168	2,409	3,909	59	269	Alcorn ST U
49	882	1,128	3,012	3,573	1,172	355	Amer Intl C
113	1,602	15,838	2,205	-1 [1]	8	16	Amer U Puerto Rico
124	1,984	864	23,176	31,352	2,237	1,397	Anderson U
143	2,884	10,309	30,960	35,038	3,183	2,146	Angelo ST U
171	1,647	6,856	20,107	24,944	935	1,660	Aquinas C MI
59	1,435	7,486	-1	37,437	1,605	3,135	Ark Tech U
156	2,936	14,100	26,681 [1]	-1 [1]	5,848	4,203	Armstrong Atlantic ST U
3	30	67	-1	17,512	190	236	Assemblies God Theo Sem
63	1,065	130	9,289	18,578	4,338	1,335	Assumption C
56	487	700	10,510	14,089	570	29	Athenaeum of Ohio
98	2,003	13,635	25,000	28,514	2,471	1,681	Auburn U Montgomery
164	3,781	9,280	25,048	29,462	2,251	1,317	Augusta ST U
121	2,533	1,976	18,862	21,094	3,209	2,821	Augustana C SF
46	713	28	-1	10,778	2,311	1,263	Austin C
10	100	20	44,508	44,508 [1]	471	36	Austin Presb Theo Sem
104	1,659	4,523 [1]	11,742	13,358	632	452	Averett C
243	5,163	4,211	-1	8,912	1,146	2,007	Babson C
922	19,807	65,254	99,424	110,466	5,683	5,505	Baker C System
53	615	825	-1 [1]	6,775	2,926	1,038	Baker U
123	2,401	572	12,259	12,560	688	233	Baptist Bible C and Sem
16	300	3,000	1,000	4,000	0	0	Bayamon Central U
96	3,072	5,005	15,079	18,120	1,904	819	Bellevue U
15	200	1,083	-1	78,163	871	2,013	Bennington C
100	3,500	896	14,765	17,387	476	1,220	Bethel C IN
69	1,582	9,120	18,787	24,104	1,783	2,304	Birmingham Southern C
33	645	1,987	5,793	7,730	2,995	4,372	Bluffton C
47 [1]	940	175	-2 [1]	4,773	1,024 [1]	2,258 [1]	BowlGrn SU Fireld
210	2,830	9,686	29,640	45,047	8,726	5,056	Bradley U
26	495	42	5,698	201	415	300	Brescia U
61	2,596	3,440	23,659	26,143	58	32	Brooks Institute
40	360	1,700	5,680	6,702	202	177	Bryn Athyn C
129	2,043	3,622	-1	17,642	2,946	2,489	Buena Vista U
167	4,132	4,706	16,882	26,521	3,985	4,986	Butler U
6	50	-1	-1 [1]	-1	481	1,675	C Atlantic
47	737	5,150	12,572	18,128	1,087	536	C Mt St Joseph

Key to Notes on Page 1   1 -- See Footnotes   -1 -- Unavailable   -2 -- Not Applicable

109

ACRL Library Data Tables 2004
PERSONNEL AND PUBLIC SERVICES

INSTITUTIONS GRANTING MASTER OF ARTS AND PROFESSIONAL DEGREES (Carnegie Code M)

Lib. No.	Institution	Notes	Professional Staff (FTE) 33	Support Staff (FTE) 34	Student Assistants (FTE) 35	Total Staff (FTE) 36	No. of Staffed Service Points 37	Weekly Public Service Hours 38
41	C Mt St Vincent	bG	5	4	2	11	1	84
42	C Our Lady Elms	bG	6	3	4	12	3	90
43	C.R. Drew U Med & Sci	bM	4	8	0	12	2	79
44	CA C Arts & Crafts	b	3	6	2	11	4	82
45	CA St Polytechnic U-Pomona	G	14	37	14	65	3	86
46	CA St U - Sacramento	bG	33	53	37	122	7	97
47	CA ST U Dominguez Hills	b	14	18	7	39	4	83
48	CA ST U Fresno		26	47	39	112	10	91
49	CA ST U Fullerton	Bb	27	43	33	103	7	84
50	CA ST U Hayward	B	14	18	15	47	3	80
51	CA ST U Long Beach	G	31	37	22	90	8	92
52	CA ST U Northridge	bG	31	58	48	137	11	91
53	CA ST U S Bernadino	f	14	29	22	64	5	86
54	CA ST U San Marcos	bG	14 [1]	26 [1]	10 [1]	50 [1]	4	69
55	CA ST U Stanislaus	B	9	17	11	37	4	87
56	CA West Sch Law	GL	9	8	2	19	6	110
57	Calvin C		8	12	12	31	6	88
58	Cameron U	Gf	7	9	24	40	2	86
59	Canisius C	G	9	10	8	27	3	99
60	Carlow C		6	2	5	13	2	90
61	Carroll C-Waukesha		6	3	6	15	2	103
62	Cedar Crest C		6	4	7	17	3	98
63	Cedarville U	G	9	16	6	31	5	85
64	Centenary C	b	3 [1]	5 [1]	3 [1]	10	1	81
65	Centenary C LA	bf	3	9	23 [1]	18	12	98
66	Central Baptist C	bf	2	1	3	5	2	72
67	Central CT ST U		20	18	4	42	7	84
68	Central MO ST U		16	31	22	69	6	96
69	Charleston Sthrn U		7	7	5	19	3	90
70	Chicago ST U	b	26	31	12	69	5	81
71	Chris Newport U		7	12	7	26	2	106
72	Christendom C	Bb	2	3	5	10	2	90
73	Christian Brothers U	b	5	3	4	12	3	83
74	Clarion U PA	Bb	11	14	74	99	92	92
75	Clarke C-IA		6	1	3	10	1	88
76	Clarkson C-NE	f	4	0	0	4	1	74
77	Colorado C	bG	10	14	6	29	5	105
78	Columbia C MO		-1	-1	-1	-1	-1	-1
79	Columbia C SC		6	4	5	15	3	84
80	Columbia Intl U	bf	5	3	4	12	3	88

Key to Notes on Page 1   1 -- See Footnotes   -1 -- Unavailable   -2 -- Not Applicable

INSTITUTIONS GRANTING MASTER OF ARTS AND PROFESSIONAL DEGREES (Carnegie Code M)

No. of Presentations to Groups 39	Participants in Group Presentations 40	No. of Reference Transactions 41	No. of Initial Circulations 42	Total Circulations 43	ILL Materials Provided 44	ILL Materials Received 45	Survey Question # Institution
46	1,322	8,480	4,377	4,440	727	231	C Mt St Vincent
39	636	560	5,006	-1	5,208	306	C Our Lady Elms
35	350	1,820	0 [1]	3,702	1,220	342	C.R. Drew U Med & Sci
31	630	1,829	37,093	51,693	6	7	CA C Arts & Crafts
332	8,105	50,492	232,305	279,988	12,303	13,737	A St Polytechnic U-Pomona
522	12,332	99,000	0 [1]	254,908	13,572	6,158	CA St U - Sacramento
119	3,327	37,842	-1	56,094	8,729	10,014	CA ST U Dominguez Hills
457	10,401	106,284	0	255,340	9,847	9,507	CA ST U Fresno
610	18,031	27,696	0 [1]	282,783	13,375	32,160	CA ST U Fullerton
425	3,653	32,062	54,611	80,545	11,072	9,131	CA ST U Hayward
650	11,061	1,730	271,616	380,698	15,492	15,495	CA ST U Long Beach
1,152	22,283	354,600	310,511	592,024	7,129	5,158	CA ST U Northridge
259	5,327	3,641	91,920	91,920	6,853	5,396	CA ST U S Bernadino
414	7,456	8,805	51,126	64,882	4,063	8,275	CA ST U San Marcos
204	3,567	11,825	-1	63,790	6,004	4,696	CA ST U Stanislaus
44	834	3,584	4,768	8,546	314	527	CA West Sch Law
159	3,180	12,498	0 [1]	118,931	5,988	4,727	Calvin C
222	3,729	12,236	-1	47,950	1,665	2,991	Cameron U
111	2,046	15,495	-1	26,254	1,642	1,747	Canisius C
59	813	4,602	5,692	10,290	5	36	Carlow C
212	4,240	2,976	-1 [1]	18,000	1,101	878	Carroll C-Waukesha
101	558	3,629	17,044	17,044 [1]	2,151	4,663	Cedar Crest C
114	1,786	5,052	-1	67,544	12,024	10,780	Cedarville U
95	1,692	5,614	-1 [1]	6,640	452	733	Centenary C
41	1,271	9,800	10,277	23,088	699	1,987	Centenary C LA
11	219	41	0	7,562	319	15	Central Baptist C
233	4,461	29,642	78,709	88,992	9,685	3,020	Central CT ST U
183	3,192	12,043	729,656	90,768	0	0	Central MO ST U
55	1,146	4,602	-1	14,633	317	228	Charleston Sthrn U
182	3,458	28,099	11,567	21,745	2,492	2,003	Chicago ST U
104	2,646	11,238	40,196	54,484	1,764	3,552	Chris Newport U
8	118	-1	-1	25,523	279	409	Christendom C
31	394	1,611	3,643	3,643	830	389	Christian Brothers U
157	3,983	32,271	72,769	72,769	3,525	1,608	Clarion U PA
34	635	100	7,223	7,223	695	242	Clarke C-IA
11	220	-1	3,108	4,024	1,497	277	Clarkson C-NE
175	2,100	9,612	65,652	65,652	8,621	10,461	Colorado C
-1	-1	-1	-1	-1	-1	-1	Columbia C MO
89	1,364	3,360	-1	-1	109	113	Columbia C SC
118	1,712	95	-1	37,285	2,062	1,102	Columbia Intl U

Key to Notes on Page 1   1 -- See Footnotes   -1 -- Unavailable   -2 -- Not Applicable

INSTITUTIONS GRANTING MASTER OF ARTS AND PROFESSIONAL DEGREES (Carnegie Code M)

Lib. No.	Survey Question # Institution	Notes	Professional Staff (FTE) 33	Support Staff (FTE) 34	Student Assistants (FTE) 35	Total Staff (FTE) 36	No. of Staffed Service Points 37	Weekly Public Service Hours 38
81	Columbus ST U	BG	17	10	4	31	5	88
82	Concordia U Irvine	b	2	1	3	6	1	73
83	Concordia U RiverF	b	4	4	2	10	3	91
84	Concordia U St Paul		5	1	3	9	2	92
85	Cooper Union	b	5	5	1	11	2	69
86	Cornerstone U	bG	4	3	6	12	1	83
87	Creighton U	b	10	10	6	27	2	104
88	Cumberland U		5	0	2	7	1	70
89	CUNY BMB C		28 1	41 1	6	75	3	119
90	CUNY C Stn Island	f	16	30	12	58	6	82
91	CUNY City C	bGM	21	18	17	56	8	88
92	CUNY HH Lehman C	bG	13	21	11	45	6	76 1
93	CUNY John Jay C Crim Just	G	16	9	8	33	1	75
94	CUNY Queens C	bG	21	34	9	64	8	78
95	Curtis Inst Music	G	4	4	2	10	2	53
96	Daniel Webster C	b	5	3	1	9	3	82
97	DeSales U		6	2	7	14	3	168
98	DN Myers C		2	1	2	5	1	73
99	Dominican C San Rafael	b	5 1	7 1	12 1	12	2 1	84 1
100	Dominican U	b	7	11	16	34	2	100
101	Drake U	b	9	13	20	42	3	105
102	Drury C	b	7	5	7	19	3	99
103	E R Aero U		19	18	18	55	3	168
104	Earlham C	Gf	6	6	8	20	1	102
105	Eastern IL U	bG	19	40	16	75	9	93
106	Eastern U	Bb	6	4	3	12	2	91
107	Eastern WA U	Bb	12	31	10	54	7	95
108	Eastrn NM U Main	BbG	11	11	12	34	6	95
109	Edinboro U PA	b	12	11	8	31	5	93
110	Elizabethtown C	b	4	5	4	13	2	107
111	Elmhurst C	b	8	11	5	24	2	94
112	Elon U	b	10	11	6	27	3	109
113	Emmanuel C MA	b	6	2	4	11	2 1	93
114	Emory & Henry C	bGf	6	8	4	18	2	95
115	Evergreen ST C	bGf	8	36	12	56	9	85
116	Fisk U	bG	4	6	3	13	3	81
117	Fitchburg ST C	G	6 1	8 1	4 1	18	2 1	85
118	FL Southern C	bG	6	4	17	27	1	82
119	Fort Hays ST U	b	9	8	19	35	6	96
120	Francis Marion U	G	9	14	8	31	3	87

Key to Notes on Page 1   1 -- See Footnotes   -1 -- Unavailable   -2 -- Not Applicable

INSTITUTIONS GRANTING MASTER OF ARTS AND PROFESSIONAL DEGREES (Carnegie Code M)

No. of Presentations to Groups 39	Participants in Group Presentations 40	No. of Reference Transactions 41	No. of Initial Circulations 42	Total Circulations 43	ILL Materials Provided 44	ILL Materials Received 45	Survey Question # Institution
230	3,021	23,996	-1 [1]	28,269	1,536	2,136	Columbus ST U
26	486	3,252	13,268	-1	2	12	Concordia U Irvine
17	374	-1	28,021	-1	1,167	367	Concordia U RiverF
105	1,600	677	6,448	8,020	313	242	Concordia U St Paul
49	841	3,168	-1	33,769	42	71	Cooper Union
87	1,779	15,704	37,539	-1	2,277	1,081	Cornerstone U
146	2,057	7,072	46,858	51,885	4,061	4,681	Creighton U
20	300	-1	1,902	-1	47	119	Cumberland U
367	5,920	36,677	-1 [1]	84,324	2,612	3,846	CUNY BMB C
220	5,798	46,551	45,157	47,079	1,245	949	CUNY C Stn Island
210	5,420	70,000	24,270	63,683	4,544	4,989	CUNY City C
262 [1]	5,531 [1]	79,144 [1]	54,414	54,414 [1]	2,167	1,699	CUNY HH Lehman C
195	3,246	48,200 [1]	32,567	37,848	1,910	723	CUNY John Jay C Crim Just
407	6,645	1,266	71,655	92,660	2,982	2,767	CUNY Queens C
1	25	130 [1]	7,488	7,488	118	31	Curtis Inst Music
72	911	2,690	10,916	9,962	508	523	Daniel Webster C
115	1,825	5,096	-1	21,022 [1]	2,777	873	DeSales U
4	23	10,400	957	972	0	0	DN Myers C
88	1,760	5,031	6,762	8,461	240	934	Dominican C San Rafael
137	2,192	12,455	15,728	23,576	3,236	4,024	Dominican U
117	1,549	10,167	21,622	35,674	4,855	2,334	Drake U
60	743	4,091	22,369	-1	-1	-1	Drury C
105	2,625	19,392	41,550	51,705	2,436	1,968	E R Aero U
161	2,648	7,852	44,583	57,794	1,789	1,989	Earlham C
168	3,752	52,900	147,476	212,268	15,357	12,248	Eastern IL U
35	750	1,000	-1	23,846	1,362	2,386	Eastern U
177	4,012	12,476	-1	68,476	4,679	6,693	Eastern WA U
50	826	9,231	40,188	43,786	1,906	2,489	Eastrn NM U Main
110	2,524	6,056	-1	62,578	5,903	2,343	Edinboro U PA
63	1,006	2,113	18,510	22,707	2,927	5,213	Elizabethtown C
196	2,940	21,250	17,098	24,707	5,525	2,328	Elmhurst C
178	3,952	6,860	55,856	67,990	4,337	5,864	Elon U
72 [1]	2,325	1,800	-1	3,979	1,162	247	Emmanuel C MA
31	558	1,608	30,816	30,816	3,174	840	Emory & Henry C
117	2,962	5,463	133,281	-1	7,560	7,991	Evergreen ST C
5	142	1,015	4,277	4,651	36	7	Fisk U
83 [1]	1,437 [1]	7,445 [1]	16,221	17,933	5,461	1,370	Fitchburg ST C
42	877	5,338	27,183	29,447	4,366	683	FL Southern C
92	1,630	2,912	234,871	234,871 [1]	5,139	5,899	Fort Hays ST U
94	1,213	5,864	12,556	17,591	1,495	509	Francis Marion U

Key to Notes on Page 1   1 -- See Footnotes   -1 -- Unavailable   -2 -- Not Applicable

INSTITUTIONS GRANTING MASTER OF ARTS AND PROFESSIONAL DEGREES (Carnegie Code M)

Lib. No.	Institution	Notes	Professional Staff (FTE) 33	Support Staff (FTE) 34	Student Assistants (FTE) 35	Total Staff (FTE) 36	No. of Staffed Service Points 37	Weekly Public Service Hours 38
121	Franklin Inst Boston	b	2	0	1	2	1	56
122	Franklin U		9	0	3	12	2	97
123	Free Will Baptist Bible C	bG	1	2	2	4	1	70
124	Frostburg ST U	bG	8	15	1	24	3	96
125	Furman U	G	13	14	9	36	4	101
126	GA SWstrn ST U	b	5	5	2	12	2 [1]	75 [1]
127	Gardner-Webb U	BbG	7	8	3	18	5	85
128	Geneva C	G	6	3	7	16	7	77
129	Georgetown C		4	7	6	-1	-1	-1
130	Goucher C	b	8	5	4	17	3	94
131	Governors ST U	bG	7	24	3	34	2	75
132	Greenville C		4	1	4	9	2	87
133	Grove City C	b	6	4	3	13	3	71
134	Harding U Main	bG	7	8	6	21	4	86
135	Hebrew C		8	3	1	12	2	59
136	Heidelberg C	Bbf	3	5	5	13	3	86
137	Hillsdale Free Will Baptist C		2	0	1	4	6	66
138	Holy Apostles C & Sem	bGf	1	2	2	5	3	78
139	Hood C	G	6 [1]	4 [1]	4 [1]	14 [1]	3	73
140	Humboldt ST U	G	15	23	10	36	4	96
141	IN Inst of Tech	bf	1	0	0	1	3	70
142	IN U Kokomo	G	5	3	5	13	2	68
143	IN U S Bend	b	15	6	9	31	4	98
144	IN U-Purdue U Ft Wayne	G	13	12	4	29	2	90
145	IN Wesleyan U	B	12	7	7	26	7	80
146	Intl Fine Arts C		1	0	6	7	10	74
147	Jacksonville ST U	bG	17	17	14	48	13	87
148	Johnson Bible C		2	3	3	8	2	73
149	Kean U		10	18	7	34	4	80
150	Keene State C	b	11	11	8	30	4	96
151	Kent ST U Stark	b	4	3	4	11	1	75
152	Kentucky Christian C	f	2 [1]	2 [1]	6	10	1	68
153	Kentucky ST U	G	10	11	6	26	4	80
154	Kettering U	b	5	8	1	14	2	87
155	King's C PA		6	8	3	16	3	90
156	LaGrange C	Bb	4	3	-1	-1	3	81
157	Lakeland C-AB		3	1	3	7	1	90
158	Lakeview C Nursing	b	1	0	1	1	1	40
159	Lancaster Bible C		4	1	4	9	1	91
160	Lander U	G	5	5	3	13	2	81

Key to Notes on Page 1   1 -- See Footnotes   -1 -- Unavailable   -2 -- Not Applicable

ACRL Library Data Tables 2004
PERSONNEL AND PUBLIC SERVICES

INSTITUTIONS GRANTING MASTER OF ARTS AND PROFESSIONAL DEGREES (Carnegie Code M)

No. of Presentations to Groups 39	Participants in Group Presentations 40	No. of Reference Transactions 41	No. of Initial Circulations 42	Total Circulations 43	ILL Materials Provided 44	ILL Materials Received 45	Survey Question # Institution
44	439	1,249	168	192	0	7	Franklin Inst Boston
-1	-1	-1	-1	-1	-1	-1	Franklin U
16	378	540	6,729	9,761	0	33	Free Will Baptist Bible C
191	3,293	4,563	17,018	21,218	2,112	2,588	Frostburg ST U
156	3,220	9,090	28,430	42,002	1,571	7,303	Furman U
41 [1]	620 [1]	2,400 [1]	5,475	8,017	1,282	1,451	GA SWstrn ST U
72	795	2,600	15,880	18,243	1,251	886	Gardner-Webb U
36	540	8,496	-1	81,626	118	119	Geneva C
-1	-1	-1	-1	-1	-1	-1	Georgetown C
91	1,130	3,213	19,166	23,077	918	1,225	Goucher C
138	1,383	27,354	28,803	33,465	8,944	2,563	Governors ST U
64	1,151	2,218	16,000	22,000	2,250	4,859	Greenville C
33	0	3,131	119,000	0	0	1,141	Grove City C
130	2,701	12,401	49,165	58,349	4,619	1,832	Harding U Main
10	240	529	7,233 [1]	9,731	9	262	Hebrew C
52	920	58	5,243	5,828	2,516	2,479	Heidelberg C
13	125	1,104	1,358	1,823	1	102	Hillsdale Free Will Baptist C
2	34	182	1,368	1,368	35	32	Holy Apostles C & Sem
85	944	390	-1 [1]	15,270	2,992	3,150	Hood C
137	3,168	14,602	-1	160,524	7,415	5,619	Humboldt ST U
30	270	40	60	60	1	1	IN Inst of Tech
128	2,918	3,864	16,834	17,733	910	298	IN U Kokomo
680	5,282	21,368	33,428	45,257	2,768	5,753	IN U S Bend
92	1,500	17,992 [1]	34,333	58,441	2,890	10,102	IN U-Purdue U Ft Wayne
251	4,616	4,116	55,757	59,765	3,078	1,581	IN Wesleyan U
14	20	1,273	3,517	4,664	0	57	Intl Fine Arts C
229	5,740	33,600	-1	63,057	2,433	585	Jacksonville ST U
45	926	560	14,892	18,179	8	46	Johnson Bible C
221	2,931	-1	-1	-1	3,674	739	Kean U
157	3,055	5,696	75,334	83,447	7,143	5,284	Keene State C
186	8,604	1,316	8,074	10,264	2,143	3,695	Kent ST U Stark
17	459	28 [1]	11,383	11,098	263	645	Kentucky Christian C
111	2,029	3,505	4,570	4,830	455	321	Kentucky ST U
27	504	1,670	16,324	17,384	2,151	1,017	Kettering U
61	1,221	0	-1	15,528	1,230	1,387	King's C PA
127 [1]	1,139	-1	-1	14,994	609	812	LaGrange C
7	104	-1	-1 [1]	8,425	135	360	Lakeland C-AB
4	61	679	1,244	1,244	173	132	Lakeview C Nursing
36	751	-1	-1	17,795	694	244	Lancaster Bible C
184	1,729	5,028	-1	11,653	400	629	Lander U

Key to Notes on Page 1   1 -- See Footnotes   -1 -- Unavailable   -2 -- Not Applicable

ACRL Library Data Tables 2004
PERSONNEL AND PUBLIC SERVICES

INSTITUTIONS GRANTING MASTER OF ARTS AND PROFESSIONAL DEGREES (Carnegie Code M)

Lib. No.	Institution	Notes	Professional Staff (FTE) 33	Support Staff (FTE) 34	Student Assistants (FTE) 35	Total Staff (FTE) 36	No. of Staffed Service Points 37	Weekly Public Service Hours 38
161	Langston U	BG	10	5	12	27	6	81
162	Laurentian U JN	bG	8 [1]	27	2	37	2	86
163	Le Moyne C	G	7	7	12	26	4	97
164	Lebanon Valley C	b	4	4	6	14	2	100
165	Lewis U		6	6	6	18	2	85
166	Lewis&Clark C	G	11	10	10	31	2	141
167	Lincoln U-MO	b	9	7	3	19	4	92
168	Lindsey Wilson C	bG	3 [1]	5 [1]	2 [1]	10	4	88
169	Lipscomb U		6	4	5	15	3	88
170	Lock Haven U PA	BbG	9	9	10	28	4	87
171	Longwood C	G	7	19	9	35	2	86
172	Lourdes C		2	1	0	4	1	63
173	Loyola Marymount U	b	17	23	17	57	4	97
174	Loyola U New Orleans	G	14	20	15	49	2	118
175	Lubbock Christian U	b	4	5	7 [1]	16	2	92
176	Luth Theo Sem Philly	bf	2	3	1	6	1	70
177	Lynchburg C		6	4	7	17	2	94
178	Malone C		5	4	3	12	2	91
179	Manchester C		4	3	3	9	2	88
180	Manhattan C		9	21	3	33	3	168
181	Marist C	G	13	6	10	28	2	96
182	Mary Baldwin C	b	5	3	5	13	4	96
183	Mary Washington C	BbG	13	13	8	34	3	92
184	Marymount U	G	10 [1]	23 [1]	-1 [1]	-1 [1]	4	91
185	Maryville U St Louis	b	5	8	3	16	2	87
186	McNeese ST U		15	11	13	39	6	80
187	Medical C Wisconsin	BbGM	14	20	0	34	4	45
188	Merrimack C	b	6	5	8	19	4	96
189	MidAmer Nazarene U		3	3	3	8	73	77
190	Millikin U	bG	5	7	4 [1]	16	2 [1]	92
191	Millsaps C	G	5	4	5	14	2	103
192	Minnesota ST U-Mankato	bG	20	21	23	64	2	93
193	Minot ST U	G	8	7	8	23	2	79
194	Monterey Inst Intl St	f	4	3	6	13	3	95
195	Moravian C		5	6	7	18	3	102
196	Morehead ST U	G	13	26	19	58	4	91
197	Morningside C	bG	3	2	2	7	3 [1]	83 [1]
198	MS Valley ST U	BG	5	13	4	22	7	78
199	Mt Holyoke C		13	18	10	41	3	109
200	Mt Marty C		2	1	2	-1	-1	-1

Key to Notes on Page 1   1 -- See Footnotes   -1 -- Unavailable   -2 -- Not Applicable

ACRL Library Data Tables 2004
PERSONNEL AND PUBLIC SERVICES

INSTITUTIONS GRANTING MASTER OF ARTS AND PROFESSIONAL DEGREES (Carnegie Code M)

No. of Presentations to Groups 39	Participants in Group Presentations 40	No. of Reference Transactions 41	No. of Initial Circulations 42	Total Circulations 43	ILL Materials Provided 44	ILL Materials Received 45	Survey Question # Institution
62	1,581	9,516	3,286	3,344	596	509	Langston U
85	1,445	-1 [1]	62,412	10,509	2,694	-1 [1]	Laurentian U JN
173	3,070	4,170	-1	38,284	2,559	2,435	Le Moyne C
82	1,120	843	38,444	38,444	1,985	4,709	Lebanon Valley C
91	1,613	2,104	8,755	10,097	1,523	324	Lewis U
67	1,019	4,783	94,393	119,356	20,609	17,139	Lewis&Clark C
107	1,605	1,780	6,137	6,728	791	1,172	Lincoln U-MO
104 [1]	1,830	3,750 [1]	-1 [1]	14,209	81	1,127	Lindsey Wilson C
72 [1]	1,155	-1	-1	28,258	1,654	440	Lipscomb U
168	3,859	2,329	22,192	22,192	3,121	1,481	Lock Haven U PA
134	3,350	19,800	122,162	122,162	5,184	1,680	Longwood C
20	251	204	2,859	3,582	1,005	1,418	Lourdes C
218	3,353	9,922	70,485	71,348	7,029	4,739	Loyola Marymount U
244	3,620	14,893	-1	83,851	2,834	3,047	Loyola U New Orleans
48	691	-1	11,567	11,567	0	8	Lubbock Christian U
3	53	260	11,447	11,447	482	113	Luth Theo Sem Philly
97	1,654	-1	22,993	26,451	2,702	2,654	Lynchburg C
27	437	7,700 [1]	17,642	18,803	6,848	4,172	Malone C
43	900	3,080	9,950	11,300	981	690	Manchester C
22	306	3,380	-1	9,827	1,583	462	Manhattan C
91	1,719	15,243	-1	16,480	752	847	Marist C
111	798	1,815	19,720	19,720 [1]	1,032	2,241	Mary Baldwin C
123	3,075	9,687	-1	67,300	4,887	4,828	Mary Washington C
145	2,410	7,028	32,082	39,107	1,399	254	Marymount U
80	1,159	6,150	-1	9,585	2,460	4,586	Maryville U St Louis
100	2,410	9,409	25,994	28,692	1,802	1,853	McNeese ST U
166	3,189	42,574	62,448	27,645	8,005	10,685	Medical C Wisconsin
127	1,807	5,878 [1]	13,476	14,173	4,240	3,432	Merrimack C
16	240	255	8,135	2,596	166	660	MidAmer Nazarene U
250 [1]	900 [1]	-1 [1]	24,398	30,877	3,087	3,887	Millikin U
39	564	2,681	-1 [1]	23,938	812	2,807	Millsaps C
308	7,297	17,702	122,077	136,029	9,535	13,244	Minnesota ST U-Mankato
168	1,971	9,828	30,521	0 [1]	4,685	6,481	Minot ST U
50	500	1,115	33,532	40,240	100	700	Monterey Inst Intl St
103	1,983	5,000	43,262	43,462	3,217	2,522	Moravian C
156	3,212	14,208	80,721	108,852	4,324	2,160	Morehead ST U
92	1,316	1,447	6,159	6,159	790	428	Morningside C
57	1,200	8,338	4,299	3,022	370	292	MS Valley ST U
109	1,635	8,000	-1	95,766	7,572	4,180	Mt Holyoke C
-1	-1	-1	-1	-1	-1	-1	Mt Marty C

Key to Notes on Page 1   1 -- See Footnotes   -1 -- Unavailable   -2 -- Not Applicable

ACRL Library Data Tables 2004
PERSONNEL AND PUBLIC SERVICES

INSTITUTIONS GRANTING MASTER OF ARTS AND PROFESSIONAL DEGREES (Carnegie Code M)

Lib. No.	Institution	Notes	Professional Staff (FTE) 33	Support Staff (FTE) 34	Student Assistants (FTE) 35	Total Staff (FTE) 36	No. of Staffed Service Points 37	Weekly Public Service Hours 38
201	Mt Mary C-WI	bf	5	3	3	11	2	79
202	MT ST U Northern	bG	2	4	5	11	2	81
203	Mt St Vincent U	Gf	4	12	2	18	2	83
204	MT Tech U Montana	bG	3	6	3	10	2 [1]	74
205	Murray ST U-KY	L	13	23	18	54	9	102
206	Muskingum C		6	2	2	10	2	89
207	Natl C Naturopathic Med	bM	2	2	3	7	1	72
208	Natl Defense U	bGf	18 [1]	10	0	28	3	63 [1]
209	NC Sch Arts		7	8	4	18	3	85
210	NEastrn IL U	B	19	38	8	64	6	78
211	Nipissing U	B	5	14	2	21	4	81
212	NJ City U		15	15	18	48	3	83
213	NM Highlands U	B	5	9	4	18	2	81
214	North Central C		7	7	7	21	4	97
215	Northern KY U	b	18	22	24	64	3	168
216	Northern ST U	bGf	5	6	6	17	2	86
217	Northwest C	b	5	4	3	12	2	91
218	Norwich U	G	6	8	7	21	3	104
219	Notre Dame C OH		3	2	4	9	1	72
220	Notre Dame Sem	b	2	-1	1 [1]	2	2 [1]	46
221	NW MO ST U	bG	9	14	7	30	3 [1]	92
222	NY Inst Tech Islip		4	2	2	8	2	70
223	NY Inst Tech Main	M	13 [1]	14 [1]	8	34	7	106
224	Oberlin C	B	18	33	29	79	7	48
225	OH U Lancaster	b	2	2	2	6	2	67
226	Olivet Nazarene U	G	6	7	10	22	2	89
227	Otterbein C	G	8	6	5	18	2	89
228	Pace U Law		26	24	9	59	8	113
229	Pacific Lutheran U	f	10	16	13	39	3	95
230	Pacific Union C		6	3	4	13	4	84
231	Palm Beach Atl C	b	5	5	5	15	1	85
232	Pfeiffer U	Bb	5	1	2	8	3	77
233	Philadelphia U	b	6	8	13	27	3	91
234	Plymouth ST C	G	8	12	3	23	4	94
235	Pont C Josephinum		2	2	1	5	1	67
236	Pope John Ntl Sem	bf	2	0	2	4	2	45
237	Prescott C	Bb	2	4	1	7	2	78
238	Providence C	b	12	17	4	33	3	107
239	Purchase C SUNY		6	16	5	26	3	105
240	Purdue U Calumet	G	9	9	3	21	3	74

Key to Notes on Page 1   1 -- See Footnotes   -1 -- Unavailable   -2 -- Not Applicable

ACRL Library Data Tables 2004
PERSONNEL AND PUBLIC SERVICES

INSTITUTIONS GRANTING MASTER OF ARTS AND PROFESSIONAL DEGREES (Carnegie Code M)

No. of Presentations to Groups 39	Participants in Group Presentations 40	No. of Reference Transactions 41	No. of Initial Circulations 42	Total Circulations 43	ILL Materials Provided 44	ILL Materials Received 45	Survey Question # Institution
52	610	990	14,550	22,242	286	132	Mt Mary C-WI
43	775	39	-1	6,370	755	475	MT ST U Northern
56	1,267	10,763	52,105 [1]	62,992 [1]	5,328	3,270	Mt St Vincent U
78	16	1,767	-1	4,827	1,248	2,794	MT Tech U Montana
191	3,760	1,462	25,597	32,357	1,998	6,421	Murray ST U-KY
130	2,300	175	8,506	10,028	161	336	Muskingum C
12	180	1,200	17,000	18,500	500	450	Natl C Naturopathic Med
350	2,500	12,000	15,000	16,200	885	474	Natl Defense U
88	755	3,725	58,200	62,100	45	95	NC Sch Arts
277	5,366	53,900	-1	79,900	15,674	6,088	NEastrn IL U
185	3,515	24,000	66,121	84,593	298	1,289	Nipissing U
210	3,887	19,440	20,000	23,500	873	249	NJ City U
27	369	11,453	4,332	4,332	902	2,106	NM Highlands U
132	2,394	3,977	-1	27,696	3,287	2,736	North Central C
213	7,455	21,350	40,711	58,652	2,847	4,174	Northern KY U
284	5,469	6,760	-1	22,871	3,294	1,295	Northern ST U
53	1,227	2,888	12,227	14,021	957	893	Northwest C
63	1,277	1,904 [1]	-1	23,674	1,426	286	Norwich U
-1	-1	-1	-1	-1	-1	-1	Notre Dame C OH
5 [1]	80	1,012	4,984	-1	8	34	Notre Dame Sem
227	3,868	2,600 [1]	-1	57,783	7,065	4,124	NW MO ST U
64	18	4,810	-1	-1	-1	-1	NY Inst Tech Islip
100	1,218	3,810	19,086	-1	1,979	1,475	NY Inst Tech Main
222	2,715	12,208	134,074	-1	16,380	19,569	Oberlin C
72	1,281	14,664	114,492	16,207	1,616	838	OH U Lancaster
112	2,434	2,236	38,083	38,083	3,830	3,047	Olivet Nazarene U
104	1,823	6,839	28,077	33,935	8,176	6,931	Otterbein C
359	6,202	51,980	33,057	39,077	2,548	6,380 [1]	Pace U Law
132	2,528	5,098 [1]	-1	44,048	4,322	7,223	Pacific Lutheran U
30	600	2,547	10,333	12,156	287	906	Pacific Union C
62	1,178	95	19,611	24,124	1,932	491	Palm Beach Atl C
29	458	20	6,204	6,204	305	485	Pfeiffer U
208	3,478	3,510	22,674	27,172	1,330	1,995	Philadelphia U
137	2,971	5,151	33,588	38,968	3,027	1,688	Plymouth ST C
19	-1	-1	-1	-1	-1	-1	Pont C Josephinum
2	40	1,000	3,563	3,563 [1]	8	18	Pope John Ntl Sem
65	1,146	730	18,538	25,324	1,549	1,093	Prescott C
93	1,209	17,784 [1]	-1	31,842	1,333	857	Providence C
55	1,030	11,340	38,795	-2	116	1,259	Purchase C SUNY
138	-1	16,329	27,677	30,527	2,420	3,299	Purdue U Calumet

Key to Notes on Page 1   1 -- See Footnotes   -1 -- Unavailable   -2 -- Not Applicable

119

INSTITUTIONS GRANTING MASTER OF ARTS AND PROFESSIONAL DEGREES (Carnegie Code M)

Lib. No.	Survey Question # / Institution	Notes	Professional Staff (FTE) 33	Support Staff (FTE) 34	Student Assistants (FTE) 35	Total Staff (FTE) 36	No. of Staffed Service Points 37	Weekly Public Service Hours 38
241	Purdue U North Central	G	3	3	3	9	2	61
242	Quincy U	b	3	4	8	15	4	84
243	R.Wesleyan C	G	5	5	3	13	2	93
244	Radford U	G	17	17	19	53	4	91
245	Ramapo C NJ	bf	9	17	21	47	4	93
246	Recnstrctnst Rabbinical C	b	2	1	0	2	2	51
247	RI Sch Design		7	13	7	27	5	88
248	Rivier C	b	12	3	4	19	3	98
249	Rockhurst U	bG	5	5	8	18	2	95
250	Roger Williams U	G	11	10	3	24	3	96
251	Roosevelt U	Bb	15	15	5	35	6	66
252	Rosemont C	b	5	4	8	17	2	134
253	Salem Teiko U	G	1	3	3	6	1	77
254	Salisbury ST U		11	10	10	31	2	100
255	San Jose ST U	bG	31	51	38	120	18	81
256	Savannah ST U	bf	5	7	2	14	6	82
257	Schreiner C		4	4	1	9	3	75
258	SE LA U	Bf	20	22	39	81	7	87
259	SE MO ST U		19	19	14	52	4	93
260	SE Oklahoma St U	b	5	4	8	17	2	83
261	Seton Hill C		5	2	3	10	1	87
262	SF Consrv Music		1	1	3	5	2	76
263	Shaw U		8	5	4	17	6	88
264	Shorter C	Bb	5	1	3	9	2	81
265	Silver Lake C	f	3	1	1	5	2 1	65
266	Sisseton-Wahpeton CC	bG	1	1	0	2	4	42
267	Southrn C Opt	M	2	1	3	6	1	85
268	Southrn IL U Edward		21	47	31	99	4	94
269	Southrn OR U	G	13 1	9	9	31	4	69
270	Spring Hill C	bf	6	7	2	15	4	90
271	St Ambrose U		8	8	6	21	4	94
272	St C.Borromeo Sem	bf	1	5	1	7	2	82
273	St Cloud ST U	b	15	20	15	50	5	93
274	St Francis C PA	G	9	9	1	19	2	100
275	St Francis-Xavier U	bf	13	19	3	35	9	92
276	St John Fisher C	bGf	7	7	6	20	2	94
277	St Joseph C Suffolk	b	8	7	4	19	6	69
278	St Joseph's C IN	bG	4	4	2	9	1	84
279	St Joseph's C NY	bf	5	6	3	14	6	82
280	St Joseph's Sem	b	2	2	0	4	2	62

Key to Notes on Page 1   1 -- See Footnotes   -1 -- Unavailable   -2 -- Not Applicable

INSTITUTIONS GRANTING MASTER OF ARTS AND PROFESSIONAL DEGREES (Carnegie Code M)

No. of Presentations to Groups 39	Participants in Group Presentations 40	No. of Reference Transactions 41	No. of Initial Circulations 42	Total Circulations 43	ILL Materials Provided 44	ILL Materials Received 45	Survey Question # Institution
82	1,538	1,306	5,547	-1	548	1,081	Purdue U North Central
50	559	1,858	13,476	16,012	1,825	762	Quincy U
89	1,150	1,310	12,750	14,588	1,687	2,009	R.Wesleyan C
308	4,411	16,609	50,861	60,560	7,679	6,066	Radford U
110	2,463	5,620	19,083	26,924	848	803	Ramapo C NJ
6	9	5,200	3,000	3,280	88	246	Recnstrctnst Rabbinical C
286	1,743	4,321	59,777	67,323	515	131	RI Sch Design
47	705	8,631	17,601	17,601	1,895	2,628	Rivier C
76	863	750	-1	11,004	565	863	Rockhurst U
423	10,998	3,630	25,357	32,023	986	1,883	Roger Williams U
178	2,670	18,128	26,117	35,205	7,029	5,888	Roosevelt U
43	393	1,070	10,000	10,204	472	442	Rosemont C
3	25	95	1,493	1,493	8	158	Salem Teiko U
85	1,847	13,091	-1	35,863	914	1,519	Salisbury ST U
736	17,069	173,553	304,418	471,269	8,172	20,140	San Jose ST U
73	812	5,027	6,480	7,194	-1 [1]	-1 [1]	Savannah ST U
52	932	325	7,153	8,171	94	456	Schreiner C
259	6,003	30,678	-1	43,866	6,426	5,618	SE LA U
206	4,223	9,579	-1	68,557	4,296	2,513	SE MO ST U
167	3,502	3,246	16,510	20,694	1,733	1,272	SE Oklahoma St U
46	1,150	520	12,673	17,363	493	670	Seton Hill C
19	150	3,500	32,552	38,600	36	48	SF Consrv Music
16	400	3,408	1,272	1,297	0 [1]	23	Shaw U
57	328	572	13,074	13,806	487	420	Shorter C
29	247	3,840 [1]	10,762	11,579	718	212	Silver Lake C
0	0	2,400 [1]	3,485	3,701	0 [1]	440 [1]	Sisseton-Wahpeton CC
2	142	1,280	1,006	1,155	22	36	Southrn C Opt
532	9,869	97,900	52,925	76,373	13,918	12,800	Southrn IL U Edward
126	2,754	8,743	47,463	70,575	8,166	9,233	Southrn OR U
80	1,729	4,385	0 [1]	7,169	653	963	Spring Hill C
434	2,497	9,931	-1 [1]	24,383	5,060	3,636	St Ambrose U
54	1,520	528	9,374	13,434	424	308	St C.Borromeo Sem
274	7,465	28,022	58,775	67,441	5,785	7,733	St Cloud ST U
239	507	2,861	15,956	19,172	598	1,342	St Francis C PA
139	2,526	14,302	86,869	95,080	4,597	5,910	St Francis-Xavier U
111	2,166	8,053	-1	40,748	2,344	2,686	St John Fisher C
147	2,425	1,300	24,187	28,075	309	206	St Joseph C Suffolk
40	610	600	9,780	-1	472	346	St Joseph's C IN
35	400	500	10,000	12,000	123	105	St Joseph's C NY
0	0	10	4,816	5,743	5	85	St Joseph's Sem

Key to Notes on Page 1   1 -- See Footnotes   -1 -- Unavailable   -2 -- Not Applicable

INSTITUTIONS GRANTING MASTER OF ARTS AND PROFESSIONAL DEGREES (Carnegie Code M)

Lib. No.	Institution	Notes	Professional Staff (FTE) 33	Support Staff (FTE) 34	Student Assistants (FTE) 35	Total Staff (FTE) 36	No. of Staffed Service Points 37	Weekly Public Service Hours 38
281	St Mary's U MN	G	5	3	2	10	2	96
282	St Meinrad Theo	b	1	4	1	6	1	68
283	St Michael's C	b	9	9	7	25	2	100
284	St Norbert C		5	8	2	15	3 [1]	100
285	St Patrick's Sem	f	3	1	2	6	3	51 [1]
286	St Peter's Abbey & C	bGf	1	1	1	3	1	45
287	ST U W GA		14	14	4	32	2	85
288	St Vincent Sem		3	0	1	3	3	101
289	St. John's C		3	3	4	13	4	88
290	Stetson U	B	10	12	6	28	3	92
291	Sthrn Polytech ST U	G	6	3	4	13	2	80
292	Stonehill C	bG	10	10	9	29	3	99
293	Sul Ross ST U	bf	8 [1]	8 [1]	18 [1]	37	3 [1]	86
294	SUNY Brockport		15	16	15	46	7	105
295	SUNY Buffalo		22	22	14	58	3	100
296	SUNY C Potsdam	G	13	10	8	30	3	94
297	SUNY IT Utica	G	7	5	4	16	2	86
298	SUNY Oneonta	G	14	17	12	43	4	100
299	SUNY Oswego	G	18	19	8	45	2	95
300	SW MO ST U	B	27	35	30	92	11	99
301	SWstrn Adventist U	b	3	1	10	14	2	77
302	SWstrn OK ST U	bf	7	11	25	43	2	85
303	Tabor C	b	1	1	2	4	1	90
304	Tiffin U	b	2	1	2	4	1	82
305	TM Cooley Law Sch	BbGL	22	28	6	56	9	124
306	Trinity Luth Sem		2	3	3	7	1	73
307	Trinity U	b	10	31	10	51	2	96
308	Trinity U		4	2	2	7	3	79
309	Troy ST U	Bb	10	9	8	27	3	86
310	Troy ST U Dothan	bG	4	4	4	12	3	64
311	Truman ST U	b	15	13	14	42	5	106
312	TX Chiro C	bM	3	2	2	7	5	81
313	U Arts	bG	6	8	3	17	4	77
314	U C Cape	bG	6	10	-1	16	2	77
315	U Charleston	b	3	2	1	6	1	80
316	U DC	b	11	20	-1	31	10	74
317	U Del Turabo		11	7	-1	18	10	86
318	U Findlay	bG	4	6	7	17	3	98
319	U Hawaii-Hilo	bG	9	12	9	30	2	81
320	U HI-Kauai CC	b	4	3	1	7	2	56

Key to Notes on Page 1   1 -- See Footnotes   -1 -- Unavailable   -2 -- Not Applicable

ACRL Library Data Tables 2004
PERSONNEL AND PUBLIC SERVICES

INSTITUTIONS GRANTING MASTER OF ARTS AND PROFESSIONAL DEGREES (Carnegie Code M)

No. of Presentations to Groups 39	Participants in Group Presentations 40	No. of Reference Transactions 41	No. of Initial Circulations 42	Total Circulations 43	ILL Materials Provided 44	ILL Materials Received 45	Survey Question # Institution
36	601	3,191	22,301	23,766	2,899	3,022	St Mary's U MN
10	10	1,500	-1	11,776	375	144	St Meinrad Theo
124	1,699	4,221	-1	30,024	2,165	4,496	St Michael's C
70	700	4,500	23,101	26,916	1,299	1,899	St Norbert C
6	180	1,500	29,705	3,307	236	21	St Patrick's Sem
-1	-1	-1	1,348	1,420	76	175	St Peter's Abbey & C
151	2,265	23,504	-1	47,612	4,948	3,024	ST U W GA
1	15	25	4,427	4,937	17	13	St Vincent Sem
20	180	658	18,678	36,785	236	715	St. John's C
79	1,185	7,271	36,738	42,734	3,635	2,117	Stetson U
21	355	1,756	11,119	16,134	1,385	344	Sthrn Polytech ST U
69	1,533	5,902	27,339 [1]	27,339	1,852	3,776	Stonehill C
120	2,220	10,424	18,939	20,070	2,788	1,812	Sul Ross ST U
120	2,400	14,427	66,600	98,273	10,984	3,975	SUNY Brockport
378 [1]	3,809 [1]	28,413 [1]	41,163	60,870	4,561	1,486	SUNY Buffalo
165	2,798	7,200	84,368	97,028	3,217	5,848	SUNY C Potsdam
38	760 [1]	7,228	-2 [1]	4,655	4,055	1,178	SUNY IT Utica
258	5,628	17,600	39,331	49,248	4,461	1,881	SUNY Oneonta
264	5,814	11,100	-1	79,836	6,836	5,606	SUNY Oswego
719	16,070	53,578	146,262	170,280	5,756	7,588	SW MO ST U
20 [1]	240 [1]	3,000 [1]	19,593	22,089	1	139	SWstrn Adventist U
186	5,042	9,454	11,898	23,959	4,752	976	SWstrn OK ST U
22	352	62	5,148	6,323	783	1,339	Tabor C
25	600	202	4,118	4,515	1,629	1,360	Tiffin U
161	2,514	6,972	9,299	12,784	865	253	TM Cooley Law Sch
30	250	4,000	8,443	11,119	162	35	Trinity Luth Sem
104	2,047	10,460	-1	72,682	5,160	3,608	Trinity U
77	700	6,000	4,278	5,499	212	2,376	Trinity U
91	2,476	237	36,606	36,606	2,066	1,332	Troy ST U
20	323	1,298	6,494	7,541	432	419	Troy ST U Dothan
169	3,451	590	-1	176,825	11,718	15,261	Truman ST U
9	370	905	5,055	7,365	592	465	TX Chiro C
53	844	2,376	54,944	-1	204	271	U Arts
73	1,127	4,325	35,534	45,005	4,441	3,509	U C Cape
29	498	3,457	2,975	2,975	174	177	U Charleston
160	4,506	9,187	-1	18,173	6,826	835	U DC
48	1,440	38,406	10,952	10,952	245	128	U Del Turabo
67	948	6,200	24,232	27,317	898	551	U Findlay
258	3,248	10,343	55,224	66,883	1,376	3,052	U Hawaii-Hilo
64	960	3,840	-1	4,927	320	153	U HI-Kauai CC

Key to Notes on Page 1   1 -- See Footnotes   -1 -- Unavailable   -2 -- Not Applicable

ACRL Library Data Tables 2004
PERSONNEL AND PUBLIC SERVICES

INSTITUTIONS GRANTING MASTER OF ARTS AND PROFESSIONAL DEGREES (Carnegie Code M)

Lib. No.	Institution	Notes	Professional Staff (FTE) 33	Support Staff (FTE) 34	Student Assistants (FTE) 35	Total Staff (FTE) 36	No. of Staffed Service Points 37	Weekly Public Service Hours 38
321	U Houston	b	15	18	10	43	3	85
322	U Mary	bGf	4	-1	2	6	2	75
323	U MI Dearborn		12	15	6	32	2	95
324	U Mobile	bG	5	3	2	10	4	72
325	U NE Kearney	b	11	15	6	32	2	92
326	U Portland	bG	7	9	14	30	4	101
327	U Richmond		20 [1]	20	15	65	5	146
328	U Rio Grande	bGf	4	3	4	11	2	81
329	U Scranton	b	19	13	15	47	2	100
330	U Sthn IN	bG	9	16	5	30	2	92
331	U Tampa	bG	7	14	6	27	3	92
332	U TN Chatt	bG	15	16	6	36	4	92
333	U TN Martin	BbG	10	16	12 [1]	38	7	85
334	U TX Tyler	BG	6	14	10	30	4	80 [1]
335	U West AL		7	1	4	12	3	83
336	U WI E Claire	b	13	18	11	42	4	112
337	U WI La Crosse	G	12	13	9	34	7	95
338	U WI Platteville	bG	9	11	9	29	6	97
339	U Winnipeg	bG	8	30	4	42	5	88
340	UNC Asheville	b	10	14	11	35	4	93
341	UNC Pembroke	bGf	12	17	15	44	4	91
342	Union C-NY		14	15	8	37	3	109
343	Valparaiso U		9	11	6	25	2	97
344	Villa Julie C	bG	7	3	1	11	2	79
345	W.Carey College	Bb	5	3	4	12	6	71
346	W.Mitchell C Law	GL	9	8	3	20	2	106
347	Walla Walla C	b	7	6	9	22	16	80
348	Walsh C Acct Bus Admin	B	4	5	11	20	3	114 [1]
349	Wartburg Theo Sem	bf	1	3	2	5	1	82
350	Washburn U Topeka	bG	10	11	5	26	3	88
351	Washington C	Gf	4	7	4	4	4	101
352	Washington Theo Union	bf	1	4	0	5	1	76
353	Wayland Bap U		5	3	4	12	2	82
354	Wayne ST C	bG	8	6	8	22	3	93
355	Webber Intl U	b	1	3	0	3	2	66
356	Wesley C	bf	3	4	0	7	1	87
357	West Chester U PA		14	26	20	60	7	94
358	West TX A & M U	bG	11	16	10	38	6	86
359	West VA Wesleyan C		3	6	8	-1	-1	-1
360	Western MD C	b	5	10	8	28	2	101

Key to Notes on Page 1   1 -- See Footnotes   -1 -- Unavailable   -2 -- Not Applicable

ACRL Library Data Tables 2004
PERSONNEL AND PUBLIC SERVICES

INSTITUTIONS GRANTING MASTER OF ARTS AND PROFESSIONAL DEGREES (Carnegie Code M)

No. of Presentations to Groups 39	Participants in Group Presentations 40	No. of Reference Transactions 41	No. of Initial Circulations 42	Total Circulations 43	ILL Materials Provided 44	ILL Materials Received 45	Survey Question # Institution
121	2,690	9,376	53,746	68,143	5,382	4,323	U Houston
43	860	150	20,745	21,875	4,344	1,429	U Mary
118	2,487	159	43,560	57,261	5,161	2,806	U MI Dearborn
65	1,625	3,100	11,761	14,595	337	367	U Mobile
207	1,410	8,054	42,102	46,093	3,395	4,241	U NE Kearney
101	1,925	9,328	42,970	54,612	6,346	6,427	U Portland
301	6,274	14,964	112,234	118,803	5,478	4,308	U Richmond
46	882	1,597	9,543	11,430	226	85	U Rio Grande
320	640	795	76,522	124,349	6,142	5,391	U Scranton
186	3,504	17,644	-1	48,568	1,625	1,112	U Sthn IN
126	2,419	4,500	12,235	12,856	1,708	2,316	U Tampa
278	5,674	15,754	29,826	36,338	2,069	9,348	U TN Chatt
129	3,225	22,800	37,515	56,229	1,757	658	U TN Martin
56	1,081	7,500 [1]	-1 [1]	23,591	2,434	2,456	U TX Tyler
75	2,500	850	5,066	5,066	642	392	U West AL
249	5,195	15,487	95,753	106,328	6,543	4,475	U WI E Claire
278	5,641	9,738	45,711	64,668	4,011	4,573	U WI La Crosse
124	1,600	13,157	29,014	32,984	1,142	733	U WI Platteville
200	4,504	34,560	106,960	121,400	2,547	11,667	U Winnipeg
221	5,947	8,190	86,835	114,401	7,398	18,216	UNC Asheville
198	3,881	290	20,462	24,462	1,498	802	UNC Pembroke
89	1,258	11,483	-1	36,565	3,694	3,739	Union C-NY
127	2,751	100	28,906	35,936	1,701	6,541	Valparaiso U
121	1,844	1,360 [1]	-1	16,352	281	136	Villa Julie C
16	137	12,000	5,540	5,540 [1]	87	25	W.Carey College
99	1,261	5,876	9,838	15,554	465	360	W.Mitchell C Law
5	1,022	4,628	-1	21,241	2,087	1,128	Walla Walla C
75	625	2,800	4,295	4,322	1,012	42	Walsh C Acct Bus Admin
33	264	430	-1	5,395	754	233	Wartburg Theo Sem
170	3,978	10,761	31,369	36,908	4,073	2,602	Washburn U Topeka
50	920	1,650 [1]	-1	18,218	443	1,863	Washington C
7	24	4,500	4,284	5,626	10	7	Washington Theo Union
16	244	-1	23,863	-1	773	561	Wayland Bap U
70	1,518	1,386	22,806	22,806	2,395	1,677	Wayne ST C
10	300	5,600	649	858	0	0	Webber Intl U
90	1,000	18,000	8,236	-1	-1	-1	Wesley C
217	4,774	16,344	46,267	52,005	5,454	6,191	West Chester U PA
175	3,137	408	15,238	19,666	2,261	4,201	West TX A & M U
-1	-1	-1	-1	-1	-1	-1	West VA Wesleyan C
64	-1	2,595	-1	36,443	1,927	2,103	Western MD C

Key to Notes on Page 1   1 -- See Footnotes   -1 -- Unavailable   -2 -- Not Applicable

ACRL Library Data Tables 2004
PERSONNEL AND PUBLIC SERVICES
INSTITUTIONS GRANTING MASTER OF ARTS AND PROFESSIONAL DEGREES (Carnegie Code M)

Lib. No.	Institution	Notes	Professional Staff (FTE) 33	Support Staff (FTE) 34	Student Assistants (FTE) 35	Total Staff (FTE) 36	No. of Staffed Service Points 37	Weekly Public Service Hours 38
	Survey Question #							
361	Western OR U	bG	10	13	12	35	3	97
362	Western Sem	b	3	1	0	4	2	51
363	Western WA U	G	19	43	16	78	5	96
364	Westfield ST C	b	8	5	5	18	4	82
365	Westminster C-UT	G	5	4	4	13	2	91
366	Wheeling Jesuit U	b	3	3	3	9	2	88
367	Whitworth C	G	5	5	4	14	2	94
368	Wilkes U	G	11	6	7	24	2	100
369	William Woods U	bL	3	3	1	7	2	87
370	Williams C		19	21	16	56	7	117
371	Wstrn IL U	Bb	18	41	22	81	11	99
372	Wstrn Theo Sem	f	2	3	2	7	1	68
373	Xavier U LA	b	14	25	21	59	8	100

Key to Notes on Page 1   1 -- See Footnotes   -1 -- Unavailable   -2 -- Not Applicable

ACRL Library Data Tables 2004
PERSONNEL AND PUBLIC SERVICES

INSTITUTIONS GRANTING MASTER OF ARTS AND PROFESSIONAL DEGREES (Carnegie Code M)

No. of Presentations to Groups 39	Participants in Group Presentations 40	No. of Reference Transactions 41	No. of Initial Circulations 42	Total Circulations 43	ILL Materials Provided 44	ILL Materials Received 45	Survey Question # Institution
118	2,799	30,660	66,845	76,818	4,380	4,940	Western OR U
3	60	560	-1	5,953	985	620	Western Sem
327	5,610	18,511	202,782	258,963	22,234	30,068	Western WA U
315	5,869	10,858	19,670	24,462	2,354	1,460	Westfield ST C
95	1,357	41,600	8,870	12,251	1,977	1,298	Westminster C-UT
0 [1]	0	100	-1	24,935	829	934	Wheeling Jesuit U
65	1,087	4,856	18,894	4,328	990	1,784	Whitworth C
179	1,878	4,519	36,461	48,087	16,610	16,200	Wilkes U
51	808	1,404	-1	20,980	2,461	1,431	William Woods U
89	1,004	155	56,504	123,565	15,794	10,627	Williams C
294	5,880	1,722	-1	39,012	15,248	7,604	Wstrn IL U
4	61	225	8,879	10,423	271	122	Wstrn Theo Sem
69	945	17,842	-1 [1]	47,748	1,595	1,199	Xavier U LA

Key to Notes on Page 1   1 -- See Footnotes   -1 -- Unavailable   -2 -- Not Applicable

ACRL LIBRARY DATA TABLES 2004

SUMMARY DATA: PH.D., FACULTY, AND ENROLLMENT STATISTICS

ALL INSTITUTIONS REPORTING

| | Ph.D.s Awarded | Ph.D. Fields | Faculty | ENROLLMENT | | | |
				Total FTE Full-time*	Total Part-time*	Grad FTE Full-time	Graduate Part-time
(Survey Question #)	46	47	48	49	50	51	52
High	814	137	4,063	46,422	38,070	12,576	9,120
Mean	28	6	284	4,879	2,327	715	636
Median	0	0	126	2,209	974	75	89
Low	0	0	0	0	0	0	0
Total	26,705	6,242	303,736	5,147,031	2,284,842	679,681	588,541
Libraries Reporting	959	961	1,068	1,055	982	951	926

ACRL LIBRARY DATA TABLES 2004

SUMMARY DATA: PH.D., FACULTY, AND ENROLLMENT STATISTICS

INSTITUTIONS GRANTING BACHELOR OF ARTS DEGREES (Carnegie Code B)

| | Ph.D.s Awarded | Ph.D. Fields | Faculty | ENROLLMENT | | | |
				Total FTE Full-time*	Total Part-time*	Grad FTE Full-time	Graduate Part-time
(Survey Question #)	46	47	48	49	50	51	52
High			1,116	30,254	35,000		
Mean			105	1,689	628		
Median			72	1,056	71		
Low			0	0	0		
Total			18,850	307,467	104,190		
Libraries Reporting			180	182	166		

ACRL LIBRARY DATA TABLES 2004

SUMMARY DATA: PH.D., FACULTY, AND ENROLLMENT STATISTICS

INSTITUTIONS GRANTING MASTER OF ARTS AND PROFESSIONAL DEGREES (Carnegie Code M)

	Ph.D.s Awarded	Ph.D. Fields	Faculty	ENROLLMENT			
				Total FTE Full-time*	Total Part-time*	Grad FTE Full-time	Graduate Part-time
(Survey Question #)	46	47	48	49	50	51	52
High			2,637	31,565	12,287	4,909	4,568
Mean			182	3,263	1,309	297	497
Median			128	2,097	648	111	246
Low			0	0	0	0	0
Total			64,933	1,154,943	422,913	100,492	159,678
Libraries Reporting			357	354	323	338	321

ACRL Library Data Tables 2004

PH.D., FACULTY, AND ENROLLMENT STATISTICS

INSTITUTIONS GRANTING BACHELOR OF ARTS DEGREES (Carnegie Code B)

Lib. No.	Institution	Notes	Ph.D.'s Awarded	Ph.D. Fields	Full-Time Faculty	ENROLLMENT Full-time, Undergrad. & Grad.	Part-time, Undergrad. & Grad.	Full-time, Grad.	Part-time, Grad.
	Survey Question #		46	47	48	49	50	51	52
1	AB C Art & Design	bf	-1	-1	82	945	-1	-1	-1
2	Adrian C		0	0	64	959	54	0	0
3	Albion C	G	0	0	124	1,715	-1	0	0
4	Amherst C	Gf	0	0	158	1,618	0	0	0
5	Aquinas C TN	G	0	0	35	619	297	0	0
6	Atlanta C Art	bG	0	0	24	293 [1]	0	0	0
7	Atlanta Christian C	bf	0	0	0	319	75	0	0
8	Augustana C RI	G	0	0	189	2,277	32	0	0
9	Barber-Scotia C		0 [1]	0 [1]	33	737	5	0 [1]	0 [1]
10	Bard C	b	0	0	160	1,526	74	202	21
11	Barton C	b	0	0	79	949	239	0	0
12	Bates C	bG	0	0	138	1,746	0	0	0
13	Benedict C	G	0	0	123	2,741	109	0	0
14	Berry C	b	0	0	148	1,872	173	17	133
15	Bethany C Bethany	b	0	0	60	893	0	0	0
16	Bethany C Lindsborg		0	0	41	579	52	0	0
17	Bethel C KS		0	0	46	435	35	0	0
18	Blackburn C	bG	0	0	35	599	16	0	0
19	Bluefield C	bf	0	0	39	821	35	0	0
20	Boise Bible C		-1	-1	-1	-1	-1	-1	-1
21	Bowdoin C		0	0	170	1,640	7	0	0
22	Bridgewater C	b	0	0	82	1,519	13	0	0
23	Bryan C	bf	0	0	44	574	0	0	0
24	C Holy Cross		0	0	265	2,748	25	-1	1
25	C Visual Arts	b	0	0	8	186	32	0	0
26	C Wooster		-1	-1	134	1,885	34	-1	-1
27	Campion C	G	0	0	21	1,184	133	0	0
28	Carroll C-Helena	b	0	0	75	1,400	-1 [1]	0	0
29	Cazenovia C	b	0	0	46	804	195	0	0
30	Centennial C	bf	0	0	432	12,000	35,000	0	0
31	Central Bible C	b	0	0	46	700	83	0	0
32	Central C		0	0	100	-1	-1	-1	-1
33	Central Christian C Bible	b	0	0	12	267	41	0	0
34	Centre C	G	0	0	92	1,062	8	0	0
35	Christian Heritage C		0	0	55	527	127	81	40
36	Clear Creek Bible		0	0	6	171	-1 [1]	0	0
37	Cmty Hosp C Health		0	0	35	401	234	0	0
38	Colby C	bG	0 [1]	0 [1]	157	1,768	0	0 [1]	0 [1]
39	Colby Sawyer C	b	0	0	47	953	27	-2	-2
40	Columbia Union C	bG	0	0	53	762	421	0	24

Key to Notes on Page 1   1 -- See Footnotes   -1 -- Unavailable   -2 -- Not Applicable

ACRL Library Data Tables 2004
PH.D., FACULTY, AND ENROLLMENT STATISTICS
INSTITUTIONS GRANTING BACHELOR OF ARTS DEGREES (Carnegie Code B)

Lib. No.	Institution	Notes	Ph.D.'s Awarded 46	Ph.D. Fields 47	Full-Time Faculty 48	ENROLLMENT Full-time, Undergrad. & Grad. 49	Part-time, Undergrad. & Grad. 50	Full-time, Grad. 51	Part-time, Grad. 52
41	Concordia C-MN	b	0	0	263	2,730	84	2	0
42	Concordia C-NY	b	0	0	33	582	41	0	0
43	Cornish C Arts		0	0	150	696 [1]	21 [1]	0	0
44	Crichton C	b	0	0	30	802	174	0	-1
45	Crown C-MN	G	0	0	35	842	264	56	3
46	Culver Stockton C	b	0	0	57	758	68	0	0
47	CUNY City C		0	0	297	7,053	4,329	0	0
48	CUNY York C	b	0	0	140	3,420	2,298	0	0
49	Dakota Wesleyan U	b	0	0	43	674	90	13	0
50	Dana C	bG	0	0	44	563	19	0	0
51	Davidson C	bG	0	0	155	1,712	0	0	0
52	Dean C	bL	0	0	23	866	473	0	0
53	Defiance C	b	0	0	49	758	280	0	90
54	Denison U		0	0	185	2,204	2,204	0	0
55	DeVry Inst Tech GA	b	0	0	1,116	30,254	13,000	3,500	4,348
56	Dickinson ST U		0	0	83	1,726	735	0	0
57	Divine Word C		0	0	16	55	0	0	0
58	East Texas Baptist U	Bb	0	0	68	1,221	35	0	0
59	Eckerd C		0	0	124	1,608	675	0	0
60	Emmanuel C GA	b	0	0	-1	-1	-1	0	0
61	Eugene Bible C		-1	-1	-1	-1	-1	-1	-1
62	Evangel U		0	0	92	0 [1]	0 [1]	0 [1]	0 [1]
63	F&M C		0	0	200	1,945	0	0	0
64	Ferrum C	bf	0	0	72	919	35	0	0
65	Finlandia U	bG	0	0	35	468	74	0	0
66	FL Christian C	b	0 [1]	0 [1]	14	200 [1]	100 [1]	0 [1]	0 [1]
67	Flagler C	bG	-2	-2	68	2,343 [1]	64 [1]	-2	-2
68	Fort Lewis C	b	0	0	176	3,317	561	0	0
69	G Adolphus C	b	0	0	178	2,555	41	0	0
70	Green Mountain C	bf	0	0	-1	589	-1	0	0
71	Grinnell C		-2	-2	139	1,498	-1	-2	-2
72	Guilford C	bG	0	0	93	1,734	367	0	0
73	H Inst Int Desgn	b	0	0	9	658	542	0	0
74	H LaGrange C	G	0	0	59	751	316	0	0
75	Hamilton C		-2	-2	203	1,782	-1	-2	-2
76	Hampshire C		-2	-2	115	1,334	0	0	0
77	Hanover C	bG	-2	-2	97	988	9	-2	-2
78	Haskell Indian Nations U	bf	0	0	57	840	86	0	0
79	Haverford C	Bb	0	0	116	1,163	0	0	0
80	Hendrix C	b	0	0	90	1,067	0	3	0

Key to Notes on Page 1   1 -- See Footnotes   -1 -- Unavailable   -2 -- Not Applicable

ACRL Library Data Tables 2004

PH.D., FACULTY, AND ENROLLMENT STATISTICS

INSTITUTIONS GRANTING BACHELOR OF ARTS DEGREES (Carnegie Code B)

Lib. No.	Institution	Notes	Ph.D.'s Awarded	Ph.D. Fields	Full-Time Faculty	ENROLLMENT			
						Full-time, Undergrad. & Grad.	Part-time, Undergrad. & Grad.	Full-time, Grad.	Part-time, Grad.
	Survey Question #		46	47	48	49	50	51	52
81	Hiram C	bG	0	0	73	891	219	0	0
82	Hobart &William Smith Cs	G	0	0	150	1,808	-1	0	0
83	Hope C		-2	-2	208	2,958	110	0	0
84	Houghton C	Bb	0	0	82	1,381	84	5	4
85	Howard Payne U	G	0	0	73	1,081	304	0	0
86	Illinois C	bGf	0	0	68	1,008	-1	0	0
87	Jamestown C	b	0	0	58	981	83	0	0
88	Johnson C Smith U	b	0	0	87	1,399	75	0	0
89	Judson C	b	0	0	68	913 [1]	260	17	9
90	Kent ST U Salem	b	0	0	34	855	477	4	15
91	Kent ST U Trumbull		-1	-1	-1	-1	-1	-1	-1
92	Kenyon C	b	0	0	155	1,601	0	0	0
93	Kettering C Med	bG	0	0	50	451	201	0	0
94	Keuka C	b	0	0	146	1,073	365	19	35
95	Knox C	G	-2	-2	89	1,106	21	0	0
96	Kwantlen UC		0	0	-1	8,674	3,859	0	0
97	Lambuth U	bGf	0	0	59	777	59	0	0
98	Lawrence U		0	0	130	1,342	65	0	0
99	Lemoyne-Owen C	Gf	0	0	51	657	106	0	0
100	Lester B Pearson C Pacific		-1	-1	-1	200	-1	-1	-1
101	LIFE Bible C	b	-2	0	17	359	87	-2	-2
102	Lyndon State C		-1	-1	-1	1,146	-1	-1	-1
103	Lyon C		0	0	45	466	1	0	0
104	Macon ST C	BbG	0	0	147	5,403	3,223	2,180	0
105	Marlboro C		0	0	40	311 [1]	0 [1]	0 [1]	0 [1]
106	Mars Hill C	b	0	0	75	1,227	157	0	0
107	Martin Luther C	bG	-2	-2	76	946	7	-2	-2
108	Mayville ST U		0	0	37	613	204	0	0
109	McKendree C	bG	0	0	66	1,594	734	0	133
110	McPherson C		-1	-1	-1	-1	-1	-1	-1
111	Methodist C	G	0	0	101	1,700	555	45	0
112	Midland Lutheran C		0	0	57	920	85	0	0
113	Milwaukee Inst Art Design	b	0	0	62	602	47	0	0
114	MO Baptist C		0	0	54	1,248	2,408	228	481
115	MO Western ST C	bG	0	0	186	3,704	1,224	0	0
116	Monmouth C	bGf	0	0	82	1,155	7	0	0
117	Mount Royal C	bG	0	0	550	7,751	-1	0	0
118	Mount Union C		0	0	125	2,110	315	0	0
119	Muhlenberg C	bG	0	0	154	2,133	8	0	0
120	NC Wesleyan C	BbG	-2	-2	49	910	785	-2	-2

Key to Notes on Page 1   1 -- See Footnotes   -1 -- Unavailable   -2 -- Not Applicable

ACRL Library Data Tables 2004
PH.D., FACULTY, AND ENROLLMENT STATISTICS
INSTITUTIONS GRANTING BACHELOR OF ARTS DEGREES (Carnegie Code B)

			Ph.D.'s Awarded	Ph.D. Fields	Full-Time Faculty	ENROLLMENT			
						Full-time, Undergrad. & Grad.	Part-time, Undergrad. & Grad.	Full-time, Grad.	Part-time, Grad.
Lib. No.	Survey Question # Institution	Notes	46	47	48	49	50	51	52
121	New C U South FL	bG	0	0	65	681	0	0	0
122	OH Dominican C	bG	0	0	112	1,899	667	221	37
123	OH Wesleyan U	b	-1	-1	142	1,911	-1	0	0
124	OK Panhandle ST U	b	0	0	57	1,012	56	0	0
125	Paier C Art		-2	-2	11	195	111	-2	-2
126	Peace C	b	0	0	42	625	24	0	0
127	Potomac C	G	0	0	5	341	0	0	0
128	Presbyterian C	bG	0	0	79	1,144	33	0	0
129	Principia C	bG	0	0	48	544	10	0	0
130	Randolph-Macon C	bf	0	0	87	1,083	24	0	0
131	Randolph-Macon WC	bG	0	0	82	705	0	0	0
132	Reformed Bible C		-2	-2	15	237	61	-2	-2
133	Reinhardt C	Bb	0	0	55	1,021	190	0	0
134	Ricks C		0	0	461	10,522 [1]	1,033 [1]	0	0
135	Ringling Sch Art & Design		0	0	63	978	-1	0	0
136	Rochester C	b	0	0	0 [1]	640	356	0	0
137	Rocky Mountain C	bGf	0	0	50	927	0 [1]	22 [1]	0
138	Rogers ST U	bG	0	0	71	1,885	1,665	0	0
139	SE C Assemblies God	bG	0	0	59	1,409 [1]	0 [1]	0	0
140	Shawnee ST U	Gf	0	0	135	3,213	585	0	0
141	Shepherd C	G	0	0	119	3,088	786	1	26
142	Siena C	G	0	0	162	3,025	354	0	0
143	Simpson C IA	bG	0	0	82	1,436	501	0	0
144	Skidmore C	b	0	0	169	2,286	298	0	52
145	Southwest U	f	-2	-2	114	1,237	27	-2	-2
146	Spartan Aero-Flight Schl	B	0 [1]	0	111 [1]	1,267 [1]	0 [1]	0 [1]	0 [1]
147	St Andrews Presby C	bG	0	0	43	629	64	0	0
148	St Gregory's U	b	0	0	32	613 [1]	-1	0	0
149	St John Vianney C Sem		0	0	6	50	1	2	0
150	St Olaf C	b	0	0	249	2,948	64	0	0
151	St. Mary's C Maryland		0	0	126	1,772	116	0	0
152	Sterling C-VT		-2	-2	17	95	7	-2	-2
153	Stillman C		0	0	72	1,092	108	0	0
154	Susquehanna U	bG	0	0	160	1,900	0	0	0
155	SW Baptist Theo Sem		-1	-1	-1	-1	-1	-1	-1
156	Swarthmore C	G	0	0	170	1,490	0	0	0
157	Sweet Briar C	bG	0	0	72	662	47	0	0
158	Talladega C	bf	0	0	46	344	344 [1]	0	0
159	Taylor U-Ft Wayne	b	0	0	133	1,859	230	8	0
160	Teikyo Post U	bL	0	0	35	719	606	0	0

Key to Notes on Page 1   1 -- See Footnotes   -1 -- Unavailable   -2 -- Not Applicable

ACRL Library Data Tables 2004
PH.D., FACULTY, AND ENROLLMENT STATISTICS
INSTITUTIONS GRANTING BACHELOR OF ARTS DEGREES (Carnegie Code B)

Lib. No.	Institution	Notes	Ph.D.'s Awarded	Ph.D. Fields	Full-Time Faculty	ENROLLMENT			
						Full-time, Undergrad. & Grad.	Part-time, Undergrad. & Grad.	Full-time, Grad.	Part-time, Grad.
	Survey Question #		46	47	48	49	50	51	52
161	TN Wesleyan C		0	0	52	645	148	-1	-1
162	Tri ST U		0	0	63	1,031	44	1	5
163	Trinity Christian C	b	0	0	65	1,050	184	0	0
164	Trinity Wstrn U	bf	0	0	130	2,593	148	307	0
165	Truett McConnell C	b	0	0	26	346	44	0	0
166	TX Lutheran U	bG	0	0	68	1,324	90	0	0
167	U Maine-Machias	G	0	0	30	577	736	0	0
168	U ME Fort Kent	b	0	0	0	1,216	666	0	0
169	U Ozarks	G	0	0	50	-1	-1	-1	-1
170	U VA C Wise	G	0	0	71	1,363	340	0	0
171	Union C-NE	b	0	0	62 [1]	793	109	0	0
172	US C Guard Acad	b	0	0	112	975	0	0	0
173	US Merchant Marine Acad	bG	0	0	70	900	0	0	0
174	US Mil Acad	f	0	0	550	4,200	0	0	0
175	US Naval Acad		0	0	550	4,200	0	0	0
176	UT Valley ST C	Bb	0	0	388	12,477	11,326	0	0
177	VA Wesleyan C	b	0	0	70	1,136	293	0	0
178	Vassar C	G	0	0	253	2,395	49	0	0
179	VMI	b	0	0	100	1,300	0	0	0
180	Wabash C	G	0	0	81	806	0	0	0
181	Warner Sthrn C	Gf	0	0	52	779	162	43	11
182	Warren Wilson C	b	0	0	61	839	0 [1]	66	0 [1]
183	Wells C	b	0	0	45	398	17	0	0
184	Western ST C	bf	0	0	81	2,040	-1	0	0
185	Westmont C	b	0	0	83	1,199	0	0	0
186	Whitman C	b	0	0	137	1,433	0	0	0
187	Wiley C	bG	0	0	47	696	11	0	0
188	Winston-Salem ST U	b	0	0	195	3,390	712	78	95
189	Wofford C	bG	0	0	81	1,127	18	0	0
190	York C		0	0	34	432	29	0	0

ACRL Library Data Tables 2004
PH.D., FACULTY, AND ENROLLMENT STATISTICS
INSTITUTIONS GRANTING MASTER OF ARTS AND PROFESSIONAL DEGREES (Carnegie Code

Lib. No.	Institution	Notes	Ph.D.'s Awarded	Ph.D. Fields	Full-Time Faculty	ENROLLMENT Full-time, Undergrad. & Grad.	Part-time, Undergrad. & Grad.	Full-time, Grad.	Part-time, Grad.
	Survey Question #		46	47	48	49	50	51	52
1	Abilene Christian U	bG	0	0	227	4,282	509	441	275
2	Agnes Scott C	G	0	0	88	893	52	24	6
3	Albany C Pharmacy		0	0	68	886	0	0	0
4	Albany Law Schl Union U	GL	-2	-2	52	717	73	717	73
5	Alcorn ST U	bG	0	0	187	2,526	783	168	479
6	Amer Intl C	b	5	1	88	1,250	350	75	225
7	Amer U Puerto Rico	Bb	0	0	40	2,539	1,106	37	6
8	Anderson U		0	0	140	2,072	824	16	309
9	Angelo ST U		0	0	234	4,728	1,315	151	274
10	Aquinas C MI	b	0	0	96	-1 [1]	-1 [1]	-1 [1]	-1 [1]
11	Ark Tech U	G	0	0	222	5,317	1,166	95	297
12	Armstrong Atlantic ST U	bG	0	0	237	3,692	2,961	246	664
13	Assemblies God Theo Sem	f	0	0	12	245	262	245	262
14	Assumption C	bG	0	0	129	2,243	527	107	185
15	Athenaeum of Ohio		0	0	26	177	90	177	90
16	Auburn U Montgomery	b	0	2	179	3,044	2,254	134	442
17	Augusta ST U	bG	0	0	111	3,787	2,348	180	318
18	Augustana C SF	bG	0	0	131	1,733	161	0	38
19	Austin C	b	0	0	92	1,316	16	38	0
20	Austin Presb Theo Sem	f	0	0	25	-1	-1	-1	-1
21	Averett C	b	0	0	66	1,522	1,327	257	505
22	Babson C	bG	0	0	193	2,143	610	426	1,199
23	Baker C System	Bb	0	0	-1	15,094	10,765	538	518
24	Baker U	G	0	0	76	1,785	466	825	411
25	Baptist Bible C and Sem	bf	2 [1]	2	26	599	106	25	45
26	Bayamon Central U	bf	0	1	4	1,500	1,500	300	400
27	Bellevue U	bf	0	0	85	3,278	1,565	856	321
28	Bennington C	b	-1	0	66	713	17	136	13
29	Bethel C IN	bf	0	0	155	1,701	-1 [1]	0	61
30	Birmingham Southern C	bG	0	0	106	1,388	77	52	38
31	Bluffton C	b	0	0	56	1,041	107	43	22
32	BowlGrn SU Fireld	b	0	0	44	912	915	0	89
33	Bradley U	b	0	0	328	5,211	858	215	539
34	Brescia U	bG	0	0	38	524	189	0	28
35	Brooks Institute	B	-2	-2	53	2,206	-2	42	-2
36	Bryn Athyn C	b	-2	-2	21	129	26	9	13
37	Buena Vista U		0	0	80	2,475	369	76	0
38	Butler U	b	0	0	269	3,815	609	70	531
39	C Atlantic	b	0	0	28 [1]	250	5 [1]	4 [1]	2 [1]
40	C Mt St Joseph	b	0	0	120	1,301	1,286	244	108

Key to Notes on Page 1   1 -- See Footnotes   -1 -- Unavailable   -2 -- Not Applicable

ACRL Library Data Tables 2004

PH.D., FACULTY, AND ENROLLMENT STATISTICS

INSTITUTIONS GRANTING MASTER OF ARTS AND PROFESSIONAL DEGREES (Carnegie Code M)

			Ph.D.'s Awarded	Ph.D. Fields	Full-Time Faculty	ENROLLMENT			
						Full-time, Undergrad. & Grad.	Part-time, Undergrad. & Grad.	Full-time, Grad.	Part-time, Grad.
	Survey Question #		46	47	48	49	50	51	52
Lib. No.	Institution	Notes							
41	C Mt St Vincent	bG	0	0	136	1,046	514	35	328
42	C Our Lady Elms	bG	-2	-2	51	574	416	9	165
43	C.R. Drew U Med & Sci	bM	0	0	285	202	53	0	1
44	CA C Arts & Crafts	b	0	0	39	1,328	156	179	10
45	CA St Polytechnic U-Pomor	G	0	0	672	14,567	4,153	314	826
46	CA St U - Sacramento	bG	0	0	2,302	20,240	8,135	3,040	2,773
47	CA ST U Dominguez Hills	b	0	0	252	7,038	5,575	1,522	2,393
48	CA ST U Fresno		0	0	704	18,166	2,260	2,042	70
49	CA ST U Fullerton	Bb	0	0	769	19,433	12,287	1,300	4,190
50	CA ST U Hayward	B	0	0	470	9,238	4,217	1,872	2,203
51	CA ST U Long Beach	G	0	0	875	23,998	10,717	2,320	4,328
52	CA ST U Northridge	bG	0	0	2,637	31,565 [1]	10,443	2,949	4,568
53	CA ST U S Bernadino	f	-1	-1	-1	12,629 [1]	-1	4,807	-1
54	CA ST U San Marcos	bG	0	0	220	5,124	2,653	642	674
55	CA ST U Stanislaus	B	0	0	285	5,049	3,023	872	1,046
56	CA West Sch Law	GL	0	0	46	837	140	837	140
57	Calvin C		0	0	307	4,096	236	4	30
58	Cameron U	Gf	0	0	192	2,669	2,963	120	307
59	Canisius C	G	0	0	205	3,860	1,233	755	804
60	Carlow C		0	0	81	1,176	951	75	296
61	Carroll C-Waukesha		0	0	100	2,099	869	37	254
62	Cedar Crest C		-1	-1	-1	798	820	-1	-1
63	Cedarville U	G	0	0	193	2,916	154	0	-1
64	Centenary C	b	0	0	42	1,040	329 [1]	119 [1]	294 [1]
65	Centenary C LA	bf	0	0	72	889	151	9	126
66	Central Baptist C	bf	0	0	16	345	81	0	0
67	Central CT ST U		0	0	395	7,284	4,847	470	762
68	Central MO ST U		0	0	430	10,351	2,805	418	1,226
69	Charleston Sthrn U		0	0	98	2,135	855	21	385
70	Chicago ST U	b	0	0	318	3,592	3,448	389	1,747
71	Chris Newport U		0	0	167	4,103	709	23	109
72	Christendom C	Bb	0	0	27	364	-1	-1	-1
73	Christian Brothers U	b	0	0	104	1,829	410 [1]	0	425
74	Clarion U PA	Bb	0	0	339	5,823	1,003	209	338
75	Clarke C-IA		-2	-2	90	856	270	57	64
76	Clarkson C-NE	f	0	0	41	362	304	1	100
77	Colorado C	bG	0	0	211	1,938	0	26	0
78	Columbia C MO		-1	-1	-1	-1	-1	-1	-1
79	Columbia C SC		0	0	94	1,184	331	261	67
80	Columbia Intl U	bf	6	2	55	864	-1	275	-1

Key to Notes on Page 1   1 -- See Footnotes   -1 -- Unavailable   -2 -- Not Applicable

			Ph.D.'s Awarded	Ph.D. Fields	Full-Time Faculty	ENROLLMENT			
						Full-time, Undergrad. & Grad.	Part-time, Undergrad. & Grad.	Full-time, Grad.	Part-time, Grad.
	Survey Question #		46	47	48	49	50	51	52
Lib. No.	Institution	Notes							
81	Columbus ST U	BG	0	0	207	4,243	2,694	262	681
82	Concordia U Irvine	b	0	0	64	1,467	280	237	173
83	Concordia U RiverF	b	-1	-1	-1	1,252	-1	-1	-1
84	Concordia U St Paul		0	0	80	1,741	236	310	0
85	Cooper Union	b	0	0	45	956	18	26	12
86	Cornerstone U	bG	0	0	83	1,703	648	88	129
87	Creighton U	b	0	0	561	3,632	611	188	319
88	Cumberland U		0	0	75	-1	-1	-1	-1
89	CUNY BMB C		0	0	453	9,771	5,355	778	1,886
90	CUNY C Stn Island	f	0	0	770	7,360	5,062	100	1,221
91	CUNY City C	bGM	0	0	584	6,187	6,363	234	3,380
92	CUNY HH Lehman C	bG	0	0	308	4,694 [1]	5,018 [1]	110 [1]	2,008 [1]
93	CUNY John Jay C Crim Ju	G	-1	-1	322	8,809	4,217	349	1,168
94	CUNY Queens C	bG	0	0	581	8,591	8,402	296	3,058
95	Curtis Inst Music	G	0	0	1	162	0	12	0
96	Daniel Webster C	b	-2	-2	32	596	438	-2	-2
97	DeSales U		0	0	88	1,718	1,196	44	697
98	DN Myers C		0	0	22	583	450	19	41
99	Dominican C San Rafael	b	0	0	69	926	577	92	285
100	Dominican U	b	0	0	96	1,450	1,738	366	1,546
101	Drake U	b	0	0	249	3,830	1,334	908 [1]	1,060 [1]
102	Drury C	b	0	0	127	2,835	1,748	229	156
103	E R Aero U		0	0	405	5,584	565	412	0
104	Earlham C	Gf	0	0	97	1,270	34	100	149
105	Eastern IL U	bG	0	0	593	9,542	1,980	652	1,025
106	Eastern U	Bb	-1	-1	100	2,960 [1]	-1	-1	-1
107	Eastern WA U	Bb	0	1	402	8,378	1,959	699	571
108	Eastrn NM U Main	BbG	0	0	140	2,723	1,236	204	581
109	Edinboro U PA	b	0	0	362	6,674	1,371	433	583
110	Elizabethtown C	b	0	0	112	1,778	210	0	0
111	Elmhurst C	b	0	0	115	1,922	671	0	197
112	Elon U	b	0	0	252	4,374	210	65	88
113	Emmanuel C MA	b	0	0	52	1,230	641	23	220
114	Emory & Henry C	bGf	0	0	77	885	96	0	39
115	Evergreen ST C	bGf	0	0	219	3,600	538	112	160
116	Fisk U	bG	0	0	52	834	39	13	10
117	Fitchburg ST C	G	-1 [1]	-1 [1]	187	2,708	2,341	272	1,398
118	FL Southern C	bG	0	0	107	1,767	681	0	39
119	Fort Hays ST U	b	0	0	277	4,500	2,873	374	1,079
120	Francis Marion U	G	0 [1]	0	167	3,073	682	180	454

Key to Notes on Page 1   1 -- See Footnotes   -1 -- Unavailable   -2 -- Not Applicable

ACRL Library Data Tables 2004

PH.D., FACULTY, AND ENROLLMENT STATISTICS

INSTITUTIONS GRANTING MASTER OF ARTS AND PROFESSIONAL DEGREES (Carnegie Code M)

Lib. No.	Institution	Notes	Ph.D.'s Awarded	Ph.D. Fields	Full-Time Faculty	Full-time, Undergrad. & Grad.	Part-time, Undergrad. & Grad.	Full-time, Grad.	Part-time, Grad.
	Survey Question #		46	47	48	49	50	51	52
121	Franklin Inst Boston	b	0	0	34	-1	-1	-1	-1
122	Franklin U		0	0	36	5,557	3,716	-1	-1
123	Free Will Baptist Bible C	bG	0	0	27	333	25	0	0
124	Frostburg ST U	bG	0	0	224	4,510	959	246	635
125	Furman U	G	0	0	216	2,778	542	83	423
126	GA SWstrn ST U	b	0	0	92	1,629	694	44	177
127	Gardner-Webb U	BbG	0	0	131	1,947	1,360	219	964
128	Geneva C	G	0	0	81	1,839	324	207	98
129	Georgetown C		0	0	105	1,292	416	49	338
130	Goucher C	b	0	0	100	1,277	870	2	830
131	Governors ST U	bG	0	0	196	1,376	4,251	525	2,433
132	Greenville C		0	0	58	1,219	-1	100	0
133	Grove City C	b	0	0	121	2,279	0	0	0
134	Harding U Main	bG	0	0	217	4,056	1,054	197	877
135	Hebrew C		0	0	7	22	105	17	104
136	Heidelberg C	Bbf	0	0	87	1,047	241	20	184
137	Hillsdale Free Will Baptist C		0	0	-1	210	66	2	9
138	Holy Apostles C & Sem	bGf	-1[1]	-1[1]	10	71	170	66	154
139	Hood C	G	0	0	76	761	1,027	74	850
140	Humboldt ST U	G	0	0	503	7,611	1,162	572	321
141	IN Inst of Tech	bf	0	0	300	3,500	2,400	100	1,400
142	IN U Kokomo	G	0	0	89	1,447	1,507	23	201
143	IN U S Bend	b	0	0	266	3,634	3,647	200	987
144	IN U-Purdue U Ft Wayne	G	0	0	376[1]	6,432	5,374	108	630
145	IN Wesleyan U	B	-1	-1	263	9,517	-1	3,213	-1
146	Intl Fine Arts C		10	16	115	1,400	100	1,500	0
147	Jacksonville ST U	bG	0	0	294	6,202	2,728	502	1,290
148	Johnson Bible C		0	0	23	748	107	30	83
149	Kean U		0	0	384	-1	-1	-1	-1
150	Keene State C	b	0	0	184	4,203	734	30	110
151	Kent ST U Stark	b	0	0	85	2,321	1,422	0	20
152	Kentucky Christian C	f	0	0	39	563	37	0	15
153	Kentucky ST U	G	1	1	151	1,731	547	73	67
154	Kettering U	b	0	0	140	2,500	660	12	660
155	King's C PA		0	-1	114	1,967	158	90	52
156	LaGrange C	Bb	0	0	79	857	163	-1	-1
157	Lakeland C-AB		0	0	52	1,381	2,448	35	395
158	Lakeview C Nursing	b	0	0	12	76	21	0	0
159	Lancaster Bible C		0	0	27	594	251	28	69
160	Lander U	G	0	0	124	2,291	691	10	306

Key to Notes on Page 1   1 -- See Footnotes   -1 -- Unavailable   -2 -- Not Applicable

ACRL Library Data Tables 2004
PH.D., FACULTY, AND ENROLLMENT STATISTICS
INSTITUTIONS GRANTING MASTER OF ARTS AND PROFESSIONAL DEGREES (Carnegie Code N

Lib. No.	Institution	Notes	Ph.D.'s Awarded 46	Ph.D. Fields 47	Full-Time Faculty 48	Full-time, Undergrad. & Grad. 49	Part-time, Undergrad. & Grad. 50	Full-time, Grad. 51	Part-time, Grad. 52
161	Langston U	BG	0	0	148	2,322	-1 [1]	-1 [1]	-1 [1]
162	Laurentian U JN	bG	3	3	301	5,100	2,682	224	176
163	Le Moyne C	G	0	0	153	2,357	1,046	91	621
164	Lebanon Valley C	b	-2	-2	100	1,530	376	-2	141
165	Lewis U		0	0	163	2,313	2,146	66	1,181
166	Lewis&Clark C	G	0	0	151	2,054	299	297	264
167	Lincoln U-MO	b	0	0	136	1,949	1,179	67	151
168	Lindsey Wilson C	bG	0	0	67	1,485	195	120	15
169	Lipscomb U		0	0	151	2,817	-1	-1	-1
170	Lock Haven U PA	BbG	0	0	220	4,383	525	116	96
171	Longwood C	G	0	0	182	3,610	309	173	182
172	Lourdes C		-2	-2	63	539	710	44	3
173	Loyola Marymount U	b	0	0	355	6,466	546	1,198	349
174	Loyola U New Orleans	G	0	0	274	4,094	1,424	791	980
175	Lubbock Christian U	b	0	0	73	1,443	494	97	77
176	Luth Theo Sem Philly	bf	0	0	21	227	0	227	0
177	Lynchburg C		0	0	124	1,759	250	104	132
178	Malone C		0	0	100	1,897	277	209	60
179	Manchester C		0	0	80	1,022	53	12	0
180	Manhattan C		0	0	211	2,886	477	92	318
181	Marist C	G	0	0	198	-1 [1]	-1	-1 [1]	-1
182	Mary Baldwin C	b	0	0	74	1,194	537	94	72
183	Mary Washington C	BbG	0	0	207 [1]	3,665	1,127	92	515
184	Marymount U	G	0	0	128	2,289	1,452	570	998
185	Maryville U St Louis	b	0	0	88	1,711	1,590	193	403
186	McNeese ST U		0	0	293	1,373	2,055	350	756
187	Medical C Wisconsin	BbGM	72	7	-1	1,200 [1]	10	200	10
188	Merrimack C	b	0	0	142	2,021	554	1	23
189	MidAmer Nazarene U		0	0	65	800	400	200	300
190	Millikin U	bG	0	0	136	2,553	104	27	0
191	Millsaps C	G	-1	-1	93	1,112	88	29	48
192	Minnesota ST U-Mankato	bG	0	0	469	11,778	2,280	589	1,084
193	Minot ST U	G	0	0	170	2,570	1,254	58	173
194	Monterey Inst Intl St	f	-1	-1	70	600	100	600	95
195	Moravian C		-2	-2	115	1,531	487	3	178
196	Morehead ST U	G	0	0	361	6,356	3,168	240	1,623
197	Morningside C	bG	0	0	65	1,176	-1	-1	61 [1]
198	MS Valley ST U	BG	0	0	110	1,836	635	50	384
199	Mt Holyoke C		-2	-2	197	2,120	0	0	0
200	Mt Marty C		0	0	44	-1	-1	-1	-1

Key to Notes on Page 1   1 -- See Footnotes   -1 -- Unavailable   -2 -- Not Applicable

ACRL Library Data Tables 2004
PH.D., FACULTY, AND ENROLLMENT STATISTICS
INSTITUTIONS GRANTING MASTER OF ARTS AND PROFESSIONAL DEGREES (Carnegie Code M)

Lib. No.	Institution	Notes	Ph.D.'s Awarded	Ph.D. Fields	Full-Time Faculty	ENROLLMENT Full-time, Undergrad. & Grad.	Part-time, Undergrad. & Grad.	Full-time, Grad.	Part-time, Grad.
Survey Question #			46	47	48	49	50	51	52
201	Mt Mary C-WI	bf	0	0	-1	755	845	47	186
202	MT ST U Northern	bG	0	0	59	1,105	411	8	106
203	Mt St Vincent U	Gf	0	0	153	2,359	2,209	67	975
204	MT Tech U Montana	bG	0	0	116	1,747	342	52	47
205	Murray ST U-KY	L	0	0	393	7,413	2,687	512	1,203
206	Muskingum C		0	0	0	-1	-1	-1	-1
207	Natl C Naturopathic Med	bM	0	0	13	400	0	400	0
208	Natl Defense U	bGf	0	0	226	938	931	938	-1
209	NC Sch Arts		0	0	150	1,061	13	82	6
210	NEastrn IL U	B	0	0	279	5,458	6,367	381	2,459
211	Nipissing U	B	-1	-1	145	2,788	1,034	692	442
212	NJ City U		0	0	238	-1 [1]	-1 [1]	-1	-1
213	NM Highlands U	B	0	0	-1	-1	-1	-1	-1
214	North Central C		0	0	125	1,837	540	49	292
215	Northern KY U	b	-2	-2	528	13,945	4,361	162	1,034
216	Northern ST U	bGf	0	0	0	1,790	1,719	0	372
217	Northwest C	b	0	0	52	1,063	98	70	11
218	Norwich U	G	0	0	112	2,289	89	566	5
219	Notre Dame C OH		0	0	83	332	623	0	158
220	Notre Dame Sem	b	0	0	16	-1	-1	111	50
221	NW MO ST U	bG	0	0	-1 [1]	-1 [1]	-1 [1]	-1 [1]	-1 [1]
222	NY Inst Tech Islip		0 [1]	0	0	0 [1]	0	0	0
223	NY Inst Tech Main	M	0	0	255	13,877	-1	3,619	-1
224	Oberlin C	B	0	0	292	2,898	-1	15	-1
225	OH U Lancaster	b	0	0	30	953	781	44	50
226	Olivet Nazarene U	G	0	0	120	3,024 [1]	-1	697 [1]	-1
227	Otterbein C	G	0	0	149	2,095	936	7	351
228	Pace U Law		-1	-1	-1	-1	-1	-1	-1
229	Pacific Lutheran U	f	0	0	237	3,105	357	183	94
230	Pacific Union C		0	0	100	1,442	11	9	0
231	Palm Beach Atl C	b	0	0	155	2,210	201	466	189
232	Pfeiffer U	Bb	0	0	65	1,128	899	136	703
233	Philadelphia U	b	0	1	110	2,560	416	205	307
234	Plymouth ST C	G	0	0	160	3,768	1,142	61	882
235	Pont C Josephinum		0	0	20	134	5	60	5
236	Pope John Ntl Sem	bf	0	0	11	71	0	71	0
237	Prescott C	Bb	0	0	71	905	131	159	72
238	Providence C	b	0	0	251	4,233 [1]	-1	358 [1]	-1
239	Purchase C SUNY		0	0	-1	3,878	-1	-1	-1
240	Purdue U Calumet	G	0	0	260	4,202	4,926	115	818

Key to Notes on Page 1   1 -- See Footnotes   -1 -- Unavailable   -2 -- Not Applicable

							ENROLLMENT			
			Ph.D.'s Awarded	Ph.D. Fields	Full-Time Faculty	Full-time, Undergrad. & Grad.	Part-time, Undergrad. & Grad.	Full-time, Grad.	Part-time, Grad.
	Survey Question #		46	47	48	49	50	51	52
Lib. No.	Institution	Notes							
241	Purdue U North Central	G	0	0	101	2,042	1,615	0	22
242	Quincy U	b	0	0	47	1,269	-1	-1	-1
243	R.Wesleyan C	G	0	0	-1	1,562 [1]	281 [1]	350	148
244	Radford U	G	0	0	340	8,165	1,054	446	606
245	Ramapo C NJ	bf	0	0	171	3,978	1,264	19	370
246	Recnstrctnst Rabbinical C	b	0	0	11	73	0	73	0
247	RI Sch Design		0	0	146	2,282	0	399	0
248	Rivier C	b	0	0	75	2,469	1,342	158	707
249	Rockhurst U	bG	0	0	128	1,366	281	500	128
250	Roger Williams U	G	0	0	186	3,837	-1	249	-1
251	Roosevelt U	Bb	0 [1]	0	208	2,664	4,860	809	2,425
252	Rosemont C	b	0	0	32	436	639	48	365
253	Salem Teiko U	G	0	0	18	364	293	28	113
254	Salisbury ST U		-2	-2	314	5,588	1,228	154	463
255	San Jose ST U	bG	0	0	29	13,781	7,552	4,909	2,690
256	Savannah ST U	bf	0	0	212	1,482	577	0	142
257	Schreiner C		0	0	49	694	86	32	0
258	SE LA U	Bf	0	0	499	11,949	3,707	529	1,500
259	SE MO ST U		0	0	389	6,788	2,782	186	901
260	SE Oklahoma St U	b	0	0	144	3,074	996	108	303
261	Seton Hill C		0	0	-1	917	661	72	305
262	SF Consrv Music		-2 [1]	-2	24	314	14	157	4
263	Shaw U		0	0	88	2,242	374	122	48
264	Shorter C	Bb	0	0	152	2,409	43	157	0
265	Silver Lake C	f	-2	-2	64	301	803	55	269
266	Sisseton-Wahpeton CC	bG	0	0	9	163	124	0	0
267	Southrn C Opt	M	0	0	44	455	0	455	0
268	Southrn IL U Edward		0	0	528	9,811	3,484	775	1,765
269	Southrn OR U	G	-2	-2	189	4,079	1,427	216	326
270	Spring Hill C	bf	0	0	69	1,112	530	22	193
271	St Ambrose U		0	0	227	2,119	1,128	336	628
272	St C.Borromeo Sem	bf	0	0	28	159	266	74	72
273	St Cloud ST U	b	0	0	625	12,463	3,668	564	906
274	St Francis C PA	G	0	0	91	1,328	563	164	369
275	St Francis-Xavier U	bf	0	0	223	4,344 [1]	859	54	3
276	St John Fisher C	bGf	0	0	135	-1 [1]	-1	-1	-1
277	St Joseph C Suffolk	b	0	0	130	2,617 [1]	1,187	8	131
278	St Joseph's C IN	bG	0	0	62	842	156	0	0
279	St Joseph's C NY	bf	0	0	130 [1]	618	608	46	54
280	St Joseph's Sem	b	0	0	9	50	0	50	0

Key to Notes on Page 1   1 -- See Footnotes   -1 -- Unavailable   -2 -- Not Applicable

PH.D., FACULTY, AND ENROLLMENT STATISTICS

INSTITUTIONS GRANTING MASTER OF ARTS AND PROFESSIONAL DEGREES (Carnegie Code M)

Lib. No.	Institution	Notes	Ph.D.'s Awarded	Ph.D. Fields	Full-Time Faculty	ENROLLMENT Full-time, Undergrad. & Grad.	Part-time, Undergrad. & Grad.	Full-time, Grad.	Part-time, Grad.
	Survey Question #		46	47	48	49	50	51	52
281	St Mary's U MN	G	0	0	104	2,318	-1	732	-1
282	St Meinrad Theo	b	0	0	23	113	-1	113	-1
283	St Michael's C	b	-2	-2	145	1,996	479	81	401
284	St Norbert C		0	0	116	2,164	153	0	74
285	St Patrick's Sem	f	0	0	15	88	3	88	3
286	St Peter's Abbey & C	bGf	0	0	0	71	33	0	0
287	ST U W GA		1	1	373	7,050	3,095	309	1,791
288	St Vincent Sem		0	0	18	71	16	71	16
289	St. John's C		0	0	75	554	15	78	13
290	Stetson U	B	0	0	201	2,167	377	93	259
291	Sthrn Polytech ST U	G	0	0	145	2,228	1,509	161	327
292	Stonehill C	bG	0	0	130	2,236	346	11	4
293	Sul Ross ST U	bf	0	0	150	2,441	-1 [1]	541	-1 [1]
294	SUNY Brockport		0	0	302	6,516	2,226	421	1,359
295	SUNY Buffalo		0	0	386	8,261	2,896	516	1,638
296	SUNY C Potsdam	G	0	0	230	3,887	420	549	274
297	SUNY IT Utica	G	-2	-2	92	1,476	1,206	191	432
298	SUNY Oneonta	G	0	0	246	5,277	385	61	189
299	SUNY Oswego	G	0	0	315	6,945	1,520	408	876
300	SW MO ST U	B	0	1	725	13,503	3,717	1,054	2,105
301	SWstrn Adventist U	b	0	0	51	719	198	10	30
302	SWstrn OK ST U	bf	0	0	230	4,768	670	58	92
303	Tabor C	b	0	0	32	415	128	4	17
304	Tiffin U	b	0	0	53	1,112	295	242	139
305	TM Cooley Law Sch	BbGL	0	0	96	-1 [1]	-1 [1]	422 [1]	1,881 [1]
306	Trinity Luth Sem		0	0	24	0 [1]	0 [1]	176 [1]	-1 [1]
307	Trinity U	b	0	0	255	2,670	184	134	92
308	Trinity U		0	0	-1	-1	-1	-1	-1
309	Troy ST U	Bb	0	0	240	4,943	3,088	787	2,039
310	Troy ST U Dothan	bG	0	0	57	864	1,035	72	246
311	Truman ST U	b	-2	-2	354	5,512	321	174	180
312	TX Chiro C	bM	0	0	36	599	19	561	4
313	U Arts	bG	0	0	114	2,058 [1]	-1	139 [1]	-1
314	U C Cape	bG	-1	-1	184	2,398	1,220	11	33
315	U Charleston	b	-1	-1	70 [1]	849	73	12	11
316	U DC	b	-1	-1	-1	1,680	3,561	60	175
317	U Del Turabo		0	0	144	10,329	2,079	1,627	406
318	U Findlay	bG	0	0	168	2,995	1,717	308	899
319	U Hawaii-Hilo	bG	0	0	168	2,627	673	50	36
320	U HI-Kauai CC	b	0	0	77	1,215	-1	-1	-1

Key to Notes on Page 1   1 -- See Footnotes   -1 -- Unavailable   -2 -- Not Applicable

ACRL Library Data Tables 2004

PH.D., FACULTY, AND ENROLLMENT STATISTICS

INSTITUTIONS GRANTING MASTER OF ARTS AND PROFESSIONAL DEGREES (Carnegie Code N

Lib. No.	Institution	Notes	Ph.D.'s Awarded 46	Ph.D. Fields 47	Full-Time Faculty 48	ENROLLMENT Full-time, Undergrad. & Grad. 49	Part-time, Undergrad. & Grad. 50	Full-time, Grad. 51	Part-time, Grad. 52
321	U Houston	b	0	0	212	3,080	4,672	1,174	2,562
322	U Mary	bGf	0	0	137	2,553	-1	-1	-1
323	U MI Dearborn		0	0	268	7,615	5,127	460	4,157
324	U Mobile	bG	0	0	88	1,273	587	53	137
325	U NE Kearney	b	0	0	296	5,025	1,354	186	820
326	U Portland	bG	0	0	179	2,787	353	135	307
327	U Richmond		0	0	329	3,075	888	88	262
328	U Rio Grande	bGf	0	0	80	1,798	368	10	249
329	U Scranton	b	0	1	247	4,003	676	230	376
330	U Sthn IN	bG	0	0	505	7,402	2,497	110	635
331	U Tampa	bG	0	0	171	2,916	-1	-1	-1
332	U TN Chatt	bG	0	1	348	7,138	2,089	469	1,331
333	U TN Martin	BbG	0	0	255	5,781	1,161	109	297
334	U TX Tyler	BG	0	0	180	2,912	1,848	246	921
335	U West AL		0	0	100	1,851	0	0	0
336	U WI E Claire	b	0	0	408	9,386	754	106	400
337	U WI La Crosse	G	0	0	487	7,875	874	319	332
338	U WI Platteville	bG	0	0	303	4,960	1,141	108	419
339	U Winnipeg	bG	0	0	246	5,804	2,817	57	167
340	UNC Asheville	b	0	0	178	2,730	716	3	33
341	UNC Pembroke	bGf	0	0	204	4,321	1,362	68	401
342	Union C-NY		0	0	196	2,154	20	0	0
343	Valparaiso U		0	0	269	3,213	567	89	86
344	Villa Julie C	bG	0	0	91	2,128	612	0	81
345	W.Carey College	Bb	0	0	96	1,908	778	420	504
346	W.Mitchell C Law	GL	-2	-2	36	630	446	630	446
347	Walla Walla C	b	-2	-2	130	1,799	-1	224	-1
348	Walsh C Acct Bus Admin	B	0	0	14	0	3,111	0	938
349	Wartburg Theo Sem	bf	-2	-2	14	165	21	165	21
350	Washburn U Topeka	bG	0	0	241	4,568	2,434	729	525
351	Washington C	Gf	-2	-2	90	1,341	17	-2	60
352	Washington Theo Union	bf	0[1]	0	17	0 [1]	0	142	89
353	Wayland Bap U		0	0	107	1,044	5,161	57	569
354	Wayne ST C	bG	0	0	239	2,915	-1	-1	-1
355	Webber Intl U	b	0	0	18	576	65	42	14
356	Wesley C	bf	0	0	62	1,723	417	59	109
357	West Chester U PA		0	0	520	9,931	2,890	524	1,654
358	West TX A & M U	bG	0	1	226	4,720	2,303	389	1,051
359	West VA Wesleyan C		0	0	108	-1	-1	-1	-1
360	Western MD C	b	0	0	90	1,840	1,452	156	1,394

Key to Notes on Page 1   1 -- See Footnotes   -1 -- Unavailable   -2 -- Not Applicable

ACRL Library Data Tables 2004

PH.D., FACULTY, AND ENROLLMENT STATISTICS

INSTITUTIONS GRANTING MASTER OF ARTS AND PROFESSIONAL DEGREES (Carnegie Code M)

Lib. No.	Institution	Notes	Ph.D.'s Awarded	Ph.D. Fields	Full-Time Faculty	ENROLLMENT Full-time, Undergrad. & Grad.	Part-time, Undergrad. & Grad.	Full-time, Grad.	Part-time, Grad.
	Survey Question #		46	47	48	49	50	51	52
361	Western OR U	bG	0	0	182	4,207	825	191	371
362	Western Sem	b	0	0	15	79	547	79	547
363	Western WA U	G	0	0	457	11,860	820	418	244
364	Westfield ST C	b	0	0	169	3,799	1,138	85	560
365	Westminster C-UT	G	0	0	120	1,903	595	115	366
366	Wheeling Jesuit U	b	0	0	84	1,080	547	55	344
367	Whitworth C	G	0	0	106	2,028	270	78	149
368	Wilkes U	G	-2	-2	184	2,026	-1	210	-1
369	William Woods U	bL	0	0	55	1,004	1,169	219	956
370	Williams C		0	0	277	2,023	-1	57	-1
371	Wstrn IL U	Bb	0	0	624	10,651	2,818	861	1,581
372	Wstrn Theo Sem	f	-1	-1	18	-1	-1	-1	-1
373	Xavier U LA	b	0	0	226	3,994	-1	810	-1

ACRL LIBRARY DATA TABLES 2004

ANALYSIS OF SELECTED VARIABLES

ALL INSTITUTIONS REPORTING

Category	High	Mean	Median	Low	Libraries Reporting
1. Professional staff as percent of Total Staff	100.00	35.97	33.33	2.77	1111
2. Support Staff as percent of Total Staff	100.00	39.20	40.00	0.00	1102
3. Student Assistant Staff as percent of Total Staff	100.00	27.17	25.02	0.00	1099
4. Ratio of Professional to Support Staff (excluding student Assistant Staff)	28.00	1.08	0.86	0.04	1080
5. Ratio of Items Loaned to Items Borrowed	647.00	2.18	1.09	0.00	1066
6. Serial Expenditures as percent of Total Library Materials Expenditures	100.00	49.69	49.74	0.00	1089
7. Total Library Material Expenditures as percent of Total Library Expenditures	95.93	33.64	33.68	1.85	1066
8. Contract Binding as percent of Total Library Expenditures	98.97	0.73	0.50	0.00	1038
9. Salary and Wages Expenditures as percent of Total Library Expenditures	100.00	58.74	56.47	7.14	1065
10. Other Operating Expenditures as percent of Total Library Expenditures	98.23	10.83	8.49	0.00	1045
11. Unit cost of monographs (per volume)	445.47	44.39	40.14	0.93	907

ACRL LIBRARY DATA TABLES 2004

ANALYSIS OF SELECTED VARIABLES

INSTITUTIONS GRANTING BACHELOR OF ARTS DEGREES (CARNEGIE CODE B)

Category	High	Mean	Median	Low	Libraries Reporting
1. Professional staff as percent of Total Staff	100.00	36.74	33.33	8.00	188
2. Support Staff as percent of Total Staff	83.33	32.41	33.33	0.00	186
3. Student Assistant Staff as percent of Total Staff	80.00	33.56	33.33	0.00	186
4. Ratio of Professional to Support Staff (excluding student Assistant Staff)	14.00	1.33	1.00	0.09	180
5. Ratio of Items Loaned to Items Borrowed	16.31	1.43	0.89	0.00	177
6. Serial Expenditures as percent of Total Library Materials Expenditures	100.00	46.67	46.11	2.77	181
7. Total Library Material Expenditures as percent of Total Library Expenditures	78.37	35.06	34.37	4.07	177
8. Contract Binding as percent of Total Library Expenditures	7.74	0.61	0.42	0.00	173
9. Salary and Wages Expenditures as percent of Total Library Expenditures	100.00	58.02	55.60	25.43	177
10. Other Operating Expenditures as percent of Total Library Expenditures	55.38	10.25	8.44	0.00	172
11. Unit cost of monographs (per volume)	211.12	39.82	38.75	1.82	156

ACRL LIBRARY DATA TABLES 2004

ANALYSIS OF SELECTED VARIABLES

INSTITUTIONS GRANTING MASTER OF ARTS AND PROFESSIONAL DEGREES (CARNEGIE CODE M)

Category	High	Mean	Median	Low	Libraries Reporting
1. Professional staff as percent of Total Staff	100.00	36.83	34.78	11.11	367
2. Support Staff as percent of Total Staff	100.00	36.48	36.84	0.00	364
3. Student Assistant Staff as percent of Total Staff	100.00	29.41	28.57	0.00	363
4. Ratio of Professional to Support Staff (excluding student Assistant Staff)	28.00	1.23	1.00	0.20	360
5. Ratio of Items Loaned to Items Borrowed	24.10	1.67	1.12	0.00	357
6. Serial Expenditures as percent of Total Library Materials Expenditures	100.00	51.73	51.91	10.25	366
7. Total Library Material Expenditures as percent of Total Library Expenditures	95.93	35.00	35.10	11.33	359
8. Contract Binding as percent of Total Library Expenditures	37.45	0.81	0.57	0.00	351
9. Salary and Wages Expenditures as percent of Total Library Expenditures	100.00	57.34	55.64	7.14	358
10. Other Operating Expenditures as percent of Total Library Expenditures	86.21	11.41	8.54	0.00	349
11. Unit cost of monographs (per volume)	262.27	44.63	40.59	2.81	331

ACRL LIBRARY DATA TABLES 2004

SUMMARY DATA: ELECTRONIC RESOURCES

ALL INSTITUTIONS REPORTING

(Survey Question #)	Electronic journals purchased 1	Electronic journals purchased 2	Electronic journals not purchased 3	Electronic reference sources 4	Electronic books 5
High	469,602	341,148	7,473,074	750,000	740,620
Mean	10,010	4,172	12,430	1,581	18,620
Median	5,675	641	24	42	4,948
Low	0	0	0	0	0
Total	8,578,829	3,441,708	9,434,188	1,413,729	17,651,451
Libraries Reporting	857	825	759	894	948

ACRL LIBRARY DATA TABLES 2004

SUMMARY DATA: NETWORKED RESOURCES AND SERVICES

ALL INSTITUTIONS REPORTING

	EXPENDITURES				
	Electronic journals purchased	Electronic full-text journals	Electronic reference sources	Electronic books	Virtual reference transactions
(Survey Question #)	6	7	8	9	10
High	8,719,188	7,296,801	4,755,311	1,676,891	117,407
Mean	246,650	156,671	153,991	18,903	784
Median	26,000	10,685	25,182	0	53
Low	0	0	0	0	0
Total	200,280,098	113,743,503	123,654,625	15,916,182	561,140
Libraries Reporting	812	726	803	842	716

ACRL LIBRARY DATA TABLES 2004

SUMMARY DATA: NETWORKED RESOURCES AND SERVICES

ALL INSTITUTIONS REPORTING

Logins to electronic databases	No. of databases reported	Queries (searches) in electronic databases	No. of databases reported	Items requested in electronic databases	No. of databases reported	Virtual visits to website	Virtual visits to catalog	
12	12a	13	13a	14	14a	15a	15b	(Survey Question #)
15,909,898	255,352	21,858,920	255,352	73,287,094	255,352	78,610,816	123,218,941	High
230,365	949	417,939	969	700,326	904	1,812,316	907,330	Mean
23,629	18	83,621	24	28,306	10	110,187	8,197	Median
0	0	0	0	0	0	0	0	Low
119,559,693	517,424	246,583,767	573,438	331,954,617	452,863	904,345,788	324,824,150	Total
519	545	590	592	474	501	499	358	Libraries Reporting

ACRL LIBRARY DATA TABLES 2004

SUMMARY DATA: DIGITIZATION ACTIVITIES

ALL INSTITUTIONS REPORTING

| (Survey Question #) | DIGITAL COLLECTIONS | | | USAGE | | DIRECT COSTS | | |
| | No. of collections | Size (MB) | Items | No. of times accessed | No. of queries | Personnel | Equipment, software, or contract services | Volume Held Collectively |
	16a	16b	16c	17a	17b	18a	18b	1
High	1,000	175,000,000	2,600,000	28,113,255	6,236,556	1,725,000	532,698	7,000,000
Mean	6	522,230	14,501	123,620	20,514	17,609	8,536	11,803
Median	0	0	0	0	0	0	0	0
Low	0	0	0	0	0	0	0	0
Total	4,968	367,127,393	10,817,690	77,262,622	12,124,065	11,745,031	5,710,577	8,261,900
Libraries Reporting	806	703	746	625	591	667	669	700

ACRL LIBRARY DATA TABLES 2004

SUMMARY DATA: ELECTRONIC RESOURCES

INSTITUTIONS GRANTING BACHELOR OF ARTS DEGREES (Carnegie Code B)

(Survey Question #)	Electronic journals purchased 1	Electronic journals purchased 2	Electronic journals not purchased 3	Electronic reference sources 4	Electronic books 5
High	32,872	64,410	120,311	12,000	147,006
Mean	6,311	3,189	3,391	133	11,694
Median	2,226	364	3	27	4,887
Low	0	0	0	0	0
Total	877,164	443,280	440,864	20,071	1,847,648
Libraries Reporting	139	139	130	151	158

ACRL LIBRARY DATA TABLES 2004

SUMMARY DATA: NETWORKED RESOURCES AND SERVICES

INSTITUTIONS GRANTING BACHELOR OF ARTS DEGREES (Carnegie Code B)

	EXPENDITURES				
	Electronic journals purchased	Electronic full-text journals	Electronic reference sources	Electronic books	Virtual reference transactions
(Survey Question #)	6	7	8	9	10
High	520,116	309,477	552,400	151,860	4,962
Mean	47,927	25,744	42,815	3,884	89
Median	17,500	7,314	8,500	0	0
Low	0	0	0	0	0
Total	6,566,024	3,243,788	5,694,428	551,571	10,061
Libraries Reporting	137	126	133	142	113

ACRL LIBRARY DATA TABLES 2004

SUMMARY DATA: NETWORKED RESOURCES AND SERVICES

INSTITUTIONS GRANTING BACHELOR OF ARTS DEGREES (Carnegie Code B)

Logins to electronic databases	No. of databases reported	Queries (searches) in electronic databases	No. of databases reported	Items requested in electronic databases	No. of databases reported	Virtual visits to website	Virtual visits to catalog	(Survey Question #)
12	12a	13	13a	14	14a	15a	15b	
309,963	32,231	620,647	112,201	931,035	201	3,745,350	15,000,000	High
25,062	374	65,750	1,435	52,371	17	189,234	296,399	Mean
4,127	5	24,028	13	4,506	4	5,872	0	Median
0	0	0	0	0	0	0	0	Low
2,205,468	34,797	6,706,495	147,838	4,294,390	1,555	14,192,554	18,080,315	Total
88	93	102	103	82	89	75	61	Libraries Reporting

155

ACRL LIBRARY DATA TABLES 2004

SUMMARY DATA: DIGITIZATION ACTIVITIES

INSTITUTIONS GRANTING BACHELOR OF ARTS DEGREES (Carnegie Code B)

	DIGITAL COLLECTIONS			USAGE		DIRECT COSTS		
	No. of collections	Size (MB)	Items	No. of times accessed	No. of queries	Personnel	Equipment, software, or services	Volumes Held Collectively
(Survey Question #)	16a	16b	16c	17a	17b	18a	18b	19
High	113	96,827	500,000	7,864,446	40,000	46,510	20,730	192,327
Mean	2	1,762	4,366	81,608	571	622	453	1,910
Median	0	0	0	0	0	0	0	0
Low	0	0	0	0	0	0	0	0
Total	289	216,705	571,970	9,221,701	62,230	70,912	53,497	242,625
Libraries Reporting	139	123	131	113	109	114	118	127

ACRL LIBRARY DATA TABLES 2004

SUMMARY DATA: ELECTRONIC RESOURCES

INSTITUTIONS GRANTING MASTER OF ARTS AND PROFESSIONAL DEGREES (Carnegie Code M)

(Survey Question #)	Electronic journals purchased 1	Electronic journals purchased 2	Electronic journals not purchased 3	Electronic reference sources 4	Electronic books 5
High	469,602	341,148	7,473,074	341,148	740,620
Mean	11,629	5,127	31,846	1,405	12,014
Median	6,408	751	26	42	3,123
Low	0	0	0	0	0
Total	3,372,513	1,445,769	7,993,420	428,589	3,856,344
Libraries Reporting	290	282	251	305	321

ACRL LIBRARY DATA TABLES 2004

SUMMARY DATA: NETWORKED RESOURCES AND SERVICES

INSTITUTIONS GRANTING MASTER OF ARTS AND PROFESSIONAL DEGREES (Carnegie Code M)

	EXPENDITURES				
	Electronic journals purchased	Electronic full-text journals	Electronic reference sources	Electronic books	Virtual reference transactions
(Survey Question #)	6	7	8	9	10
High	683,257	1,122,827	700,000	123,000	117,407
Mean	71,578	50,663	71,113	3,083	826
Median	40,620	19,924	33,250	0	40
Low	0	0	0	0	0
Total	19,111,437	12,209,685	18,631,683	823,152	189,984
Libraries Reporting	267	241	262	267	230

ACRL LIBRARY DATA TABLES 2004

SUMMARY DATA: NETWORKED RESOURCES AND SERVICES

INSTITUTIONS GRANTING MASTER OF ARTS AND PROFESSIONAL DEGREES (Carnegie Code M)

Logins to electronic databases	No. of databases reported	Queries (searches) in electronic databases	No. of databases reported	Items requested in electronic databases	No. of databases reported	Virtual visits to website	Virtual visits to catalog	
12	12a	13	13a	14	14a	15a	15b	(Survey Question #)
6,532,315	255,352	7,121,775	255,352	70,127,972	255,352	15,245,249	655,403	High
116,786	1,774	264,642	1,732	653,040	1,746	568,003	87,670	Mean
25,540	25	104,300	33	50,212	13	98,696	11,821	Median
0	0	0	0	0	0	0	0	Low
19,853,686	319,246	51,605,255	339,399	102,527,309	291,582	88,040,482	9,731,368	Total
170	180	195	196	157	167	155	111	Libraries Reporting

ACRL LIBRARY DATA TABLES 2004

SUMMARY DATA: DIGITIZATION ACTIVITIES

INSTITUTIONS GRANTING MASTER OF ARTS AND PROFESSIONAL DEGREES (Carnegie Code M)

	DIGITAL COLLECTIONS			USAGE		DIRECT COSTS		
	No. of collections	Size (MB)	Items	No. of times accessed	No. of queries	Personnel	Equipment, software, or contract	Volu Collecti
(Survey Question #)	16a	16b	16c	17a	17b	18a	18b	
High	1,000	83,502,663	1,051,194	748,673	632,464	300,000	200,000	193,
Mean	5	611,716	4,723	4,105	3,015	2,924	2,337	1,
Median	0	0	0	0	0	0	0	
Low	0	0	0	0	0	0	0	
Total	1,415	142,529,863	1,161,919	870,220	636,142	649,053	530,598	283,
Libraries Reporting	268	233	246	212	211	222	227	

ACRL Library Data Tables 2004
ELECTRONIC RESOURCES

INSTITUTIONS GRANTING BACHELOR OF ARTS DEGREES (Carnegie Code B)

Lib. No.	Survey Question # Institution	Electronic journals purchased 1	Electronic full-text journals purchased 2	Electronic journals not purchased 3	Electronic Reference Sources 4	Electronic books 5
1	AB C Art & Design	-1	-1	-1	3	-1
2	Adrian C	41	37	0	70	0
3	Albion C	-1	-1	-1	41	6,350
4	Amherst C	-1	5,002	0	-1	73,079
5	Aquinas C TN	-1	-1	-1	-1	-1
6	Atlanta C Art	0	0	0	160	0
7	Atlanta Christian C	-1	-1	-1	-1	-1
8	Augustana C RI	-1	-1	-1	81	0
9	Barber-Scotia C	20,459	2	0	2	0
10	Bard C	700	-1	-1	-1	-1
11	Barton C	13,053	0	20	20	22,581
12	Bates C	-1	-1	-1	-1	-1
13	Benedict C	5	4	4	9	0
14	Berry C	22,125	2,032	1,432	127	15,000
15	Bethany C Bethany	13,043	682	0	44	30,000
16	Bethany C Lindsborg	0	0	0	7	0
17	Bethel C KS	19,177	62	6,101	61	6,686
18	Blackburn C	0	0	0	5	329
19	Bluefield C	28	10,400	25	527	42,000
20	Boise Bible C	2	2	0	1	0
21	Bowdoin C	22,321	1,897	2,338	166	81,664
22	Bridgewater C	-1	42	-1	59	0
23	Bryan C	13	10,000	0	50	36,000
24	C Holy Cross	11,934	594	75	46	4,917
25	C Visual Arts	0	0	0	5	1,045
26	C Wooster	0	6,566	0	200	14,598
27	Campion C	-1	-1	-1	-1	-1
28	Carroll C-Helena	5	15	0	33	0
29	Cazenovia C	-1	-1	-1	-1	1,500
30	Centennial C	43	-1	0	27	4,857
31	Central Bible C	2,226	2,226	0	0	7,736
32	Central C	12,748	32	-1	14	11,373
33	Central Christian C Bible	2	0	0	0	0
34	Centre C	0	72	56	3	4,000
35	Christian Heritage C	0	0	7,400	112	13,836
36	Clear Creek Bible	0	0	6	3	9,493
37	Cmty Hosp C Health	0	0	0	0	0
38	Colby C	2,720	0	0	90	114,953
39	Colby Sawyer C	-1	0	0	27	744
40	Columbia Union C	-1	-1	-1	50	-1

-1 -- Unavailable   -2 -- Not Applicable

ACRL Library Data Tables 2004
ELECTRONIC RESOURCES
INSTITUTIONS GRANTING BACHELOR OF ARTS DEGREES (Carnegie Code B)

Lib. No.	Survey Question # Institution	Electronic journals purchased 1	Electronic full-text journals purchased 2	Electronic journals not purchased 3	Electronic Reference Sources 4	Electronic books 5
41	Concordia C-MN	24,409	6,900	17,442	67	11,586
42	Concordia C-NY	-1	-1	-1	0	0
43	Cornish C Arts	0	0	12	2	2,852
44	Crichton C	-1	-1	26	25	10,768
45	Crown C-MN	5,000	0	10,000	65	35,000
46	Culver Stockton C	-1	-1	-1	2	5,936
47	CUNY City C	-1	-1	-1	-1	-1
48	CUNY York C	0	0	0	0	0
49	Dakota Wesleyan U	256	239	0	18	11,580
50	Dana C	6,675	283	0	21	13,598
51	Davidson C	-1	1,010	17,527	264	147,006
52	Dean C	23	2	21	22	0
53	Defiance C	-1	7	1	123	17,000
54	Denison U	-1	-1	-1	-1	-1
55	DeVry Inst Tech GA	6,200	144	2,200	17	13,000
56	Dickinson ST U	-1	-1	-1	-1	-1
57	Divine Word C	0	0	0	2	0
58	East Texas Baptist U	1,000	15,000	2,000	165	25,000
59	Eckerd C	13,375	501	0	282	3,733
60	Emmanuel C GA	0	0	0	12	28,072
61	Eugene Bible C	0	0	0	0	0
62	Evangel U	8,000	6,000	0	10	0
63	F&M C	1,030	1,030	0	73	0
64	Ferrum C	40	10,300	447	120	43,899
65	Finlandia U	501	500	5	53	12,445
66	FL Christian C	18,298	13,285	0	0	0
67	Flagler C	12,714	0	87	9	31,000
68	Fort Lewis C	16,753	70	10	48	0
69	G Adolphus C	8,005	364	-1	77	5,334
70	Green Mountain C	0	0	0	5	18,000
71	Grinnell C	2,264	2,264	0	147	7,767
72	Guilford C	9,271	645	5,567	166	37,237
73	H Inst Int Desgn	1	1,500	0	9	5,000
74	H LaGrange C	14,400	0	5,315	66	9,329
75	Hamilton C	2,330	-1	1,000	180	0
76	Hampshire C	8,319	7,823	9,137	4	0
77	Hanover C	-1	686	-1	1	0
78	Haskell Indian Nations U	0	0	0	0	0
79	Haverford C	10,074	2,584	-1	85	1,895
80	Hendrix C	38	1,300	0	3	500

-1 -- Unavailable   -2 -- Not Applicable

ACRL Library Data Tables 2004
ELECTRONIC RESOURCES

INSTITUTIONS GRANTING BACHELOR OF ARTS DEGREES (Carnegie Code B)

Lib. No.	Survey Question # Institution	Electronic journals purchased 1	Electronic full-text journals purchased 2	Electronic journals not purchased 3	Electronic Reference Sources 4	Electronic books 5
81	Hiram C	-1	-1	-1	-1	-1
82	Hobart &William Smith Cs	9,854	1,325	3,915	33	3,577
83	Hope C	3,139	1,964	1,175	37	11,530
84	Houghton C	-1	-1	-1	-1	0
85	Howard Payne U	-1	-1	-1	-1	-1
86	Illinois C	-1	-1	-1	-1	-1
87	Jamestown C	18,130	110	0	2	10,413
88	Johnson C Smith U	18,250	13,569	0	21	21,000
89	Judson C	32,872	14	33,740	45	0
90	Kent ST U Salem	3	3	0	1	0
91	Kent ST U Trumbull	-1	-1	-1	-1	-1
92	Kenyon C	14,104	6,645	-1	138	20,857
93	Kettering C Med	-1	-1	-1	-1	-1
94	Keuka C	15,000	12,000	0	25	10,600
95	Knox C	3,213	1,928	7,463	59	0
96	Kwantlen UC	7,750	-1	-1	35	550
97	Lambuth U	22,694	0	120,311	331	36,750
98	Lawrence U	763	763	0	77	6,515
99	Lemoyne-Owen C	6	1	2	2	0
100	Lester B Pearson C Pacific	-1	-1	-1	-1	-1
101	LIFE Bible C	1,722	0	0	7	0
102	Lyndon State C	-1	-1	-1	-1	-1
103	Lyon C	9	17,109	0	17	19,859
104	Macon ST C	1	-2	-2	-2	15,000
105	Marlboro C	6,857	6,857	0	9	30,000
106	Mars Hill C	13,144	0	0	87	41,194
107	Martin Luther C	-1	592	714	9	11,615
108	Mayville ST U	29,506	20,182	44	9	7,424
109	McKendree C	20	8,000	8,000	40	1,000
110	McPherson C	-1	-1	0	51	5,871
111	Methodist C	9,773	194	5,487	0	24,128
112	Midland Lutheran C	11,000	-1	-1	-1	-1
113	Milwaukee Inst Art Design	0	0	0	4	0
114	MO Baptist C	200	195	39	12	0
115	MO Western ST C	11,515	180	423	47	1,800
116	Monmouth C	767	755	67	103	5,467
117	Mount Royal C	17,525	-1	-1	-1	0
118	Mount Union C	18,000	6,000	1,500	12,000	20,000
119	Muhlenberg C	10,354	447	0	67	0
120	NC Wesleyan C	6,000	-1	10	74	22,000

-1 -- Unavailable   -2 -- Not Applicable

ACRL Library Data Tables 2004
ELECTRONIC RESOURCES
INSTITUTIONS GRANTING BACHELOR OF ARTS DEGREES (Carnegie Code B)

Lib. No.	Survey Question # Institution	Electronic journals purchased 1	Electronic full-text journals purchased 2	Electronic journals not purchased 3	Electronic Reference Sources 4	Electronic books 5
121	New C U South FL	-1	-1	-1	-1	-1
122	OH Dominican C	875	-1	-1	5	820
123	OH Wesleyan U	-1	6,670	253	27	17,000
124	OK Panhandle ST U	1,942	1,942	9,974	40	18,297
125	Paier C Art	0	0	0	0	0
126	Peace C	4,000	4,000	0	2	23,000
127	Potomac C	0	0	0	2	0
128	Presbyterian C	-1	-1	-1	-1	-1
129	Principia C	17,373	-1	-1	43	-1
130	Randolph-Macon C	654	654	0	0	0
131	Randolph-Macon WC	13,000	10,000	100	50	10,000
132	Reformed Bible C	4	2	17	5	11,400
133	Reinhardt C	15,000	15,000	0	0	0
134	Ricks C	-1	-1	-1	175	33,335
135	Ringling Sch Art & Design	0	0	0	10	0
136	Rochester C	0	1,773	1,911	11	10,919
137	Rocky Mountain C	0	36	0	12	0
138	Rogers ST U	-1	-1	0	59	29,131
139	SE C Assemblies God	8,000	8,000	50	25	2,300
140	Shawnee ST U	4,246	4,246	8,954	55	16,828
141	Shepherd C	6,500	0	0	5	0
142	Siena C	5,529	4,304	3,072	65	4,068
143	Simpson C IA	15,150	150	54	8	7,487
144	Skidmore C	22,302	1,307	18	161	3,599
145	Southwest U	1,699	-1	-1	123	33,941
146	Spartan Aero-Flight Schl	0	0	6,474	1	0
147	St Andrews Presby C	9,921	9,921	4,051	60	22,751
148	St Gregory's U	0	0	1,933	-1	3,947
149	St John Vianney C Sem	-1	-1	-1	-1	0
150	St Olaf C	0	0	0	55	0
151	St. Mary's C Maryland	-1	-1	-1	-1	-1
152	Sterling C-VT	24,015	312	-1	1	0
153	Stillman C	3,252	2,297	83,455	7	0
154	Susquehanna U	3	15,185	0	327	0
155	SW Baptist Theo Sem	-1	-1	-1	-1	-1
156	Swarthmore C	16,874	2,955	-1	145	3,486
157	Sweet Briar C	-1	64,410	-1	-1	-1
158	Talladega C	-1	-1	-1	-1	-1
159	Taylor U-Ft Wayne	133	4,897	3,628	18	5,621
160	Teikyo Post U	0	0	17	10	0

-1 -- Unavailable   -2 -- Not Applicable

ACRL Library Data Tables 2004

ELECTRONIC RESOURCES

INSTITUTIONS GRANTING BACHELOR OF ARTS DEGREES (Carnegie Code B)

Lib. No.	Survey Question # Institution	Electronic journals purchased 1	Electronic full-text journals purchased 2	Electronic journals not purchased 3	Electronic Reference Sources 4	Electronic books 5
161	TN Wesleyan C	8,500	538	-1	-1	20,000
162	Tri ST U	205	147	-1	21	2,375
163	Trinity Christian C	9,255	174	520	53	80
164	Trinity Wstrn U	0	15,989	0	100	2,577
165	Truett McConnell C	-1	-1	-1	-1	-1
166	TX Lutheran U	18,161	-1	-1	51	27,450
167	U Maine-Machias	122	53	-1	-1	-1
168	U ME Fort Kent	-1	16,703	246	45	7,400
169	U Ozarks	-1	-1	-1	-1	-1
170	U VA C Wise	10,354	885	279	62	0
171	Union C-NE	3,158	3,143	3,543	52	16,856
172	US C Guard Acad	-1	-1	-1	-1	-1
173	US Merchant Marine Acad	-1	-1	-1	-1	4
174	US Mil Acad	-1	-1	-1	-1	-1
175	US Naval Acad	-1	-1	-1	-1	-1
176	UT Valley ST C	-1	6,975	-1	114	6,398
177	VA Wesleyan C	9,500	518	0	26	0
178	Vassar C	16,724	2,378	8,909	130	6,000
179	VMI	800	518	16,022	11	0
180	Wabash C	5,735	5,735	0	14	4,617
181	Warner Sthrn C	16,567	10,371	0	6	0
182	Warren Wilson C	-1	9,823	-1	50	35,000
183	Wells C	0	0	-1	4	0
184	Western ST C	1	1	0	3	0
185	Westmont C	15,817	330	1	33	14,400
186	Whitman C	-1	-1	-1	-1	-1
187	Wiley C	0	0	74	2	27,450
188	Winston-Salem ST U	0	0	0	-1	14,000
189	Wofford C	1	1	8,821	239	37,485
190	York C	0	0	7,344	20	40,198

-1 -- Unavailable   -2 -- Not Applicable

ACRL Library Data Tables 2004
NETWORKED ELECTRONIC RESOURCES AND SERVICES
INSTITUTIONS GRANTING BACHELOR OF ARTS DEGREES (Carnegie Code B)

Lib. No.	Institution	Notes	EXPENDITURES				Virtual reference transactions 10	Federated searching across networked electronic resources? 11
	Survey Question #		Electronic journals purchased 6	Electronic full-text journals 7	Electronic reference sources 8	Electronic books 9		
1	AB C Art & Design	C	-1	10,000	-1	-1	-1	
2	Adrian C		22,871	1,048	31,749	0	-1	Y
3	Albion C		121,810	56,465	121,810	120	118	N
4	Amherst C		-1	164,377	-1	2,890	-1	N
5	Aquinas C TN		-1	-1	-1	-1	-1	
6	Atlanta C Art		0	0	8,500	0	0	N
7	Atlanta Christian C		-1	-1	-1	-1	-1	
8	Augustana C RI		-1	-1	104,113	0	0	N
9	Barber-Scotia C		14,500	11,410	3,617	0	2	N
10	Bard C		27,036	-1	-1	-1	0	N
11	Barton C		20,584	0	0	0	26	N
12	Bates C		-1	-1	-1	-1	-1	N
13	Benedict C		34,337	32,315	34,337	0	0	N
14	Berry C		143,070	35,205	149,976	0	-1	N
15	Bethany C Bethany		43,634	3,684	39,950	0	0	N
16	Bethany C Lindsborg		0	0	6,006	0	0	Y
17	Bethel C KS		8,710	-1	0	0	314	N
18	Blackburn C		0	0	9,787	1,000	0	N
19	Bluefield C		9,000	3,000	2,000	1,500	56	
20	Boise Bible C		-1	-1	-1	-1	-1	
21	Bowdoin C		235,206	-1	-1	16,130	383	N
22	Bridgewater C		23,100	18,000	26,872	0	0	N
23	Bryan C		558	24,000	1,600	1,150	0	N
24	C Holy Cross		25,866	10,555	130,577	0	195	N
25	C Visual Arts		0	0	3,210	0	0	Y
26	C Wooster		304,498	0	0	0	0	Y
27	Campion C	C	-1	-1	-1	-1	-1	
28	Carroll C-Helena		200	-1	0	0	-1	
29	Cazenovia C		18,650	-1	-1	-1	0	N
30	Centennial C	C	147,000	-1	-1	-1	-1	N
31	Central Bible C		7,628	7,628	0	0	10	Y
32	Central C		18,859	1,925	638	897	-1	N
33	Central Christian C Bible		0	0	0	0	0	N
34	Centre C		0	53,609	27,613	1,000	0	N
35	Christian Heritage C		0	0	11,092	970	0	N
36	Clear Creek Bible		0	0	8,782	250	0	N
37	Cmty Hosp C Health		0	0	0	0	-1	
38	Colby C		492,104	0	200,000	151,860	0	N
39	Colby Sawyer C		31,844	0	48,028	1,111	0	Y
40	Columbia Union C		-1	-1	77,008	-1	-1	N

C -- Reported in Canadian $ -1 -- Unavailable   -2 -- Not Applicable

INSTITUTIONS GRANTING BACHELOR OF ARTS DEGREES (Carnegie Code B)

Logins to electronic databases 12	No. of databases reported 12a	Queries (searches) in electronic databases 13	No. of databases reported 13a	Items requested in electronic databases 14	No. of databases reported 14a	Virtual visits to website 15a	Virtual visits to catalog 15b	Excl. visits fr. inside library 15c	Survey Question # Institution
1	7	30,512	7	-1	-1	-1	-1		AB C Art & Design
-1	0	63,337	34	-1	0	-1	-1	N	Adrian C
-1	-1	-1	-1	-1	-1	-1	-1	N	Albion C
-1	-1	-1	-1	-1	-1	-1	-1		Amherst C
-1	-1	-1	-1	-1	-1	-1	-1		Aquinas C TN
-1	-1	-1	-1	-1	-1	-1	-1	Y	Atlanta C Art
-1	-1	-1	-1	-1	-1	-1	-1		Atlanta Christian C
-1	-1	-1	-1	-1	-1	-1	-1		Augustana C RI
1,171	21	1,523	233	446	15	0	87	Y	Barber-Scotia C
0	0	0	0	0	0	0	0	Y	Bard C
21,633	5	23,372	5	-1	-1	25,340	10,776	N	Barton C
-1	-1	-1	-1	-1	-1	-1	-1	N	Bates C
-1	-1	-1	-1	-1	-1	-1	-1	N	Benedict C
26,986	27	221,648	27	146,937	27	196,172	-1	N	Berry C
42,844	-1	-1	-1	0	0	53,371	0	N	Bethany C Bethany
5,832	5	32,457	5	11,422	2	-1	-1	N	Bethany C Lindsborg
13,994	10	35,917	10	55,226	10	15,306	-1	N	Bethel C KS
0	0	0	0	0	0	0	0	N	Blackburn C
890	45	0	467	0	0	5,000	6,500	N	Bluefield C
-1	-1	-1	-1	0	0	0	0	Y	Boise Bible C
119,826	144	-1	-1	-1	-1	496,678	-1	N	Bowdoin C
-1	-1	78,954	58	-1	-1	70,880	-1	N	Bridgewater C
20,850	17	14,534	17	16,584	17	0	0	N	Bryan C
-1	-1	152,563	46	-1	-1	92,383	-1	N	C Holy Cross
5,436	4	17,698	5	7,396	2	0	0	N	C Visual Arts
0	0	69,262	49	0	0	868,570	0	Y	C Wooster
-1	-1	-1	-1	-1	-1	-1	-1		Campion C
-1	-1	-1	-1	-1	-1	-1	-1		Carroll C-Helena
-1	-1	-1	-1	-1	-1	-1	-1		Cazenovia C
66,755	27	-1	-1	-1	-1	28,247	-1	Y	Centennial C
4,623	3	13,523	3	0	0	0	0	N	Central Bible C
-1	-1	206,532	14	-1	-1	212,174	173,090	N	Central C
0	0	0	0	0	0	0	0	Y	Central Christian C Bible
-1	-1	126,618	27	93,759	27	-1	-1	N	Centre C
-1	-1	26,717	24	-1	-1	-1	-1		Christian Heritage C
971	2	3,863	2	0	2	-1	-1		Clear Creek Bible
0	0	0	0	0	0	0	0	Y	Cmty Hosp C Health
0	0	0	0	0	0	0	0		Colby C
24,339	-1	154,940	-1	117,388	-1	359,385	-1	N	Colby Sawyer C
-1	-1	-1	-1	-1	-1	-1	-1	N	Columbia Union C

-1 -- Unavailable   -2 -- Not Applicable

ACRL Library Data Tables 2004
NETWORKED ELECTRONIC RESOURCES AND SERVICES
INSTITUTIONS GRANTING BACHELOR OF ARTS DEGREES (Carnegie Code B)

Lib. No.	Institution	Notes	Electronic journals purchased 6	Electronic full-text journals 7	Electronic reference sources 8	Electronic books 9	Virtual reference transactions 10	Federated searching across networked electronic resources? 11
			EXPENDITURES					
41	Concordia C-MN		37,774	35,206	72,980	9,932	-1	Y
42	Concordia C-NY		-1	-1	0	0	-1	N
43	Cornish C Arts		0	0	1,500	0	65	N
44	Crichton C		-1	-1	36,287	1,000	0	N
45	Crown C-MN		10,860	0	20,161	10,123	0	N
46	Culver Stockton C		21,657	17,135	1,395	1,000	-1	Y
47	CUNY City C		-1	-1	-1	-1	-1	Y
48	CUNY York C		0	0	0	0	0	N
49	Dakota Wesleyan U		10,000	3,000	10,000	1,500	450	Y
50	Dana C		13,734	2,250	602	1,035	0	N
51	Davidson C		-1	73,232	222,238	4,499	110	N
52	Dean C		6,384	175	6,209	0	0	N
53	Defiance C		-1	-1	-1	-1	-1	Y
54	Denison U		-1	-1	-1	-1	-1	
55	DeVry Inst Tech GA		475,000	7,000	475,000	114,000	4,962	Y
56	Dickinson ST U		-1	-1	-1	-1	-1	
57	Divine Word C		0	0	997	0	4	N
58	East Texas Baptist U		5,000	10,000	68,000	5,000	0	N
59	Eckerd C		97,643	70,501	4,640	7,925	48	N
60	Emmanuel C GA		0	0	19,397	0	-1	N
61	Eugene Bible C		-1	-1	-1	-1	-1	
62	Evangel U		24,746	24,746	0	0	0	N
63	F&M C		87,475	87,475	163,675	0	185	N
64	Ferrum C		5,000	34,887	0	0	0	N
65	Finlandia U		6,613	5,955	8,122	500	-1	N
66	FL Christian C		3,564	0	0	0	5	Y
67	Flagler C		34,560	0	6,285	2,400	0	N
68	Fort Lewis C		70,982	35,264	70,982	0	420	N
69	G Adolphus C		38,303	34,234	127,810	300	24	N
70	Green Mountain C		15,200	-1	-1	1,200	0	N
71	Grinnell C		177,218	-1	-1	950	0	N
72	Guilford C		58,110	41,995	72,887	1,948	0	N
73	H Inst Int Desgn		1,000	6,000	2,520	1,100	1	N
74	H LaGrange C		-1	-1	11,417	1,000	-1	N
75	Hamilton C		-1	-1	268,540	0	0	N
76	Hampshire C		89,944	83,799	1,917	0	150	N
77	Hanover C		101,355	29,764	912	0	0	N
78	Haskell Indian Nations U		0	0	0	-1	0	Y
79	Haverford C		241,185	232,880	128,599	0	186	N
80	Hendrix C		17,500	45,100	3,000	5,000	0	N

C -- Reported in Canadian $ -1 -- Unavailable   -2 -- Not Applicable

ACRL Library Data Tables 2004
NETWORKED RESOURCES AND SERVICES

INSTITUTIONS GRANTING BACHELOR OF ARTS DEGREES (Carnegie Code B)

Logins to electronic databases 12	No. of databases reported 12a	Queries (searches) in electronic databases 13	No. of databases reported 13a	Items requested in electronic databases 14	No. of databases reported 14a	Virtual visits to website 15a	Virtual visits to catalog 15b	Excl. visits fr. inside library 15c	Survey Question # Institution
152,930	67	620,647	67	346,602	67	-1	1,497,421	N	Concordia C-MN
-1	-1	-1	-1	-1	-1	-1	-1	N	Concordia C-NY
1	3	1	3	1	1	1	1	N	Cornish C Arts
6,985	4	12,410	4	164	1	-1	-1	N	Crichton C
-1	-1	-1	-1	-1	-1	-1	-1	N	Crown C-MN
-1	-1	16,880	17	-1	-1	-1	-1	N	Culver Stockton C
-1	-1	-1	-1	-1	-1	-1	-1		CUNY City C
0	0	0	0	-1	0	0	0	Y	CUNY York C
5,557	14	31,432	22	28,462	14	0	0		Dakota Wesleyan U
3,500	4	13,388	4	8,468	4	28,638	14,250	N	Dana C
104,571	182	-1	-1	-1	-1	111,332	207,944	N	Davidson C
-1	-1	-1	-1	-1	-1	-1	-1		Dean C
-1	-1	-1	-1	-1	-1	20,398	-1	N	Defiance C
-1	-1	-1	-1	-1	-1	-1	-1		Denison U
-1	-1	600,000	5	500,000	5	-1	-1	N	DeVry Inst Tech GA
-1	-1	-1	-1	-1	-1	-1	-1		Dickinson ST U
0	0	0	0	0	0	0	0	Y	Divine Word C
11,155	49	46,095	49	19,616	49	0	0	N	East Texas Baptist U
-1	69	-1	69	-1	69	-1	-1	N	Eckerd C
3,796	12	10,720	12	17,128	12	-1	-1		Emmanuel C GA
-1	-1	-1	-1	-1	-1	-1	-1		Eugene Bible C
0	0	0	-1	0	0	0	0	N	Evangel U
97,436	19	132,655	19	194,328	19	67,226	-1	N	F&M C
56,375	13	0	0	0	0	0	0	N	Ferrum C
-1	-1	15,445	12	-1	-1	-1	-1	N	Finlandia U
0	0	0	0	0	0	0	0	N	FL Christian C
-1	-1	-1	-1	-1	-1	-1	-1	N	Flagler C
0	0	174,967	48	112,006	19	0	0	N	Fort Lewis C
52,915	47	145,369	24	60,995	31	171,853	22,266	N	G Adolphus C
-1	-1	-1	-1	-1	-1	-1	-1		Green Mountain C
-2	-2	-2	-2	-2	-2	-1	-1	N	Grinnell C
-1	-1	94,901	112	-1	-1	-1	-1	N	Guilford C
1,620	2	-1	2	-1	-1	-1	-1	N	H Inst Int Desgn
2,964	7	12,758	8	7,182	8	-1	-1	N	H LaGrange C
-1	-1	-1	-1	-1	-1	-1	-1		Hamilton C
36,895	24	121,700	41	89,368	26	308,854	-2	N	Hampshire C
-1	-1	-1	-1	-1	-1	-1	-1		Hanover C
-1	1	-1	-1	-1	-1	-1	-1	N	Haskell Indian Nations U
-1	-1	-1	-1	-1	-1	332,503	-1	N	Haverford C
189,861	46	229,847	46	200,501	27	46,189	38,601	Y	Hendrix C

-1 -- Unavailable   -2 -- Not Applicable

ACRL Library Data Tables 2004

NETWORKED ELECTRONIC RESOURCES AND SERVICES

INSTITUTIONS GRANTING BACHELOR OF ARTS DEGREES (Carnegie Code B)

Lib. No.	Institution	Notes	EXPENDITURES Electronic journals purchased 6	Electronic full-text journals 7	Electronic reference sources 8	Electronic books 9	Virtual reference transactions 10	Federated searching across networked electronic resources? 11
81	Hiram C		-1	-1	52,066	-1	-1	N
82	Hobart &William Smith Cs		179,664	91,578	88,086	0	-1	Y
83	Hope C		50,338	20,541	98,283	2,034	-1	Y
84	Houghton C		-1	-1	-1	0	0	N
85	Howard Payne U		-1	-1	-1	-1	-1	N
86	Illinois C		-1	-1	-1	-1	-1	
87	Jamestown C		22,955	3,400	7,150	1,500	36	N
88	Johnson C Smith U		22,597	-1	-1	-1	0	Y
89	Judson C		35,587	453	2,613	0	160	N
90	Kent ST U Salem		-1	1,731	-1	0	-1	N
91	Kent ST U Trumbull		-1	-1	-1	-1	-1	
92	Kenyon C		209,031	162,733	67,875	29,116	-1	N
93	Kettering C Med		-1	-1	-1	-1	-1	
94	Keuka C		30,000	27,000	12,300	3,100	0	Y
95	Knox C		48,579	27,041	37,743	0	-1	N
96	Kwantlen UC	C	-1	-1	96,279	0	141	N
97	Lambuth U		8,702	8,702	6,127	0	0	N
98	Lawrence U		103,327	-1	-1	1,798	-1	N
99	Lemoyne-Owen C		19,643	6,000	2,600	0	50	N
100	Lester B Pearson C Pacific	C	-1	-1	-1	-1	-1	
101	LIFE Bible C		7,568	0	7,568	0	10	Y
102	Lyndon State C		-1	-1	-1	-1	-1	
103	Lyon C		11,000	35,000	7,000	1,000	0	N
104	Macon ST C		-2	-2	-2	-2	-2	N
105	Marlboro C		9,626	9,626	3,917	417	-1	N
106	Mars Hill C		25,346	0	28,500	-1	0	N
107	Martin Luther C		2,025	5,200	7,567	1,500	-2	N
108	Mayville ST U		8,701	8,701	9,182	1,500	90	N
109	McKendree C		500	47,722	3,000	275	350	N
110	McPherson C		-1	-1	-1	-1	10	N
111	Methodist C		36,136	6,955	0	0	-1	N
112	Midland Lutheran C		5,500	-1	-1	-1	-1	
113	Milwaukee Inst Art Design		0	0	4,709	0	0	N
114	MO Baptist C		27,900	22,400	28,869	0	0	N
115	MO Western ST C		27,172	5,960	75,263	3,938	95	N
116	Monmouth C		57,991	26,705	63,178	0	-1	N
117	Mount Royal C	C	166,000	-1	-1	0	-1	N
118	Mount Union C		96,360	54,807	103,185	2,485	-1	N
119	Muhlenberg C		84,929	13,479	145,975	0	0	N
120	NC Wesleyan C		-1	-1	32,891	-1	10	N

C -- Reported in Canadian $ -1 -- Unavailable   -2 -- Not Applicable

ACRL Library Data Tables 2004
NETWORKED RESOURCES AND SERVICES

INSTITUTIONS GRANTING BACHELOR OF ARTS DEGREES (Carnegie Code B)

Logins to electronic databases 12	No. of databases reported 12a	Queries (searches) in electronic databases 13	No. of databases reported 13a	Items requested in electronic databases 14	No. of databases reported 14a	Virtual visits to website 15a	Virtual visits to catalog 15b	Excl. visits fr. Inside library 15c	Survey Question # Institution
-1	-1	43,896	-1	29,805	-1	-1	-1		Hiram C
-1	33	117,748	33	-1	33	-1	-1	N	obart &William Smith Cs
-1	-1	-1	-1	-1	-1	-1	-1	N	Hope C
0	0	0	0	0	0	0	0	Y	Houghton C
-1	-1	-1	-1	-1	-1	-1	-1		Howard Payne U
-1	-1	-1	-1	-1	-1	-1	-1		Illinois C
-1	-1	47,453	30	28,511	22	19,122	-1	N	Jamestown C
64,909	9	-1	9	-1	9	-1	-1	N	Johnson C Smith U
26,408	45	43,392	45	931,035	45	-1	-1	Y	Judson C
-1	-1	-1	-1	-1	-1	-1	-1		Kent ST U Salem
-1	-1	-1	-1	-1	-1	-1	-1	N	Kent ST U Trumbull
-1	-1	90,524	70	-1	-1	-1	-1	N	Kenyon C
-1	-1	-1	-1	-1	-1	-1	-1		Kettering C Med
2,200	2	154,209	23	55,408	6	0	0		Keuka C
-1	-1	-1	-1	-1	-1	-1	-1		Knox C
-1	-1	-1	-1	-1	-1	-1	-1	N	Kwantlen UC
0	0	0	0	0	0	17,366	0	N	Lambuth U
-1	-1	-1	-1	-1	-1	-1	-1	N	Lawrence U
100	500	100	500	3,000	200	3,500	5,000	N	Lemoyne-Owen C
-1	-1	-1	-1	-1	-1	-1	-1		ster B Pearson C Pacific
-1	5	-1	5	-1	5	-1	-1	N	LIFE Bible C
-1	-1	-1	-1	-1	-1	-1	-1		Lyndon State C
7,920	5	23,634	5	1	1	9,099	1	Y	Lyon C
-2	-2	-2	-2	-2	-2	-2	-2	Y	Macon ST C
-1	-1	87,279	11	21,815	11	-1	-1		Marlboro C
-1	0	-1	0	-1	0	-1	-1	N	Mars Hill C
-1	13	-1	13	-1	-1	-1	-1	Y	Martin Luther C
4,938	19	18,371	19	22,675	18	-1	-1	N	Mayville ST U
-1	-1	174,641	55	77,459	37	411,571	-1	N	McKendree C
-1	-1	-1	-1	-1	-1	-1	-1	N	McPherson C
-1	-1	-1	-1	-1	-1	-1	-1	N	Methodist C
-1	-1	-1	-1	-1	-1	-1	-1	N	Midland Lutheran C
0	0	0	0	0	0	0	0	N	ilwaukee Inst Art Design
0	0	0	0	0	0	0	0	N	MO Baptist C
54,161	31	235,315	35	152,631	25	-1	-1	N	MO Western ST C
34,111	95	93,412	95	64,103	21	-1	-1	N	Monmouth C
-1	-1	-1	-1	-1	-1	3,745,350	-1	N	Mount Royal C
-1	-1	84,122	200	-1	-1	-1	-1	N	Mount Union C
0	0	203,717	38	0	0	0	0		Muhlenberg C
-1	-1	-1	-1	-1	-1	-1	-1	N	NC Wesleyan C

-1 -- Unavailable   -2 -- Not Applicable

ACRL Library Data Tables 2004
NETWORKED ELECTRONIC RESOURCES AND SERVICES
INSTITUTIONS GRANTING BACHELOR OF ARTS DEGREES (Carnegie Code B)

Lib. No.	Survey Question # Institution	Notes	Electronic journals purchased 6	Electronic full-text journals 7	Electronic reference sources 8	Electronic books 9	Virtual reference transactions 10	Federated searching across networked electronic resources? 11
			EXPENDITURES					
121	New C U South FL		-1	-1	-1	-1	-1	Y
122	OH Dominican C		-1	-1	-1	-1	-1	Y
123	OH Wesleyan U		35,772	114,589	12,105	-1	66	Y
124	OK Panhandle ST U		10,977	10,977	25,563	2,800	50	Y
125	Paier C Art		0	0	0	0	0	N
126	Peace C		21,690	20,690	-1	0	0	N
127	Potomac C		0	0	15,280	0	0	N
128	Presbyterian C		-1	-1	-1	-1	-1	
129	Principia C		46,962	-1	-1	-1	-1	N
130	Randolph-Macon C		42,836	42,836	0	0	0	N
131	Randolph-Macon WC		30,000	25,000	4,000	1,000	0	N
132	Reformed Bible C		4,257	2,290	3,529	125	-1	N
133	Reinhardt C		22,428	22,428	0	0	0	N
134	Ricks C		-1	-1	-1	112,488	0	Y
135	Ringling Sch Art & Design		0	0	12,953	0	0	N
136	Rochester C		0	20,038	1,000	500	0	N
137	Rocky Mountain C		0	0	12,000	0	150	Y
138	Rogers ST U		-1	-1	82,799	2,800	-1	N
139	SE C Assemblies God		25,000	25,000	50,000	4,000	0	N
140	Shawnee ST U		10,276	10,276	49,773	1,019	351	Y
141	Shepherd C		14,906	0	64,695	0	0	N
142	Siena C		115,552	90,475	3,430	0	20	N
143	Simpson C IA		25,296	15,349	2,975	0	50	N
144	Skidmore C		246,496	67,079	179,417	8,269	-1	N
145	Southwest U		-1	-1	-1	-1	-1	N
146	Spartan Aero-Flight Schl		0	0	0	0	0	Y
147	St Andrews Presby C		7,710	7,710	292	0	14	N
148	St Gregory's U		0	0	0	0	-1	N
149	St John Vianney C Sem		-1	-1	5,224	0	-1	N
150	St Olaf C		0	0	196,606	0	150	N
151	St. Mary's C Maryland		-1	-1	-1	0	-1	Y
152	Sterling C-VT		15,000	14,950	200	0	0	N
153	Stillman C		5,524	2,000	552,400	0	5	N
154	Susquehanna U		1,835	0	156,999	0	27	N
155	SW Baptist Theo Sem		-1	-1	-1	-1	-1	
156	Swarthmore C		314,111	309,477	165,295	1,979	62	N
157	Sweet Briar C		90,912	-1	-1	-1	-1	N
158	Talladega C		-1	-1	-1	-1	-1	
159	Taylor U-Ft Wayne		-2	-1	2,540	1,100	-2	Y
160	Teikyo Post U		0	0	25,799	0	-1	N

C -- Reported in Canadian $ -1 -- Unavailable   -2 -- Not Applicable

172

INSTITUTIONS GRANTING BACHELOR OF ARTS DEGREES (Carnegie Code B)

Logins to electronic databases 12	No. of databases reported 12a	Queries (searches) in electronic databases 13	No. of databases reported 13a	Items requested in electronic databases 14	No. of databases reported 14a	Virtual visits to website 15a	Virtual visits to catalog 15b	Excl. visits fr. inside library 15c	Survey Question # Institution
									New C U South FL
-1	-1	-1	-1	-1	-1	-1	-1		OH Dominican C
-1	-1	-1	-1	-1	-1	-1	-1	N	OH Wesleyan U
-1	-1	118,811	61	380,654	28	3,571,912	-1	N	OK Panhandle ST U
16,852	40	16,852	40	99,074	40	56,507	25,983	Y	Paier C Art
0	0	0	0	0	0	0	0	N	Peace C
22,000	0	9,182	0	9,182	-1	-1	-1	N	Potomac C
2,121	2	7,720	2	0	0	0	0		Presbyterian C
-1	-1	-1	-1	-1	-1	-1	-1	N	Principia C
-1	-1	-1	-1	-1	-1	-1	-1		Randolph-Macon C
-1	-1	-1	-1	-1	-1	-1	-1	N	Randolph-Macon WC
4,000	50	5,000	50	5,000	50	4,000	3,000	Y	Reformed Bible C
1,853	53	6,467	53	2,501	53	-1	-1		Reinhardt C
-1	-1	-1	-1	-1	-1	-1	-1	N	Ricks C
-1	-1	-1	-1	-1	-1	196,411	15,000,000	Y	ingling Sch Art & Design
-1	-1	-1	-1	-1	-1	-1	-1	N	Rochester C
0	0	50,793	18	29,473	18	0	5,719	N	Rocky Mountain C
5,233	2	16,325	2	0	2	20,000	0	N	Rogers ST U
-1	-1	-1	-1	-1	-1	-1	-1	N	SE C Assemblies God
-1	-1	-1	-1	-1	-1	-1	-1		Shawnee ST U
28,817	201	122,844	112,201	2,380	201	19,866	268,212	N	Shepherd C
0	0	99,159	6	0	0	0	0		Siena C
-1	-1	209,110	27	60,733	3	122,209	104,386	N	Simpson C IA
-1	-1	103,997	11	67,312	11	-1	-1	N	Skidmore C
128,152	200	-1	-1	-1	-1	-1	185,827	N	Southwest U
-1	-1	-1	-1	-1	-1	-1	-1	N	Spartan Aero-Flight Schl
3,139	20	21,351	20	4,012	20	0	0	Y	St Andrews Presby C
8,924	4	-1	-1	-1	-1	-1	27,743	N	St Gregory's U
3,963	30	17,832	30	9,425	24	-1	7,568	N	St John Vianney C Sem
-1	-1	-1	-1	-1	-1	-1	-1		St Olaf C
69,833	10	168,589	10	-1	1	281,441	360,000	N	St. Mary's C Maryland
-1	-1	-1	-1	-1	-1	-1	-1	N	Sterling C-VT
3,036	3	6,032	3	14,885	3	5,872	-1	N	Stillman C
0	0	0	0	0	0	0	0	Y	Susquehanna U
309,963	25	214,859	25	0	0	120,981	74,814	N	SW Baptist Theo Sem
-1	-1	-1	-1	-1	-1	-1	-1		Swarthmore C
-1	-1	-1	-1	-1	-1	495,289	-1	N	Sweet Briar C
-1	-1	-1	-1	-1	-1	-1	-1	N	Talladega C
-1	-1	-1	-1	-1	-1	-1	-1		Taylor U-Ft Wayne
-1	88	-1	-1	118,146	88	165,686	-1	N	Teikyo Post U
4,254	5	18,460	5	-1	5	-1	-1	N	

-1 -- Unavailable   -2 -- Not Applicable

INSTITUTIONS GRANTING BACHELOR OF ARTS DEGREES (Carnegie Code B)

Lib. No.	Survey Question # Institution	Notes	EXPENDITURES				Virtual reference transactions 10	Federated searching across networked electronic resources? 11
			Electronic journals purchased 6	Electronic full-text journals 7	Electronic reference sources 8	Electronic books 9		
161	TN Wesleyan C		-1	-1	-1	-1	-1	Y
162	Tri ST U		14,646	3,092	13,379	1,140	-1	Y
163	Trinity Christian C		17,741	3,048	22,512	1,723	-1	N
164	Trinity Wstrn U	C	0	70,000	2,500	0	0	N
165	Truett McConnell C		-1	-1	-1	-1	-1	
166	TX Lutheran U		22,479	3,000	6,500	6,500	-1	N
167	U Maine-Machias		4,000	3,675	0	0	0	Y
168	U ME Fort Kent		-1	-1	-1	-1	68	Y
169	U Ozarks		-1	-1	-1	-1	-1	
170	U VA C Wise		24,731	0	0	0	0	N
171	Union C-NE		35	14,487	705	848	-1	N
172	US C Guard Acad		-1	-1	-1	-1	-1	N
173	US Merchant Marine Acad		-1	-1	-1	0	-1	N
174	US Mil Acad		-1	-1	-1	-1	-1	
175	US Naval Acad		-1	-1	-1	-1	-1	
176	UT Valley ST C		-1	-1	-1	-1	-1	Y
177	VA Wesleyan C		15,655	11,727	2,814	0	0	N
178	Vassar C		520,116	297,406	-1	3,815	189	N
179	VMI		22,465	10,200	23,671	0	0	N
180	Wabash C		68,784	67,784	-1	1,000	0	Y
181	Warner Sthrn C		20,721	0	0	0	10	N
182	Warren Wilson C		38,998	-1	-1	-1	-1	N
183	Wells C		0	0	-1	0	0	N
184	Western ST C		166	166	20,443	0	-1	N
185	Westmont C		8,897	27,298	69,312	2,512	0	N
186	Whitman C		-1	-1	-1	-1	-1	
187	Wiley C		0	0	2,500	0	0	N
188	Winston-Salem ST U		0	0	0	0	182	Y
189	Wofford C		1	31,188	56,018	0	1	N
190	York C		0	0	3,937	0	0	Y

C -- Reported in Canadian $ -1 -- Unavailable   -2 -- Not Applicable

ACRL Library Data Tables 2004
NETWORKED RESOURCES AND SERVICES

INSTITUTIONS GRANTING BACHELOR OF ARTS DEGREES (Carnegie Code B)

Logins to electronic databases 12	No. of databases reported 12a	Queries (searches) in electronic databases 13	No. of databases reported 13a	Items requested in electronic databases 14	No. of databases reported 14a	Virtual visits to website 15a	Virtual visits to catalog 15b	Excl. visits fr. inside library 15c	Survey Question # Institution
167,325	-1	-1	-1	-1	-1	-1	-1		TN Wesleyan C
-1	-1	-1	-1	-1	-1	-1	-1	N	Tri ST U
-1	-1	45,351	44	29,740	44	-1	-1		Trinity Christian C
0	0	0	0	0	0	0	0	Y	Trinity Wstrn U
-1	-1	-1	-1	-1	-1	-1	-1		Truett McConnell C
2,047	1	53,144	4	-1	-1	-1	-1		TX Lutheran U
3,835	-1	12,421	-1	-1	-1	-1	-1	N	U Maine-Machias
5,944	34	28,949	34	0	0	6,320	1,135	Y	U ME Fort Kent
-1	-1	-1	-1	-1	-1	-1	-1		U Ozarks
0	0	0	0	0	0	1,332,032	13,093	N	U VA C Wise
8,444	18	26,773	18	21,207	18	-1	-1	Y	Union C-NE
-1	50	37,849	50	-1	50	-1	-1		US C Guard Acad
-1	-1	18,374	-1	-1	-1	-1	822	Y	S Merchant Marine Acad
-1	-1	-1	-1	-1	-1	-1	-1		US Mil Acad
-1	-1	-1	-1	-1	-1	-1	-1		US Naval Acad
-1	-1	-1	-1	-1	-1	-1	-1		UT Valley ST C
-1	-1	-1	-1	-1	-1	-1	-1		VA Wesleyan C
50,502	52	158,944	63	-1	-1	-1	-1	N	Vassar C
1,955	3	17,183	7	-1	-1	-1	-1		VMI
-1	-1	-1	-1	-1	-1	-1	-1	N	Wabash C
22,707	4	41,470	6	18,445	6	72,519	-1	N	Warner Sthrn C
-1	-1	-1	-1	-1	-1	-1	-1		Warren Wilson C
-1	0	-1	0	-1	0	-1	-1	N	Wells C
-1	-1	-1	-1	-1	-1	-1	-1		Western ST C
33,969	28	49,209	28	-1	-1	-1	-1	Y	Westmont C
-1	-1	-1	-1	-1	-1	-1	-1		Whitman C
2,053	3	2,385	3	1,798	3	-1	-1		Wiley C
12,827	32,231	24,421	32,231	0	0	0	0	N	Winston-Salem ST U
1	-1	1	-1	1	-1	1	26,076	N	Wofford C
4,260	3	5,640	3	0	0	5,000	0	N	York C

-1 -- Unavailable   -2 -- Not Applicable

ACRL Library Data Tables 2004
DIGITIZATION ACTIVITIES
INSTITUTIONS GRANTING BACHELOR OF ARTS DEGREES (Carnegie Code B)

		DIGITAL COLLECTIONS			USAGE		DIRECT COSTS		
		No. of collections	Size (MB)	Items	No. of times accessed	No. of queries	Personnel	Equipment, software, or contract services	Volumes Held Collectively
Lib. No.	Survey Question # Institution	16a	16b	16c	17a	17b	18a	18b	19
1	AB C Art & Design	-1	-1	-1	-1	-1	-1	-1	-1
2	Adrian C	0	0	0	0	0	0	0	0
3	Albion C	0	0	0	0	0	0	0	0
4	Amherst C	0	-1	-1	-1	-1	-1	-1	-1
5	Aquinas C TN	-1	-1	-1	-1	-1	-1	-1	-1
6	Atlanta C Art	0	0	0	0	0	0	0	0
7	Atlanta Christian C	-1	-1	-1	-1	-1	-1	-1	-1
8	Augustana C RI	-1	-1	-1	-1	-1	-1	-1	0
9	Barber-Scotia C	0	0	0	0	0	0	0	0
10	Bard C	0	0	0	0	0	0	0	0
11	Barton C	0	0	0	0	0	0	0	0
12	Bates C	-1	-1	-1	-1	-1	-1	-1	-1
13	Benedict C	-1	-1	-1	-1	-1	17,000	3,250	-1
14	Berry C	1	-1	895	-1	-1	-1	-1	0
15	Bethany C Bethany	0	0	0	0	0	0	0	0
16	Bethany C Lindsborg	0	0	0	0	0	0	0	0
17	Bethel C KS	112	2,584	12,101	-1	-1	-1	-1	0
18	Blackburn C	0	0	0	0	0	0	0	0
19	Bluefield C	0	0	0	0	0	0	0	0
20	Boise Bible C	0	0	0	0	0	0	0	0
21	Bowdoin C	2	112	3,042	-1	-1	-1	-1	0
22	Bridgewater C	0	-1	-1	-1	-1	-1	-1	-1
23	Bryan C	0	0	0	0	0	0	0	0
24	C Holy Cross	1	-1	1,227	-1	-1	-1	-1	0
25	C Visual Arts	0	0	0	0	0	0	0	0
26	C Wooster	0	0	0	0	0	0	0	0
27	Campion C	-1	-1	-1	-1	-1	-1	-1	-1
28	Carroll C-Helena	-1	-1	-1	-1	-1	-1	-1	-1
29	Cazenovia C	-1	-1	-1	-1	-1	-1	-1	-1
30	Centennial C	0	0	0	0	0	0	0	0
31	Central Bible C	0	0	0	0	0	0	0	0
32	Central C	0	0	0	0	0	0	0	0
33	Central Christian C Bible	0	0	0	0	0	0	0	0
34	Centre C	1	200	2,900	-1	-1	-1	1,500	0
35	Christian Heritage C	0	0	0	0	0	0	0	0
36	Clear Creek Bible	0	0	0	0	0	0	0	0
37	Cmty Hosp C Health	0	0	0	0	0	0	0	0
38	Colby C	0	0	0	0	0	0	0	0
39	Colby Sawyer C	0	0	0	0	0	0	0	0
40	Columbia Union C	0	0	0	0	0	0	0	0

-1 -- Unavailable   -2 -- Not Applicable

ACRL Library Data Tables 2004
DIGITIZATION ACTIVITIES

INSTITUTIONS GRANTING BACHELOR OF ARTS DEGREES (Carnegie Code B)

	DIGITAL COLLECTIONS			USAGE		DIRECT COSTS		
	No. of collections	Size (MB)	Items	No. of times accessed	No. of queries	Personnel	Equipment, software, or contract services	Volumes Held Collectively
Survey Question # Institution	16a	16b	16c	17a	17b	18a	18b	19
Concordia C-MN	0	-1	-1	-1	-1	-1	-1	-1
Concordia C-NY	0	0	0	0	0	0	0	0
Cornish C Arts	1	1	1	1	1	1	1	1
Crichton C	0	0	0	0	0	0	0	0
Crown C-MN	0	0	0	0	0	0	0	0
Culver Stockton C	0	0	0	0	0	0	0	0
CUNY City C	0	0	0	0	0	0	0	0
CUNY York C	0	0	0	0	0	0	0	0
Dakota Wesleyan U	0	0	0	0	0	0	0	0
Dana C	0	0	0	0	0	0	0	0
Davidson C	1	180	132	-1	-1	-1	-1	0
Dean C	0	0	0	0	0	0	0	0
Defiance C	0	0	0	0	0	0	0	-1
Denison U	-1	-1	-1	-1	-1	-1	-1	-1
DeVry Inst Tech GA	-1	-1	-1	-1	-1	-1	-1	-1
Dickinson ST U	-1	-1	-1	-1	-1	-1	-1	-1
Divine Word C	0	0	0	0	0	0	0	0
East Texas Baptist U	0	0	0	0	0	0	0	0
Eckerd C	0	0	0	0	0	0	0	0
Emmanuel C GA	0	0	0	0	0	0	0	0
Eugene Bible C	-1	-1	-1	-1	-1	-1	-1	-1
Evangel U	0	0	0	0	0	0	0	0
F&M C	2	-1	6,154	5,200	5,200	0	20,730	-1
Ferrum C	0	0	0	0	0	0	0	0
Finlandia U	0	0	0	0	0	0	0	0
FL Christian C	1	0	220	0	0	0	0	0
Flagler C	0	-2	-2	-2	-2	-2	-2	-2
Fort Lewis C	-1	-1	-1	-1	-1	-1	-1	-1
G Adolphus C	1	-1	329	-1	-1	-1	149	-1
Green Mountain C	-1	-1	-1	-1	-1	-1	-1	-1
Grinnell C	-2	-2	-2	-2	-2	-2	-2	-2
Guilford C	0	0	0	0	0	0	0	0
H Inst Int Desgn	0	0	0	0	0	0	0	0
H LaGrange C	0	0	0	0	0	0	0	0
Hamilton C	2	-1	-1	-1	-1	-1	-1	0
Hampshire C	8	22	69	13,929	-2	-2	-2	192,327
Hanover C	-2	-2	-2	-2	-2	-2	-2	0
Haskell Indian Nations U	0	0	0	0	0	-1	-1	0
Haverford C	3	-1	783	-1	-1	0	0	0
Hendrix C	0	0	0	0	0	0	0	0

-1 -- Unavailable   -2 -- Not Applicable

ACRL Library Data Tables 2004
DIGITIZATION ACTIVITIES

INSTITUTIONS GRANTING BACHELOR OF ARTS DEGREES (Carnegie Code B)

Lib. No.	Survey Question # Institution	DIGITAL COLLECTIONS No. of collections 16a	Size (MB) 16b	Items 16c	USAGE No. of times accessed 17a	No. of queries 17b	DIRECT COSTS Personnel 18a	Equipment, software, or contract services 18b	Volumes Held Collectively 19
81	Hiram C	-1	-1	-1	-1	-1	-1	-1	-1
82	Hobart &William Smith Cs	4	2,424	1,492	-1	-1	-1	-1	-1
83	Hope C	-2	-2	-2	-2	-2	-2	-2	0
84	Houghton C	0	0	0	0	0	0	0	0
85	Howard Payne U	0	-1	-1	-1	-1	-1	-1	-1
86	Illinois C	-1	-1	-1	-1	-1	-1	-1	-1
87	Jamestown C	0	0	0	0	0	0	0	0
88	Johnson C Smith U	1	239	1,304	-1	-1	46,510	14,266	0
89	Judson C	0	0	0	0	0	0	0	0
90	Kent ST U Salem	0	0	0	0	0	0	0	0
91	Kent ST U Trumbull	-1	-1	-1	-1	-1	-1	-1	-1
92	Kenyon C	-1	-1	-1	-1	-1	-1	-1	32,000
93	Kettering C Med	-1	-1	-1	-1	-1	-1	-1	-1
94	Keuka C	0	0	0	0	0	0	0	0
95	Knox C	-1	-1	-1	-1	-1	-1	-1	0
96	Kwantlen UC	-1	-1	-1	-1	-1	-1	-1	-1
97	Lambuth U	0	0	0	0	0	0	0	0
98	Lawrence U	0	0	0	0	0	0	0	0
99	Lemoyne-Owen C	0	0	0	0	75	0	0	0
100	Lester B Pearson C Pacific	-1	-1	-1	-1	-1	-1	-1	-1
101	LIFE Bible C	-2	-2	-2	-2	-2	-2	-2	-2
102	Lyndon State C	-1	-1	-1	-1	-1	-1	-1	-1
103	Lyon C	0	0	0	0	0	0	0	0
104	Macon ST C	0	0	0	0	0	0	0	0
105	Marlboro C	0	0	0	0	0	0	0	0
106	Mars Hill C	0	0	0	0	0	0	0	0
107	Martin Luther C	0	0	0	0	0	0	0	0
108	Mayville ST U	0	0	0	-1	-1	-1	-1	-1
109	McKendree C	-1	-1	-1	-1	-1	-1	-1	-1
110	McPherson C	0	0	0	0	-1	-1	-1	-1
111	Methodist C	1	1	19	-1	-1	0	0	0
112	Midland Lutheran C	-1	-1	-1	-1	-1	-1	-1	-1
113	Milwaukee Inst Art Design	0	0	0	0	0	0	0	0
114	MO Baptist C	0	0	0	0	0	0	0	0
115	MO Western ST C	1	40,960	500	0	0	-1	8,000	0
116	Monmouth C	-1	-1	-1	-1	-1	0	0	-1
117	Mount Royal C	0	0	0	0	0	0	0	0
118	Mount Union C	0	-1	-1	-1	-1	-1	-1	-1
119	Muhlenberg C	0	0	0	0	0	0	0	0
120	NC Wesleyan C	0	0	0	0	0	0	0	0

-1 -- Unavailable   -2 -- Not Applicable

ACRL Library Data Tables 2004
DIGITIZATION ACTIVITIES

INSTITUTIONS GRANTING BACHELOR OF ARTS DEGREES (Carnegie Code B)

	DIGITAL COLLECTIONS			USAGE		DIRECT COSTS		
	No. of collections	Size (MB)	Items	No. of times accessed	No. of queries	Personnel	Equipment, software, or contract services	Volumes Held Collectively
Survey Question #	16a	16b	16c	17a	17b	18a	18b	19
Institution								
New C U South FL	0	0	0	0	0	0	0	0
OH Dominican C	-1	-1	-1	-1	-1	-1	-1	-1
OH Wesleyan U	-1	-1	-1	-1	-1	-1	-1	-1
OK Panhandle ST U	4	-1	18,297	455	455	1,400	0	18,297
Paier C Art	0	0	0	0	0	0	0	0
Peace C	0	0	0	0	0	0	0	0
Potomac C	0	0	0	0	0	0	0	0
Presbyterian C	-1	-1	-1	-1	-1	-1	-1	-1
Principia C	0	0	0	0	0	0	0	0
Randolph-Macon C	0	0	0	0	0	0	0	0
Randolph-Macon WC	0	0	0	0	0	0	0	0
Reformed Bible C	0	0	0	0	0	0	0	0
Reinhardt C	0	0	0	-1	-1	-1	-1	-1
Ricks C	12	-1	500,000	7,864,446	-1	-1	-1	0
Ringling Sch Art & Design	-1	-1	-1	-1	-1	-1	-1	-1
Rochester C	0	0	0	0	0	0	0	0
Rocky Mountain C	0	0	0	0	0	0	0	0
Rogers ST U	0	0	0	0	0	0	0	-1
SE C Assemblies God	0	0	0	0	0	0	0	-1
Shawnee ST U	-1	-1	-1	-1	-1	-1	-1	-1
Shepherd C	0	0	0	0	0	0	0	0
Siena C	0	0	0	-1	-1	0	0	0
Simpson C IA	0	0	0	0	0	0	0	0
Skidmore C	-1	40	11,000	-1	40,000	-1	4,000	-1
Southwest U	-1	-1	-1	-1	-1	-1	-1	-1
Spartan Aero-Flight Schl	0	0	0	0	0	0	0	0
St Andrews Presby C	-2	-2	-2	-2	-2	-2	-2	0
St Gregory's U	0	0	0	0	0	0	0	0
St John Vianney C Sem	-1	-1	-1	-1	-1	-1	-1	-1
St Olaf C	-1	-1	-1	-1	-1	-1	-1	-1
St. Mary's C Maryland	4	96,827	2,116	-1	-1	6,000	1,500	-1
Sterling C-VT	0	0	0	-2	-2	-2	-2	-2
Stillman C	0	0	0	0	0	0	0	0
Susquehanna U	0	0	0	0	0	0	0	0
SW Baptist Theo Sem	-1	-1	-1	-1	-1	-1	-1	-1
Swarthmore C	0	0	0	0	0	0	0	0
Sweet Briar C	-1	-1	-1	-1	-1	-1	-1	-1
Talladega C	-1	-1	-1	-1	-1	-1	-1	-1
Taylor U-Ft Wayne	-1	-1	-1	-1	-1	-1	-1	-1
Teikyo Post U	0	0	0	0	0	0	0	0

-1 -- Unavailable   -2 -- Not Applicable

ACRL Library Data Tables 2004
DIGITIZATION ACTIVITIES

INSTITUTIONS GRANTING BACHELOR OF ARTS DEGREES (Carnegie Code B)

Lib. No.	Survey Question # Institution	DIGITAL COLLECTIONS			USAGE		DIRECT COSTS		Volumes Held Collectively
		No. of collections 16a	Size (MB) 16b	Items 16c	No. of times accessed 17a	No. of queries 17b	Personnel 18a	Equipment, software, or contract services 18b	19
161	TN Wesleyan C	1	-1	205	-1	-1	-1	-1	-1
162	Tri ST U	0	0	0	0	0	0	0	0
163	Trinity Christian C	0	0	0	0	0	0	0	0
164	Trinity Wstrn U	0	0	0	0	0	0	0	0
165	Truett McConnell C	-1	-1	-1	-1	-1	-1	-1	-1
166	TX Lutheran U	0	0	0	0	0	0	0	0
167	U Maine-Machias	0	0	0	0	0	0	0	0
168	U ME Fort Kent	0	0	0	0	0	0	0	0
169	U Ozarks	-1	-1	-1	-1	-1	-1	-1	-1
170	U VA C Wise	0	0	0	0	0	0	0	0
171	Union C-NE	0	0	0	0	0	0	0	0
172	US C Guard Acad	0	0	0	0	0	0	0	0
173	US Merchant Marine Acad	0	0	0	0	0	0	0	0
174	US Mil Acad	-1	-1	-1	-1	-1	-1	-1	-1
175	US Naval Acad	-1	-1	-1	-1	-1	-1	-1	-1
176	UT Valley ST C	0	-1	-1	0	-1	0	0	0
177	VA Wesleyan C	0	0	0	0	0	0	0	0
178	Vassar C	2	72,005	4,238	-1	-1	-1	-1	0
179	VMI	113	240	4,907	1,337,659	16,489	-1	-1	0
180	Wabash C	0	0	0	0	0	0	0	0
181	Warner Sthrn C	0	0	0	0	0	0	0	0
182	Warren Wilson C	-1	-1	-1	-1	-1	-1	-1	-1
183	Wells C	0	0	0	0	0	0	0	0
184	Western ST C	0	0	0	0	0	0	0	0
185	Westmont C	0	0	0	-1	-1	-1	-1	-1
186	Whitman C	-1	-1	-1	-1	-1	-1	-1	-1
187	Wiley C	0	0	0	0	0	0	0	0
188	Winston-Salem ST U	0	0	0	0	0	0	0	0
189	Wofford C	1	-1	-1	1	-1	1	1	0
190	York C	9	870	39	10	10	0	100	0

-1 -- Unavailable   -2 -- Not Applicable

ACRL Library Data Tables 2004
ELECTRONIC RESOURCES

INSTITUTIONS GRANTING MASTER OF ARTS AND PROFESSIONAL DEGREES (Carnegie Code M)

Lib. No.	Survey Question # Institution	Electronic journals purchased 1	Electronic full-text journals purchased 2	Electronic journals not purchased 3	Electronic Reference Sources 4	Electronic books 5
1	Abilene Christian U	20,322	720	1,782	115	34,050
2	Agnes Scott C	13,000	1,263	2,500	171	37,917
3	Albany C Pharmacy	-1	-1	-1	-1	-1
4	Albany Law Schl Union U	-1	-1	0	13	0
5	Alcorn ST U	12,350	8,766	27,554	77	0
6	Amer Intl C	3,194	3,194	4,747	16	0
7	Amer U Puerto Rico	18,833	18,833	0	8	4,000
8	Anderson U	-1	-1	-1	-1	-1
9	Angelo ST U	-1	-1	-1	-1	-1
10	Aquinas C MI	-1	-1	-1	-1	-1
11	Ark Tech U	-1	-1	-1	-1	-1
12	Armstrong Atlantic ST U	7,988	463	0	0	0
13	Assemblies God Theo Sem	0	0	0	7	0
14	Assumption C	-1	-1	-1	4	0
15	Athenaeum of Ohio	-1	-1	-1	-1	-1
16	Auburn U Montgomery	212	10,436	0	0	40,000
17	Augusta ST U	5,316	4,430	1,830	201	15,054
18	Augustana C SF	542	16,820	7	29	11,521
19	Austin C	1,857	1,857	25	16	9,500
20	Austin Presb Theo Sem	0	0	0	5	0
21	Averett C	14,564	10,782	207	90	37,673
22	Babson C	33,051	150	33,051	111	5,225
23	Baker C System	1,800	96	0	13	8,000
24	Baker U	18,248	213	14,031	19	6,382
25	Baptist Bible C and Sem	0	11,152	0	0	0
26	Bayamon Central U	10,000	5,000	10,000	4,000	40
27	Bellevue U	17,579	15,470	0	27	14,105
28	Bennington C	13,347	9,857	1	2	894
29	Bethel C IN	4,896	212	32	32	0
30	Birmingham Southern C	558	558	0	114	114
31	Bluffton C	-1	-1	-1	-1	-1
32	BowlGrn SU Fireld	0	0	-2	-1	-1
33	Bradley U	13,000	1,400	9,000	125	1,900
34	Brescia U	19,942	19,942	0	15	37,624
35	Brooks Institute	-2	-2	-2	18	5,453
36	Bryn Athyn C	0	0	69	6	0
37	Buena Vista U	14,929	-1	-1	55	8,485
38	Butler U	361	8,475	149	27	0
39	C Atlantic	-1	12	-1	20	5,000
40	C Mt St Joseph	9,000	30	0	16	14,000

-1 -- Unavailable   -2 -- Not Applicable

ACRL Library Data Tables 2004
ELECTRONIC RESOURCES

INSTITUTIONS GRANTING MASTER OF ARTS AND PROFESSIONAL DEGREES (Carnegie Code M)

Lib. No.	Survey Question # Institution	Electronic journals purchased 1	Electronic full-text journals purchased 2	Electronic journals not purchased 3	Electronic Reference Sources 4	Electronic books 5
41	C Mt St Vincent	10,901	10,901	0	-1	0
42	C Our Lady Elms	2,120	2,114	6,190	38	1,170
43	C.R. Drew U Med & Sci	-1	97	-1	18	84
44	CA C Arts & Crafts	0	0	1	9	1
45	CA St Polytechnic U-Pomona	732	-1	-1	99	11,675
46	CA St U - Sacramento	469,602	0	0	0	12,202
47	CA ST U Dominguez Hills	11,269	4,990	17,846	50	3,332
48	CA ST U Fresno	0	0	0	0	0
49	CA ST U Fullerton	-1	-1	-1	-1	-1
50	CA ST U Hayward	-1	-1	-1	-1	-1
51	CA ST U Long Beach	-1	-1	-1	-1	7,556
52	CA ST U Northridge	14,984	14,984	-1	45	6,079
53	CA ST U S Bernadino	-1	-1	-1	-1	7,582
54	CA ST U San Marcos	22,124	-1	-1	-1	-1
55	CA ST U Stanislaus	11,100	11,100	400	74	4,000
56	CA West Sch Law	427	427	-1	48	0
57	Calvin C	-1	-1	-1	-1	-1
58	Cameron U	27,068	27,044	0	2	0
59	Canisius C	1,218	-1	12,921	22	4,156
60	Carlow C	12,534	0	29	12	0
61	Carroll C-Waukesha	9,794	4,200	18,051	3	6,213
62	Cedar Crest C	5,158	689	-1	23	1,442
63	Cedarville U	-1	-1	-1	170	17,000
64	Centenary C	0	0	0	25	0
65	Centenary C LA	0	46,396	43	7	638
66	Central Baptist C	0	0	0	0	0
67	Central CT ST U	-1	-1	-1	-1	-1
68	Central MO ST U	26,500	600	26	125	4,959
69	Charleston Sthrn U	571	592	-1	890	25,799
70	Chicago ST U	32	12,196	0	97	5,379
71	Chris Newport U	7,931	7,931	50	49	0
72	Christendom C	-1	252	38	14	-1
73	Christian Brothers U	1	1	1	1	28,204
74	Clarion U PA	341,148	341,148	0	341,148	0
75	Clarke C-IA	16,000	15,971	2,000	18	14,046
76	Clarkson C-NE	550	-1	-1	-1	0
77	Colorado C	21,577	2,175	0	166	4,190
78	Columbia C MO	9	2	4	5	7,462
79	Columbia C SC	271	271	13,498	30	0
80	Columbia Intl U	0	0	-1	-1	0

-1 -- Unavailable   -2 -- Not Applicable

ACRL Library Data Tables 2004
ELECTRONIC RESOURCES

INSTITUTIONS GRANTING MASTER OF ARTS AND PROFESSIONAL DEGREES (Carnegie Code M)

Lib. No.	Survey Question # Institution	Electronic journals purchased 1	Electronic full-text journals purchased 2	Electronic journals not purchased 3	Electronic Reference Sources 4	Electronic books 5
81	Columbus ST U	-1	-1	-1	-1	-1
82	Concordia U Irvine	-1	7,850	0	294	0
83	Concordia U RiverF	-1	8,000	-1	-1	12,980
84	Concordia U St Paul	-1	-1	-1	75	50
85	Cooper Union	1,732	1,732	3,130	23	387
86	Cornerstone U	498	498	-1	118	19,318
87	Creighton U	12,657	2,422	18	73	2,847
88	Cumberland U	0	0	30	30	35,000
89	CUNY BMB C	-1	22,437	-1	80	31
90	CUNY C Stn Island	-1	16,000	-1	77	3,000
91	CUNY City C	20,119	10,000	7,963	50	6,111
92	CUNY HH Lehman C	-1	-1	-1	-1	-1
93	CUNY John Jay C Crim Just	21,489	3,613	1,853	99	5,771
94	CUNY Queens C	25,500	2,700	2,000	150	5,352
95	Curtis Inst Music	0	0	0	1	0
96	Daniel Webster C	133,763	0	0	0	0
97	DeSales U	8,400	239	600	38	40,000
98	DN Myers C	8,139	11,046	2,907	144	17,000
99	Dominican C San Rafael	0	0	0	0	1,510
100	Dominican U	13,092	-1	-1	97	0
101	Drake U	25,000	808	500	80	27,364
102	Drury C	10,840	463	9,591	52	16,326
103	E R Aero U	-1	-1	-1	30	0
104	Earlham C	17,818	1,303	-1	134	56,964
105	Eastern IL U	-1	-1	-1	-1	-1
106	Eastern U	12,000	12,000	1,000	20	53,000
107	Eastern WA U	6,186	667	8,450	6	1,597
108	Eastrn NM U Main	13,601	8,074	1,312	1,615	11,000
109	Edinboro U PA	-1	-1	-1	95	12,213
110	Elizabethtown C	13,932	55	1,424	45	1,295
111	Elmhurst C	2,919	432	8,715	30	22,401
112	Elon U	-1	957	-1	157	24,674
113	Emmanuel C MA	18	9	15	13	0
114	Emory & Henry C	9,946	622	-1	69	45,000
115	Evergreen ST C	-1	-1	19	116	1,311
116	Fisk U	3,120	1,157	707	5	11,173
117	Fitchburg ST C	17,004	811	13,202	117	3,412
118	FL Southern C	-1	-1	-1	-1	-1
119	Fort Hays ST U	0	0	0	95	7,690
120	Francis Marion U	0	0	-1	4	27,946

-1 -- Unavailable   -2 -- Not Applicable

INSTITUTIONS GRANTING MASTER OF ARTS AND PROFESSIONAL DEGREES (Carnegie Code M)

Lib. No.	Survey Question # Institution	Electronic journals purchased 1	Electronic full-text journals purchased 2	Electronic journals not purchased 3	Electronic Reference Sources 4	Electronic books 5
121	Franklin Inst Boston	-1	-1	-1	-1	-1
122	Franklin U	0	0	0	3	17,323
123	Free Will Baptist Bible C	5,491	2	-1	-1	3,744
124	Frostburg ST U	25,182	367	0	57	0
125	Furman U	11,872	1,273	1,890	95	2,588
126	GA SWstrn ST U	2	2	44	100	27,417
127	Gardner-Webb U	12,500	0	0	60	24,130
128	Geneva C	3	13	0	6	0
129	Georgetown C	-1	24,773	-1	-1	39,258
130	Goucher C	22,066	11,113	1,895	80	1,410
131	Governors ST U	0	3	0	14,303	130
132	Greenville C	5,035	35	3,000	20	-1
133	Grove City C	132	1,009	0	25	0
134	Harding U Main	7,873	-1	-1	57	8,841
135	Hebrew C	4	69	12	1,583	21,100
136	Heidelberg C	0	0	0	90	0
137	Hillsdale Free Will Baptist C	3,400	850	2,050	5,450	0
138	Holy Apostles C & Sem	0	0	-1	-1	0
139	Hood C	-1	18,031	4,618	57	1,751
140	Humboldt ST U	1	1	1	48	3,752
141	IN Inst of Tech	4,000	4,000	7,473,074	1	3,500
142	IN U Kokomo	19,993	1,272	6,262	36	243,272
143	IN U S Bend	24,199	1,072	-1	114	5,367
144	IN U-Purdue U Ft Wayne	13,516	6,247	20,479	120	4,876
145	IN Wesleyan U	37	32,182	-1	28,010	4,753
146	Intl Fine Arts C	10	4	10	15	25
147	Jacksonville ST U	-1	-1	-1	-1	11,173
148	Johnson Bible C	60	60	5,468	62	0
149	Kean U	-1	-1	-1	-1	-1
150	Keene State C	12,000	60	2	64	0
151	Kent ST U Stark	13	0	0	13	0
152	Kentucky Christian C	5,157	5,157	0	3	44,139
153	Kentucky ST U	389	389	477	91	16,362
154	Kettering U	200	-1	5	15	50
155	King's C PA	-1	-1	-1	-1	-1
156	LaGrange C	25	25	-1	145	-1
157	Lakeland C-AB	292	292	0	11	7,153
158	Lakeview C Nursing	18,215	6,443	0	3	0
159	Lancaster Bible C	8,268	0	0	15	3,407
160	Lander U	0	0	127	23	25,420

-1 -- Unavailable   -2 -- Not Applicable

ELECTRONIC RESOURCES

INSTITUTIONS GRANTING MASTER OF ARTS AND PROFESSIONAL DEGREES (Carnegie Code M)

Lib. No.	Survey Question # Institution	Electronic journals purchased 1	Electronic full-text journals purchased 2	Electronic journals not purchased 3	Electronic Reference Sources 4	Electronic books 5
161	Langston U	18,439	10,253	1,901	203	0
162	Laurentian U JN	24,952	12,945	351	34	6,161
163	Le Moyne C	15,620	4,405	0	105	6,640
164	Lebanon Valley C	-1	-1	-1	-1	120
165	Lewis U	7,415	7,050	4	78	53
166	Lewis&Clark C	-1	-1	-1	-1	0
167	Lincoln U-MO	0	0	0	33	0
168	Lindsey Wilson C	19,622	-1	0	16	50,000
169	Lipscomb U	2	128	8	34	0
170	Lock Haven U PA	24,404	0	0	0	0
171	Longwood C	6,629	764	5,276	146	0
172	Lourdes C	-1	0	0	171	2,350
173	Loyola Marymount U	15,316	-1	0	120	-1
174	Loyola U New Orleans	21,500	-1	-1	-1	27,037
175	Lubbock Christian U	1	19,023	-1	307	27,450
176	Luth Theo Sem Philly	1	0	-1	1	0
177	Lynchburg C	-1	-1	-1	-1	-1
178	Malone C	18,151	6,088	1,500	744	24,599
179	Manchester C	-1	-1	-1	-1	-1
180	Manhattan C	327	327	-1	-1	1,757
181	Marist C	-1	-1	-1	57	22,600
182	Mary Baldwin C	15,513	74	15	37	13,542
183	Mary Washington C	28,148	3,596	967	117	35,654
184	Marymount U	1,656	15,095	1,530	33	900
185	Maryville U St Louis	24,780	169	-1	77	20,956
186	McNeese ST U	-1	-1	-1	7	18,497
187	Medical C Wisconsin	1,900	1,900	3,500	45	500
188	Merrimack C	19,374	147	-1	30	6,902
189	MidAmer Nazarene U	5	0	0	0	0
190	Millikin U	-1	-1	-1	-1	-1
191	Millsaps C	11,559	316	1,401	89	500
192	Minnesota ST U-Mankato	16,895	3,095	2,028	167	10,650
193	Minot ST U	5,741	149	2	20	5,000
194	Monterey Inst Intl St	185	185	0	25	50
195	Moravian C	579	579	1,476	4	11,238
196	Morehead ST U	22,288	1,987	2,253	67	38,332
197	Morningside C	-1	15,265	-1	2	7,334
198	MS Valley ST U	6,000	4,200	400	102	32,158
199	Mt Holyoke C	-1	-1	-1	-1	-1
200	Mt Marty C	-1	-1	-1	-1	-1

-1 -- Unavailable   -2 -- Not Applicable

ACRL Library Data Tables 2004
ELECTRONIC RESOURCES

INSTITUTIONS GRANTING MASTER OF ARTS AND PROFESSIONAL DEGREES (Carnegie Code M)

Lib. No.	Survey Question # Institution	Electronic journals purchased 1	Electronic full-text journals purchased 2	Electronic journals not purchased 3	Electronic Reference Sources 4	Electronic books 5
201	Mt Mary C-WI	-1	-1	-1	15	7,100
202	MT ST U Northern	32	1	30,410	39	550
203	Mt St Vincent U	10,823	3,463	-1	26	302
204	MT Tech U Montana	21,644	21,644	2,871	22	7,438
205	Murray ST U-KY	345	11,450	3,288	9	0
206	Muskingum C	6,020	6,000	20	100	20,000
207	Natl C Naturopathic Med	400	400	-1	12	45
208	Natl Defense U	96	6	8	198	0
209	NC Sch Arts	0	0	0	0	0
210	NEastrn IL U	17,428	5,958	-1	92	9,660
211	Nipissing U	13,350	7,648	2,400	86	-1
212	NJ City U	22,500	-1	-1	3	0
213	NM Highlands U	-1	-1	-1	-1	17,203
214	North Central C	778	5,448	76	8	1,974
215	Northern KY U	298	-1	-1	-1	12,600
216	Northern ST U	9,445	1,500	1,200	45	12,062
217	Northwest C	0	0	121	0	4,149
218	Norwich U	11,054	38	101	-1	-1
219	Notre Dame C OH	20,859	20,859	0	161	18,709
220	Notre Dame Sem	0	0	0	0	0
221	NW MO ST U	-1	-1	0	-1	0
222	NY Inst Tech Islip	0	0	0	0	0
223	NY Inst Tech Main	12,152	11,960	4,696	46	10,293
224	Oberlin C	18,951	11,081	-1	243	18,000
225	OH U Lancaster	0	6,200	0	0	21,640
226	Olivet Nazarene U	684	684	9,701	20	3,000
227	Otterbein C	7,506	5,650	-1	1,686	16,650
228	Pace U Law	58	23,470	282	128	10,766
229	Pacific Lutheran U	-1	-1	-1	-1	-1
230	Pacific Union C	12,337	165	137	79	3,805
231	Palm Beach Atl C	0	0	0	8	38,504
232	Pfeiffer U	10,949	0	1	67	20,000
233	Philadelphia U	15,126	1,380	1,500	43	7,785
234	Plymouth ST C	45,937	1,439	86	36	0
235	Pont C Josephinum	1,938	1,155	0	12	0
236	Pope John Ntl Sem	-1	-1	-1	-1	-1
237	Prescott C	17	3	12	4	0
238	Providence C	-1	11,809	-1	117	8,450
239	Purchase C SUNY	14,957	2,201	1,508	28	8,149
240	Purdue U Calumet	418	418	1,384	139	1,294

-1 -- Unavailable   -2 -- Not Applicable

ACRL Library Data Tables 2004

ELECTRONIC RESOURCES

INSTITUTIONS GRANTING MASTER OF ARTS AND PROFESSIONAL DEGREES (Carnegie Code M)

Lib. No.	Survey Question # Institution	Electronic journals purchased 1	Electronic full-text journals purchased 2	Electronic journals not purchased 3	Electronic Reference Sources 4	Electronic books 5
241	Purdue U North Central	12,424	1,026	19,731	1	0
242	Quincy U	-1	-1	-1	-1	-1
243	R.Wesleyan C	20,000	157	1,000	27	0
244	Radford U	7,712	1,597	9,773	175	38,590
245	Ramapo C NJ	32	28	5	10	1,767
246	Recnstrctnst Rabbinical C	0	0	0	5	0
247	RI Sch Design	5,400	0	0	15	0
248	Rivier C	0	0	0	63	4,100
249	Rockhurst U	14,000	425	0	120	0
250	Roger Williams U	17,534	875	52	112	205
251	Roosevelt U	8,347	-1	10,224	42	0
252	Rosemont C	362	362	0	7	0
253	Salem Teiko U	0	0	-1	0	0
254	Salisbury ST U	1,802	1,780	576	64	318
255	San Jose ST U	37,217	37,217	4,331	192	4,622
256	Savannah ST U	-1	4,401	1	27	27,441
257	Schreiner C	241	241	13,072	10	29,467
258	SE LA U	985	985	41	74	38,829
259	SE MO ST U	14,334	486	320	1	0
260	SE Oklahoma St U	8	41	-1	10	8,000
261	Seton Hill C	2	8,783	80	3	0
262	SF Consrv Music	0	0	0	4	0
263	Shaw U	-1	18,852	-1	22	22,243
264	Shorter C	-1	-1	-1	-1	-1
265	Silver Lake C	4	4	1	1	0
266	Sisseton-Wahpeton CC	0	0	0	0	0
267	Southrn C Opt	0	0	2	0	0
268	Southrn IL U Edward	-1	9,169	334	62	2,453
269	Southrn OR U	25,785	504	19	60	0
270	Spring Hill C	16,835	724	1,403	375	14,879
271	St Ambrose U	-1	302	0	77	13,854
272	St C.Borromeo Sem	10,928	6,250	60	3,362	88
273	St Cloud ST U	18,333	2,194	0	76	13,776
274	St Francis C PA	6,872	5,881	6,001	41	40,000
275	St Francis-Xavier U	5,267	5,267	15	45	0
276	St John Fisher C	10,000	-1	-1	15	3,000
277	St Joseph C Suffolk	15	7	1	33	7
278	St Joseph's C IN	0	0	0	29	0
279	St Joseph's C NY	15	7	1	33	740,620
280	St Joseph's Sem	0	0	0	3	0

-1 -- Unavailable   -2 -- Not Applicable

ACRL Library Data Tables 2004
ELECTRONIC RESOURCES

INSTITUTIONS GRANTING MASTER OF ARTS AND PROFESSIONAL DEGREES (Carnegie Code M

Lib. No.	Survey Question # Institution	Electronic journals purchased 1	Electronic full-text journals purchased 2	Electronic journals not purchased 3	Electronic Reference Sources 4	Electronic books 5
281	St Mary's U MN	-1	-1	-1	-1	-1
282	St Meinrad Theo	2	0	3	22	3,417
283	St Michael's C	17,800	458	67	97	7,853
284	St Norbert C	13,000	-1	-1	-1	7,566
285	St Patrick's Sem	0	0	0	4	0
286	St Peter's Abbey & C	-1	-1	-1	-1	0
287	ST U W GA	2,264	3,756	2,175	229	65,788
288	St Vincent Sem	0	0	0	37	0
289	St. John's C	-1	-1	-1	-1	-1
290	Stetson U	19,792	176	308	117	151
291	Sthrn Polytech ST U	-1	-1	-1	-1	-1
292	Stonehill C	967	1	1	25	0
293	Sul Ross ST U	12,500	12,500	0	5	40,000
294	SUNY Brockport	13,556	13,556	-1	99	928
295	SUNY Buffalo	19,398	-1	-1	35	5,415
296	SUNY C Potsdam	4,604	-1	15,363	68	5,693
297	SUNY IT Utica	15,206	2,623	0	51	1,400
298	SUNY Oneonta	17,446	4,177	1,510	100	4,268
299	SUNY Oswego	-1	-1	-1	-1	-1
300	SW MO ST U	737	737	183	111	0
301	SWstrn Adventist U	0	-1	-1	-1	27,000
302	SWstrn OK ST U	-1	5,200	-1	52	24,000
303	Tabor C	-1	-1	-1	-1	-1
304	Tiffin U	2,500	2,500	0	150	17,000
305	TM Cooley Law Sch	-1	-1	-1	14	-1
306	Trinity Luth Sem	200	175	0	5	0
307	Trinity U	17,026	970	2,340	164	27,681
308	Trinity U	9,086	-1	0	15	500
309	Troy ST U	10,000	3,000	0	49	32,191
310	Troy ST U Dothan	-1	-1	-1	-1	-1
311	Truman ST U	-1	-1	-1	-1	-1
312	TX Chiro C	-1	-1	-1	-1	-1
313	U Arts	-1	-1	-1	-1	-1
314	U C Cape	20,960	-1	-1	110	50
315	U Charleston	14,603	-1	-1	32	40,416
316	U DC	-1	-1	-1	-1	-1
317	U Del Turabo	9,371	9,180	-1	80	21,609
318	U Findlay	28,046	5,661	840	143	17,002
319	U Hawaii-Hilo	18,700	1,850	2,215	38	3,123
320	U HI-Kauai CC	0	0	0	4	0

-1 -- Unavailable   -2 -- Not Applicable

ACRL Library Data Tables 2004

ELECTRONIC RESOURCES

INSTITUTIONS GRANTING MASTER OF ARTS AND PROFESSIONAL DEGREES (Carnegie Code M)

Lib. No.	Survey Question # Institution	Electronic journals purchased 1	Electronic full-text journals purchased 2	Electronic journals not purchased 3	Electronic Reference Sources 4	Electronic books 5
321	U Houston	1	1	1	108	50,249
322	U Mary	-1	-1	-1	-1	-1
323	U MI Dearborn	25	18	-1	128	7,020
324	U Mobile	19,640	5,000	3,000	1,500	0
325	U NE Kearney	15,034	1,338	2,076	105	2,346
326	U Portland	19,000	525	0	90	116
327	U Richmond	17,319	2,043	1,292	202	42,287
328	U Rio Grande	13,960	5,900	0	968	21,300
329	U Scranton	15,000	15,000	1,520	11	1,900
330	U Sthn IN	7,700	3,327	3,307	10	2,294
331	U Tampa	-1	-1	-1	-1	-1
332	U TN Chatt	10,210	454	0	44	0
333	U TN Martin	24,533	15,283	9,791	40	26,767
334	U TX Tyler	41,600	6,185	0	1	20,658
335	U West AL	5,000	5,000	0	1,000	1,500
336	U WI E Claire	12,697	-1	-1	60	9,616
337	U WI La Crosse	1,550	1,550	0	50	7,337
338	U WI Platteville	123	123	0	21	0
339	U Winnipeg	6,710	2,543	1,190	179	1,921
340	UNC Asheville	16,100	2,175	535	81	100
341	UNC Pembroke	0	0	0	130	1,500
342	Union C-NY	-1	1,627	195	188	0
343	Valparaiso U	9,117	217	19,119	109	0
344	Villa Julie C	-1	12,088	-1	33	755
345	W.Carey College	303	718	0	8	0
346	W.Mitchell C Law	2,715	2	139	35	0
347	Walla Walla C	12	213	709	65	11
348	Walsh C Acct Bus Admin	12,000	8,134	0	28	5,713
349	Wartburg Theo Sem	-1	-1	-1	-1	0
350	Washburn U Topeka	18,211	1,048	0	89	8,818
351	Washington C	15,076	-1	-1	93	0
352	Washington Theo Union	1	1	8	4	0
353	Wayland Bap U	0	-1	-1	88	36,388
354	Wayne ST C	-1	-1	-1	-1	0
355	Webber Intl U	0	0	0	15	0
356	Wesley C	0	-1	0	-1	0
357	West Chester U PA	22,803	1,173	730	156	5,917
358	West TX A & M U	4,984	3,318	6,884	87	24,511
359	West VA Wesleyan C	-1	-1	-1	-1	40,045
360	Western MD C	17,636	1,202	62	37	0

-1 -- Unavailable   -2 -- Not Applicable

INSTITUTIONS GRANTING MASTER OF ARTS AND PROFESSIONAL DEGREES (Carnegie Code M

Lib. No.	Survey Question # Institution	Electronic journals purchased 1	Electronic full-text journals purchased 2	Electronic journals not purchased 3	Electronic Reference Sources 4	Electronic books 5
361	Western OR U	8,415	520	185	90	1,823
362	Western Sem	0	0	0	2	0
363	Western WA U	1,841	-1	582	63	-1
364	Westfield ST C	0	13,829	4,828	10	3,400
365	Westminster C-UT	15,199	1,570	2,175	95	30,588
366	Wheeling Jesuit U	-1	-1	-1	-1	-1
367	Whitworth C	12,585	585	0	83	2,947
368	Wilkes U	11,132	920	-1	97	-1
369	William Woods U	15,430	-1	-1	71	9,339
370	Williams C	10,377	4,323	1,642	5,520	4,937
371	Wstrn IL U	609	376	53	-1	1,972
372	Wstrn Theo Sem	87	87	2	17	-1
373	Xavier U LA	16,238	647	0	36	10,081

-1 -- Unavailable   -2 -- Not Applicable

ACRL Library Data Tables 2004
NETWORKED RESOURCES AND SERVICES

INSTITUTIONS GRANTING MASTER OF ARTS AND PROFESSIONAL DEGREES (Carnegie Code M

Lib. No.	Institution	Notes	Electronic journals purchased 6	Electronic full-text journals 7	Electronic reference sources 8	Electronic books 9	Virtual reference transactions 10	Federated searching across networked electronic resources? 11
			EXPENDITURES					
1	Abilene Christian U		63,149	66,321	63,149	0	306	Y
2	Agnes Scott C		96,486	91,569	151,337	950	70	N
3	Albany C Pharmacy		-1	-1	-1	-1	-1	
4	Albany Law Schl Union U		-1	-1	437,049	0	240	Y
5	Alcorn ST U		69,838	52,377	20,112	0	1,133	N
6	Amer Intl C		43,000	43,000	12,000	0	0	N
7	Amer U Puerto Rico		125,000	50,000	7,121	5,000	20	N
8	Anderson U		-1	-1	-1	-1	-1	
9	Angelo ST U		-1	-1	202,562	-1	150	N
10	Aquinas C MI		-1	-1	-1	-1	-1	
11	Ark Tech U		-1	-1	-1	-1	-1	N
12	Armstrong Atlantic ST U		85,665	12,000	0	0	-1	N
13	Assemblies God Theo Se		0	0	7,000	0	-1	N
14	Assumption C		-1	-1	68,842	0	40	N
15	Athenaeum of Ohio		-1	-1	-1	-1	-1	N
16	Auburn U Montgomery		16,300	109,648	0	3,496	95	N
17	Augusta ST U		28,635	23,177	65,991	7,624	18	Y
18	Augustana C SF		47,507	39,646	2,799	4,000	75	N
19	Austin C		68,782	68,782	33,245	0	0	N
20	Austin Presb Theo Sem		-1	-1	-1	-1	-1	
21	Averett C		46,719	46,042	72,325	0	690	N
22	Babson C		125,796	4,850	387,322	2,656	-1	N
23	Baker C System		5,000	5,000	131,548	0	2,824	N
24	Baker U		51,624	6,750	1,650	0	171	N
25	Baptist Bible C and Sem		0	16,474	0	0	0	N
26	Bayamon Central U		70,000	5,000	30	123,000	7,000	N
27	Bellevue U		85,399	85,399	13,975	6,000	2,533	Y
28	Bennington C		25,000	15,085	3,000	960	0	N
29	Bethel C IN		-1	-1	31,514	-1	0	N
30	Birmingham Southern C		29,538	29,538	87,154	0	0	N
31	Bluffton C		-1	-1	-1	-1	-1	Y
32	BowlGrn SU Fireld		-2	-2	-2	-2	6	Y
33	Bradley U		103,000	72,000	280,000	8,000	-1	N
34	Brescia U		10,814	10,814	14,468	750	-1	N
35	Brooks Institute		-2	-2	1,672	-2	-2	N
36	Bryn Athyn C		0	0	10,152	0	246	N
37	Buena Vista U		85,976	-1	82,636	0	19	N
38	Butler U		28,421	136,427	44,883	0	70	Y
39	C Atlantic		-1	24,640	56,048	330	-1	N
40	C Mt St Joseph		38,000	0	2,000	2,500	89	N

C -- Reported in Canadian $ -1 -- Unavailable   -2 -- Not Applicable

INSTITUTIONS GRANTING MASTER OF ARTS AND PROFESSIONAL DEGREES (Carnegie Code M)

Logins to electronic databases 12	No. of databases reported 12a	Queries (searches) in electronic databases 13	No. of databases reported 13a	Items requested in electronic databases 14	No. of databases reported 14a	Virtual visits to website 15a	Virtual visits to catalog 15b	Excl. visits fr. inside library 15c	Survey Question # Institution
-1	-1	209,650	26	-1	-1	126,064	-1	N	Abilene Christian U
26,562	68	112,396	78	135,221	77	-1	-1		Agnes Scott C
-1	-1	-1	-1	-1	-1	-1	-1		Albany C Pharmacy
-1	-1	-1	-1	-1	-1	-1	-1	N	Albany Law Schl Union U
11,112	75	44,695	75	81,645	75	118,205	86,234	N	Alcorn ST U
63,331	33	104,975	48	70,127,972	8,937	63,929	2,200	Y	Amer Intl C
-1	-1	-1	-1	125	25	207	125	Y	Amer U Puerto Rico
-1	-1	-1	-1	-1	-1	-1	-1		Anderson U
-1	-1	211,098	175	281,331	175	880,900	-1		Angelo ST U
-1	-1	-1	-1	-1	-1	-1	-1		Aquinas C MI
-1	-1	-1	-1	-1	-1	-1	-1	N	Ark Tech U
-1	-1	-1	-1	-1	-1	-1	-1		Armstrong Atlantic ST U
-1	-1	-1	-1	-1	-1	-1	-1		semblies God Theo Sem
-1	-1	149,058	31	-1	-1	-1	-1	N	Assumption C
-1	-1	-1	-1	-1	-1	-1	-1	Y	Athenaeum of Ohio
152,678	110	165,503	110	432,786	110	-1	-1		Auburn U Montgomery
82,886	201	231,570	201	342,883	201	96,000	97,127	N	Augusta ST U
32,146	87	112,234	87	93,425	87	-1	248,434	N	Augustana C SF
-1	0	-1	0	-1	0	-1	-1		Austin C
-1	-1	-1	-1	-1	-1	-1	-1		Austin Presb Theo Sem
-1	-1	270,362	59	176,285	29	-1	-1		Averett C
82,976	7	198,815	10	753,057	18	249,774	-1	N	Babson C
-1	33	274,623	33	1,688	33	62,709	-1	N	Baker C System
34,812	53	137,789	53	121,543	53	-1	-1		Baker U
68,374	8	683,297	8	376,112	8	0	0	N	Baptist Bible C and Sem
10,000	4,000	7,000	7,000	10,000	10,000	15,000	5,000	N	Bayamon Central U
68,050	9	68,841	9	361,516	9	22,155	16,616	N	Bellevue U
-1	-1	26,179	8	27,867	4	-1	-1		Bennington C
18,936	26	75,355	46	37,845	41	0	0	N	Bethel C IN
-1	114	-1	-1	-1	-1	-1	-1	Y	Birmingham Southern C
-1	0	-1	0	-1	0	-1	0	N	Bluffton C
-1	-1	-1	-1	-1	-1	-1	-2	N	BowlGrn SU Fireld
-1	-1	349,000	100	-1	-1	-1	-1	N	Bradley U
-1	-1	-1	-1	-1	-1	-1	-1	N	Brescia U
864	1	-1	-2	-1	-2	-2	-2	Y	Brooks Institute
-1	-1	-1	-1	-1	-1	3,000	-1	Y	Bryn Athyn C
-1	-1	128,824	53	-1	-1	-1	-1	Y	Buena Vista U
-1	-1	-1	-1	-1	-1	-1	-1	N	Butler U
-1	-1	-1	-1	-1	-1	-1	-1		C Atlantic
0	0	0	0	0	0	100,428	43,009	N	C Mt St Joseph

-1 -- Unavailable   -2 -- Not Applicable

ACRL Library Data Tables 2004

NETWORKED RESOURCES AND SERVICES

INSTITUTIONS GRANTING MASTER OF ARTS AND PROFESSIONAL DEGREES (Carnegie Code M)

Lib. No.	Survey Question # Institution	Notes	Electronic journals purchased 6	Electronic full-text journals 7	Electronic reference sources 8	Electronic books 9	Virtual reference transactions 10	Federated searching across networked electronic resources? 11
			EXPENDITURES					
41	C Mt St Vincent		45,615	45,615	-1	0	0	N
42	C Our Lady Elms		22,923	22,755	63,344	0	0	N
43	C.R. Drew U Med & Sci		-1	146,525	131,575	12,800	0	N
44	CA C Arts & Crafts		0	0	9,064	7	-1	N
45	CA St Polytechnic U-Pomo		271,794	-1	-1	14,431	1,132	Y
46	CA St U - Sacramento		469,602	0	0	0	1,248	N
47	CA ST U Dominguez Hills		136,302	62,773	219,480	0	3,237	Y
48	CA ST U Fresno		0	0	0	0	0	N
49	CA ST U Fullerton		-1	-1	-1	-1	-1	
50	CA ST U Hayward		-1	-1	-1	-1	-1	
51	CA ST U Long Beach		-1	-1	-1	-1	-1	
52	CA ST U Northridge		194,191	-1	5,000	-1	1,480	Y
53	CA ST U S Bernadino		-1	-1	-1	-1	-1	N
54	CA ST U San Marcos		174,198	-1	-1	-1	548	N
55	CA ST U Stanislaus		110,192	110,192	56,477	3,023	79	Y
56	CA West Sch Law		21,348	21,348	119,475	0	-1	Y
57	Calvin C		-1	-1	-1	-1	-1	
58	Cameron U		60,521	-1	-1	-1	28	N
59	Canisius C		-1	-1	6,045	32,262	-1	N
60	Carlow C		22,239	0	31,055	0	60	N
61	Carroll C-Waukesha		47,019	0	1,600	4,000	50	Y
62	Cedar Crest C		15,040	40,372	3,728	1,284	-1	N
63	Cedarville U		-1	30,614	75,170	-1	-1	Y
64	Centenary C		0	0	516	0	0	N
65	Centenary C LA		0	35,710	13,858	0	20	N
66	Central Baptist C		0	0	5,149	0	-1	N
67	Central CT ST U		-1	-1	-1	-1	-1	N
68	Central MO ST U		238,879	159,631	230,129	702	299	N
69	Charleston Sthrn U		20,372	158,622	20,372	2,418	-1	N
70	Chicago ST U		14,508	12,508	135,006	-1	-1	N
71	Chris Newport U		-1	4,090	63,106	0	87	N
72	Christendom C		-1	1,875	3,972	-1	-1	N
73	Christian Brothers U		0	0	0	3,000	117,407	N
74	Clarion U PA		112,947	112,947	112,947	0	0	Y
75	Clarke C-IA		2,500	31,911	10,000	1,962	-1	N
76	Clarkson C-NE		3,868	3,868	8,363	0	0	Y
77	Colorado C		89,199	65,407	287,027	0	96	N
78	Columbia C MO		-1	-1	-1	-1	-1	
79	Columbia C SC		7,776	7,776	32,537	0	0	N
80	Columbia Intl U		-1	-1	-1	0	-1	Y

C -- Reported in Canadian $ -1 -- Unavailable   -2 -- Not Applicable

INSTITUTIONS GRANTING MASTER OF ARTS AND PROFESSIONAL DEGREES (Carnegie Code M)

Logins to electronic databases 12	No. of databases reported 12a	Queries (searches) in electronic databases 13	No. of databases reported 13a	Items requested in electronic databases 14	No. of databases reported 14a	Virtual visits to website 15a	Virtual visits to catalog 15b	Excl. visits fr. inside library 15c	Survey Question # Institution
134,600	12	-1	-1	-1	-1	-1	-1	N	C Mt St Vincent
-1	-1	-1	-1	-1	-1	-1	-1	N	C Our Lady Elms
-1	-1	-1	-1	-1	-1	-1	-1		C.R. Drew U Med & Sci
1,624	5	-1	-1	-1	-1	-1	-1		CA C Arts & Crafts
-1	-1	899,027	83	-1	-1	1,048,647	315,892	N	St Polytechnic U-Pomona
64,641	159	1,219,887	62	0	0	1,205,659	67,017	N	CA St U - Sacramento
126,621	37	759,414	60	830,479	50	1,381,454	1	N	CA ST U Dominguez Hills
0	0	0	0	0	0	0	0	N	CA ST U Fresno
-1	-1	-1	-1	-1	-1	-1	-1		CA ST U Fullerton
-1	-1	-1	-1	-1	-1	-1	-1		CA ST U Hayward
-1	-1	-1	-1	-1	-1	-1	-1		CA ST U Long Beach
-1	-1	7,121,775	-1	-1	-1	7,121,775	-1	Y	CA ST U Northridge
-1	-1	-1	-1	-1	-1	-1	-1	N	CA ST U S Bernadino
171,908	102	587,342	102	-1	102	465,053	82,392	N	CA ST U San Marcos
300,326	63	-1	-1	-1	-1	143,672	-1	Y	CA ST U Stanislaus
-1	-1	-1	-1	-1	-1	35,112	-1	N	CA West Sch Law
-1	-1	-1	-1	-1	-1	-1	-1		Calvin C
209,891	27,068	209,891	27,068	-1	-1	219,388	655,403	N	Cameron U
-1	-1	-1	-1	426,221	106	251,646	32,083	N	Canisius C
-1	-1	35,571	8	740	3	22,994	-1	N	Carlow C
135,621	34	135,621	34	99,245	34	500,000	483,787	Y	Carroll C-Waukesha
-1	-1	-1	-1	-1	-1	-1	-1		Cedar Crest C
-1	-1	-1	-1	-1	-1	-1	-1	N	Cedarville U
0	25	70,995	25	0	0	18,194	0	N	Centenary C
37,194	241	97,276	241	73,436	241	100,000	100,000	N	Centenary C LA
-1	-1	-1	-1	-1	-1	-1	-1		Central Baptist C
-1	-1	-1	-1	-1	-1	-1	-1		Central CT ST U
-1	125	-1	0	-1	0	1,458,107	505,560	Y	Central MO ST U
66,781	48	-1	-1	-1	-1	-1	-1		Charleston Sthrn U
20,000	110	40,000	110	75,000	110	-1	-1		Chicago ST U
-1	-1	257,437	18	168,712	12	98,696	-1	N	Chris Newport U
201	6	366	6	-1	-1	-1	-1		Christendom C
22,858	35	67,746	35	103,151	35	117,407	0	N	Christian Brothers U
-1	-1	-1	-1	-1	-1	-1	-1		Clarion U PA
-1	-1	-1	-1	-1	-1	-1	-1	N	Clarke C-IA
-1	-1	-1	-1	-1	-1	-1	-1	N	Clarkson C-NE
0	0	0	0	0	0	0	0		Colorado C
-1	-1	-1	-1	-1	-1	-1	-1	N	Columbia C MO
29,720	20	170,893	20	141,822	20	-1	-1	Y	Columbia C SC
12,476	12	47,730	42	2,174	-1	-1	5,493	N	Columbia Intl U

-1 -- Unavailable   -2 -- Not Applicable

NETWORKED RESOURCES AND SERVICES

INSTITUTIONS GRANTING MASTER OF ARTS AND PROFESSIONAL DEGREES (Carnegie Code M

Lib. No.	Survey Question # Institution	Notes	EXPENDITURES				Virtual reference transactions 10	Federated searching across networked electronic resources? 11
			Electronic journals purchased 6	Electronic full-text journals 7	Electronic reference sources 8	Electronic books 9		
81	Columbus ST U		-1	-1	-1	-1	-1	
82	Concordia U Irvine		33,054	-1	-1	0	-1	N
83	Concordia U RiverF		-1	20,626	6,534	-1	-1	Y
84	Concordia U St Paul		69,604	54,919	121,482	-1	15	N
85	Cooper Union		44,174	44,174	64,304	1,575	-1	Y
86	Cornerstone U		-1	-1	-1	-1	-1	N
87	Creighton U		131,221	63,950	206,626	627	19	N
88	Cumberland U		0	0	0	1,000	0	N
89	CUNY BMB C		-1	148,852	339,925	0	3,078	Y
90	CUNY C Stn Island		-1	204,831	25,044	-1	419	Y
91	CUNY City C		643,115	300,000	160,000	0	2	N
92	CUNY HH Lehman C		-1	-1	-1	-1	-1	N
93	CUNY John Jay C Crim J		154,319	66,998	76,099	16,397	298	N
94	CUNY Queens C		306,415	202,822	151,562	0	-1	N
95	Curtis Inst Music		0	0	0	0	38	N
96	Daniel Webster C		42,182	0	0	0	71	N
97	DeSales U		41,198	3,000	6,202	500	258	N
98	DN Myers C		4,023	4,023	14,543	213	260	N
99	Dominican C San Rafael		0	0	0	0	0	N
100	Dominican U		75,000	-1	-1	-1	-1	N
101	Drake U		228,030	56,967	171,064	5,668	145	N
102	Drury C		32,178	14,745	53,371	0	-1	N
103	E R Aero U		0	0	313,033	0	3,894	N
104	Earlham C		-1	32,351	141,793	12,911	-1	N
105	Eastern IL U		-1	-1	-1	-1	-1	
106	Eastern U		-1	-1	-1	-1	-1	N
107	Eastern WA U		62,450	91,000	42,000	0	-1	Y
108	Eastrn NM U Main		62,384	-1	-1	-1	721	N
109	Edinboro U PA		-1	-1	-1	-1	-1	
110	Elizabethtown C		79,730	35,054	82,765	1,745	47	N
111	Elmhurst C		-1	-1	-1	2,235	50	N
112	Elon U		244,455	-1	-1	4,313	90	N
113	Emmanuel C MA		95,000	-1	-1	0	0	Y
114	Emory & Henry C		45,000	-1	-1	-1	-1	N
115	Evergreen ST C		-1	59,327	96,681	-1	-1	Y
116	Fisk U		15,500	15,500	1,500	850	0	N
117	Fitchburg ST C		72,068	17,623	82,138	0	-1	N
118	FL Southern C		-1	-1	-1	-1	-1	
119	Fort Hays ST U		0	0	125,922	533	0	N
120	Francis Marion U		-1	-1	-1	-1	-1	

C -- Reported in Canadian $ -1 -- Unavailable   -2 -- Not Applicable

INSTITUTIONS GRANTING MASTER OF ARTS AND PROFESSIONAL DEGREES (Carnegie Code M)

Logins to electronic databases 12	No. of databases reported 12a	Queries (searches) in electronic databases 13	No. of databases reported 13a	Items requested in electronic databases 14	No. of databases reported 14a	Virtual visits to website 15a	Virtual visits to catalog 15b	Excl. visits fr. inside library 15c	Survey Question # Institution
-1	-1	-1	-1	-1	-1	-1	-1		Columbus ST U
-1	-1	-1	-1	-1	-1	-1	-1		Concordia U Irvine
10,798	11	46,304	11	-1	-1	-1	-1		Concordia U RiverF
2,168	4	818,820	6	388,763	6	-1	-1		Concordia U St Paul
-1	-1	-1	-1	-1	-1	-1	-1		Cooper Union
-1	-1	367,823	34	-1	-1	-1	-1	N	Cornerstone U
92,958	46	404,579	66	764,584	40	862,353	-1	N	Creighton U
-1	-1	-1	-1	-1	-1	-1	-1		Cumberland U
-1	-1	-1	-1	-1	-1	503,868	44,236	Y	CUNY BMB C
-1	-1	-1	-1	-1	-1	-1	-1		CUNY C Stn Island
-1	75	610,000	75	805,000	75	-1	-1	N	CUNY City C
-1	-1	-1	-1	-1	-1	-1	-1	N	CUNY HH Lehman C
193,118	99	-1	-1	-1	-1	431,926	-1	N	NY John Jay C Crim Just
-1	-1	-1	-1	-1	-1	-1	-1		CUNY Queens C
0	0	0	0	0	0	-2	-2	N	Curtis Inst Music
20,119	19	63,822	19	130,277	19	-1	-1		Daniel Webster C
34,658	38	-1	-1	-1	-1	35,267	19,790	N	DeSales U
-1	-1	3,723	142	4,662	142	-1	-1	N	DN Myers C
0	0	0	0	0	0	0	0		Dominican C San Rafael
-1	-1	-1	-1	-1	-1	-1	-1		Dominican U
45,513	31	241,276	39	39,186	11	409,155	83,343	N	Drake U
24,839	60	135,565	60	226,164	60	99,800	-1	Y	Drury C
-1	-1	-1	-1	-1	-1	-1	-1	N	E R Aero U
-1	-1	151,579	53	-1	-1	1,100,000	-1	N	Earlham C
-1	-1	-1	-1	-1	-1	-1	-1		Eastern IL U
-1	-1	-1	-1	-1	-1	-1	-1		Eastern U
-1	-1	-1	-1	-1	-1	-1	-1	N	Eastern WA U
-1	9,386	84,038	9,386	40,761	9,386	-1	-1	Y	Eastrn NM U Main
-1	-1	-1	-1	-1	-1	-1	-1		Edinboro U PA
38,602	33	134,935	33	55,023	33	-1	-1	Y	Elizabethtown C
-1	-1	-1	-1	-1	-1	-1	-1		Elmhurst C
535,701	70	-1	-1	-1	-1	-1	-1	N	Elon U
30,715	33	89,623	33	71,452	33	-2	-2	Y	Emmanuel C MA
-1	0	29,555	8	-1	-1	-1	-1		Emory & Henry C
49,263	38	168,255	31	153,117	29	-1	-1	N	Evergreen ST C
-1	-1	-1	-1	-1	-1	0	0	Y	Fisk U
12,618	134	178,785	134	402,486	56	86,572	-1	N	Fitchburg ST C
-1	-1	-1	-1	-1	-1	-1	-1		FL Southern C
0	0	0	0	0	0	0	0	Y	Fort Hays ST U
-1	-1	-1	-1	-1	-1	-1	-1		Francis Marion U

-1 -- Unavailable   -2 -- Not Applicable

ACRL Library Data Tables 2004
NETWORKED RESOURCES AND SERVICES

INSTITUTIONS GRANTING MASTER OF ARTS AND PROFESSIONAL DEGREES (Carnegie Code M

			EXPENDITURES				
Lib. No.	Institution	Notes	Electronic journals purchased 6	Electronic full-text journals 7	Electronic reference sources 8	Electronic books 9	Virtual reference transactions 10	Federated searching across networked electronic resources? 11
121	Franklin Inst Boston		-1	-1	-1	-1	-1	
122	Franklin U		-1	-1	-1	5,623	300	Y
123	Free Will Baptist Bible C		120	45	0	333	0	N
124	Frostburg ST U		53,600	24,610	109,486	0	225	Y
125	Furman U		-1	-1	213,781	0	-1	N
126	GA SWstrn ST U		6,455	6,455	0	0	9	Y
127	Gardner-Webb U		63,300	0	63,300	63,300	20	Y
128	Geneva C		1,930	1,005	57,759	0	0	N
129	Georgetown C		-1	-1	-1	1,426	0	N
130	Goucher C		109,976	72,989	140,544	0	0	N
131	Governors ST U		95	345	153,793	14,807	930	N
132	Greenville C		16,273	1,100	5,000	0	250	N
133	Grove City C		85,500	21,000	39,000	0	0	N
134	Harding U Main		67,044	-1	89,607	-1	100	N
135	Hebrew C		4,142	4,142	540	457	260	N
136	Heidelberg C		0	0	12,000	0	0	Y
137	Hillsdale Free Will Baptist C		3,922	3,575	3,922	0	-1	Y
138	Holy Apostles C & Sem		0	0	0	0	-1	Y
139	Hood C		-1	39,249	53,563	0	-1	N
140	Humboldt ST U		72,247	72,247	25,182	0	65	Y
141	IN Inst of Tech		28,000	28,000	2,200	1,100	40	N
142	IN U Kokomo		43,412	7,186	47,393	1,382	218	N
143	IN U S Bend		74,974	44,562	182,674	2,290	198	N
144	IN U-Purdue U Ft Wayne		134,924	103,322	180,907	-1	-1	N
145	IN Wesleyan U		10,566	129,250	2,441	11,892	-1	Y
146	Intl Fine Arts C		1,000	7,500	8,000	0	0	N
147	Jacksonville ST U		-1	-1	-1	6,880	0	N
148	Johnson Bible C		2,100	2,100	8,213	0	-2	N
149	Kean U		-1	-1	-1	-1	-1	
150	Keene State C		92,567	59,313	33,254	0	-1	N
151	Kent ST U Stark		18,052	0	0	0	-1	N
152	Kentucky Christian C		0	0	0	0	0	N
153	Kentucky ST U		11,512	11,512	34,161	1	1	Y
154	Kettering U		100,000	100,000	120,000	1,000	0	N
155	King's C PA		-1	-1	-1	-1	-1	
156	LaGrange C		-1	-1	-1	-1	-1	
157	Lakeland C-AB		5,291	5,291	34,820	1,267	0	N
158	Lakeview C Nursing		3,350	3,350	0	0	0	N
159	Lancaster Bible C		22,755	0	17,369	627	0	N
160	Lander U		0	0	25,062	2,455	-1	N

C -- Reported in Canadian $ -1 -- Unavailable   -2 -- Not Applicable

198

ACRL Library Data Tables 2004
NETWORKED RESOURCES AND SERVICES

INSTITUTIONS GRANTING MASTER OF ARTS AND PROFESSIONAL DEGREES (Carnegie Code M)

Logins to electronic databases 12	No. of databases reported 12a	Queries (searches) in electronic databases 13	No. of databases reported 13a	Items requested in electronic databases 14	No. of databases reported 14a	Virtual visits to website 15a	Virtual visits to catalog 15b	Excl. visits fr. inside library 15c	Survey Question # Institution
-1	-1	-1	-1	-1	-1	-1	-1		Franklin Inst Boston
14,378	148	84,799	148	-1	148	-1	14,376	N	Franklin U
-1	-1	-1	-1	-1	-1	-1	-1		Free Will Baptist Bible C
49,118	57	444,494	57	1	0	266,613	20,136	N	Frostburg ST U
-1	-1	-1	-1		-1	150,747	-1	N	Furman U
81,968	100	198,532	100	-1	100	-1	536,825	N	GA SWstrn ST U
120,408	33	166,066	33	190,050	33	32,128	11,821	N	Gardner-Webb U
0	-1	0	0	0	0	0	0	N	Geneva C
-1	-1	-1	-1	-1	-1	190,400	-1		Georgetown C
60,003	32	242,862	55	693,636	46	-1	-1	N	Goucher C
-1	-1	-1	-1	-1	-1	-1	-1		Governors ST U
18,735	6	91,366	6	36,267	6	-1	-1	N	Greenville C
0	0	0	0	0	0	0	0	N	Grove City C
-1	-1	216,254	56	-1	-1	132,761	132,761	N	Harding U Main
1,096	7,695	1,096	7,695	0	0	10,584	0	N	Hebrew C
-1	90	-1	90	-1	90	-1	-1		Heidelberg C
-1	-1	-1	-1	-1	-1	-1	-1		Ilsdale Free Will Baptist C
-1	-1	-1	-1	0	0	-1	-1	N	Holy Apostles C & Sem
-1	-1	77,687	57	57,086	57	-1	-1		Hood C
206,847	136	1	136	1	136	1	1	Y	Humboldt ST U
0	0	0	0	0	0	0	0	N	IN Inst of Tech
22,198	31	86,038	31	-1	-1	-1	-1	N	IN U Kokomo
72,829	57	335,966	47	259,563	47	2,634,695	-1	N	IN U S Bend
160,986	63	751,339	63	444,412	63	-1	-1		IN U-Purdue U Ft Wayne
109,905	255,352	418,784	255,352	707,436	255,352	-1	-1	N	IN Wesleyan U
300	300	300	300	1	1	0	0	Y	Intl Fine Arts C
-1	-1	-1	-1	-1	-1	15,245,249	-1	N	Jacksonville ST U
-2	-2	-2	-2	-2	-2	-2	-2	N	Johnson Bible C
-1	-1	-1	-1	-1	-1	-1	-1		Kean U
307,311	64	307,311	64	-1	-1	171,993	-1	N	Keene State C
14,636	9	68,454	9	50,212	9	-1	-1	N	Kent ST U Stark
-1	-1	-1	-1	-1	-1	-1	-1		Kentucky Christian C
10,362	27	42,617	27	27,379	27	1	1		Kentucky ST U
-1	-1	-1	-1	-1	-1	-1	-1		Kettering U
-1	-1	-1	-1	-1	-1	-1	-1		King's C PA
-1	-1	-1	-1	-1	-1	-1	-1		LaGrange C
-1	-1	-1	-1	-1	-1	-1	-1		Lakeland C-AB
1,258	6,768	5,773	6,768	0	0	0	0	N	Lakeview C Nursing
16,479	5	54,778	5	16,782	3	-1	-1		Lancaster Bible C
27,106	17	215,146	18	84,355	19	-1	-1	N	Lander U

-1 -- Unavailable   -2 -- Not Applicable

NETWORKED RESOURCES AND SERVICES

INSTITUTIONS GRANTING MASTER OF ARTS AND PROFESSIONAL DEGREES (Carnegie Code M

			EXPENDITURES					
Lib. No.	Survey Question # / Institution	Notes	Electronic journals purchased 6	Electronic full-text journals 7	Electronic reference sources 8	Electronic books 9	Virtual reference transactions 10	Federated searching across networked electronic resources? 11
161	Langston U		0	0	0	0	0	Y
162	Laurentian U JN	C	-1	-1	-1	-1	-1	Y
163	Le Moyne C		19,928	76,832	214,124	15,520	0	N
164	Lebanon Valley C		77,506	-1	500	1,600	-1	N
165	Lewis U		158,500	143,705	6,192	815	517	Y
166	Lewis&Clark C		-1	-1	-1	0	174	N
167	Lincoln U-MO		0	0	33,759	0	10	Y
168	Lindsey Wilson C		22,291	-1	11,037	8,946	40	N
169	Lipscomb U		60	-1	-1	-1	-1	
170	Lock Haven U PA		129,071	0	0	0	22	N
171	Longwood C		67,408	38,326	92,800	0	96	N
172	Lourdes C		2,722	0	0	270	0	Y
173	Loyola Marymount U		250,000	-1	-1	-1	0	N
174	Loyola U New Orleans		197,322	-1	-1	-1	704	Y
175	Lubbock Christian U		17,367	-1	-1	-1	0	N
176	Luth Theo Sem Philly		4,200	-1	-1	0	20	N
177	Lynchburg C		-1	-1	-1	-1	-1	N
178	Malone C		69,908	32,635	72,030	10,115	25	Y
179	Manchester C		-1	-1	-1	-1	-1	
180	Manhattan C		-1	84,324	-1	3,353	-1	N
181	Marist C		-1	-1	-1	11,053	-1	N
182	Mary Baldwin C		5,406	18,124	14,004	0	605	N
183	Mary Washington C		-1	-1	-1	4,065	-1	Y
184	Marymount U		30,000	38,990	63,089	1,000	278	Y
185	Maryville U St Louis		59,197	-1	62,641	0	23	N
186	McNeese ST U		-1	-1	-1	-1	0	N
187	Medical C Wisconsin		-1	-1	-1	-1	1,800	N
188	Merrimack C		-1	27,336	70,206	0	-1	N
189	MidAmer Nazarene U		30,000	0	0	0	0	N
190	Millikin U		-1	-1	-1	-1	-1	N
191	Millsaps C		41,570	32,950	23,033	0	-1	N
192	Minnesota ST U-Mankato		198,232	94,735	381,437	17,073	475	N
193	Minot ST U		20,383	6,583	70,000	0	0	N
194	Monterey Inst Intl St		18,500	18,500	50,000	3,000	0	N
195	Moravian C		3,414	3,414	2,118	4,335	0	N
196	Morehead ST U		111,400	56,412	113,076	5,258	200	N
197	Morningside C		13,957	10,000	2,000	0	-1	Y
198	MS Valley ST U		74,500	14,000	500	5,000	50	Y
199	Mt Holyoke C		-1	-1	-1	-1	-1	
200	Mt Marty C		-1	-1	-1	-1	-1	N

C -- Reported in Canadian $ -1 -- Unavailable   -2 -- Not Applicable

ACRL Library Data Tables 2004
NETWORKED RESOURCES AND SERVICES

INSTITUTIONS GRANTING MASTER OF ARTS AND PROFESSIONAL DEGREES (Carnegie Code M)

Logins to electronic databases 12	No. of databases reported 12a	Queries (searches) in electronic databases 13	No. of databases reported 13a	Items requested in electronic databases 14	No. of databases reported 14a	Virtual visits to website 15a	Virtual visits to catalog 15b	Excl. visits fr. inside library 15c	Survey Question # Institution
15,086	5	45,292	5	0	0	0	0	N	Langston U
158,913	39	408,567	39	263,809	39	315,416	134,232	N	Laurentian U JN
118,055	69	553,256	69	-1	-1	298,654	-1	N	Le Moyne C
-1	-1	150,000	7	-1	-1	71,000	-1	N	Lebanon Valley C
115,440	77	163,105	77	241,799	77	-1	-1	N	Lewis U
74,000	167	-1	-1	-1	-1	242,766	-1		Lewis&Clark C
-1	-1	-1	-1	-1	-1	92,000	-1	N	Lincoln U-MO
-1	-1	-1	-1	-1	-1	-1	-1	Y	Lindsey Wilson C
-1	-1	-1	-1	-1	-1	-1	-1	Y	Lipscomb U
0	0	317,112	95	168,876	95	163,128	0	N	Lock Haven U PA
53,783	38	207,438	94	107,197	34	-1	579,474	N	Longwood C
4,190	3	17,490	8	23,259	6	-1	-1		Lourdes C
-1	-1	-1	-1	-1	-1	-1	311,135	N	Loyola Marymount U
-1	-1	-1	-1	-1	-1	615,802	-1	N	Loyola U New Orleans
4,019	40	63,525	95	36,670	95	-1	-1	N	Lubbock Christian U
3,492	1	8,803	1	0	0	-1	-1		Luth Theo Sem Philly
-1	-1	-1	-1	-1	-1	-1	-1	Y	Lynchburg C
-1	-1	66,419	87	136,422	79	-1	-1	Y	Malone C
-1	-1	-1	-1	-1	-1	-1	-1		Manchester C
-1	-1	-1	-1	-1	-1	705,144	-1		Manhattan C
-1	-1	-1	-1	-1	-1	-1	-1		Marist C
-1	-1	-1	-1	-1	-1	-1	-1	Y	Mary Baldwin C
-1	-1	-1	-1	-1	-1	-1	-1	N	Mary Washington C
-1	-1	-1	-1	-1	-1	37,777	-1	N	Marymount U
24,086	77	177,987	77	191,943	8	-1	7,350	N	Maryville U St Louis
-1	-1	-1	-1	-1	-1	-1	-1	Y	McNeese ST U
297,149	1,945	139,857	25	633,478	1,800	482,895	265,643	N	Medical C Wisconsin
-1	-1	78,967	22	-1	-1	71,854	-1	N	Merrimack C
0	0	0	0	0	0	0	0	N	MidAmer Nazarene U
-1	-1	-1	-1	-1	-1	-1	-1		Millikin U
-1	-1	-1	-1	-1	-1	-1	54,214	Y	Millsaps C
166,713	107	785,103	133	729,566	69	536,335	0	N	Minnesota ST U-Mankato
30,000	20	130,000	20	0	0	0	0	N	Minot ST U
10,000	25	20,000	20	800	20	50,000	30,000	Y	Monterey Inst Intl St
29,816	6	223,054	9	123,375	5	-1	-1	N	Moravian C
-1	-1	319,640	-1	229,829	-1	90,347	-1	N	Morehead ST U
62,574	6	62,574	6	62,574	6	-1	-1	N	Morningside C
25,000	60	80,000	60	95,000	60	0	0	N	MS Valley ST U
-1	-1	-1	-1	-1	-1	-1	-1	N	Mt Holyoke C
-1	-1	-1	-1	-1	-1	-1	-1		Mt Marty C

-1 -- Unavailable   -2 -- Not Applicable

INSTITUTIONS GRANTING MASTER OF ARTS AND PROFESSIONAL DEGREES (Carnegie Code M

Lib. No.	Institution (Survey Question #)	Notes	Electronic journals purchased 6	Electronic full-text journals 7	Electronic reference sources 8	Electronic books 9	Virtual reference transactions 10	Federated searching across networked electronic resources? 11
201	Mt Mary C-WI		23,000	-1	-1	-1	-1	Y
202	MT ST U Northern		12,836	-1	16,284	1,840	-2	Y
203	Mt St Vincent U	C	106,952	21,860	136,864	-1	-1	Y
204	MT Tech U Montana		51,599	40,641	10,958	0	-1	N
205	Murray ST U-KY		83,431	1	1	0	0	N
206	Muskingum C		-1	-1	-1	-1	-1	Y
207	Natl C Naturopathic Med		30,000	28,000	-1	2,000	80	N
208	Natl Defense U		0	0	700,000	-1	10,000	N
209	NC Sch Arts		0	0	0	0	0	N
210	NEastrn IL U		-1	-1	-1	-1	-1	N
211	Nipissing U	C	87,401	36,813	266,299	9,662	0	N
212	NJ City U		-1	-1	-1	-1	-1	N
213	NM Highlands U		-1	-1	-1	-1	-1	N
214	North Central C		-1	-1	-1	-1	18	N
215	Northern KY U		-1	-1	-1	13,291	219	N
216	Northern ST U		0	24,825	79,078	1,500	32	N
217	Northwest C		0	0	0	2,290	0	N
218	Norwich U		85,874	-1	-1	-1	-1	Y
219	Notre Dame C OH		33,559	32,151	0	556	520	
220	Notre Dame Sem		0	0	0	0	0	N
221	NW MO ST U		1	-1	-1	0	-1	N
222	NY Inst Tech Islip		0	0	0	0	0	Y
223	NY Inst Tech Main		159,000	163,000	171,250	28,200	-1	N
224	Oberlin C		412,573	412,573	-1	18,927	126	Y
225	OH U Lancaster		0	2,500	0	0	0	N
226	Olivet Nazarene U		22,024	22,024	8,479	0	45	N
227	Otterbein C		115,932	-1	-1	-1	170	Y
228	Pace U Law		37,912	205,084	87,004	18,753	515	Y
229	Pacific Lutheran U		-1	-1	-1	-1	84	N
230	Pacific Union C		27,716	6,410	58,370	2,835	-1	N
231	Palm Beach Atl C		0	0	19,449	0	0	N
232	Pfeiffer U		23,230	0	-1	-1	-1	N
233	Philadelphia U		132,740	23,575	109,165	2,000	-1	N
234	Plymouth ST C		45,101	-1	53,054	0	0	N
235	Pont C Josephinum		6,938	3,698	15,648	0	0	N
236	Pope John Ntl Sem		-1	-1	-1	-1	-1	
237	Prescott C		26,000	3,000	2,000	0	-1	Y
238	Providence C		-1	332,925	-1	-1	-1	N
239	Purchase C SUNY		112,610	55,163	38,329	2,973	-1	N
240	Purdue U Calumet		34,902	34,902	35,508	1,100	18	N

C -- Reported in Canadian $ -1 -- Unavailable   -2 -- Not Applicable

ACRL Library Data Tables 2004
NETWORKED RESOURCES AND SERVICES

INSTITUTIONS GRANTING MASTER OF ARTS AND PROFESSIONAL DEGREES (Carnegie Code M)

Logins to electronic databases 12	No. of databases reported 12a	Queries (searches) in electronic databases 13	No. of databases reported 13a	Items requested in electronic databases 14	No. of databases reported 14a	Virtual visits to website 15a	Virtual visits to catalog 15b	Excl. visits fr. inside library 15c	Survey Question # Institution
13,480	5	-1	-1	-1	-1	-1	-1		Mt Mary C-WI
10,357	30	40,930	30	16,849	15	-1	-1		MT ST U Northern
-1	-1	-1	-1	-1	-1	-1	-1	N	Mt St Vincent U
-1	-1	-1	-1	-1	-1	-1	15,090	N	MT Tech U Montana
1	1	386,196	77	1	1	125,357	55,985	N	Murray ST U-KY
-1	-1	-1	-1	-1	-1	-1	-1	N	Muskingum C
700	12	1,600	12	3,500	12	28,000	21,000	N	Natl C Naturopathic Med
0	0	0	0	0	0	1,500,000	115,200	N	Natl Defense U
0	0	0	0	0	0	0	0	N	NC Sch Arts
-1	-1	555,270	68	423,615	43	-1	-1		NEastrn IL U
-1	-1	-1	-1	-1	-1	-1	-1		Nipissing U
-1	-1	-1	-1	-1	-1	2,976,290	-1	N	NJ City U
-1	-1	-1	-1	-1	-1	-1	-1	N	NM Highlands U
-1	-1	188,246	56	-1	-1	597,312	-1	N	North Central C
-1	-1	-1	-1	-1	-1	-1	-1	N	Northern KY U
-1	-1	-1	-1	-1	-1	-1	-1		Northern ST U
14,420	11	52,767	17	69,956	17	-1	-1		Northwest C
-1	-1	80,726	-1	-1	-1	-1	-1		Norwich U
2,264	30	7,532	79	9,821	38	-1	16,622	N	Notre Dame C OH
0	0	0	0	0	0	0	0		Notre Dame Sem
-1	-1	397,777	55	-1	-1	-1	-1	N	NW MO ST U
0	0	0	0	0	0	0	0	Y	NY Inst Tech Islip
43,625	78	159,041	78	147,644	78	62,499	41,937	N	NY Inst Tech Main
-1	-1	-1	-1	24,852	-1	-1	-1	N	Oberlin C
0	0	0	0	0	0	0	0	N	OH U Lancaster
-1	-1	-1	-1	-1	-1	-1	-1		Olivet Nazarene U
-1	-1	-1	-1	-1	-1	250,767	-1	N	Otterbein C
0	0	632,464	90	0	0	0	31,900	Y	Pace U Law
-1	-1	-1	-1	-1	-1	-1	-1	N	Pacific Lutheran U
-1	-1	-1	-1	-1	-1	-1	-1		Pacific Union C
0	0	0	0	0	0	0	0	N	Palm Beach Atl C
24,261	58	-1	-1	-1	-1	-1	-1		Pfeiffer U
82,715	32	-1	-1	-1	-1	784,961	-1	N	Philadelphia U
74,009	8	238,127	8	292,887	8	437,672	502,853	N	Plymouth ST C
-1	0	-1	0	-1	0	-1	-1	Y	Pont C Josephinum
-1	-1	-1	-1	-1	-1	-1	-1		Pope John Ntl Sem
-2	-2	-2	-2	-2	-2	-2	-2	Y	Prescott C
-1	-1	-1	-1	-1	-1	-1	-1		Providence C
-1	-1	-1	-1	54,191	18	-1	-1	N	Purchase C SUNY
-1	47	-1	47	-1	47	-1	-1	N	Purdue U Calumet

-1 -- Unavailable   -2 -- Not Applicable

ACRL Library Data Tables 2004
NETWORKED RESOURCES AND SERVICES

INSTITUTIONS GRANTING MASTER OF ARTS AND PROFESSIONAL DEGREES (Carnegie Code M)

Lib. No.	Survey Question # Institution	Notes	Electronic journals purchased 6	Electronic full-text journals 7	Electronic reference sources 8	Electronic books 9	Virtual reference transactions 10	Federated searching across networked electronic resources? 11
			EXPENDITURES					
241	Purdue U North Central		33,937	-1	900	0	345	Y
242	Quincy U		-1	-1	-1	-1	-1	
243	R.Wesleyan C		31,391	5,829	68,005	0	26	N
244	Radford U		158,589	91,834	148,154	21,919	-1	N
245	Ramapo C NJ		105,327	73,752	23,628	0	-1	Y
246	Recnstrctnst Rabbinical C		0	0	8,000	0	25	N
247	RI Sch Design		11,324	0	26,846	0	0	N
248	Rivier C		0	0	55,915	4,145	23	N
249	Rockhurst U		59,000	22,000	103,000	0	0	N
250	Roger Williams U		83,632	30,325	196,015	13,865	274	N
251	Roosevelt U		58,309	-1	122,652	0	354	N
252	Rosemont C		22,136	22,136	15,909	0	0	N
253	Salem Teiko U		0	0	0	0	3	N
254	Salisbury ST U		208,184	130,652	220,140	0	327	Y
255	San Jose ST U		683,257	683,257	683,892	0	4,970	Y
256	Savannah ST U		135,649	140,249	0	0	0	Y
257	Schreiner C		5,882	5,882	0	0	18	N
258	SE LA U		-1	-1	-1	-1	1,418	N
259	SE MO ST U		116,700	35,792	188,298	0	76	N
260	SE Oklahoma St U		1,340	16,474	44,883	0	-1	N
261	Seton Hill C		0	0	0	0	-1	N
262	SF Consrv Music		0	0	5,000	-1	0	N
263	Shaw U		-1	29,662	17,528	-1	-1	N
264	Shorter C		-1	-1	-1	-1	-1	
265	Silver Lake C		2,205	2,205	890	0	0	N
266	Sisseton-Wahpeton CC		0	0	0	0	0	N
267	Southrn C Opt		0	0	0	0	0	N
268	Southrn IL U Edward		440,828	-1	-1	18,976	542	N
269	Southrn OR U		36,196	15,958	64,414	0	-1	N
270	Spring Hill C		15,621	4,380	1,179	1,710	0	
271	St Ambrose U		39,327	4,768	61,863	2,370	121	N
272	St C.Borromeo Sem		10,928	7,897	14,290	0	200	Y
273	St Cloud ST U		50,006	37,697	253,453	7,500	161	N
274	St Francis C PA		39,149	39,149	63,865	0	172	Y
275	St Francis-Xavier U	C	219,048	219,048	-1	0	-1	N
276	St John Fisher C		156,000	-1	-1	-1	30	N
277	St Joseph C Suffolk		40,620	7,662	54,401	2,868	0	N
278	St Joseph's C IN		0	0	16,543	0	0	N
279	St Joseph's C NY		40,620	7,662	54,401	2,868	0	N
280	St Joseph's Sem		0	0	7,100	0	0	N

C -- Reported in Canadian $ -1 -- Unavailable   -2 -- Not Applicable

INSTITUTIONS GRANTING MASTER OF ARTS AND PROFESSIONAL DEGREES (Carnegie Code M)

Logins to electronic databases 12	No. of databases reported 12a	Queries (searches) in electronic databases 13	No. of databases reported 13a	Items requested in electronic databases 14	No. of databases reported 14a	Virtual visits to website 15a	Virtual visits to catalog 15b	Excl. visits fr. inside library 15c	Survey Question # Institution
8,935	1	35,199	2	16,778	1	-1	-1		Purdue U North Central
-1	-1	-1	-1	-1	-1	-1	-1		Quincy U
-1	-1	-1	-1	-1	0	-1	-1		R.Wesleyan C
120,620	14	482,068	20	360,379	16	484,524	145,380	N	Radford U
-1	-1	-1	-1	-1	-1	-1	-1		Ramapo C NJ
0	0	0	0	0	0	0	0	Y	ecnstrctnst Rabbinical C
36,515	15	36,515	15	109,966	10	0	0	N	RI Sch Design
25,436	3	148,828	3	103,247	3	112,534	112,534	N	Rivier C
-1	-1	-1	-1	-1	-1	46,000	-1	N	Rockhurst U
31,427	15	183,511	100	79,395	19	1,189,708	-1	Y	Roger Williams U
-1	-1	-1	-1	-1	-1	573,309	-1		Roosevelt U
0	16	31,167	16	31,307	16	0	0	Y	Rosemont C
0	0	0	0	0	0	0	0	N	Salem Teiko U
25,644	11	123,888	27	-1	-1	-1	-1		Salisbury ST U
681,314	138	1	1	1	1	2,789,439	1	N	San Jose ST U
27,306	3	59,440	3	28,682	3	-1	-1		Savannah ST U
4,784	22	21,505	22	50,050	22	40,000	10,000	Y	Schreiner C
-1	-1	-1	-1	-1	-1	8,089,591	-1	N	SE LA U
195,691	57	2,980,582	57	835,551	57	-1	-1	N	SE MO ST U
29,751	12	150,000	12	-1	12	377,662	12,635	N	SE Oklahoma St U
-1	-1	56,453	2	0	0	-1	14,420	N	Seton Hill C
-1	-1	-1	-1	-1	-1	0	-1		SF Consrv Music
5,104	210	5,104	210	-1	-1	-1	-1	N	Shaw U
-1	-1	-1	-1	-1	-1	-1	-1		Shorter C
-1	-1	-1	-1	-1	-1	-1	-1		Silver Lake C
0	0	0	0	0	0	0	0	N	Sisseton-Wahpeton CC
0	0	0	0	0	0	2,850	18,285	Y	Southrn C Opt
-1	-1	-1	-1	-1	-1	301,858	103,369	N	Southrn IL U Edward
-1	-1	-1	-1	-1	-1	-1	-1	Y	Southrn OR U
0	0	0	0	0	0	0	0		Spring Hill C
-1	-1	-1	-1	-1	-1	-1	-1	N	St Ambrose U
2,966	5	12,787	5	9,578	5	57,224	49,870	N	St C.Borromeo Sem
573,351	76	573,351	76	494,168	76	324,055	-1	N	St Cloud ST U
-1	41	144,367	41	-1	41	-1	-1	Y	St Francis C PA
-1	-1	-1	-1	-1	-1	4,227,991	-1	N	St Francis-Xavier U
-1	-1	-1	-1	-1	-1	-1	-1		St John Fisher C
153,470	64	561,209	64	1,064,252	64	-1	-1	N	St Joseph C Suffolk
33,065	-1	-1	-1	-1	-1	-1	-1	N	St Joseph's C IN
153,470	64	561,209	64	1,064,252	64	-1	-1	N	St Joseph's C NY
-1	3	-1	3	-1	3	-1	-1	N	St Joseph's Sem

-1 -- Unavailable   -2 -- Not Applicable

ACRL Library Data Tables 2004

NETWORKED RESOURCES AND SERVICES

INSTITUTIONS GRANTING MASTER OF ARTS AND PROFESSIONAL DEGREES (Carnegie Code M

			EXPENDITURES					
Lib. No.	Survey Question # Institution	Notes	Electronic journals purchased 6	Electronic full-text journals 7	Electronic reference sources 8	Electronic books 9	Virtual reference transactions 10	Federated searching across networked electronic resources? 11
281	St Mary's U MN		-1	-1	-1	-1	-1	Y
282	St Meinrad Theo		-1	-1	0	0	-1	N
283	St Michael's C		23,487	14,715	34,750	176	27	N
284	St Norbert C		65,210	-1	-1	1,177	-1	N
285	St Patrick's Sem		0	0	4,000	0	0	N
286	St Peter's Abbey & C	C	-1	-1	-1	0	-1	Y
287	ST U W GA		208,425	7,455	69,126	2,150	-1	Y
288	St Vincent Sem		0	0	10,264	0	0	N
289	St. John's C		-1	-1	-1	-1	-1	
290	Stetson U		50,514	6,230	158,103	8,903	140	N
291	Sthrn Polytech ST U		-1	-1	-1	-1	-1	N
292	Stonehill C		58,721	1	20,129	0	0	N
293	Sul Ross ST U		46,023	46,023	1,200	2,800	10	N
294	SUNY Brockport		197,692	197,692	196,696	157	288	Y
295	SUNY Buffalo		300,466	-1	-1	0	271	N
296	SUNY C Potsdam		45,836	-1	88,366	3,487	142	N
297	SUNY IT Utica		171,850	113,789	87,724	0	5	N
298	SUNY Oneonta		48,952	22,733	90,950	0	122	N
299	SUNY Oswego		-1	-1	-1	-1	-1	
300	SW MO ST U		498,600	498,600	307,000	0	106	N
301	SWstrn Adventist U		-1	-1	-1	-1	-1	Y
302	SWstrn OK ST U		-1	-1	-1	-1	-1	
303	Tabor C		-1	-1	-1	-1	-1	
304	Tiffin U		13,000	56,571	2,000	2,000	0	N
305	TM Cooley Law Sch		109,890	5,241	115,283	0	101	N
306	Trinity Luth Sem		500	4,235	300	0	0	N
307	Trinity U		161,734	100,584	262,335	0	-1	N
308	Trinity U		-1	-1	21,750	0	0	N
309	Troy ST U		111,573	28,356	111,573	5,366	1,462	N
310	Troy ST U Dothan		-1	-1	-1	-1	-1	
311	Truman ST U		-1	-1	-1	-1	-1	
312	TX Chiro C		-1	-1	-1	-1	-1	
313	U Arts		-1	-1	-1	-1	-1	
314	U C Cape	C	93,466	-1	-1	-1	225	N
315	U Charleston		-1	-1	21,762	-1	44	N
316	U DC		-1	-1	-1	-1	-1	
317	U Del Turabo		45,687	80,000	90,000	10,000	-1	Y
318	U Findlay		85,979	28,000	47,500	2,400	-1	Y
319	U Hawaii-Hilo		46,245	22,792	75,381	10,278	166	N
320	U HI-Kauai CC		0	0	2,500	0	-1	Y

C -- Reported in Canadian $ -1 -- Unavailable   -2 -- Not Applicable

ACRL Library Data Tables 2004
NETWORKED RESOURCES AND SERVICES

INSTITUTIONS GRANTING MASTER OF ARTS AND PROFESSIONAL DEGREES (Carnegie Code M)

Logins to electronic databases 12	No. of databases reported 12a	Queries (searches) in electronic databases 13	No. of databases reported 13a	Items requested in electronic databases 14	No. of databases reported 14a	Virtual visits to website 15a	Virtual visits to catalog 15b	Excl. visits fr. inside library 15c	Survey Question # Institution
-1	-1	-1	-1	-1	-1	-1	-1		St Mary's U MN
-1	-1	-1	-1	-1	-1	-1	-1	Y	St Meinrad Theo
-1	-1	132,402	59	-1	-1	-1	-1	Y	St Michael's C
-1	-1	-1	-1	-1	-1	-1	-1		St Norbert C
0	0	0	0	0	0	0	0	N	St Patrick's Sem
-1	-1	-1	-1	-1	-1	-1	-1	N	St Peter's Abbey & C
-1	-1	-1	-1	-1	-1	-1	-1		ST U W GA
0	0	0	0	0	0	0	0	Y	St Vincent Sem
-1	-1	-1	-1	-1	-1	-1	-1		St. John's C
45,504	21	459,627	32	613,426	45	308,248	42,415	N	Stetson U
-1	-1	-1	-1	-1	-1	-1	-1		Sthrn Polytech ST U
1	1	47,661	2	1	1	1	1	N	Stonehill C
73,128	106	90,282	106	46,127	106	92,812	-1	N	Sul Ross ST U
-1	-1	-1	-1	-1	-1	-1	-1	N	SUNY Brockport
74,619	23	499,176	28	456,680	31	666,722	556,852	N	SUNY Buffalo
-1	-1	248,281	66	-1	-1	6,825,000	-1	N	SUNY C Potsdam
10,000	38	84,410	5	71,711	4	-1	-1		SUNY IT Utica
277,000	8	-1	-1	-1	-1	600,000	-1	Y	SUNY Oneonta
-1	-1	-1	-1	-1	-1	-1	-1		SUNY Oswego
-1	-1	-1	-1	-1	-1	1,322,937	-1	N	SW MO ST U
-1	-1	24,944	-1	14,770	-1	-1	-1	N	SWstrn Adventist U
-1	-1	-1	-1	-1	-1	443,444	262,579	N	SWstrn OK ST U
-1	-1	-1	-1	-1	-1	-1	-1		Tabor C
0	0	0	0	0	0	0	0	N	Tiffin U
-1	-1	-1	-1	-1	-1	-1	-1	N	TM Cooley Law Sch
0	0	0	0	0	0	0	0	N	Trinity Luth Sem
-1	-1	276,733	105	-1	-1	-1	-1		Trinity U
-1	-1	-1	-1	-1	-1	-1	-1	Y	Trinity U
0	0	0	0	0	0	0	0	N	Troy ST U
-1	-1	-1	-1	-1	-1	-1	-1	N	Troy ST U Dothan
-1	-1	-1	-1	-1	-1	-1	-1		Truman ST U
-1	-1	-1	-1	-1	-1	-1	-1		TX Chiro C
-1	-1	-1	-1	-1	-1	-1	-1		U Arts
-1	-1	-1	-1	-1	-1	45,068	-1	N	U C Cape
-1	-1	-1	-1	-1	-1	-1	-1		U Charleston
-1	-1	-1	-1	-1	-1	-1	-1		U DC
-1	-1	-1	-1	-1	-1	-1	-1		U Del Turabo
44,586	33	456	1	1,694	1	-1	-1	N	U Findlay
-1	-1	-1	-1	-1	-1	-1	-1	N	U Hawaii-Hilo
-1	-1	-1	-1	-1	-1	238,042	-1	N	U HI-Kauai CC
-1	-1	-1	-1	-1	-1	-1	-1	N	

-1 -- Unavailable   -2 -- Not Applicable

INSTITUTIONS GRANTING MASTER OF ARTS AND PROFESSIONAL DEGREES (Carnegie Code M

Lib. No.	Survey Question # Institution	Notes	Electronic journals purchased 6	Electronic full-text journals 7	Electronic reference sources 8	Electronic books 9	Virtual reference transactions 10	Federated searching across networked electronic resources? 11
			EXPENDITURES					
321	U Houston		1	1	1	1	143	N
322	U Mary		-1	-1	16,872	-1	-1	N
323	U MI Dearborn		137,028	74,818	250,939	7,565	214	N
324	U Mobile		35,000	18,000	5,000	0	0	Y
325	U NE Kearney		114,860	38,819	18,244	0	129	N
326	U Portland		-1	-1	-1	-1	-1	N
327	U Richmond		188,648	63,890	-1	3,702	161	N
328	U Rio Grande		14,739	-1	-1	-1	38	Y
329	U Scranton		45,289	1,122,827	25,274	990	234	Y
330	U Sthn IN		240,384	136,679	23,816	3,090	103	Y
331	U Tampa		-1	-1	-1	-1	-1	N
332	U TN Chatt		158,212	79,218	190,342	0	170	N
333	U TN Martin		155,740	97,026	49,017	5,500	-1	Y
334	U TX Tyler		133,273	18,754	1,072	-1	-1	N
335	U West AL		0	74,423	0	0	0	N
336	U WI E Claire		73,000	58,400	73,000	-1	466	N
337	U WI La Crosse		33,165	19,924	116,448	0	229	Y
338	U WI Platteville		7,670	7,670	19,942	0	1,500	N
339	U Winnipeg	C	459,091	-1	2,092	-1	1,553	N
340	UNC Asheville		77,796	77,796	215,399	2,098	107	N
341	UNC Pembroke		0	0	181,806	0	120	Y
342	Union C-NY		-1	-1	235,191	0	0	N
343	Valparaiso U		167,245	31,102	21,378	0	95	N
344	Villa Julie C		-1	-1	55,245	0	-1	N
345	W.Carey College		31,539	12,170	26,587	0	0	Y
346	W.Mitchell C Law		88,338	260	118,719	0	-1	N
347	Walla Walla C		96,727	-1	86,708	0	-2	N
348	Walsh C Acct Bus Admin		22,000	3,000	106,000	1,000	187	N
349	Wartburg Theo Sem		-1	-1	-1	0	0	N
350	Washburn U Topeka		-1	-1	-1	0	-1	Y
351	Washington C		80,128	-1	-1	0	0	N
352	Washington Theo Union		945	945	0	0	0	N
353	Wayland Bap U		-1	-1	-1	-1	-1	N
354	Wayne ST C		-1	-1	-1	-1	-1	
355	Webber Intl U		0	0	19,000	0	0	N
356	Wesley C		-1	-1	-1	0	0	N
357	West Chester U PA		324,169	204,194	234,823	24,172	147	Y
358	West TX A & M U		113,867	102,899	39,617	-1	50	N
359	West VA Wesleyan C		-1	-1	-1	-1	123	N
360	Western MD C		81,944	-1	81,944	0	98	N

C -- Reported in Canadian $ -1 -- Unavailable   -2 -- Not Applicable

ACRL Library Data Tables 2004
NETWORKED RESOURCES AND SERVICES

NSTITUTIONS GRANTING MASTER OF ARTS AND PROFESSIONAL DEGREES (Carnegie Code M)

Logins to electronic databases 12	No. of databases reported 12a	Queries (searches) in electronic databases 13	No. of databases reported 13a	Items requested in electronic databases 14	No. of databases reported 14a	Virtual visits to website 15a	Virtual visits to catalog 15b	Excl. visits fr. inside library 15c	Survey Question # Institution
1	1	1	1	1	1	1	1		U Houston
-1	-1	-1	-1	-1	-1	-1	-1		U Mary
107,181	16	790,392	15	253,085	8	2,601,653	214,806	N	U MI Dearborn
25,000	100	114,080	75	82,295	75	75,000	45,000	Y	U Mobile
2,046,432	-1	365,495	61	963,072	59	340,357	282,730	Y	U NE Kearney
-1	-1	-1	-1	-1	-1	-1	-1		U Portland
235,804	202	316,186	202	-1	-1	-1	591,500	N	U Richmond
-1	-1	-1	-1	-1	-1	23,526	-1	Y	U Rio Grande
595,195	110	1,190,390	110	2,380,780	110	159,718	0	N	U Scranton
79,000	40	-1	-1	-1	-1	110,443	190,000	N	U Sthn IN
-1	-1	-1	-1	-1	-1	-1	-1	Y	U Tampa
103,085	43	376,335	70	300,360	12	547,546	-1	Y	U TN Chatt
-1	-1	279,106	85	-1	-1	-1	-1	Y	U TN Martin
13,341	13	55,511	13	44,502	13	1,311,762	-1	N	U TX Tyler
0	0	0	0	0	0	0	0	N	U West AL
424,757	146	824,459	151	1,637,737	1,021	513,248	77,732	N	U WI E Claire
115,458	81	560,776	142	295,346	59	305,020	-1	N	U WI La Crosse
-1	-1	-1	-1	-1	-1	-1	-1		U WI Platteville
-1	-1	-1	-1	-1	-1	-1	-1		U Winnipeg
67,272	96	-1	-1	-1	-1	400,000	-1	N	UNC Asheville
6,532,315	44	4,300,000	44	3,150,000	44	182,040	175,000	N	UNC Pembroke
-1	-1	-1	-1	-1	-1	-1	-1	N	Union C-NY
87,037	4	178,998	7	219,038	5	299,355	343,602	N	Valparaiso U
79,711	9	96,130	15	-1	-1	-1	-1	N	Villa Julie C
59,085	4	86,036	7	71,959	5	26,132	-1	N	W.Carey College
-1	-1	981,569	12	-1	-1	78,854	-1	Y	W.Mitchell C Law
-1	-1	-1	-1	-1	-1	3,168	-1	N	Walla Walla C
87,000	17	0	0	0	0	0	8,500	Y	Walsh C Acct Bus Admin
-1	-1	-1	-1	-1	-1	-1	-1		Wartburg Theo Sem
-1	-1	101,729	89	-1	89	-1	-1	N	Washburn U Topeka
-1	-1	358,566	93	-1	-1	-1	-1		Washington C
0	0	0	0	0	0	0	0		Washington Theo Union
-1	-1	-1	-1	-1	-1	-1	-1	N	Wayland Bap U
-1	-1	-1	-1	-1	-1	-1	-1		Wayne ST C
-1	-1	-1	-1	-1	-1	0	-1	N	Webber Intl U
0	0	0	0	0	0	0	0	N	Wesley C
383,576	66	918,719	82	1,000,291	52	102	118,482	N	West Chester U PA
85,559	7	296,286	11	348,975	7	811,775	503,376	N	West TX A & M U
17,392	68	83,204	68	52,061	68	-1	-1		West VA Wesleyan C
-1	0	24,251	17,636	-1	0	-1	-1		Western MD C

-1 -- Unavailable   -2 -- Not Applicable

ACRL Library Data Tables 2004
NETWORKED RESOURCES AND SERVICES

INSTITUTIONS GRANTING MASTER OF ARTS AND PROFESSIONAL DEGREES (Carnegie Code M

			EXPENDITURES					
Lib. No.	Survey Question # Institution	Notes	Electronic journals purchased 6	Electronic full-text journals 7	Electronic reference sources 8	Electronic books 9	Virtual reference transactions 10	Federated searching across networked electronic resources? 11
361	Western OR U		93,647	78,304	165,171	0	-1	N
362	Western Sem		0	0	6,681	0	0	N
363	Western WA U		-1	-1	287,850	-1	237	Y
364	Westfield ST C		0	62,116	32,671	0	350	N
365	Westminster C-UT		83,986	-1	76,486	9,563	-1	Y
366	Wheeling Jesuit U		-1	-1	-1	-1	-1	N
367	Whitworth C		-1	17,123	-1	2,700	-1	N
368	Wilkes U		179,569	30,385	154,355	2,700	322	N
369	William Woods U		25,919	-1	-1	1,512	59	Y
370	Williams C		160,004	463,795	154,348	31,552	502	N
371	Wstrn IL U		213,041	-1	156,303	-1	-1	N
372	Wstrn Theo Sem		7,443	7,443	2,285	-1	-1	N
373	Xavier U LA		38,913	20,418	67,777	0	0	N

INSTITUTIONS GRANTING MASTER OF ARTS AND PROFESSIONAL DEGREES (Carnegie Code M)

Logins to electronic databases 12	No. of databases reported 12a	Queries (searches) in electronic databases 13	No. of databases reported 13a	Items requested in electronic databases 14	No. of databases reported 14a	Virtual visits to website 15a	Virtual visits to catalog 15b	Excl. visits fr. inside library 15c	Survey Question # Institution
75,300	90	-1	-1	-1	-1	-1	-1		Western OR U
2,425	1	8,433	1	3,154	1	-1	-1	N	Western Sem
-1	-1	-1	-1	-1	-1	975,105	-1	N	Western WA U
143,032	77	489,575	77	1,234,689	60	766,585	60,000	N	Westfield ST C
-1	-1	160,541	54	-1	-1	-1	-1	N	Westminster C-UT
-1	-1	-1	-1	-1	-1	-1	-1	Y	Wheeling Jesuit U
-1	-1	-1	-1	-1	-1	-1	-1		Whitworth C
5,942	3	104,300	64	-1	-1	-1	-1		Wilkes U
14,391	-1	30,280	-1	19,099	-1	-1	-1	N	William Woods U
-1	-1	382,816	-1	-1	-1	-1	-1		Williams C
-1	-1	714,186	113	-1	-1	523,809	-1	N	Wstrn IL U
2,378	17	6,304	17	-1	-1	-1	-1		Wstrn Theo Sem
-1	-1	-1	-1	-1	-1	-1	-1		Xavier U LA

-1 -- Unavailable   -2 -- Not Applicable

ACRL Library Data Tables 2004
DIGITIZATION ACTIVITIES

INSTITUTIONS GRANTING MASTER OF ARTS AND PROFESSIONAL DEGREES (Carnegie Code

Lib. No.	Survey Question # Institution	DIGITAL COLLECTIONS			USAGE		DIRECT COSTS		Volumes Held Collectively
		No. of collections	Size (MB)	Items	No. of times accessed	No. of queries	Personnel	Equipment, software, or contract services	
		16a	16b	16c	17a	17b	18a	18b	19
1	Abilene Christian U	-1	-1	-1	-1	-1	-1	-1	-1
2	Agnes Scott C	0	0	0	0	0	0	0	0
3	Albany C Pharmacy	-1	-1	-1	-1	-1	-1	-1	-1
4	Albany Law Schl Union U	0	0	0	0	0	-1	-1	-1
5	Alcorn ST U	0	0	0	0	0	0	0	0
6	Amer Intl C	0	0	0	0	0	0	0	0
7	Amer U Puerto Rico	2	900,000	14,000	150	105	77,000	30,500	4,000
8	Anderson U	-1	-1	-1	-1	-1	-1	-1	-1
9	Angelo ST U	-1	-1	-1	-1	-1	-1	-1	-1
10	Aquinas C MI	-1	-1	-1	-1	-1	-1	-1	-1
11	Ark Tech U	-1	-1	-1	-1	-1	-1	-1	-1
12	Armstrong Atlantic ST U	3	57,237,236	522	-1	-1	-1	-1	-1
13	Assemblies God Theo Sem	-1	-1	-1	-1	-1	-1	-1	-1
14	Assumption C	-2	-2	-2	-2	-2	-2	-2	0
15	Athenaeum of Ohio	-1	-1	-1	-1	-1	-1	-1	-1
16	Auburn U Montgomery	-1	-1	-1	-1	-1	-1	-1	-1
17	Augusta ST U	1	1,360	50	0	0	600	0	0
18	Augustana C SF	0	0	0	0	0	0	0	0
19	Austin C	0	0	0	0	0	0	0	0
20	Austin Presb Theo Sem	-1	-1	-1	-1	-1	-1	-1	-1
21	Averett C	-1	-1	-1	-1	-1	-1	-1	-1
22	Babson C	1	483	75	-1	-1	-1	-1	-1
23	Baker C System	-1	-1	-1	-1	-1	-1	-1	-1
24	Baker U	0	0	0	0	0	0	0	0
25	Baptist Bible C and Sem	0	0	0	0	0	0	0	0
26	Bayamon Central U	1,000	-1	-1	-1	-1	300,000	200,000	-1
27	Bellevue U	-1	-1	-1	-1	-1	-1	-1	-1
28	Bennington C	0	0	0	0	0	0	0	0
29	Bethel C IN	0	0	0	0	0	0	0	0
30	Birmingham Southern C	0	0	0	0	0	0	0	0
31	Bluffton C	0	0	0	0	0	0	0	0
32	BowlGrn SU Fireld	0	-2	0	-2	-2	-2	-2	525
33	Bradley U	-1	-1	-1	-1	-1	-1	-1	-1
34	Brescia U	0	0	0	0	0	0	0	0
35	Brooks Institute	0	-2	-2	-2	-2	-2	-2	-2
36	Bryn Athyn C	1	77	-1	-1	-1	16,670	5,000	0
37	Buena Vista U	0	0	0	0	0	0	0	0
38	Butler U	0	0	0	0	0	0	0	0
39	C Atlantic	-2	-2	-2	-2	-2	-2	-2	-2
40	C Mt St Joseph	0	0	0	0	0	0	0	0

-1 -- Unavailable   -2 -- Not Applicable

ACRL Library Data Tables 2004
DIGITIZATION ACTIVITIES

INSTITUTIONS GRANTING MASTER OF ARTS AND PROFESSIONAL DEGREES (Carnegie Code M)

	DIGITAL COLLECTIONS			USAGE		DIRECT COSTS		
	No. of collections	Size (MB)	Items	No. of times accessed	No. of queries	Personnel	Equipment, software, or contract services	Volumes Held Collectively
Survey Question #	16a	16b	16c	17a	17b	18a	18b	19
Institution								
C Mt St Vincent	0	0	0	0	0	0	0	0
C Our Lady Elms	-2	-2	-2	-2	-2	-2	-2	-2
C.R. Drew U Med & Sci	0	0	0	0	0	0	0	-1
CA C Arts & Crafts	3	4,722	4,718	-1	-1	-2	-2	0
CA St Polytechnic U-Pomon	-1	-1	-1	-1	-1	-1	-1	-1
CA St U - Sacramento	2	120,000	1,687	20,667	0	59,028	0	0
CA ST U Dominguez Hills	0	0	0	0	0	0	0	0
CA ST U Fresno	0	0	0	0	0	0	0	0
CA ST U Fullerton	-1	-1	-1	-1	-1	-1	-1	-1
CA ST U Hayward	-1	-1	-1	-1	-1	-1	-1	-1
CA ST U Long Beach	-1	-1	-1	-1	-1	-1	-1	-1
CA ST U Northridge	5	-1	-1	-1	-1	-1	-1	-1
CA ST U S Bernadino	-1	-1	-1	-1	-1	-1	-1	-1
CA ST U San Marcos	0	0	0	0	0	0	0	0
CA ST U Stanislaus	0	0	0	0	0	0	0	0
CA West Sch Law	1	-1	418	-1	-1	-1	-1	-1
Calvin C	-1	-1	-1	-1	-1	-1	-1	-1
Cameron U	-1	-1	-1	-1	-1	-1	-1	-1
Canisius C	1	200	500	-1	-1	-1	1,500	0
Carlow C	0	0	0	0	0	0	0	0
Carroll C-Waukesha	0	0	0	0	0	0	0	0
Cedar Crest C	-1	-1	-1	-1	-1	-1	-1	-1
Cedarville U	0	0	0	0	0	0	0	0
Centenary C	0	0	0	0	0	0	0	0
Centenary C LA	2	250	2	0	0	0	0	0
Central Baptist C	0	-1	-1	-1	-1	-1	-1	-1
Central CT ST U	-1	-1	-1	-1	-1	-1	-1	-1
Central MO ST U	0	0	0	-1	0	-1	0	-1
Charleston Sthrn U	0	0	0	0	0	0	0	0
Chicago ST U	-1	-1	-1	-1	-1	-1	-1	-1
Chris Newport U	0	0	0	0	0	0	-1	0
Christendom C	-1	-1	-1	-1	-1	-1	-1	-1
Christian Brothers U	0	0	0	0	0	0	0	0
Clarion U PA	-1	-1	-1	-1	-1	-1	-1	-1
Clarke C-IA	-2	-2	-2	-2	-2	-2	-2	0
Clarkson C-NE	0	0	0	0	0	0	0	0
Colorado C	8	600	11,000	0	0	0	0	0
Columbia C MO	0	-1	-1	-1	-1	-1	-1	-1
Columbia C SC	0	0	0	0	0	0	0	0
Columbia Intl U	0	0	0	0	0	0	0	193,163

-1 -- Unavailable   -2 -- Not Applicable

213

INSTITUTIONS GRANTING MASTER OF ARTS AND PROFESSIONAL DEGREES (Carnegie Code

		DIGITAL COLLECTIONS			USAGE		DIRECT COSTS		
		No. of collections	Size (MB)	Items	No. of times accessed	No. of queries	Personnel	Equipment, software, or contract services	Volumes Held Collectively
Lib. No.	Survey Question # Institution	16a	16b	16c	17a	17b	18a	18b	19
81	Columbus ST U	-1	-1	-1	-1	-1	-1	-1	-1
82	Concordia U Irvine	0	0	0	0	0	0	0	0
83	Concordia U RiverF	-1	-1	-1	-1	-1	-1	-1	-1
84	Concordia U St Paul	0	-1	-1	-1	-1	-1	-1	-1
85	Cooper Union	-1	-1	-1	-1	-1	-1	-1	-1
86	Cornerstone U	0	0	0	0	0	0	0	0
87	Creighton U	2	-1	-1	-1	-1	-1	20,000	-1
88	Cumberland U	0	-1	-1	0	0	0	0	0
89	CUNY BMB C	17	-1	-1	-1	-1	-1	-1	-1
90	CUNY C Stn Island	-1	-1	-1	-1	-1	-1	-1	-1
91	CUNY City C	11	1,620	5,667	-1	272	3,440	0	0
92	CUNY HH Lehman C	-1	-1	-1	-1	-1	-1	-1	-1
93	CUNY John Jay C Crim Ju	-1	-1	-1	-1	-1	-1	-1	-1
94	CUNY Queens C	-1	-1	-1	-1	-1	-1	-1	-1
95	Curtis Inst Music	0	0	0	0	0	0	0	0
96	Daniel Webster C	0	0	0	0	0	0	0	0
97	DeSales U	0	0	0	0	0	0	0	0
98	DN Myers C	0	0	0	-1	-1	-1	-1	-1
99	Dominican C San Rafael	0	0	0	0	0	0	0	0
100	Dominican U	-1	-1	-1	-1	-1	-1	-1	-1
101	Drake U	0	0	0	0	0	0	0	0
102	Drury C	0	0	0	0	0	0	0	0
103	E R Aero U	2	-1	1,500	-1	-1	-1	-1	-1
104	Earlham C	-1	-1	-1	-1	-1	-1	-1	-1
105	Eastern IL U	-1	-1	-1	-1	-1	-1	-1	-1
106	Eastern U	1	-1	-1	-1	-1	-1	-1	-1
107	Eastern WA U	0	0	0	0	0	0	0	0
108	Eastrn NM U Main	0	0	0	0	0	0	0	0
109	Edinboro U PA	-1	-1	-1	-1	-1	-1	-1	-1
110	Elizabethtown C	2	37,000	2,300	-1	-1	-1	-1	0
111	Elmhurst C	-1	-1	-1	-1	-1	-1	-1	-1
112	Elon U	0	0	0	0	0	0	0	0
113	Emmanuel C MA	0	-2	-2	-2	-2	-2	-2	0
114	Emory & Henry C	0	0	0	0	0	0	0	0
115	Evergreen ST C	-1	-1	-1	-1	-1	-1	-1	-1
116	Fisk U	0	0	0	0	0	0	0	0
117	Fitchburg ST C	0	0	0	0	0	0	0	0
118	FL Southern C	-1	-1	-1	-1	-1	-1	-1	-1
119	Fort Hays ST U	0	0	0	0	0	0	0	0
120	Francis Marion U	-1	-1	-1	-1	-1	-1	-1	-1

-1 -- Unavailable   -2 -- Not Applicable

ACRL Library Data Tables 2004
DIGITIZATION ACTIVITIES

INSTITUTIONS GRANTING MASTER OF ARTS AND PROFESSIONAL DEGREES (Carnegie Code M)

	DIGITAL COLLECTIONS			USAGE		DIRECT COSTS		
	No. of collections	Size (MB)	Items	No. of times accessed	No. of queries	Personnel	Equipment, software, or contract services	Volumes Held Collectively
Survey Question #	16a	16b	16c	17a	17b	18a	18b	19
Institution								
Franklin Inst Boston	-1	-1	-1	-1	-1	-1	-1	-1
Franklin U	0	0	0	0	0	0	0	0
Free Will Baptist Bible C	0	0	0	0	0	0	0	0
Frostburg ST U	1	570	368	0	0	20,250	28,377	0
Furman U	0	0	0	0	0	0	0	0
GA SWstrn ST U	-1	-1	-1	-1	-1	-1	-1	-1
Gardner-Webb U	0	0	0	0	0	0	0	0
Geneva C	0	0	0	0	0	0	0	0
Georgetown C	0	0	0	0	0	0	0	-1
Goucher C	-1	-1	-1	-1	-1	-1	-1	-1
Governors ST U	0	-1	-1	-1	-1	-1	-1	-1
Greenville C	0	0	0	0	0	0	0	0
Grove City C	0	0	0	0	0	0	0	0
Harding U Main	0	-1	-1	-1	-1	-1	-1	-1
Hebrew C	-1	-1	-1	-1	-1	-1	-1	-1
Heidelberg C	0	0	0	0	0	0	0	0
Hillsdale Free Will Baptist C	0	0	0	0	0	0	0	0
Holy Apostles C & Sem	0	0	0	0	0	0	0	0
Hood C	0	0	0	0	0	0	0	0
Humboldt ST U	5	60	3,973	1	1	4,000	1	1
IN Inst of Tech	0	0	0	0	0	0	0	0
IN U Kokomo	0	0	0	0	0	0	0	0
IN U S Bend	0	0	0	0	0	0	0	0
IN U-Purdue U Ft Wayne	-1	-1	-1	-1	-1	-1	-1	-1
IN Wesleyan U	-1	-1	-1	-1	-1	-1	-1	-1
Intl Fine Arts C	0	0	0	0	0	0	0	0
Jacksonville ST U	2	-1	2	-1	-1	-1	-1	-1
Johnson Bible C	0	-2	-2	-2	-2	-2	-2	0
Kean U	0	-1	-1	-1	-1	-1	-1	-1
Keene State C	0	0	0	0	0	0	0	0
Kent ST U Stark	0	0	0	0	0	0	0	0
Kentucky Christian C	0	0	0	0	0	0	0	0
Kentucky ST U	1	1	1	1	1	1	1	1
Kettering U	-1	-1	-1	-1	-1	-1	-1	-1
King's C PA	-1	-1	-1	-1	-1	-1	-1	-1
LaGrange C	0	0	0	0	0	0	0	0
Lakeland C-AB	0	0	0	0	0	0	0	0
Lakeview C Nursing	0	0	0	0	0	0	0	0
Lancaster Bible C	0	0	0	0	0	0	0	0
Lander U	0	0	0	0	0	0	0	0

-1 -- Unavailable   -2 -- Not Applicable

INSTITUTIONS GRANTING MASTER OF ARTS AND PROFESSIONAL DEGREES (Carnegie Code

		DIGITAL COLLECTIONS			USAGE		DIRECT COSTS		
		No. of collections	Size (MB)	Items	No. of times accessed	No. of queries	Personnel	Equipment, software, or contract services	Volumes Held Collectively
Lib. No.	Survey Question # Institution	16a	16b	16c	17a	17b	18a	18b	19
161	Langston U	0	0	0	0	0	0	0	0
162	Laurentian U JN	-2	-2	-2	-2	-2	-2	-2	-2
163	Le Moyne C	1	-1	3,024	36,408	-1	-1	-1	0
164	Lebanon Valley C	-1	-1	-1	-1	-1	-1	-1	-1
165	Lewis U	-1	-1	-1	-1	-1	-1	-1	-1
166	Lewis&Clark C	-1	-1	-1	-1	-1	-1	-1	-1
167	Lincoln U-MO	3	1,632	67	-1	-1	-1	-1	-1
168	Lindsey Wilson C	-1	-1	-1	-1	-1	-1	-1	-1
169	Lipscomb U	0	-1	-1	-1	-1	-1	-1	-1
170	Lock Haven U PA	0	0	0	0	0	0	0	0
171	Longwood C	0	-1	-1	-1	-1	-1	-1	-1
172	Lourdes C	-2	-2	-2	-2	-2	-2	-2	-2
173	Loyola Marymount U	0	0	0	0	0	0	0	0
174	Loyola U New Orleans	-1	-1	-1	-1	-1	-1	-1	-1
175	Lubbock Christian U	0	0	0	-1	-1	0	0	0
176	Luth Theo Sem Philly	0	0	0	0	0	0	0	0
177	Lynchburg C	0	0	0	0	0	0	0	0
178	Malone C	0	0	0	0	0	0	0	0
179	Manchester C	0	0	0	0	0	0	0	0
180	Manhattan C	-1	-1	-1	-1	-1	-1	-1	-1
181	Marist C	-1	-1	-1	-1	-1	-1	-1	-1
182	Mary Baldwin C	0	0	0	0	0	0	0	0
183	Mary Washington C	0	0	0	0	0	0	0	0
184	Marymount U	0	0	0	-1	-1	-1	-1	-1
185	Maryville U St Louis	0	0	0	0	0	0	0	0
186	McNeese ST U	1	159	750	-1	3,189	-1	-1	-1
187	Medical C Wisconsin	0	0	0	0	0	0	0	0
188	Merrimack C	0	0	0	0	0	0	0	0
189	MidAmer Nazarene U	0	0	0	0	0	0	0	0
190	Millikin U	0	0	0	0	0	0	0	0
191	Millsaps C	-1	-1	-1	-1	-1	-1	-1	-1
192	Minnesota ST U-Mankato	0	0	0	0	0	0	0	0
193	Minot ST U	0	0	0	0	0	0	0	0
194	Monterey Inst Intl St	10	100	10	20	5	1,000	3,000	10
195	Moravian C	-1	-1	-1	-1	-1	-1	-1	-1
196	Morehead ST U	4	-1	1,693	-1	-1	0	0	0
197	Morningside C	0	0	0	0	0	0	0	0
198	MS Valley ST U	0	0	0	0	0	0	0	0
199	Mt Holyoke C	-1	-1	-1	-1	-1	-1	-1	-1
200	Mt Marty C	-1	-1	-1	-1	-1	-1	-1	-1

-1 -- Unavailable   -2 -- Not Applicable

ACRL Library Data Tables 2004
DIGITIZATION ACTIVITIES

INSTITUTIONS GRANTING MASTER OF ARTS AND PROFESSIONAL DEGREES (Carnegie Code M)

	DIGITAL COLLECTIONS			USAGE		DIRECT COSTS		
	No. of collections	Size (MB)	Items	No. of times accessed	No. of queries	Personnel	Equipment, software, or contract services	Volumes Held Collectively
Survey Question #	16a	16b	16c	17a	17b	18a	18b	19
Institution								
Mt Mary C-WI	0	0	0	0	0	0	0	0
MT ST U Northern	-2	-2	-2	-2	-2	-2	-2	-2
Mt St Vincent U	0	-1	-1	-1	-1	-1	-1	0
MT Tech U Montana	1	-1	45	0	0	-1	1,000	0
Murray ST U-KY	0	0	0	0	0	0	0	0
Muskingum C	0	0	0	0	0	0	0	0
Natl C Naturopathic Med	0	0	0	0	0	0	0	0
Natl Defense U	101	245,854	0	0	0	0	66,000	0
NC Sch Arts	0	0	0	0	0	0	0	0
NEastrn IL U	0	0	0	0	0	0	0	0
Nipissing U	0	0	0	0	0	0	0	0
NJ City U	0	0	0	0	0	0	0	-1
NM Highlands U	0	0	0	0	0	0	0	0
North Central C	-1	-1	-1	-1	-1	-1	-1	-1
Northern KY U	-1	-1	-1	-1	-1	-1	-1	-1
Northern ST U	0	0	0	0	0	0	0	0
Northwest C	0	0	0	0	0	0	0	0
Norwich U	0	0	0	0	0	0	0	0
Notre Dame C OH	0	0	0	0	0	0	0	0
Notre Dame Sem	0	0	0	0	0	0	0	0
NW MO ST U	0	0	0	0	0	0	0	0
NY Inst Tech Islip	0	0	0	0	0	0	0	0
NY Inst Tech Main	0	0	0	0	0	0	0	0
Oberlin C	7	3,000	1,500	-1	-1	10,000	1,000	0
OH U Lancaster	0	0	0	0	0	0	0	0
Olivet Nazarene U	0	0	0	0	0	0	0	0
Otterbein C	1	-1	9	-1	-1	-1	-1	0
Pace U Law	15	2,485	355	342	632,464	0	0	0
Pacific Lutheran U	-1	-1	-1	-1	-1	-1	-1	-1
Pacific Union C	0	0	0	0	0	0	0	0
Palm Beach Atl C	0	0	0	0	0	0	0	38,204
Pfeiffer U	2	-1	250	-1	-1	-1	-1	0
Philadelphia U	0	0	0	0	0	0	0	0
Plymouth ST C	0	0	0	0	0	0	0	0
Pont C Josephinum	0	0	0	0	0	0	0	0
Pope John Ntl Sem	-1	-1	-1	-1	-1	-1	-1	-1
Prescott C	0	0	0	0	0	0	0	0
Providence C	0	0	0	0	0	0	0	0
Purchase C SUNY	0	0	0	0	0	0	0	0
Purdue U Calumet	2	134	5,216	-1	-1	5,000	0	-1

-1 -- Unavailable   -2 -- Not Applicable

217

INSTITUTIONS GRANTING MASTER OF ARTS AND PROFESSIONAL DEGREES (Carnegie Code

Lib. No.	Survey Question # Institution	DIGITAL COLLECTIONS			USAGE		DIRECT COSTS		Volumes Held Collectively
		No. of collections	Size (MB)	Items	No. of times accessed	No. of queries	Personnel	Equipment, software, or contract services	
		16a	16b	16c	17a	17b	18a	18b	19
241	Purdue U North Central	0	0	0	0	0	0	0	0
242	Quincy U	-1	-1	-1	-1	-1	-1	-1	-1
243	R.Wesleyan C	0	0	0	0	0	0	0	0
244	Radford U	1	10,189	596	367	103	0	0	0
245	Ramapo C NJ	-1	-1	439	-1	-1	-1	-1	-1
246	Recnstrctnst Rabbinical C	0	0	0	0	0	0	0	0
247	RI Sch Design	0	0	0	0	0	0	0	0
248	Rivier C	0	0	0	0	0	0	0	0
249	Rockhurst U	-1	-1	-1	-1	-1	0	0	0
250	Roger Williams U	1	103,350	5,783	-1	-1	-1	-1	0
251	Roosevelt U	0	0	0	0	0	0	0	0
252	Rosemont C	0	0	0	0	0	0	0	0
253	Salem Teiko U	0	0	0	0	0	0	0	0
254	Salisbury ST U	0	0	0	0	0	-2	-2	-2
255	San Jose ST U	1	1	1	1	1	1	1	1
256	Savannah ST U	0	0	0	0	0	0	0	0
257	Schreiner C	0	0	0	0	0	0	0	0
258	SE LA U	-1	-1	-1	-1	-1	-1	-1	-1
259	SE MO ST U	0	0	0	0	0	0	0	0
260	SE Oklahoma St U	0	0	0	0	0	0	0	0
261	Seton Hill C	0	0	0	0	0	0	0	0
262	SF Consrv Music	0	0	0	-2	-2	0	0	0
263	Shaw U	-1	-1	-1	-1	-1	-1	-1	-1
264	Shorter C	-1	-1	-1	-1	-1	-1	-1	-1
265	Silver Lake C	0	-1	-1	0	0	-1	-1	-1
266	Sisseton-Wahpeton CC	0	0	0	0	0	0	0	0
267	Southrn C Opt	0	0	0	0	0	0	0	0
268	Southrn IL U Edward	0	0	0	0	0	0	0	0
269	Southrn OR U	2	19	1,484	61,916	-1	42,680	19,132	-2
270	Spring Hill C	0	0	0	0	0	0	0	0
271	St Ambrose U	1	20,600	1,211	-1	-1	3,600	19,728	0
272	St C.Borromeo Sem	0	0	0	0	0	0	0	0
273	St Cloud ST U	0	0	0	0	0	0	0	13,376
274	St Francis C PA	0	0	0	0	0	0	0	0
275	St Francis-Xavier U	0	0	0	0	0	0	0	0
276	St John Fisher C	-1	-1	-1	-1	-1	-1	-1	-1
277	St Joseph C Suffolk	0	0	0	0	0	0	0	0
278	St Joseph's C IN	0	0	0	0	0	0	0	0
279	St Joseph's C NY	0	0	0	0	0	0	0	0
280	St Joseph's Sem	0	0	0	0	0	0	0	0

-1 -- Unavailable   -2 -- Not Applicable

ACRL Library Data Tables 2004
DIGITIZATION ACTIVITIES

INSTITUTIONS GRANTING MASTER OF ARTS AND PROFESSIONAL DEGREES (Carnegie Code M)

	DIGITAL COLLECTIONS			USAGE		DIRECT COSTS		
	No. of collections	Size (MB)	Items	No. of times accessed	No. of queries	Personnel	Equipment, software, or contract services	Volumes Held Collectively
Survey Question #	16a	16b	16c	17a	17b	18a	18b	19
Institution								
St Mary's U MN	-1	-1	-1	-1	-1	-1	-1	-1
St Meinrad Theo	0	0	0	0	0	0	0	0
St Michael's C	0	0	0	0	0	0	0	0
St Norbert C	1	-1	6,000	-1	-1	-1	-1	0
St Patrick's Sem	0	0	0	-1	-1	-1	-1	-1
St Peter's Abbey & C	0	0	0	0	0	0	0	0
ST U W GA	0	0	0	0	0	0	0	0
St Vincent Sem	0	0	0	0	0	0	0	0
St. John's C	-1	-1	-1	-1	-1	-1	-1	-1
Stetson U	0	-2	-2	-2	-2	-2	-2	-2
Sthrn Polytech ST U	-1	-1	-1	-1	-1	-1	-1	-1
Stonehill C	0	0	0	0	0	0	0	0
Sul Ross ST U	0	0	0	0	0	0	0	0
SUNY Brockport	0	0	0	0	0	0	0	0
SUNY Buffalo	0	0	0	0	0	0	0	0
SUNY C Potsdam	0	0	0	0	0	0	0	0
SUNY IT Utica	0	-2	-2	-2	-2	-2	-2	0
SUNY Oneonta	0	0	0	0	0	0	0	0
SUNY Oswego	-1	-1	-1	-1	-1	-1	-1	-1
SW MO ST U	1	9,180	817	895	-1	-1	69,923	0
SWstrn Adventist U	0	0	0	0	0	0	0	0
SWstrn OK ST U	-1	-1	-1	-1	-1	-1	-1	-1
Tabor C	-1	-1	-1	-1	-1	-1	-1	-1
Tiffin U	0	0	0	0	0	0	0	0
TM Cooley Law Sch	0	0	0	0	0	0	0	0
Trinity Luth Sem	0	0	0	0	0	0	0	0
Trinity U	3	9	4	522	0	500	5,000	-1
Trinity U	0	0	0	0	0	0	0	0
Troy ST U	0	0	0	0	0	0	0	0
Troy ST U Dothan	-1	-1	-1	-1	-1	-1	-1	-1
Truman ST U	-1	-1	-1	-1	-1	-1	-1	-1
TX Chiro C	-1	-1	-1	-1	-1	-1	-1	-1
U Arts	-1	-1	-1	-1	-1	-1	-1	-1
U C Cape	-1	-1	-1	-1	-1	-1	-1	-1
U Charleston	-1	-1	-1	-1	-1	-1	-1	-1
U DC	-1	-1	-1	-1	-1	-1	-1	-1
U Del Turabo	-1	-1	-1	-1	-1	-1	-1	-1
U Findlay	0	0	0	0	0	0	0	0
U Hawaii-Hilo	-1	-1	-1	-1	-1	-1	-1	-1
U HI-Kauai CC	0	0	0	0	0	0	0	0

-1 -- Unavailable   -2 -- Not Applicable

ACRL Library Data Tables 2004
DIGITIZATION ACTIVITIES

INSTITUTIONS GRANTING MASTER OF ARTS AND PROFESSIONAL DEGREES (Carnegie Code

		DIGITAL COLLECTIONS			USAGE		DIRECT COSTS		
		No. of collections	Size (MB)	Items	No. of times accessed	No. of queries	Personnel	Equipment, software, or contract services	Volumes Held Collectively
Lib. No.	Survey Question # Institution	16a	16b	16c	17a	17b	18a	18b	19
321	U Houston	0	0	0	0	0	0	0	0
322	U Mary	0	0	0	0	0	0	0	0
323	U MI Dearborn	1	1,300	4,593	748,673	-2	41,878	597	0
324	U Mobile	0	0	0	0	0	0	0	0
325	U NE Kearney	-1	-1	-1	-1	-1	0	0	-1
326	U Portland	0	0	0	0	0	0	0	0
327	U Richmond	2	187,904	25,332	-1	-1	37,000	43,287	0
328	U Rio Grande	0	0	0	0	0	0	0	0
329	U Scranton	1	3	32	0	0	0	0	1,900
330	U Sthn IN	-1	-1	-1	-1	-1	-1	-1	-1
331	U Tampa	0	0	0	-1	-1	-1	-1	-1
332	U TN Chatt	1	25	35	1	1	60	40	0
333	U TN Martin	-1	-1	-1	-1	-1	-1	-1	0
334	U TX Tyler	0	0	0	0	0	0	0	0
335	U West AL	0	0	0	0	0	0	0	0
336	U WI E Claire	-1	-1	-1	-1	-1	-1	-1	0
337	U WI La Crosse	3	25,000	91	-1	-1	1,300	2,000	0
338	U WI Platteville	0	0	0	0	0	0	0	0
339	U Winnipeg	0	0	0	0	0	0	0	0
340	UNC Asheville	161	97,800	1,051,194	-1	-1	-1	-1	0
341	UNC Pembroke	0	0	0	0	0	0	0	0
342	Union C-NY	0	0	0	0	0	0	0	0
343	Valparaiso U	0	0	0	0	0	0	0	0
344	Villa Julie C	-1	-1	-1	-1	-1	-1	-1	-1
345	W.Carey College	0	0	0	0	0	0	0	0
346	W.Mitchell C Law	1	-1	40	-1	-1	-1	-1	0
347	Walla Walla C	2	14,277	1,483	256	-1	-1	-1	-2
348	Walsh C Acct Bus Admin	0	0	0	0	0	0	0	32,000
349	Wartburg Theo Sem	0	0	0	0	0	0	0	0
350	Washburn U Topeka	0	0	0	0	0	0	0	0
351	Washington C	0	0	0	0	0	0	0	0
352	Washington Theo Union	0	0	0	0	0	0	0	0
353	Wayland Bap U	0	0	0	0	0	0	0	0
354	Wayne ST C	-1	-1	-1	-1	-1	-1	-1	-1
355	Webber Intl U	0	0	0	0	0	0	0	0
356	Wesley C	0	0	0	0	0	0	0	0
357	West Chester U PA	0	0	-1	-1	0	0	0	0
358	West TX A & M U	0	0	0	0	0	0	0	0
359	West VA Wesleyan C	1	-1	167	-1	-1	-1	-1	-1
360	Western MD C	-2	-2	-2	-2	-2	-2	-2	0

-1 -- Unavailable   -2 -- Not Applicable

ACRL Library Data Tables 2004
DIGITIZATION ACTIVITIES

INSTITUTIONS GRANTING MASTER OF ARTS AND PROFESSIONAL DEGREES (Carnegie Code M)

	DIGITAL COLLECTIONS			USAGE		DIRECT COSTS		
	No. of collections	Size (MB)	Items	No. of times accessed	No. of queries	Personnel	Equipment, software, or contract services	Volumes Held Collectively
Survey Question #	16a	16b	16c	17a	17b	18a	18b	19
Institution								
Western OR U	-1	-1	-1	-1	-1	-1	-1	0
Western Sem	0	0	0	0	0	0	0	0
Western WA U	-1	-1	-1	-1	-1	-1	-1	-1
Westfield ST C	0	0	0	0	0	0	0	0
Westminster C-UT	1	-1	157	-1	-1	-1	7,690	-1
Wheeling Jesuit U	-1	-1	-1	-1	-1	-1	-1	-1
Whitworth C	0	0	0	0	0	0	0	0
Wilkes U	-1	-1	-1	-1	-1	-1	-1	-1
William Woods U	1	-1	95	-1	-1	2,545	5,121	0
Williams C	7	83,502,663	2,663	-1	-1	22,500	1,700	-1
Wstrn IL U	0	0	0	0	0	0	0	0
Wstrn Theo Sem	-1	-1	-1	-1	-1	-1	-1	-1
Xavier U LA	0	0	0	0	0	0	0	0

-1 -- Unavailable   -2 -- Not Applicable

2004

FOOTNOTES TO THE ACRL STATISTICS

Footnotes are listed for any institution included in this volume that provided a text footnote to one or more questions in the survey. The notes are arranged alphabetically by the abbreviated institution name and then ordered by question number. For a listing of abbreviated names and full institution names, including schools not listed in this volume, see the "Key to Participating Institutions" that follows this section.

Stray clicks on the footnote indicator button during the survey may have left a few footnote indicators in the data where no actual note exists. The footnotes have been formatted and some were edited for publication.

Institution	Q. No	Note
B C Art & Design	13	35mm slides
	30A	Membership in consortia
drian C	19	OCLC Bibliographic Databases; Online Services
gnes Scott C	Trends Note	"Even with the instructions given
mer U Puerto Rico	43	This information is not available at this moment
mherst C	42	not available
quinas C MI	2A	The library initiated a comprehensive weeding project in preparation for our move into a new building.
	49	IPEDS data not available.
	50	IPEDS data not available.
	51	IPEDS data not available.
	52	IPEDS data not available.
	54	We do not receive government documents.
quinas C TN	5	print only
	7	284
rk Tech U	Trends Note	"Our statistics for electronic resources are not differentiated this way
Armstrong Atlantic ST U	30B	University System Galileo program provides several databases. We don't have cost figures.
	42	includes renewals. Initial circulations not counted separately
	43	see 42 footnote
	54	We are not a depository and subscribe to very few government publications
	Trends Note	"We don't have separate statistics for 10
Assumption C	30B	I do not know this amount
	54	If we have any government documents of a serial nature.
	Trends Note	We have not been counting our electronic transactions in this way.
Atlanta C Art	13	Number is approximate as 2/3 of the collection is not on our database
	22	We do not separate out professional from support staff pay in our budget.
	31	Purchases of hardware are under the college's overall budget and therefore not included.
	37	"Circulation desk
	41	We do not keep statistics on this task
	42	We do not keep statistics on reserves vs. circulation borrowing.
	49	We do not distinguish in our records between full and part-time students.
	54	We do not collect these.
	Trends Note	Note for Item 4: The Atlanta College of Art is a member of the GALILEO consortium operated by the University System of Georgia. Count is approximate based on current holdings of GALILEO plus 3 databases we purchase to supplement their offerings.
Auburn U Montgomery	19	All materials are included in either of the two categories above.
	Trends Note	"For 14a
Austin Presb Theo Sem	43	do not have figures for renewals
Averett C	4	Monographic titles purchased.
	13	Exludes items in the Archives
	30A	SOLINET: $600 associate membership. SWING consortium dues: $1000.
	30B	"VIVA consortium: $7750 state match
	31	"Hardware and software purchases are centralized through the Computer Center
	32	"Interlibrary loan shipping
	41	Staff are trained to answer simple reference questions during 18 hrs per week when librarians are not present. These questions are not tallied.
	54	We are not a depository.
	Trends Note	Web site visits and initial hits on the library catalog will be reported for 2004-05.
Babson C	Trends Note	http://dibinst.mit.edu/BURNDY/Collections/Babson/Babson.htm The Grace K. Babson Collection of the Works of Sir Isaac Newton are on permanent loan to the Burndy Library of the Dibner Institute for the History of Science and Technology. The Online Newton
Baker U	18	Other materials are inseparable from the monographs in the budget.
	30B	"We take advantage of state purchases for libraries

Institution	Q. No	Note
Baker U	42	renewals not tracked separately
	Trends Note	The library web site comes up automatically in all labs across campus whenever a stude faculty member access the web -- this is not a useful number.
Barber-Scotia C	4	These are reported as volumes.
	11	unknown
	12	These materials are not housed in the library. Access to these are from another area.
	13	Not a part of the Library.
	14	Accessed from another area of campus.
	15	This number only reflect videos. No films are housed here.
	26	Maintenance Fees for machines and equipment
	30A	OCLC Services and databases
	30B	NC LIVE- State electronic library access to databases
	32	Amount allocated for postage
	46	Undergraduate Institution
	47	Does not apply.
	51	This is a four year liberal arts undergraduate institution.
	52	Does not apply
	Trends Note	"12a. Users accessed NCLIVE
Bates C	7	Includes 24137 titles in electronic format
	31	Library budget includes no expenditures for computing.
	Trends Note	"These questions ask for answers that we don't keep track of
Benedict C	5	Includes 186 titles and 43 supplements.
	6	Includes 46 government documents and 5 gifts.
	15	An additional category in our audiovisual materials collection includes Kits which totals 14
	30B	"DISCUSS cost $13
	31	"Computer hardware cost $12
	32	For postage.
	37	"Includes: Reference desk
	43	Renewal statistics not currently kept.
	Survey Note	Not any.
	Trends Note	"Considering the new questions added to this year's Academic Library Trends section of th survey
Berry C	22	Wages for professional staff and support staff are combined.
	Trends Note	"12. Does not include figures for all consortium-supplied databases. 12a. Number of vend (not separate products) 13. Partial count 13a. Number of vendors (not separate products 14. Figure only includes full-text
Bethany C Bethany	8	approximate
	42	unavailable
	Trends Note	"I would have preferred to put 'unavailable' (u/a) for: 13
Bethel C IN	26	Preservation
	50	we do not have separate figures for part-time students
	Trends Note	Items requested are Full text requests only (PDF and HTML full text retrievals)
Bethel C KS	18	Question 16 includes all library materials except current serials.
Birmingham Southern C	7	Does not include aggregated databases
	11	Archives volumes are included in Respsonse #1A
	13	"Includes 6
	18	"Microforms $20
	33	Incl. 5FTE professional librarians
Blackburn C	Trends Note	12-14a. Unable to determine
Bluffton C	1A	adjusted figure
	17	"Print periodicals
	18	"A/V

Institution	Q. No	Note
Huffton C	19	"Databases and search services
	29	"Databases
	30A	Bibliographic utilities (Q19)
Boise Bible C	41	weekly transactions
Bowdoin C	15	Includes all audiovisual materials
	Trends Note	"Question #6: includes all electronic resources Question #11: Planning to select and implement 05/06 Question #12: Data from login script
BowlGrn SU Fireld	1A	This is a corrected figure.
	11	Based on actual measure. I believe last year's reported figure of was in error.
	39	Not included are five sections of a one-credit course-- Intro. to the Electronic Library-- taught to 49 students.
	42	Renewals are not counted separatly.
	44	"Includes materials sent to our Main Campus
	45	"Includes materials received from our Main Campus
	54	Five government documents are included; the majority are not.
	Trends Note	"We have access to many electronic resources through our Main Campus and OhioLINK
Bradley U	1A	New figure from online catalog
	5	includes electronic serials
	6	electronic journals that are not purchased
	9	inadvertently omitted these last year
	17	includes electronic resources
	Trends Note	E books are included in question 4
Brescia U	1A	Included Netlibrary records here last year--have removed them this year.
	Survey Note	"Question 30b. We are part of a statewide consortium
Bryan C	Trends Note	"15a 15b our IT is currently unable to furnish stats regarding web
Buena Vista U	1A	includes A/V materials
	2A	Weeded and recounted serials
	Trends Note	1. Anything with electronic access in any full-text database. 2. This one excludes any journals on partially covered in the aggregators. 3. Unable to measure this. 6. This amount includes the amount on question #8. 10. April-June 2004
Butler U	19	Bibliographic utility - 25041
C Holy Cross	18	Included in 16 and 17.
	31	In ITS Budget.
C Wooster	37	Circ Desk - ILL Circ Desk - Reserves Reference Desk Special Collections Gov't Information
	Trends Note	We do not keep statistics for anything marked with a '0'
C.R. Drew U Med & Sci	42	Can't provide this information with our current ILS.
	57	Our library is a health sciences library and the scope of our collection reflects this.
	Trends Note	"Can't answer questions 12-15
CA St Polytechnic U-Pomona	18	"Other library materials consists of: E-books (14
	26	"Other operating expenditures consist of: furniture & equipment ((8221); Innovative Interfaces maintenance (122
	30B	"Not reported: External funding of $114
	Trends Note	13A: The types of resources included are: ABC-CLIO; AIP Journal Center; EBSCOHOST; First Search; Gale Group; ProQuest; Silver Platter; and WilsonWeb.
CA St U - Sacramento	11	.
	42	"CSU
CA ST U Dominguez Hills	19	"Electronic databases = $227
	Trends Note	"#4. Includes e-books; #12a. Licensed citation indexes
CA ST U Fresno	Trends Note	We do not have these items readily available.
CA ST U Fullerton	5	includes gifts--don't have information broken down
	6	see above
	21	"$31
	30B	we do have system shared resources but do not have $ figure for them

Institution	Q. No	Note
CA ST U Fullerton	42	don't have this statistic
	54	"some are in monographs
CA ST U Hayward	Trends Note	We have not begun collecting data for emetrics.
CA ST U Long Beach	3	"As a result of weeding projects
	19	"Computer files/search services (including e-serials): $697
CA ST U Northridge	2A	Not recorded
	6	not recorded
	12	not recorded
	17	702165 for print periodicals and serials and 194191 for electronic serial subscriptions
	19	Document delivery/interlibrary loan
	22	All professionals in this field; librarians only: 1843326
	49	FTE
	Trends Note	Data revealing number of resources accessed and number of sessions is not available. on digital collections and resources to support them not available.
CA ST U S Bernadino	49	Fall 2003
	Survey Note	-1
	Trends Note	Developing Statistical methods
CA ST U San Marcos	5	print only
	6	print only
	7	print only
	16	includes pre-pays
	17	includes pre-pays
	19	ILL/DD
	20	includes pre-pays
	33	Actual: 13.8
	34	Actual: 25.5
	35	Actual: 9.58
	36	Actual: 48.86
	Trends Note	#14 - Not counted
CA West Sch Law	4	Titles purchased.
	25	Salary/fringe benefits information is confidential and not generally distributed.
	27	Salary/fringe benefits not included.
	Survey Note	Fiscal Year: August 1-July 31.
Calvin C	42	Can't gather this figure
	Trends Note	"Sorry
Campion C	18	Included in other expenditures
	22	"1/2 year at 80% of salary due to sabbatical
	24	Higher salary figure to cover more hours during librarian sabbatical
	28	Computer files and electronic materials are handled by the Main university library on camp
	39	Instruction sessions are booked on demand - no record is kept of the number performed e semester
	41	Figures not kept
	Trends Note	These figures are only available from the Main university library
Carlow C	Trends Note	For question #1 duplicates are not removed.
Carroll C-Helena	18	ILL 63.50
	19	"MEMBERSHIP 213 OCLC 19
	22	U/A
	23	U/A
	30A	U/A
	30B	U/A
	31	U/A

Institution	Q. No	Note
Carroll C-Helena	41	Q/A
	42	Q/A
	43	Q/A
	44	Q/A
	45	Q/A
	50	Q/A
Carroll C-Waukesha	42	unknown
Cedar Crest C	19	Computer equipent
	43	Our system does not provide separate statistics.
Centenary C	4	records not kept
	11	We do not know the extent of this collection
	13	We do not know the extent of this collection
	15	All AV combined
	26	We are not provided with the costs of benefits
	30B	we do not know the amounts expended on these subsidies. We receive
	33	Two Full time one part time
	34	Three full time and three part time
	35	Not paid from library budget. 12 student working 8 hours per week
	42	Do not track
	50	dont know
	51	don't know
	52	don't know
	Survey Note	The main campus library services two off campus site that do not have libraries.
	Trends Note	Some of the items are answered with 0 because we do not track the amounts
Centenary C LA	26	Salary benifits come from main budget.
	30A	OCLC/AMIGOS Interlibrary Loan and Cataloging esxpenses are together.
	35	Funds come through Department of Financial Aid.
	Survey Note	N/A
	Trends Note	N/A
Central Christian C Bible	32	This is an estimate by the number of Interlibrary loans made.
	34	This includes one person who volunteered time at .25
Central CT ST U	15	Includes audio.
Central MO ST U	7	in 2003 total should have been 3599 instead of 3699 as reported
	19	information report in previous years in line 19 are now reported in other lines
	Trends Note	"#4 - yes
Centre C	Trends Note	URL: http://www.centre.edu/web/library/sc/digital.html THE CENTRE COLLEGE DIGITAL ARCHIVES is a growing collection of electronic versions of manuscript and printed items primarily relating to Centre College and Kentucky College for Women. Included a
Charleston Sthrn U	1A	"Adjusted includes 14
Chicago ST U	10	Data not available
	13	data unavailable
	28	data unavailable
	30B	data unavailable
	32	data unavailable
	Trends Note	The library is currently working on digitization. Digitization data is currently unavailable for this survey but should be available for the next survey.
Chris Newport U	15	We do not maintain separate totals by category; this represents our total audio visual collection.
	19	"Electronic online services $106
	26	"This includes $994
Christendom C	22	estimate
	23	estimate

Institution	Q. No	Note
Christendom C	24	estimate
	Trends Note	The Library does no work digitally as of yet: we are small liberal arts college. To date the has been little interest in digital matters
Christian Brothers U	10	not counted separately
	14	counted as video
	50	not available
Clarkson C-NE	1	Estimate is based on an estimate of 10 'traditional' volumes per foot.
Clear Creek Bible	50	"I have not been able to get this information
	53	"Our access to ebooks are also in our catalog
	54	We don't have government documents.
	55	"Fringe benefits were paid from the library budget in the amount of $18
	Trends Note	We did not have the capability to monitor number of visits to the website and the online c until June 2004.
Columbia C MO	17	Serial database costs not included in 2002-2003 survey
Columbia C SC	54	No government documents
Columbus ST U	30B	This is the amount that the GALILEO iniative paid on behalf of CSU.
	42	Unable to separate out renewals.
Concordia C-NY	3	We did extensive weeding in our Curriculum Materials Center.
Concordia U Irvine	54	Not applicable.
Concordia U St Paul	15	Question 15 includes audio--we do not separate them out.
Cooper Union	3	We withdrew 323 more volumes than we added
	19	Bibliographic Utilities: 61437 Literature Searching + ILL: 1120 Security Devices/Services 3055 Memberships: 1490
Cornish C Arts	1A	11561 volumes held s of June 2002.
	13	Slides.
	14	"CD
	15	VHS and DVD
	16	Included in question 20.
	17	Included in question 20.
	18	Included in question 20.
	31	Lab computers.
	37	"Circulation desk
	38	"96 circulation
	39	Exact count.
	40	Exact count.
	41	Statistics kept daily.
	42	Cannot separate reserves transactions.
	44	Do not loan.
	45	Do not have ILL service.
	49	Undergraduate only.
	50	Non-matriculated.
	53	Based on copy records in database.
Crichton C	22	Professional staff and support staff are not separated
	25	Added total professional/support plus student
	43	Our system does not distinguish between initial circulations and renewals
	Trends Note	#14. Only one of the databases actually gave statistics for documents requested.
Crown C-MN	1	The numbers do not add up because the number reported in 1a was from a manual count the last 100 years or so. The number reported here is an accurate count from the online catalog (we just finished our recon project this past year).
	4	This is an estimate. Nearly all of our volumes are purchased.
	18	Electronic books
	19	Bibliographic utilities

Institution	Q. No	Note
Brown C-MN	22	The figure reported is for all library staff. The college does not distinguish between professional and support staff in the library for budget purposes
	23	See note 22.
	25	excludes fringe benefits
	26	"Includes fringe benefits
	42	We do not distinguish between initial circulations and renewals
	43	We do not distinguish between initial circulations and renewals
Culver Stockton C	4	We do not have figures that differentiate between purchased and non-purchased volumes.
	19	Databases - 21657 Consortiums - 20603
	30A	Consortiums
	37	Circulation & Reference
	38	During academic year
CUNY BMB C	33	"25 full time
	34	"24 full time
	42	cannot distinguish first time borrowings from renewals
CUNY City C	Trends Note	"Q 19 seems out of order
CUNY HH Lehman C	17	CUNY Office of Library Services assumed some costs formerly paid directly by Lehman.
	18	"Microfilm 13
	19	"NYLINK $17
	22	Used somewhat fewer adjunct (Part-time)librarian hours this year.
	24	"Includes $8
	29	"$139
	38	72 at the beginning of the semester. 76 from mid-term to end of semester.
	39	Actual count.
	40	Actual count.
	41	"1
	43	We cannot separate renewals from initial circulations.
	49	Fall 2003 figures used. 4584 FT Undergrads 110 FT Grad Students
	50	Fall 2003 figures used. 3010 PT Undergrads 2008 PT Grad Students
	51	Fall 2003 figures used.
	52	Fall 2003 figures used.
	Trends Note	"We are not yet counting the items you requested in Trends in the way in which you requested them
CUNY NYC Tech C	17	excluded CUNY paid electronic serials
	19	NYLINK
	22	figure is lower than last time - 3 new professional staff members with lower salaries
	24	figure higher - expanded Internet Lab and staffing need increased
	26	"postage
	30A	NYLINK
	30B	CUNY CENTRAL electronic resources
	42	excluded reserves which were previously included in figure
	43	don't have count for renewals
	44	numbers increased since we expanded service
	45	numbers increased since we expanded service
	Trends Note	For FY03-04 we did not compile statistics in this area. We are just beginning to look at counting these numbers.
CUNY York C	42	Circulation and reserve are not separated in this system
	43	See above note
	Survey Note	none
	Trends Note	The statistics requested are NOT available at this time. Please see note on survey: York College's WWW resources are provided primarily by the central CUNY Library system and are thus not counted here at York.
Curtis Inst Music	11	est.

Institution	Q. No	Note
Curtis Inst Music	41	Only ref. transactions requiring written replies are tracked.
Dakota Wesleyan U	1A	This number includes e-books.
Daniel Webster C	2A	Weeding for inventory
	10	Databases produced in-house; available on Web Aircraft Review Index Aircraft Acciden Index
	13	Art slides
	16	Library budget was frozen in October 2003
	21	Who cares? This is a dated area of inquiry.
	29	Should change description to electronic resources or something more inclusive than elec serials that can be mistaken for electronic collections or not deemed to include electronic databases.
DeSales U	5	In our number for the previous survey we did not include our electronic journal subscriptio
	13	This number includes 401 slides and 733 paintings and art reproductions.
	14	2286 of these are LPs
	25	We do not separate professional staff from support staff in our salary line.
	26	"These expenses include costs for our Innovative Interfaces maintenance fees
	30B	We receive almost the entire collection of netLibrary titles via the Pennyslvania Power Lib program (ACCESS PA) We do not pay a fee for that service.
	43	We do not separate reserves from other circulation figures.
	Trends Note	"Q8 This figure includes database subscriptions to citation or abstract only. It includes Ca Periodical Index
Dickinson ST U	1A	figure corrected from last year
	2	includes 2173 e-books
	4	includes 2173 e-books purchased this year
	5	includes 1670 full-text journals and newspapers (does not include Gale full-text title count)
	9	"discontinued depository status
	16	includes $6572 for e-books as reported above
	17	includes $28.741 for full-text journals
	43	includes 72302 licensed databases searches
Divine Word C	43	Renewals are not counted.
	Trends Note	We do not maintain statistics on use of our electronic reference sources or OPAC.
Dominican C San Rafael	5	420 Journals: Reference comprises remainder
	15	"Plus 1
	33	Reference/Acquisitions Librarians Dean
	34	"Techinical Support including cataloging
	35	Average per semester
	37	Circ and Reference
	38	83.5 during academic year 64 during summer session (May-August)
Drake U	7	Includes electronic full-test access
	51	Includes Law and Pharmacy students.
	52	Includes Law and Pharmacy students.
	55	"Benefit allocation for year was $258
	Survey Note	"Fiscal year is June 1
	Trends Note	"A digitization web site was developed during the summer
Drury C	1A	Figure reported last year erroneously included microform titles.
	2A	Ceased depository status and withdrew large numbers of print documents.
	4	We can report titles only.
E R Aero U	1A	Does not include approx. 33000 vols. (previously reported) in distributed reference/branch libraries (see final footnote).
	22	Professional and support staff reported combined.
	23	Professional and support staff reported combined.

Institution	Q. No	Note
R Aero U	Survey Note	"We have not included approx 33000 volumes (line 1a.) that reside in our extended campus reference collections. These remotely located collections meet all of the IPEDS criteria for a branch library
arlham C	30B	"We get databases from INSPIRE
	31	Most computer equipment is purchased through central institutional funds. This figure is an estimate.
	Trends Note	#6 These expenditures are all associated with the purchase of electronic databases and cannot be disaggregated.
ast Texas Baptist U	8	This is just an estimate at this time. Once these have been added to our system we'll have a much better handle on this number.
	14	Includes recordings found in the main library and the music library.
	16	"We originally had over $125
	17	We didn't cut any out of our serials budget.
	18	Electronic resources were not cut.
	21	This line was cut entirely due to the budget cuts.
	26	"Includes supplies
	28	NetLibrary and ebrary.
	33	Includes library director.
	Trends Note	"Statistics on sessions
astern U	11	University and institutional archives
	16	Excludes online journals
	19	"Online aggragators
	49	Total FTE
astrn NM U Main	21	"$15
	31	68 computers were replaced under the university's cyclical rotation plan at no cost to library budget
ckerd C	Trends Note	"We do not maintain usage figures for our electronic resources to the extent requested. Electronic resources are heavily used. Ansers to #12-14 would add up to 100
lizabethtown C	Trends Note	The digitization project took place in 1999. Users can read information about the collection but must contact the staff for assistance. Description of the collection and sample photos are available on the web at www2etown.edu/library/SpC/SpC.htm. Q 12a
lmhurst C	4	"Titles
mmanuel C GA	22	Estimate based on May 2004 figures
	23	Estimate based on May 2004 figures
	24	Estimated
	31	Not part of library budget
	32	Amount not reported separately from other operating expenditures
mmanuel C MA	18	"microfilm
	19	electronic database subscriptions
	37	Circulation and Reference desks
	39	library instruction sessions
	Survey Note	-2
	Trends Note	-2
Emory & Henry C	4	titles
	19	electronic resources
	26	"equipment
	Trends Note	Amount for #6 also includes #7-9.
Evangel U	18	Microforms expendatures are included in current serials costs.
	41	We do not keep this figure.
	49	Do not have those figures available.
	50	Do not have those figures
	51	Do not have those figures
	52	Do not have those figures

Institution	Q. No	Note
F&M C	Trends Note	"13A. A selected list of the most popular research databases we have. 14A. These are commercial citation and full text databases
Ferrum C	42	Information lost during system migration.
	43	Information lost during system migration.
	Trends Note	We should be able to have much more complete data next year as we finish our migration an Innovative system and add counters to our home and catalog pages.
Finlandia U	23	"Total for full-time staff is $99
	43	Separate figure for renewals is unavailable.
Fitchburg ST C	6	These stats are not kept
	13	Paitnings: 223 Archival Photos:2296
	17	"Print Subs. $185
	18	"Microfiche: $432 Audio CDs $609 Pamphlets: $215 Electronic Databses: $54
	19	Interlibrary Loans: $37
	22	1 Director 5 Librarians .37 Part-tiem Librarian
	23	8 FTE staff members
	24	Grad Asst. $7500
	26	"ADMINISTRATIVE EXPENSES: Office Supplies
	29	"Online databases Indexes
	30A	"NELINET Membership: $1000 OCLC usage: $18
	30B	"The library is a member of the Central Massachsuetts Regional Library System and the M Board of Library Commissioners. As a result
	31	"ARIEL: $2370 Serials Solutions:$3152 VOYAGER Maint: $14
	33	1 Director 5 FT Librarians .37 PT weekend librarian
	34	5 full time assts 3 fte
	35	Includes 1 Grad Asst
	37	Reference Desk Circulation Desk
	39	Includes Distance Learning on-site classes
	40	Includes Distance Learning on-site classes
	41	"Includes in perons
	46	Do not award Doctorates
	47	Do not award Doctorates
	Trends Note	I fail to see the importance of some of these questions. There is no standard definition of 'search' used by the vendors. You (the editors) need to warn us a year in advance to colle some of these statistics. #14 my statistics are the number of i
FL Christian C	16	"This is the complete book expenditure; transfers from our bookstore are not counted in lir but were charged to the library budget. For only books counted on line 4 the amt. is $12
	20	These may not be the final audited numbers.
	30B	"We are a Selective User of OCLC services through CFLC
	31	IT hardware expenses not part of library budget therefore not reported to me. The amount one handheld device and software only.
	42	Total figure includes reserves; calculation omitting reserves from our system is too time-consuming to be useful.
	43	"Additionally
	46	We are an undergraduate institution
	47	We are an undergraduate institution
	49	Estimated numbers in 49 and 50. I do not have access to IPEDS. FTE for Fall 2003 was
	50	I do not have access to IPEDS. FTE for Fall 2003 was 254
	51	We are an undergraduate institution
	52	We are an undergraduate institution
	Trends Note	"All our databases are through consortia so we do not get any individualized usage statistic know they are regularly used
Flagler C	49	Includes main campus and 2 satellite programs
	50	Includes main campus and 2 satellite programs
Fort Hays ST U	6	Are not counted

Institution	Q. No	Note
Fort Hays ST U	15	Cannout break out these statistics with current software.
	43	Library software does not make distinctions.
	Trends Note	We have not been counting any of these questions. Sorry
Fort Lewis C	Trends Note	Note to #10. 348 of these were part of the AskColorado consortium Note to #14 This number is for full text only. It does not include citations or abstracts.
Francis Marion U	12	The campus has a separate media center
	13	see enote in Q12
	14	see note in Q12
	15	see note in Q12
	19	Electronic Resources
	46	no Ph.D. program
Free Will Baptist Bible C	22	This includes our para-professional staff as well; we cannot break these numbers apart
	31	"Our computer equipment and software
	55	"Fringe benefits totaled (an additional) $21
Frostburg ST U	1A	Reflects new baseline counts based on inventory.
G Adolphus C	30B	"There are more
	33	This is really 7.5
	34	This is really 8.5
	35	This is really 14.6
	36	This really should be 31
	Survey Note	Our fiscal year ended 5/31/04
	Trends Note	We are using PastPerfect archives and museum software to scan photographs in the Lutheran Minnesota Conference and Synod Archives. We are scheduled to submit photos to the Minnesota Digital Library as an MDL Coalition member. See http://www.mndigital.or
GA SWstrn ST U	5	collection development purchased
	6	"Government Documents-40
	10	"Government Documents-3695
	12	Government Documents-Maps
	14	Audio video included together. The count is not separated. Cataloging-9313 & Governments Documents-43.
	15	Included in 14 as A-V.
	22	Reference Librarian position frozen. Government Documents librarian left and it was 10 months before we could fill the Government Documents position.
	24	Wise program was discontinued in this year.
	32	Not exact figure. Added fax expenditures.
	37	Circulation desk. Reference desk staffed in the afternoons.
	38	Opening hours were reduced because of 1 full time professional position was frozen and 1 full time professional position was vacant.
	39	Figure based on actual statistical data.
	40	Figure based on actual statistical data.
	41	Figure based on actual statistical data.
	Trends Note	Questions 1 & 2....Number of electronic journals purchased is also number of electronic 'full text' journals. Question 4..No exact number but an estimate would be more than 100 number of electronic reference sources. Questions 6 & 7....The expenditures
Gardner-Webb U	4	No separate count of gift/purchased volumes
	17	Includes NCLIVE bundle with databases including serial and non-serial material
	29	Includes NCLIVE bundle with databases including serial and non-serial material
Governors ST U	Trends Note	"Where there is no information
Guilford C	3	Chiefly bound periodicals withdrawn after the addition of JSTOR.
	6	"74 print
	19	"Bibliographic utilities $8
	32	"$550 Interlibrary loan; $5
	42	System does not differentiate between first-time transactions and renewals.

Institution	Q. No	Note
Guilford C	Trends Note	Q. 13: Note all resources provide usage statistics.
H Inst Int Desgn	Trends Note	-1
H LaGrange C	26	Does not include fringe benefits.
	27	Does not include fringe benefits.
	30B	This figure is unknown
	42	System stats do not separate initial from renewals.
Hamilton C	15	"Includes all AV formats
	54	no separate government documents collection
Hanover C	2	Unable to provide due to mid-year switch in library automated system.
	2A	Unable to provide due to mid-year switch in library automated system.
	3	Estimated figure based on subtracting previous year's holdings from holdings from this reporting year.
	8	Adjusted 'correct' figure from last reporting period.
	9	Adjusted 'correct' figure from last reporting period.
	26	"Includes items such as consortial/membership fees
	33	We had a vacant librarian line for the year.
	37	"Circulation
	38	Hours open per week during academic year.
	41	Typical week.
	53	This figure is not highly reliable due to mid-year switch in library automated system.
	54	Some government documents are included in the above count (from 2000 onward).
	Survey Note	"Due to a mid-year switch in our consortia-purchased library automated system
	Trends Note	"Many of these questions involve a level of detail that we do not collect
Harding U Main	3	Withdrawing physical government documents; adding Marcive records and linking to Government information
Haverford C	Survey Note	none
	Trends Note	The library has three digital collections. The senior thesis archive is an OAI-compliant database of metadata and full-text digital copies (PDF format) of Haverford College senior theses which currently has 96 records. (URL: http://thesis.haverford.edu/
Hebrew C	7	Including Electronic serials acquired as part of an aggregated package we have 7418 titles
	25	"Does not include benefits which total 53
	42	"3823 & 3
Hobart &William Smith Cs	Trends Note	"16c: Item count does not include thumbnail versions of images
Holy Apostles C & Sem	17	Extra payment this year due to the FAXON bankruptcy.
	18	Included elsewhere with monographs; microforms are no longer purchased by our Library
	46	We do not offer PhD degrees.
	47	We do not offer PdD degrees.
	Trends Note	We participate in the iCONN databases available to Connecticut Universities. As this was relatively new to us during the 2003 academic year I have no real statistics to report at this time. I will keep abreast of these figures for next year's reporting.
Hood C	5	This represents 672 paper serial subscriptions plus full-text electronic subs.
	6	This represents 5 free paper subscriptions plus free electronic ful-text subs.
	18	This is A/V only. Our microforms expenditures are calculated as part of serials costs.
	33	It is really 5.6.
	34	It is really 3.5.
	35	It is really 4.28.
	36	Total is really 13.38. WE'd love to have that other '.62' person!
	42	We do not separate this figure from total circulation transactions.
Hope C	11	Archives is a separate unit from the library.
Houghton C	21	only in-house binding $2183
	25	fringe benefits $147779 not included in total
Howard Payne U	17	"The NCES directions indicated databases such as Project MUSE was to be counted as 1
	30B	I have absolutely no clue.

Institution	Q. No	Note
Howard Payne U	31	None paid out of library budget; all from IT budget.
	53	"Perhaps a mix
	54	"Yes
	Trends Note	"The last time we accurately gathered these statistics was over two years ago
Humboldt ST U	1	An actual count of periodical volumes was taken and it was less than previously reported
	26	"furniture
	Trends Note	Additional collections are represented by digital samples and finding aids.
IN U Kokomo	55	"Fringe benefits amount to $80
IN U S Bend	8	410504 Cataloged; 735184 Uncataloged
IN U-Purdue U Ft Wayne	4	orders placed & received
	5	1509 print
	6	173 print
	41	based on typical week during middle of semester
	48	includes 20 administrative staff with faculty rank
Jacksonville ST U	5	"Includes aggregated online collections
Johnson Bible C	2	Volume counts are based on volumes accessioned during the year.
	23	One position was filled with paid staff for only 4 months out of the year.
Johnson C Smith U	Trends Note	The library's digitization project was made possible by a grant from the NC ECHO division of the North Carolina State Library. The materials that were digitized relate to the establishment and early history of Johnson C. Smith University. The URL for the
Judson C	19	"Online Databases+$38199 Equipment=$4251 Membership Dues=$1072 The instruction for Question 19 indicate that bibliogrpahic utilities should go here. However
	26	"Bibliographic utilities=$12784 Office Supplies=$4782 Staff Improvement=$980 Travel=$672 Equipment Repair=$700 Archival Supplies=$49 The instruction for Question 19 indicate that bibliogrpahic utilities should go here. However
	30A	"The instruction for Question 19 indicate that bibliogrpahic utilities should go here. However
	49	I couldn't tell from the instructions whether you were after headcount or FTE. 913 is headcount of full-time students. The FTE is 971.1
	Trends Note	"Statistics for Q12 and Q13 are somewhat meaningless
Kent ST U Salem	Trends Note	"Questions 1
Kent ST U Trumbull	54	No government documents.
Kentucky Christian C	2	Includes 230 bound periodicals
	14	"Includes 2
	15	"Includes 1
	29	See 30b
	30A	"Solinet OCLC Database development $12
	30B	"Appalachian College Association $16
	32	"Courier Service $1
	33	1 Professional Position remained vacant
	34	A vacancy of .625 FTE existed during the reporting period.
	41	"Week of October 13 - 17
Kentucky ST U	11	154844 sq. ft.We don't have this information in linear ft.
	Survey Note	N.A.
	Trends Note	"4. NetLibrary is included as an e-books aggregate service; no individual reference sources were counted from NetLibrary. 9. NetLibrary collection was purchased previously
Keuka C	1A	I do not think we supplied a survey last year
Lakeland Sheboygan	42	We are unable to differential between initial circulation and renewal.
Lambuth U	9	also includes Center for Jewish Research and storage books not cataloged.
	10	Main collection and government documents
	22	Includes fringe benefits
	23	Includes fringe benefits
	25	Includes fringe benefits
	27	Salaries do not come out of library budget.

Institution	Q. No	Note
Lambuth U	28	All other CD-ROMs accompanied books and are included in the monographic entry (#16)
Lancaster Bible C	19	12187 CD-ROM subscriptions 6652 Conservation 9135 Databases-not full text
	21	We do send materials to a contract bindery but we did not send anything that was paid d... the 2003-2004 fiscal year.
Langston U	30B	Funding from state -- amount unknown.
	31	Paid by separate campus department.
	50	Cannot get data
	51	Cannot get data
	52	Cannot get data
	Trends Note	Data on visits to library web page and catalog are unavailable.
Laurentian U JN	2	New system and was not collecting data properly
	2A	New system and was not collecting data properly
	3	New system and was not collecting data properly
	9	New system and was not collecting data properly
	18	Included in 16 and 17
	19	CNFS
	28	Included in number 20
	29	Included in number 20
	30A	Included in number 20
	30B	Included in number 20
	31	Included in number 20
	32	Included in number 20
	33	This does not include the Director 7 Librarians and 1 Archivist
	41	Stats are not kept
	45	New system and was not collecting data properly
	55	342004 - total of Fringe Benefits
Le Moyne C	19	Interlibrary Loan document delivery expense 7259 + Copyright Clearance expense 329
	Survey Note	"Fiscal Year end May 31
Lewis&Clark C	4	Does not include monographic standing orders
	16	"Includes AV
	19	Doc. Del.$476 In-house binding $950
LIFE Bible C	1	Unclassified bound serials arranged in alphabetical order are not included.
	7	232 print serials + 1722 electronic fulltext journals in ProQuest & ATLAS not duplicated in serials.
	27	"Health insurance
	55	"Fringe benefits = health insurance
Lindsey Wilson C	1A	From previous year's survey.
	2	"titles 1410 titles X 1.1 = conversion for vol count of 1552 + gifts added
	4	1410 titles purchased X 1.1 vol / title. I have found that the ratio of volumes to titles 1.1 : ... seems to carry over from year to year.
	5	"Includes periodicals in online
	8	"Includes reels
	9	Kim's figures from Government Documents
	10	Primarily government docs CD ROMS
	11	Includes college archives and oral history collection.
	12	All in government documents
	13	Framed pictures on library wall
	14	Musical CDs
	15	VHS tapes and a growing number of DVD recordings.
	16	Amount spent on print materials. This excludes the portion of ACA (Appalachian College Association)fees allocated to e-books in m
	17	"Amount spent on journals in print

Institution	Q. No	Note
Lindsey Wilson C	18	"$5
	19	"ACA Consortium fees for Central Library: this covers a host of of reference and full-text databases
	26	Benefits
	31	Support for online catalog
	33	Three full-time librarians
	34	"Five library assistants
	35	Actually 1.6 FTE
	39	Includes extended campus visits.
	41	We note that this is down. The Internet has made so many students self-directed learners. We received many more non-reference type requests
	42	Unable to determine
Lipscomb U	39	increase due to implementing programs in information literacy broadly
Lourdes C	12	uncataloged
	15	Does not include 1126 evideos
Lubbock Christian U	16	see line 26
	17	see line 26
	18	see line 26
	19	see line 26
	20	see line 26
	24	This is the 100% amount. Last year's survey had only listed the 40% amount that the library's pays for.
	26	"Includes lines 16
	29	this total is also included in line 26
	35	"On last year's survey we listed a headcount
	Trends Note	"#'s7
Luth Theo Sem Philly	Survey Note	The Krauth Memorial Library is attached to the Lutheran Theological Seminary at Philadelphia.
Lyndon State C	7	This is the total number of subscriptions. We don't count individual copies or bound volumes.
Malone C	1	"Includes 14
	1A	"Includes 74
	41	Our typical fall week reference transaction was 214. We multiplied this by 36 weeks to get an overall estimate (many weeks will be less)
	Trends Note	"No. 3 was an estimate of the number of government document journals and periodicals that are listed in our catalog that are available online--the total number of government documents serials and journals total was about 3
Manhattan C	Trends Note	"Due to new system migration of library catalog
Marist C	28	JSTOR one time payment
	32	Does not include fees paid to bibliographic utilities
	49	Undergraduate FTE was 4389
	51	Graduate FTE was 527
Marlboro C	1A	"FY03 report wasn't accurate because inventory hadn't occured. This 64
	2A	Found missing during summer 2003 inventory
	7	Hard copy subscriptions only. Does not include electronic journal titles.
	14	From catalog holdings -- music sound recordings and audiobooks.
	15	From catalog holdings.
	16	Excludes AV.
	17	Hard copy subscriptions only.
	18	Audiovisual only.
	19	Electronic resources.
	22	Library Director Technical Services/Reference Librarian Acqusitions/Systems Librarian (10 mo.)
	23	Library Assistant (10 mo.)
	26	"Supplies

Institution	Q. No	Note
Marlboro C	29	"MLA
	30A	"Nelinet
	31	"Sirsi
	32	"OCLC ILL costs
	33	"Two full-time
	34	10 months
	43	We don't keep track of renewals.
	49	Does not include Marlboro College Graudate Center.
	50	Ditto.
	51	Ditto.
	52	Ditto.
	53	Based upon inventory done summer 2003.
Mars Hill C	Survey Note	Our fiscal year runs from June 1 to May 31.
Mary Washington C	18	included in Q. 26
	27	Last report probably included benefits in this total. Benefits are not included here.
	48	last year was reported in FTE. FTE this year is 238
	Trends Note	"Total for lines 6
Marymount U	14	Included in #4
	15	Included in #4
	22	"Includes library
	23	"Includes library
	24	"Includes in library
	25	"Includes library
	26	"Includues library
	27	I
	33	Includes librarians and staff in library and one in learning resource center.
	34	"Includes staff in library
	35	This figure will be emailed as soon as possible.
	36	This figure will be emailed as soon as possible.
	Trends Note	#2 - Duplicate titles not removed. #10 - We provide virtual reference to a consortium.
Maryville U St Louis	4	"Figure is Titles purchased
	8	Government documents are excluded from this figure
	19	Access Charges for materials: $1826
	Survey Note	"Fiscal Year is June 1
	Trends Note	Q.2 ECO subscriptions; does not include JSTOR. Q.4 Does not include e-books. Q. Resources reported are all library databases and electronic resources excluding the online library catalog Q. 13a Resources reported are all library databases
Mayville ST U	32	"In the process of changing to a state-wide computer system
	Survey Note	-1
	Trends Note	"12a. Included in the count are two online encyclopedias
McNeese ST U	1A	A more accurate volume count (and one that differs from last reported) was obtained by us the SIRSI report module.
	5	Includes electronic journals
	11	Reported elsewhere
	19	Electronic resources purchased through consortium
	26	"Includes computer hardware and software
	Trends Note	The number reported in 17b is the number of queries conducted for the whole Louisiana D Library Collection which contains our (1) collection.
McPherson C	12	Total for 12-15 is 4471. We don't keep separate counts.
Medical C Wisconsin	6	"State supported electronic access via Badgerlink to over 3
	9	We ceased being a depository library and weeded the collection. All physical items kept ar cataloged and counted as monographs.
	10	CD's

Institution	Q. No	Note
Medical C Wisconsin	49	"we are a medical school with PhD's in the basic sciences. Our medical students are 200 per class x4 = 800
	57	We are a medical library only.
Merrimack C	32	cannot separate out
	41	Average 113/week times 52 weeks
	Trends Note	Found this section confusing to fill out.
Methodist C	5	Does not include titles in electronic aggregators. Does include subscriptions only obtained on microform.
	16	Includes purchases handled by the library but paid for from academic department funds
	18	Instructions not clear on handling of microforms. Some of our microforms are unique subscriptions. all microform cost included in serials Q17
	35	Actual number is .55 FTE
	54	We treat some as current serials and others are cataloged as monographs.
Millikin U	11	"Manual measure Feb.2005
	18	microforms (film & fiche). No other formats are disaggregated in our accounting.
	19	All-inclusive figure for databases & bib utilities - we do not differentiate in our accounting.
	26	"Benefits $107
	28	All-inclusive figure for databases & bib utilities - we do not differentiate in our accounting.
	30A	Not disaggregated from Q28
	30B	State-wide free databases via Illinois State Library cannot be calculated.
	32	"These expenses (OCLC
	35	18 students @ 11 hours average/week 40 hour work week
	37	"Circ
	39	Likely a more accurate number for earlier years too... Multiple sessions for all freshmen along with significant numbers for upper classes; also orientations for university faculty & staff
	40	This remains accurate.
	41	Not tracked
	55	"Fringe benfits = 107
Millsaps C	14	Includes all AV material.
	18	Included in line 16 and 17.
	42	Initial circulation is not counted separately from renewals.
Milwaukee Inst Art Design	13	2895 added FY includes both retro & new slides shot(36282 in FilemakerPro plus estimate of uncat slides included)
	33	2.5
	35	1.4
	36	3.9
	Survey Note	MIAD Fiscal year June 2003- May 2004 reported
	Trends Note	Reporting fiscal year June 2003 - May 2004
Minnesota ST U-Mankato	1A	"Previous year were reported in error as 782
	5	`
	30B	Value of resources provided by MINITEX
	32	Includes new ILLiad startup and subscription costs
MO Baptist C	Trends Note	No statistics are kept re the above.
MO Western ST C	42	We no not report out reserve totals separately.
	Trends Note	Question 17 figure is '0' because the collection was not mounted and available online during FY 03-04.
Monmouth C	5	Includes 377 Print 40 Standing Orders 636 JSTOR 80 ACS 10 ECO 53 PsycARTICLES
	6	24 Gift 31 Govt Doc in print
	18	"10
	19	"4
	28	4800 JSTOR Archival Fees 5000 NYTimes Out-of-copyright fee
	Trends Note	Q1-4. Would it be any more helpful or consistent to provide a checklist of databases that most of us subscribe to? I'm thinking of something like Serials Solutions provides in their Overlap Analysis. Q16-19. Digital Collections. We have provided a f
Moravian C	1A	"Last year's figure (220

Institution	Q. No	Note
Morningside C	3	"Due to extensive weeding we had a minus of 1
	37	includes Media Center/IT area which is no longer part of the library operations or operatic budget
	38	Media Center and Reference desk have fewer hours staffed weekly
	52	fte count
Mount Union C	Trends Note	Answers to questions 1-5 are estimates.
MT ST U Northern	Survey Note	-2
	Trends Note	-2
Mt St Vincent U	42	This total includes Reserves
	43	This total includes Reserves
MT Tech U Montana	8	Number lower than previously reported. All drawers were individually measured to arrive number. Previously it was not taken into account that all drawers are not full.
	9	Number lower due to weeding and new measurement that did not count documents previ reported.
	11	Many of these items are barcoded and already reported.
	12	The number here is for our collection of flat and folded maps.
	37	Reference Desk Public Services Desk
	54	Limited number of government documents processed and shelved with current serials inc in this count.
	Trends Note	We have chosen Contentdm software for our digital collection. We are still in the process developing our first digital collection which contains images of our campus history. We ha not yet released this collection for public viewing.
Muhlenberg C	8	Includes governemnt documents
	12	Includes government documents
	Trends Note	"There are a number of questions in this section where the information may have been available to us
Muskingum C	4	approximate
	8	approximate
	29	approximate
	30B	approximate
Natl Defense U	1	"6
	22	One librarians salary is paid by a componenet outisde the library
	26	MERLN Website and outreach activities
	33	One FTE is paid by a componenet outside the library
	38	Monday-Friday 0700-1800 hrs. and 2 Saturdays per month
	Trends Note	"MERLN website
NC Sch Arts	5	"Includes access to online full-text database aggregators
	17	"Includes electronic journals. However
	18	"Includes music scores as well as moving image materials
NJ City U	49	Figures not available
	50	Figrues not available
NM Highlands U	Survey Note	None
Notre Dame C OH	19	"This figure includes OhioLINK database fees 34
Notre Dame Sem	8	Microfilms were discontinued for this fiscal year.
	11	Archive is maintained by this figure is not available.
	26	This includes Computer Services and Other Expenses.
	30B	Automation provider yearly contract and cataloging utility.
	35	Total student hours per week are 24 (6 hours times 4 students). Total is approximately .5 F
	37	"Librarian's Office Circulation desk (staffed 4 hours per day
	39	Two new student orientation workshops are given each semester. Smaller group presenta are give to individual classes as needed.
NW MO ST U	1A	physical inventory at mid-year caused an adjustment of figures
	5	"we do not separate gift subscriptions from those purchased
	7	"About 10

Institution	Q. No	Note
W MO ST U	8	vast bulk of these are ERIC fiche
	9	All our documents are cataloged.
	22	Fringe benefits excluded.
	23	Fringe benefits excluded.
	25	Fringe benefits excluded.
	28	"We have no exact figures
	37	"circulation/reference
	41	We record only questions for which professional help is required. Directional and computer questions are handled by students and I.T. staff.
	48	"Here at the last minute
	49	"See note 48. In Fall of '03
	50	see 49
	51	see 49
	52	see 49
	55	"Fringe benefits for library employees totaled $220
	Trends Note	"Question 13 and 13a. These are aggregator databases such as J-Stor
NY Inst Tech Islip	9	Government documents are cataloged as part of the general collection
	16	Budget is centrally administered
	17	Serials purchased from centralized book budget
	18	Included in periodicals budget
	28	Included in costs for monographs
	29	Budget centralized for all libraries
	46	NYIT does have a Ph.D degree program
	49	Breakdown of students between campuses not available
	Trends Note	Electronic purchases are made from the institutional budget and cover the five libraries in the system.
NY Inst Tech Main	22	Last year's figures did not include staff in the technical services dept.
	23	Last year's figures did not include staff in the technical services dept.
	24	The Student Affairs office manages student workers and they now manage the budget. The library no longer has a budget line for student aides.
	33	One frozen/unfilled professional position
	34	One frozen/unfilled support staff position
Oberlin C	11	Held in separately administered Oberlin College Archives.
OH Dominican C	Survey Note	-1
	Trends Note	-1
Olivet Nazarene U	49	Represents FTE
	51	Represents FTE
Otterbein C	1	"We also have 17
	6	U/A
	11	Approximate.
	27	"Employee Fringe Benefits = $124
	30B	"To determine
	32	Only a portion; our ILL OCLC expenses are included in Line 30a.
	55	"The directions said not to include. Our fringe benefits = $124
	Trends Note	"Getting this type of statistics for a small private college is almost impossible!!! The questions asked on this survey would take hours to obtain
Pace U-NY	30A	OCLC
	45	Does not include items received from commercial document suppliers:481
	Trends Note	18a-18b: We are using a hosted repository for digitized objects-Proquest UMI Administration became an added task for systems administrator. 20. Our digitization activities are tied to our Pilot Project on Digital Commons/Digital Repository Pilot cost is
Pacific Lutheran U	3	1549 -# of Archives & Special Collections bib records deleted but not yet replaced by new cataloging records.
	12	"This number includes all a/v materials: cartographic

Institution	Q. No	Note
Pacific Lutheran U	21	"$1
	25	"This is the first year that audio and TV services are included in our data
	41	full year
	Survey Note	Our fiscal year runs from June 1-May 31. This is the first year that audio and TV service is included in all areas.
	Trends Note	"This section requires a lot of research. If the questions had been anticipated or request other surveys at the beginning of the fiscal year
Paier C Art	7	One newspaper subscription cancelled.
	35	Actual = .4
Peace C	5	4000 electronic titles from periodical aggregators
	8	estimate from lineal inches of microfiche.
Plymouth ST C	1	Excludes bound periodicals Includes cataloged a/v material
	1A	Excludes bound periodicals Includes cataloged a/v material
	2	Includes cataloged a/v material
	2A	Includes cataloged a/v material
	3	Includes cataloged a/v material
	4	Includes single volumes purchased plus volumes received from continuation orders
	5	Includes 18 unnumbered monographic & publishers' series
	7	Includes 18 unnumbered monographic & publishers' series
	16	Includes expenditures for 380 continuation orders (number included in line 5)
	17	Excludes expenditures for 380 continuation orders (included in line 16)
	18	A/v included in line 16; microforms included in line 17
Potomac C	31	Provided through the Systems Administrator
	43	We don't separate renewals from initial circulation.
	Trends Note	We have purchased the EBSCO Business Source ELite/Health Business Full text and th Wilson Business FullText for our students. Access is anywhere with Internet access and appropriate user ID and password
Prescott C	31	Comes out of the Research and Technology Dept. budget.
Principia C	1	This year we made a switch from statistics that had always been gathered manually and h never been audited nor inventoried.
	26	"This expenditure included a one-time expense for a carpeting project
Providence C	1A	We have undergone a lot of work to get our #'s right and I have no accurate # to report fo year requested.
	4	an estimated figure
	22	an estimate - we don't keep separate salary data by category
	23	an estimate - we don't keep separate salary data by category
	31	budgeted by IT
	41	"342 x 52 = 17
	49	fte figure
	51	fte figure
	Trends Note	There are data element categories in which we simply do not collect the information this s is asking for (no need on our part).
Purdue U Calumet	Survey Note	"Q19: Document Delivery: $32
R.Wesleyan C	5	"Includes 157 electronic serials (via ATLAS
	17	Includes electronic subscriptions and databases
	49	Does not include Northeastern Seminary students also served by the library.
	50	Does not include Northeastern Seminary students
Radford U	Trends Note	1. May include duplicate titles in aggregated databases. 12. Full-text DB's and Abs & Cita DB's are included. 13. Full-text DB's and Abs & Citation DB's are included. 14. Full-text D and Abs & Citation DB's are included. 16. Photographic DB -
Ramapo C NJ	4	We do not track the number of gift items that have been cataloged.
Randolph-Macon WC	41	We don't track reference transactions.
Recnstrctnst Rabbinical C	Survey Note	"Our fiscal year

Institution	Q. No	Note
eformed Bible C	Trends Note	"For question 12: These statistics are for the number of sessions conducted in the state consortia of databases available through FirstSearch The students have access to additional databases
Sch Design	4	titles
	32	Records not kept separately; costs are minimal.
	Trends Note	I have no data for number 15.
icks C	1A	Catalogued Government Documents were not included in last year's total.
	16	Included in Book Budget.
	17	Included in Book Budget.
	18	Included in Book Budget.
	19	Included in Book Budget.
	20	Total Book Budget.
	30A	See 30b footnote.
	30B	"Total for Bibliographic Utilities
	49	The enrollment figure is for Fall 2004. (Our calendar/budget year runs from January 1 through December 31.)
	50	The enrollment figure is for Fall 2004. (Our calendar/budget year runs from January 1 through December 31.)
	Trends Note	Questions 1-14: We apologize for the large number of -1 notes in this section. There are two reasons for this. 1. We are part of a consortium of universities that are sponsored by The Church of Jesus Christ of Latter-day Saints.
ivier C	Survey Note	n/a
	Trends Note	n/a
ochester C	39	figure not available
	40	figure not available
	41	figure not available
	48	figure not available
	Survey Note	Salaries for professional and paraprfessional staff are estimated because separate figures for the two categories of employees are not available.
ockhurst U	Trends Note	Some of these statistics are not available to us at this time.
ocky Mountain C	42	We do not track renewals.
	43	Includes all renewals.
	50	I do not have that figure.
	51	New Masters program.
	Trends Note	We do not keep track of specific electronic media.
ogers ST U	19	Electronic materials and bibliographic utilities
	42	can not separate out renewals and initial circulations
oosevelt U	1A	Number submitted last year included AV and did not include bound volumes of periodicals.
	5	"Number reflects Total Holdings calculated by Serials Solutions
	31	These items are purchased from a university-wide technology budget.
	46	We do award EdD and PsyD degrees.
	Survey Note	"Statistics reported reflect data from all four Roosevelt Library facilities - the Murray-Green Library
Salem Teiko U	5	Use Ebscohost online
	22	not available as separate entry
Salisbury ST U	28	"included is one-time purchase cost of JSTOR (Arts & Humanities I
	29	"included is $90
	Trends Note	"#4 - in absence of directions
Savannah ST U	11	Number of boxes
	44	Unable to respond due to webservef malfunction.
	45	Unable to respond due to webservef malfunction.
Schreiner C	10	Includes NetLibrary holdings
SE C Assemblies God	43	we do not have separate statistics for renewals
	49	FTE students

Institution	Q. No	Note
SE C Assemblies God	50	I do not have this information
SE MO ST U	19	Interlibrary Loan = $1658 and Electronic Retrieval = $294
SF Consrv Music	18	Audio visual materials
	46	Master of Music is the highest degree awarded.
	54	We do not own government documents
Shaw U	5	Hardcopy
	12	Atlas
	19	Supplies
	29	Databases
	31	Computers for Staff and for public use
	44	We are selective users in the consortium (Borrowers only)
	Trends Note	"Resources reported are from: NC LIVE JSTOR
Shawnee ST U	Trends Note	Yes. EBOOKS are included CQ Reseacher EBSCO
Shepherd C	Trends Note	"13a. Access Science
Siena C	2A	Including periodical volumes withdrawn
	18	Audiovisual materials only
	19	Includes bibliographic utilities
	Trends Note	#1 includes all electronic journals purchased regardless in all databases #6 includes expenditures for all databases with full-text journals.
Silver Lake C	1A	Small adjustment from last year
	3	Withdrew more than we added
	13	Larger amount because we had not included postcards last year
	19	bibliographic utilities $11800 memberships with periodicals 400
	37	Reference desk and Circulation desk
	41	About 80 per week
	Trends Note	No 12-14 cannot be answered. Our machinery does not keep track No 15 At this time do not take part in virtual visits etc No 18-19 We do not have any digital collections
Simpson C IA	Trends Note	"encyclopedias
Skidmore C	31	software only
	37	Circulation Desk Reference Desk
	Trends Note	#7 & 8 =#6 16 b & c Visual Resources Collection #17 Estimate 18b Estimate
Southrn C Opt	1A	Adjusted up from last year's figure by 314 volumes not included on last survey
Southrn IL U Edward	30B	-1 (NA)
Southrn OR U	26	"$380
	33	Really 12.5 with the .5 paid with IMLS grant funds.
	Trends Note	16b. No.of GB not megabytes. 18a. Includes OPE. 16.So. Or. Digital Archives contains 2 collections: Bioregion and First Nations. Both are available at: soda.sou.edu. The Bioregi collection contains federal & state pubs. pertaining to the So. Oregon reg
Southwest U	27	Employee fringe benefits are paid from the library budget.
Spartan Aero-Flight Schl	31	This figure is low but I can only report what I know I have been involved with. We have be unable to get records from the financial dept.
	46	No Ph.D.'s Degrees offered.
	48	This does not reflect the on-call instructors.
	49	This is the Fall 2003 count.
	50	This is not applicable.
	51	This is not applicable.
	52	This is not applicable.
Spring Hill C	30B	Information not available.
	31	Not part of the Library budget
	42	Not available
	Trends Note	N0t digitizing at present. virtual Data collection unavailable.
St Ambrose U	32	ILL postage expense is not included because it is applied at a University central site and integrated with all other library postage expense.

Institution	Q. No	Note
St Ambrose U	42	New library automated system acquired and started midyear. Circulation report without renewals was not provided by new system.
St Andrews Presby C	1A	Volumes and Electronic Books
	Survey Note	FY ends May 31st
St C.Borromeo Sem	1A	Last year's figure included microforms and AV
	5	"Added Atlas
St Cloud ST U	Trends Note	"#10 - Virtual reference service started in February 2004. #15b - Due to migration to a new library system
St Francis-Xavier U	49	ß
St John Fisher C	5	Print and microform subscriptions.
	18	AV only. Microforms cannot be disaggregated from periodicals.
	19	Electronic databases and miscellaneous.
	25	Includes fringe benefits.
	49	Fall 2003 FTE (all students) 2669 Undergrad FTE 2329 Grad FTE 340
	53	System counted items in collection.
	Trends Note	I don't have most of these stats you are requesting.
St John Vianney C Sem	23	"One support staff's library degree is from Chile and has not been validated
St Joseph C Suffolk	5	Includes only print subscriptions and individual electronic titles. Does not include number of titles in aggregated databases.
	14	"32 is the total held and refers to titles
	15	"Refers to titles
	17	"Includes: $28
	29	"Includes: Individual Electronic Journal Titles
	49	"In error
	Trends Note	"Responses to questions 12
St Joseph's C NY	11	1foot=52 pieces
	19	"33
	48	Total faculty includes both campuses - Brooklyn and Patchogue.
	Trends Note	I have spent a good deal of time attempting to answer the questions in Trends. It is very difficult dealing with multiple vendors and databases to figure out what the questions are and how to answer them and to separate expenses in so many categories..
St Joseph's Sem	2A	These volumes from an off-campus collection.
St Meinrad Theo	4	ca. 80 percent
St Michael's C	4	Number of monographic TITLES purchased.
	19	Document Delivery/Interlibrary Loan: $13631
St Norbert C	29	includes question 28
	37	Circulation Desk Reference Desk Reserves Desk
	Trends Note	Question 6: This is our database expenditure. Question 16: Our digital collection is a group of scanned photographs from our archives. Question 18a: Our photographs have been scanned by volunteers. Question 18b: No new software or equipment was pur
St Olaf C	Trends Note	"#1 We do not purchase electronic journals separately - only when included in a database or collection. #5 NetLibrary through Minitex. #12a and 13a Vendor
St Patrick's Sem	38	"Library is open to students and staff 24 hours per day
	Survey Note	"The figures do not include a special collection which is housed in the library but not owned by the library. This collection is owned by the Archives of the Archdiocese of San Francisco
St Peter's Abbey & C	Survey Note	Fiscal year ends April 30.
ST U W GA	19	"$8
St. Mary's C Maryland	5	"Includes print
	30A	OCLC
	31	Includes library and media hardware and software and LIS maintenance
	33	"Includes one digital media specialist
	43	Reflects library items circulated at any circulation point in 16-member academic library consortium.
Sterling C-VT	26	Postage -- 362 Telephone -- 5 Memberships -- 219 Copier -- 196 Prof Meetings -- 43 Tech Support -- 480 Supplies -- 432

Institution	Q. No	Note
Sterling C-VT	31	Tech support for Follett library software
	38	Whole library is open 24/7 for students
	Trends Note	"Questions regarding sessions
Stetson U	1A	"Federal documents historically counted as 2.5 docs/vol. Totals do not include minimal-le cataloged documents
	4	"Titles
	5	"Includes full text journals from aggregators which we add to our All Journals page - excl Lexis-Nexis
	14	Does not include 601 locally produced compact disk recordings of local recitals which are minimally cataloged
	18	Incl. non-journal online resources
	22	Excl. fringe benefits
	23	Excl. fringe benefits
	25	Excl. fringe benefits
	27	Excl. personnel fringe benefits
	30B	"We have access to several First Search databases through the State of Florida Library
	53	Except for Federal documents
	Survey Note	"Fiscal year is June 1
	Trends Note	"Fiscal year June 1
Stonehill C	2	includes gov documents added to the online catalog
	7	Included gov doc serials
	8	includes gov documents
	27	"Excludes fringe benefits
	42	Includes renewals. Currently unable to pull from circulation data.
	Trends Note	"I do not understand the breakdown for electronic resources (journals
Sul Ross ST U	18	Microform and a/v cannot be totally disaggtregated so are included in 16 and 17 above.
	19	Electronic subscriptions
	22	Media Center and Systems employees moved to OIT -- one unfilled Librarian position
	23	Media Center and Systems employees moved to OIT
	24	Media Center and Systems student employees moved to OIT
	26	Media Center and Systems M&O moved to OIT
	33	Media Center and System staff moved to OIT. One Frozen Librarian Position.
	34	Media Center and System staff moved to OIT.
	35	Media Center and System student moved to OIT.
	37	Media Center moved to OIT
	50	Unavailable
	52	Unavailable
SUNY Brockport	1	Figure is that reported in other reports
	1A	"Figures were to be taken from last year's report. We could not find the report
	Trends Note	"For items 12-15 above
SUNY Buffalo	18	"Includes curriculum materials
	19	"Includes document delivery
	26	"Includes service and maintenance contracts
	39	Includes library courses offered for credit
	40	Includes students enrolled in library courses offered for credit
	41	Includes only questions asked at the Reference Desk; does not include questions asked a other service points not computer questions
SUNY C Potsdam	19	This is the total amount from lines 28-32.
	Trends Note	"#2: Cannot provide this
SUNY IT Utica	28	Included with monograph total
	30A	"NYLINK
	31	Hardware purchase and LMS maintenance fee

Institution	Q. No	Note
SUNY IT Utica	32	ILL and delivery charges
	40	20 students per class
	42	statistics do not allow for counting initial charge out.
	Trends Note	Data for accessing electronic resources is incomplete or limited in how to extract relative information. Questions 12-15
SUNY Oswego	Trends Note	"We made an attempt to fill out the Metrics portion of the survey
Swarthmore C	6	Gov Doc serials
	30A	"The survey says this data should be from question 26
	Trends Note	"Question 15- the number here is the number of visits to the a page on the library site listing all available databases. Users can access library resources from many locations and do not necessarily start at the library home page
Sweet Briar C	1	Figure of 266064 reported last year included an estimate of bound journal volumes since corrected to actual figures for 2004 year end. Science Branch was also in process of closing and all volumes were counted in report but many withdrawn between May an
	1A	Figure of 266064 reported last year included an estimate of bound journal volumes since corrected to actual figures for 2004 year end. Science Branch was also in process of closing and all volumes were counted in report but many withdrawn between May an
SWstrn Adventist U	29	An estimate.
	30B	An estimate.
	39	An estimate.
	40	An estimate.
	41	An estimate.
Tabor C	1	Line 1 based on an estimate
	1A	61518 non-av materials in OPAC. Estimated 19000 items on shelves which are not yet in the OPAC
	11	We also hold county records which make up 318 linear feet.
	16	includes AV materials -- could not split out for this year. I will in the future.
	Trends Note	I am frustrated by the lack of representation for aggregated databases. We use aggregated databases almost exclusively for access to journal material. According to your counts our numbers show about 23 total electronic journals purchased (poor choice of
Talladega C	30A	Reported in #26
	31	Reported in #21
	38	Extended 1.6 hours during finals
	50	No part-time or graduate
Teikyo Post U	2A	Weeding of cataloged government documents;finished inventory--purged missing materials files.
	30A	Institutional capital expense
	30B	Nelinet
	31	Institutional capital expense
Tiffin U	Trends Note	Are numbers of OPAL and OhioLink. Many of these statistics (questions 10-19) are not available.
TM Cooley Law Sch	4	This figure represents titles.
	19	"Computer databases
	49	Thomas M Cooley is a Law School only. we have no undergraduates
	50	Thomas M Cooley is a Law School only. we have no undergraduates
	51	Includes both JD and LLM (Masters of Law) students.
	52	Includes both JD and LLM (Masters of Law) students.
	55	Fringe Benefit figure is included in Question 26 - Other operating expenses
	56	We are only a Law Library
Tri ST U	1	"Held May 31
	1A	"Held May 31
	8	Includes 46760 uncataloged fiche
	19	E-book consortial purchase
	30B	Unknown
	32	Also reported 30a

Institution	Q. No	Note
Trinity C DC	30B	estimate
	Trends Note	#1 Number reported was generated from database title counts which most likely contain duplication
Trinity Luth Sem	49	Not Available
	50	Not Available
	51	Full-time equivalents
	52	Not Available
Trinity U	Trends Note	Cover page http://digitalcommons.trinity.edu
Troy ST U	Trends Note	"# 1
Truett McConnell C	Trends Note	Electronic resources in library collection are not ableto be counted in this manner.
TX Lutheran U	1A	Our fiscal year ends May 31
	8	estimate - method of counting was changed
	9	all are counted in #1 or #8
	22	salaries are reported on calendar year exact figures for FY not available
	23	same as above
	42	we do not separate figures for initial charges and renewals
	54	some of them are
	Trends Note	Q6-9 each contains $6500 TexShare consortium fee
U Arts	4	Titles
	49	2058 is the number of FTE. I am waiting on the numbers exactly as they are requested on form.
	51	139 is the number of FTE. I am waiting on the numbers exactly as they are requested on form.
U Charleston	48	FTE figure.
U DC	15	these are media materials in all formats.
U Del Turabo	Trends Note	Use of networked electronic resource based on a sample of 33 databases. Library Digitiz Activities not yet available.
U Houston	1	31-Aug-04
	1A	"Volumes held August 31
U Maine - Machias	41	"estimated at 6 questions per day X 330 days open (as noted above
U Mary	3	We did some extensive weeding
U MI Dearborn	30A	BY04 contract wasn't paid until BY05.
	31	Contract was paid for two-years in BY04 in error. So this is double our usual charge.
	Trends Note	"13(a) electronic journal databases
U NE Kearney	19	Memberships only
	Trends Note	"For 15a
U Portland	Trends Note	Q1--estimate Q6-9--figure cannot be separated from larger expenditures for e-resources
U Richmond	17	"Includes all electronic resources
	29	includes all electronic formats and includes both one-time and subscription purchases; als included in response to line 17
	31	"computer hardware and software is paid out of Information Services budget
	33	Includes one position paid for by an IMLS grant
U Scranton	5	Print subscriptions. Print titles have been canceled to get fulltext online.
	27	"With fringes $2
	31	"Computers in the Library are purchased by the Information Resources budget
	Trends Note	"Virtual visits to Library's website refer only to home page and not to catalog
U TN Martin	5	This figure relects 04 conversion of approximately 30 ACS (Chemistry) journals from print electronic access.
	14	"Our response for fiscal 03 neglected to report phonorecordings
	15	Much of our current growth in media is in the area of DVD's.
	17	This reflects 04 transfer of $28738 from periodicals to database expenditures when library' American Chemical Society journals were switched from print-based to online access.
	30A	Includes charges for SOLINET and Ariel.

Institution	Q. No	Note
TN Martin	30B	Estimated value of various databases received through state Tenn-Share network.
	31	"Includes Innovative maintenance charges + all staff and service desk computer replacements and software. As instructed
	35	Note: Last year the total number of student workers were reported rather than FTE students. This error was corrected for the 2004 survey.
TX Tyler	17	"Includes database expenditures (see Q.29
	29	Also included in Q.17
	38	Hours expanded to 85.5 during Fall 04
	41	University enrollment growth of 68% since 2000 so increased Reference transactions.
	42	Migrated to new library system during this time--stats unavailable
VA C Wise	1A	Adjusted
	Trends Note	Question 15B refers to number of visits from sites outside of Library.
WI E Claire	28	"We don't have a seperate budget line for these
	30B	Cannot be calculated accurately; dollar value shown is for our state consortial arrangement
	Trends Note	"Many of the statistics asked for in this collection are not ones the library currently collects and it's difficult to calculate them
WI La Crosse	Trends Note	"University of Wisconsin Digital Collections digitizes
Winnipeg	Survey Note	"Figures based on a fiscal year ending March 31
US Merchant Marine Acad	1	"Fiscal year ended Sept. 30
	Survey Note	Fiscal year runs from October 1st to September 30th.
US Naval Acad	1	"As of Sept. 30
	1A	"As of September 30
	27	Not including fringe benefits or computer maintenance.
UT Valley ST C	16	Includes expenditures for new cartographic materials.
Valparaiso U	Trends Note	"It is very difficult to measure the database statistics because different vendors calculate those statistics differently
Vassar C	4	figure for titles
	Trends Note	4. E-boooks are not included 7. does not include electronic formats that come with print subscriptions
Villa Julie C	16	This year's figure reflects a more accurate picture due to improved accuracy in our Acquisitions work flow.
	31	Most other computer purchases are paid for by a non-library budget line.
	32	Photocopy costs not included.
	41	We are receiving more requests for reference help via email and Reference Chat. The figure reported does not relect Virtual Transactions.
	Trends Note	"The College recently switched to a new web system
VMI	24	This is for summer student workers - Student workers are not paid out of library funds during regular school year
	30A	There is a 0 balance because SOLINET as paid out of previous fiscal yeara budget from surplus money at end of year.
W.Carey College	22	That information is not available to me separated from support staff.
	23	That information is not available to me separated from professional staff
	25	Salaries for professional staff and support staff is $240191.
	43	Cannot separate renewals from initial circulations.
W.Mitchell C Law	4	titles
	19	oclc = 12000;educational software=420;document delivery=1
	56	We are a free standing law school
	Trends Note	We track searches on our catalog (29516) but not visits to the catalog.
Walla Walla C	4	"This is a title count
	Trends Note	17a is the number of times accessed within the last 90 days. 2/18/05
Walsh C Acct Bus Admin	26	Part-time librarians
	38	80 hours at main branch 34 hours at campus branch
	Trends Note	We are migrating more to electronic reference sources

Institution	Q. No	Note
Warner Sthrn C	Trends Note	THE EXPENDITURE TOTALS FOR QUESTIONS 7 AND 8 ARE INCLUDED IN THE TO EXPENDITURES FOR CURRENT ELECTRONIC JOURNALS PURCHASED LISTED IN QUESTION 6.
Warren Wilson C	1A	did not report last year
	4	This number is an estimate since we do not keep this statistic.
	9	we do not keep this statistic
	10	these are unique full text titles
	11	not available
	12	we do not have
	13	we do not have
	22	includes support staff
	23	is included in 22
	28	we do not keep this statistic
	31	not purchased from library budget
	37	Circulation Reference Archives
	42	we do not keep this statistic
	50	we do not keep this statistic
	52	we do not keep this statistic
Washington C	17	backfiles are included
	18	microforms only. A/V included in monographs expenditure
	23	professional and non-professional included
	31	IT Department takes care of network maintainance
	41	e-mail queries included
	Trends Note	We did not have enough detailed statistics to accurately complete this section.
Washington Theo Union	46	Institution does not offer Ph.D.s
	49	WTU is a graduate school only.
Wayne ST C	15	Total of all AV Materials
Wesley C	22	Only have aggregrate salary figures. No breakdown by category of employee.
West Chester U PA	Trends Note	"Q. 4 Includes E-books. Q 12a: Includes E-Jrnl Aggregators - E*Subscribe
West TX A & M U	6	"Includes approximtely 7
	Trends Note	"Q. 4. ebooks are not included in the total. Q. 12.
West VA Wesleyan C	2A	Includes purge of 'missing book' records as well as discards.
	5	We have no mechanism for counting titles in electronic aggregate packages.
	9	"We have a small
Western OR U	4	Titles
	Trends Note	We do not collected statistics in many of these areas at this time.
Western Sem	1A	"The figure for June 30
	8	We don't count book units: We have 26674 vols of books; Periodicals: 1257 reels (3492 vc and 28893 sheets (3614 vols)
Western WA U	4	"Represents titles
	5	Includes some 'bundled' purchases.
Westfield ST C	Trends Note	"12a
Wheeling Jesuit U	19	Put aggregated databases here for lack of knowing where else to put them.
	39	Restructuring & hiring freeze--no library instructional services in 03-04.
Whitworth C	18	Microforms included in line 17.
	Trends Note	Ebooks not included in Q4
William Woods U	2	Includes acquisition of 9339 e-books
	4	Includes 9339 e-books
	19	Bib Util - $5599 Doc Del- $2295
	Trends Note	Question 15 is difficult to answer with any degree of accuracy because our library shares a catalog with a cluster of libraries within a statewide catalog and a visit to our library's catalo subset is difficult to determine because of the multiple ways i
Williams C	16	Includes computer files and e-books

Institution	Q. No	Note
Williams C	17	Includes electronic subscriptions
	Trends Note	19. Shared storage institued in FY '05.
Wofford C	4	We do not separate purchased from gift additions in our accounting.
Wstrn Theo Sem	26	contract for archival services
Xavier U LA	5	Includes electronic serial subscriptions
	24	Students paid through a federal grant program that is not part of the library's budget.
	29	This does not include e-serials that come as part of the subscription price for print serials.
	42	Figure for initial circulations not known due to software problem.
	Trends Note	"We did not begin electronic reference service until 2004-05. Up until now
York C	1	This figure includes 13668 electronic books and 40198 electronic government documents.
	1A	This figure contains 4073 electronic book and 1350 electronic government documents.
	2	This figure includes 9595 electronic books and 38848 electronic government documents.
	3	This figure includes 9595 electronic books and 38848 electronic government documents.
	16	"This figure includes $1375 for government documents
	19	Bibliographic utilities $4626.
	30B	Paid for by Nebraska Library Commission.
	34	A half-time person in audio-visual department.
	43	We checked books out for five weeks and did not renew them.

KEY TO PARTICIPATING INSTITUTIONS

Institution	Full Name of Institution	Location	Ca Cla
A Baldwin Agrl C	Abraham Baldwin Abricultural College	Tifton, GA	A
AB C Art & Design	Alberta College of Art & Design	Calgary, AB	B
Abilene Christian U	Abilene Christian University	Abilene, TX	M
Adelphi U	Adelphi University	Garden City, NY	D
Adrian C	Adrian College	Adrian, MI	B
Agnes Scott C	Agnes Scott College	Atlanta/Decatur, GA	M
Aiken Tech C	Aiken Technical College	Aiken, SC	A
Albany C Pharmacy	Albany College of Pharmacy	Albany, NY	M
Albany Law Schl Union U	Albany Law School	Albany, NY	M
Albion C	Albion College	Albion, MI	B
Alcorn ST U	Alcorn State University	Lorman, MS	M
Alfred U-Herrick	Alfred University	Alfred, NY	D
Algonqn C Appl A&T	Algonquin College Applied Arts and Technology	Nepean, ON	A
Alliant Intl U	Alliant International University-Los Angeles	Alhambra, CA	D
Alliant Intl U-San Dieg	Alliant International University-San Diego	San Diego, CA	D
Alvin CC	Alvin Community College	Alvin, TX	A
Amer Intl C	American International College	Springfield, MA	M
Amer U Puerto Rico	American University of Puerto Rico	Bayamon, PR	M
American River C	American River College	Sacramento, CA	A
Amherst C	Amherst College	Amherst, MA	B
Anderson U	Anderson University	Anderson, IN	M
Andover C	Andover College	Portland, ME	A
Angelo ST U	Angelo State University	San Angelo, TX	M
Anne Arundel CC	Anne Arundel Community College	Arnold, MD	A
Anoka Ramsey C C	Anoka Ramsey Community College Coon Rapids Campus	Coon Rapids, MN	A
Aquinas C MI	Aquinas College	Grand Rapids, MI	M
Aquinas C TN	Aquinas College	Nashville, TN	B
AR ST U Beebe	Arkansas State University Beebe	Beebe, AR	A
Arizona State U	Arizona State University	Tempe, AZ	D
Ark Tech U	Arkansas Tech University	Russellville, AR	M
Armstrong Atlantic ST U	Armstrong Atlantic State University	Savannah, GA	M
Ashland U	Ashland University	Ashland, OH	D
Assemblies of God Theo Sem	Assemblies of God Theological Seminary	Springfield, MO	M
Assumption C	Assumption College	Worcester, MA	M
Athenaeum of Ohio	Athenaeum of Ohio	Cincinnati, OH	M
Atlanta C Art	Atlanta College of Art	Atlanta, GA	B
Atlanta Christian C	Atlanta Christian College	East Point, GA	B
Auburn U	Auburn University	Auburn, Al	D
Auburn U Montgomery	Auburn University at Montgomery	Montgomery, AL	M
Augusta ST U	Augusta State University	Augusta, GA	M
Augustana C RI	Augustana College	Rock Island, IL	B

A=Associates   B=Bachelors   M=Masters   D=Doctorate

KEY TO PARTICIPATING INSTITUTIONS

Institution	Full Name of Institution	Location	Carnegie Class
Augustana C SF	Augustana College	Sioux Falls, SD	M
Austin C	Austin College	Sherman, TX	M
Austin Presb Theo Sem	Austin Presbyterian Theological Seminary	Austin, TX	M
Averett C	Averett University	Danville, VA	M
AZ Western C	Arizona Western College	Yuma, AZ	A
Azusa Pacific U	Azusa Pacific University	Azusa, CA	D
Babson C	Babson College	Babson Park, MA	M
Bacone C	Bacone College	Muskogee, OK	A
Bainbridge C	Bainbridge College	Bainbridge, GA	A
Baker C	Baker College	Flint, MI	M
Baker U	Baker University	Baldwin City, KS	M
Baptist Bible C and Graduate Schoc	Baptist Bible College and Graduate School	Springfield, MO	M
Barber-Scotia C	Barber-Scotia College	Concord, NC	B
Bard C	Bard College	Annandale-On-Hudson	B
Barry U	Barry University	Miami Shores, FL	D
Barton C	Barton College	Wilson, NC	B
Bates C	Bates College	Lewiston, ME	B
Bayamon Central U	Bayamon Central University	Bayamon, PR	M
Baylor U	Baylor University	Waco, TX	D
Bellevue U	Bellevue University	Bellevue, NE	M
Bellingham Tech C	Bellingham Technical College	Bellingham, WA	A
Belmont Tech C	Belmont Technical College	Saint Clairsville,	A
Belmont U	Belmont University	Nashville, TN	D
Benedict C	Benedict College	Columbia, SC	B
Benedictine U	Benedictine University	Lisle, IL	D
Bennington C	Bennington College	Bennington, VT	M
Bergen CC	Bergen Community College	Paramus, NJ	A
Berry C	Berry College	Mount Berry, GA	B
Bethany C Bethany	Bethany College	Bethany, WV	B
Bethany C Lindsborg	Bethany College	Lindsborg, KS	B
Bethel C IN	Bethel College	Mishawaka, IN	M
Bethel C KS	Bethel College	North Newton, KS	B
Biola U	Biola University	La Mirada, CA	D
Birmingham Southern C	Birmingham-Southern College	Birmingham, AL	M
Black Hawk C	Black Hawk College	Moline, IL	A
Blackburn C	Blackburn College	Carlinville, IL	B
Blessed John XXIII National Sem	Blessed John XXIII National Seminary	Weston, MA	M
Blue Mountain CC	Blue Mountain Community College	Pendleton, OR	A
Blue Ridge CC	Blue Ridge Community College	Weyers Cave, VA	A
Bluefield C	Bluefield College	Bluefield, VA	B
Bluffton C	Bluffton University	Bluffton, OH	M

A=Associates   B=Bachelors   M=Masters   D=Doctorate

KEY TO PARTICIPATING INSTITUTIONS

Institution	Full Name of Institution	Location	Carnegie Class
Boise Bible C	Boise Bible College	Boise, ID	B
Boise ST U	Boise State University	Boise, ID	D
Boston C	Boston College	Chestnut Hill, MA	D
Bowdoin C	Bowdoin College	Brunswick, ME	B
BowlGrn SU Fireld	Bowling Green State University Firelands College	Huron, OH	M
Bradley U	Bradley University	Peoria, IL	M
Brandeis U	Brandeis University	Waltham, MA	D
Brazosport C	Brazosport College	Lake Jackson, TX	A
Brescia U	Brescia University	Owensboro, KY	M
Bridgewater C	Bridgewater College	Bridgewater, VA	B
Brigham Young U	Brigham Young University	Provo, UT	D
Brookdale CC	Brookdale Community College	Lincroft, NJ	A
Brooklyn Law School	Brooklyn Law School	Brooklyn, NY	D
Brooks Institute	Brooks Institute of Photography	Santa Barbara, CA	M
Broward CC	Broward Community College	Davie, FL	A
Brown U	Brown University	Providence, RI	D
Bryan C	Bryan College	Dayton, TN	B
Bryn Athyn C New Church	Bryn Athyn College of the New Church	Bryn Athyn, PA	M
Bryn Mawr C	Bryn Mawr College	Bryn Mawr, PA	D
Buena Vista U	Buena Vista University Library	Storm Lake, IA	M
Bunker Hill CC	Bunker Hill Community College	Boston, MA	A
Butler U	Butler University	Indianapolis, IN	M
C Atlantic	College of the Atlantic	Bar Harbor, ME	M
C Holy Cross	College of the Holy Cross	Worcester, MA	B
C Mainland	College of the Mainland	Texas City, TX	A
C Merici	Collège Mérici	Quebec, QC	A
C Mt St Joseph	College of Mount Saint Joseph	Cincinnati, OH	M
C New Caledonia	College of New Caledonia	Prince George, BC	A
C of Mount St. Vincent	College of Mount Saint Vincent	Riverdale, NY	M
C of Southern Idaho	College of Southern Idaho	Twin Falls, ID	A
C Our Lady Elms	College of Our Lady of the Elms	Chicopee, MA	M
C Redwoods	College of the Redwoods	Eureka, CA	A
C Visual Arts	College of Visual Arts	St. Paul, MN	B
C William & Mary	College of William and Mary	Williamsburg, VA	D
C Wooster	The College of Wooster	Wooster, OH	B
C.R. Drew U Med & Sci	Charles R. Drew University of Medicine and Science	Los Angeles, CA	M
CA Prof Psych Berkeley	Alliant International University-Berkeley/Alameda	Alameda, CA	D
CA St Polytechnic U-Pom	California State Polytechnic University-Pomona	Pomona, CA	M
CA St U - Sacramento	California State University-Sacramento	Sacramento, CA	M
CA ST U Dominguez Hills	California State University-Dominguez Hills	Carson, CA	M
CA ST U Fresno	California State University-Fresno	Fresno, CA	M

A=Associates   B=Bachelors   M=Masters   D=Doctorate

254

KEY TO PARTICIPATING INSTITUTIONS

Institution	Full Name of Institution	Location	Carnegie Class
CA ST U Fullerton	California State University-Fullerton	Fullerton, CA	M
CA ST U Hayward	California State University-Hayward	Hayward, CA	M
CA ST U Long Beach	California State University-Long Beach	Long Beach, CA	M
CA ST U Northridge	California State University-Northridge	Northridge, CA	M
CA ST U S Bernadino	California State University-San Bernardino	San Bernardino, CA	M
CA ST U San Marcos	California State University-San Marcos	San Marcos, CA	M
CA ST U Stanislaus	California State University, Stanislaus	Turlock, CA	M
CA West Sch Law	California Western School of Law	San Diego, CA	M
California C Arts	California College Of The Arts	Oakland, CA	M
Calvin C	Calvin College	Grand Rapids, MI	M
Camden County C	Camden County College	Blackwood, NJ	A
Cameron U	Cameron University	Lawton, OK	M
Campion C	Campion College	Regina, SK	B
Cape Cod CC	Cape Cod Community College	West Barnstable, MA	A
Cape Fear CC	Cape Fear Community College	Wilmington, NC	A
Capital CC	Capital Community College	Hartford, CT	A
Carl Sandburg C	Carl Sandburg College	Galesburg, IL	A
Carlow C	Carlow University	Pittsburgh, PA	M
Carnegie Mellon U	Carnegie Mellon University	Pittsburgh, PA	D
Carroll C-Helena	Carroll College	Helena, MT	B
Carroll C-Waukesha	Carroll College	Waukesha, WI	M
Carteret CC	Carteret Community College	Morehead City, NC	A
Case Western Reserve U	Case Western Reserve University	Cleveland, OH	D
Catholic U Am	The Catholic University of America	Washington, DC	D
Cazenovia C	Cazenovia College	Cazenovia, NY	B
CC Allegheny Co-Alleghe	Community College of Allegheny County Allegheny Campus	Pittsburgh, PA	A
CC Allegheny Co-Boyce	Community College of Allegheny County Boyce Campus	Monroeville, PA	A
CC of Baltimore Co-Dundalk	The Community College of Baltimore County-Dundalk Campus	Baltimore, MD	A
Cedar Crest C	Cedar Crest college	Allentown, PA	M
Cedar Valley	Cedar Valley College	Lancaster, TX	A
Cedarville U	Cedarville University	Cedarville, OH	M
CEGEP Beauce-Appalaches	CEGEP de Beauce-Appalaches	Saint-Georges, QC	A
CEGEP Chicoutimi	CEGEP de Chicoutimi	Chicoutimi, QC	A
Centenary C	Centenary College	Hackettstown, NJ	M
Centenary C LA	Centenary College of Louisiana	Shreveport, LA	M
Centennial C	Centennial College	Scarborough, ON	B
Central Alabama C C	Central Alabama Community College	Alexander City, AL	A
Central Baptist C	Central Baptist College	Conway, AR	M
Central Bible C	Central Bible College	Springfield, MO	B
Central C	Central College	Pella, IA	B
Central Christian C Bib	Central Christian College of the Bible	Moberly, MO	B

A=Associates   B=Bachelors   M=Masters   D=Doctorate

255

KEY TO PARTICIPATING INSTITUTIONS

Institution	Full Name of Institution	Location	Carnegie Class
Central CT ST U	Central Connecticut State University	New Britain, CT	M
Central MI U	Central Michigan University	Mount Pleasant, MI	D
Central MO ST U	Central Missouri State University	Warrensburg, MO	M
Central OR CC	Central Oregon Community College	Bend, OR	A
Centralia C	Centralia College	Centralia, WA	A
Centre C	Centre College	Danville, KY	B
Charleston Sthrn U	Charleston Southern University	Charleston, SC	M
Chatfield C	Chatfield College	Saint Martin, OH	A
Chatt St Tech CC	Chattanooga State Technical Community College	Chattanooga, TN	A
Chattahoochee Tech	Chattahoochee Technical College	Marietta, GA	A
Chicago ST U	Chicago State University	Chicago, IL	M
Chippewa V Tech C	Chippewa Valley Technical College	Eau Claire, WI	A
Chris Newport U	Christopher Newport University	Newport News, VA	M
Christendom C	Christendom College	Front Royal, VA	M
Christian Brothers U	Christian Brothers University	Memphis, TN	M
Christian Heritage C	Christian Heritage College	El Cajon, CA	B
Clackamas CC	Clackamas Community College	Oregon City, OR	A
Clarion U PA	Clarion University of Pennsylvania	Clarion, PA	M
Clarke C-IA	Clarke College	Dubuque, IA	M
Clarkson C-NE	Clarkson College	Omaha, NE	M
Clarkson U-NY	Clarkson University	Potsdam, NY	D
Clear Creek Bible	Clear Creek Baptist Bible College	Pineville, KY	B
Cleveland ST U	Cleveland State University	Cleveland, OH	D
Clovis CC	Clovis Community College	Clovis, NM	A
Coastal GA CC	Coastal Georgia Community College	Brunswick, GA	A
Colby C	Colby College	Waterville, ME	B
Colby-Sawyer C	Colby-Sawyer College	New London, NH	B
Colorado C	Colorado College	Colorado Springs, C	M
Colorado Northwestern C C	Colorado Northwestern Community College	Rangely, CO	A
Columbia C CA	Columbia College	Sonora, CA	A
Columbia C MO	Columbia College	Columbia, MO	M
Columbia C SC	Columbia College	Columbia, SC	M
Columbia Intl U	Columbia International University	Columbia, SC	M
Columbia ST CC	Columbia State Community College	Columbia, TN	A
Columbia U	Columbia University	New York, NY	D
Columbia Union C	Columbia Union College	Takoma Park, MD	B
Columbus ST U	Columbus State University	Columbus, GA	M
Concordia C	Concordia College-Moorhead	Moorhead, MN	B
Concordia C-NY	Concordia College	Bronxville, NY	B
Concordia Theo Sem	Concordia Theological Seminary	Fort Wayne, IN	D
Concordia U	Concordia University	Seward, NE	M

A=Associates   B=Bachelors   M=Masters   D=Doctorate

256

KEY TO PARTICIPATING INSTITUTIONS

Institution	Full Name of Institution	Location	Carnegie Class
Concordia U Irvine	Concordia University	Irvine, CA	M
Concordia U St Paul	Concordia University, St. Paul	Saint Paul, MN	M
Concordia U-QC	Concordia University	Montreal, QC	D
Connors ST C	Connors State College	Warner, OK	A
Cooper Union	Cooper Union	New York, NY	M
Cornell U	Cornell University	Ithaca, NY	D
Cornell U Med	Cornell University	New York, NY	D
Cornerstone U	Cornerstone University	Grand Rapids, MI	M
Cornish C Arts	Cornish College of the Arts	Seattle, WA	B
Cosumnes River C	Cosumnes River College	Sacramento, CA	A
Creighton U	Creighton University	Omaha, NE	M
Crichton C	Crichton College Library	Memphis, TN	B
Crowder C	Crowder College	Neosho, MO	A
Crown C-MN	Crown College	St. Bonifacius, MN	B
Cuesta C	Cuesta College Library	San Luis Obispo, CA	A
Culver Stockton C	Culver-Stockton College	Canton, MO	B
Cumberland Co C	Cumberland County College	Vineland, NJ	A
Cumberland U	Cumberland University	Lebanon, TN	M
CUNY BMB C	City University of New York Bernard M. Baruch College	New York, NY	M
CUNY Borough Manhattan	City University of New York Borough of Manhattan Communi	New York, NY	A
CUNY C Stn Island	City University of New York College of Staten Island	Staten Island, NY	M
CUNY City C	City University of New York City College	New York, NY	M
CUNY Grad Ctr	City University of New York Graduate Center	New York, NY	D
CUNY HH Lehman C	City University of New York Herbert H. Lehman College	Bronx, NY	M
CUNY John Jay C Criminal Justice	City University of New York John Jay College of Criminal Justice	New York, NY	M
CUNY LaGuardia CC	City University of New York,La Guardia Community Colleg	Long Island City, N	A
CUNY NYC Tech C	New York City College of Technology (City University of	Brooklyn, NY	B
CUNY Queens C	City University of New York Queens College	Flushing, NY	M
CUNY Queensborough CC	City University of New York Queensborough Community Coll	Bayside, NY	A
CUNY York C	City University of New York York College	Jamaica, NY	B
Curtis Inst Music	Curtis Institute of Music	Philadelphia, PA	M
Cuyamaca C	Cuyamaca College	El Cajon, CA	A
Dakota Wesleyan U	Dakota Wesleyan University	Mitchell, SD	B
Dana C	Dana College	Blair, NE	B
Daniel Webster C	Daniel Webster College	Nashua, NH	M
Darton C	Darton College	Albany, GA	A
Davidson C	Davidson College	Davidson, NC	B
Davidson Cnty CC	Davidson County Community College	Lexington, NC	A
DE Tech CC Stanton	Delaware Technical and Community College	Newark, DE	A
Dean C	Dean College	Franklin, MA	B
Defiance C	The Defiance College	Defiance, OH	B

A=Associates   B=Bachelors   M=Masters   D=Doctorate

257

KEY TO PARTICIPATING INSTITUTIONS

Institution	Full Name of Institution	Location	Campus Class
Del Mar C	Del Mar College	Corpus Christi, TX	A
Delaware County C C	Delaware County Community College	Media, PA	A
Delta C	Delta College	University Center,	A
Delta ST U	Delta State University	Cleveland, MS	D
Denison U	Denison University	Granville, OH	B
DePaul U	DePaul University	Chicago, IL	D
DeSales U	DeSales University	Center Valley, PA	M
DeVry IT-Chicago	DeVry University	Oakbrook Terrace, I	B
Dickinson ST U	Dickinson State University	Dickinson, ND	B
Divine Word C	Divine Word College	Epworth, IA	B
DN Myers C	David N. Myers University	Cleveland, OH	M
Dodge City CC	Dodge City Community College	Dodge City, KS	A
Dominican C San Rafael	Dominican University of San Rafael	San Rafael, CA	M
Dominican U	Dominican University	River Forest, IL	M
Drake U	Drake University	Des Moines, IA	M
Drexel MCPH	Drexel University Libraries	Philadelphia, PA	D
Drury C	Drury University	Springfield, MO	M
Duke U	Duke University	Durham, NC	D
Dyersburg ST CC	Dyersburg State Community College	Dyersburg, TN	A
E R Aero U	Embry Riddle Aeronautical University	Daytona Beach, FL	M
Earlham C	Earlham College	Richmond, IN	M
East Central C	East Central College	Union, MO	A
East Georgia C	East Georgia College	Swainsboro, GA	A
East Los Angeles C	East Los Angeles College	Monterey Park, CA	A
East Tenn ST U	East Tennessee State University	Johnson City, TN	D
East Texas Baptist U	East Texas Baptist University	Marshall, TX	B
Eastern IL U	Eastern Illinois University	Charleston, IL	M
Eastern Michigan U	Eastern Michigan University	Ypsilanti, MI	D
Eastern U	Eastern University	St Davids, PA	M
Eastern WA U	Eastern Washington University	Cheney, WA	M
Eastrn NM U Main	Eastern New Mexico University Main Campus	Portales, NM	M
Eckerd C	Eckerd College	Saint Petersburg, F	B
Ecole Polytech Mtl	Ecole polytechnique de Montreal	Montreal, QC	D
Eden Theo Sem	Webster University and Eden Theological Seminary	Webster Groves, MO	D
Edinboro U PA	Edinboro University of Pennsylvania	Edinboro, PA	M
Elizabethtown C	Elizabethtown College	Elizabethtown, PA	M
Elmhurst C	Elmhurst College	Elmhurst, IL	M
Elon U	Elon University	Elon, NC	M
Emmanuel C GA	Emmanuel College	Franklin Springs, G	B
Emmanuel C MA	Emmanuel College	Boston, MA	M
Emory & Henry C	Emory & Henry College	Emory, VA	M

A=Associates   B=Bachelors   M=Masters   D=Doctorate

258

KEY TO PARTICIPATING INSTITUTIONS

Institution	Full Name of Institution	Location	Carnegie Class
Emporia ST U	Emporia State University	Emporia, KS	D
Erie CC City	Erie Community College City Campus	Buffalo, NY	A
Estrn Baptist Theo Sem	Eastern Baptist Theological Seminary	Wynnewood, PA	D
Eugene Bible C	Eugene Bible College	Eugene, OR	B
Evangel U	Evangel University	Springfield, MO	B
Evergreen ST C	The Evergreen State College	Olympia, WA	M
F&M C	Franklin & Marshall College	Lancaster, PA	B
Fayetteville Tech C C	Fayetteville Technical Community College	Fayetteville, NC	A
Fergus Falls C C	Fergus Falls Community College	Fergus Falls, MN	A
Ferris ST U	Ferris State University	Big Rapids, MI	D
Ferrum C	Ferrum College	Ferrum, VA	B
Finlandia U	Finlandia University	Hancock, MI	B
Fisk U	Fisk University	Nashville, TN	M
Fitchburg ST C	Fitchburg State College	Fitchburg, MA	M
FL A & M U	Florida Agricultural and Mechanical University	Tallahassee, FL	D
FL Atlantic U	Florida Atlantic University	Boca Raton, FL	D
FL Christian C	Florida Christian College	Kissimmee, FL	B
FL Southern C	Florida Southern College	Lakeland, FL	M
Flagler C	Flagler College	St. Augustine, FL	B
Florida Inst Tech	Florida Institute of Technology	Melbourne, FL	D
Florida Keys C C	Florida Keys Community College	Key West, FL	A
Florida State U	Florida State University	Tallahassee, FL	D
Floyd C	Floyd College	Rome, GA	A
Fort Belknap C	Fort Belknap College	Harlem, MT	T
Fort Hays ST U	Fort Hays State University	Hays, KS	M
Fort Lewis C	Fort Lewis College	Durango, CO	B
Francis Marion U	Francis Marion University	Florence, SC	M
Franklin Inst Boston	Benjamin Franklin Institute of Technology	Boston, MA	M
Franklin U	Franklin University	Columbus, OH	M
Frederick C C	Frederick Community College	Frederick, MD	A
Free Will Baptist Bible	Free Will Baptist Bible College	Nashville, TN	M
Frostburg ST U	Frostburg State University	Frostburg, MD	M
Furman U	Furman University	Greenville, SC	M
G Adolphus C	Gustavus Adolphus College	Saint Peter, MN	B
G.C. Wallace ST CC-Doth	George C. Wallace State Community College - Dothan	Dothan, Al	A
GA ST U	Georgia State University	Atlanta, GA	D
GA SWstrn ST U	Georgia Southwestern State University	Americus, GA	M
Gainesville C	Gainesville College	Gainesville, GA	A
Gannon U	Gannon University	Erie, PA	D
Gardner-Webb U	Gardner-Webb University	Boiling Springs, NC	M
Gavilan C	Gavilan College	Gilroy, CA	A

A=Associates   B=Bachelors   M=Masters   D=Doctorate

KEY TO PARTICIPATING INSTITUTIONS

Institution	Full Name of Institution	Location	Carnegie Class
Geneva C	Geneva College	Beaver Falls, PA	M
George Corley Wallace State C C	George Corley Wallace State Community College - Selma	Selma, AL	A
George Fox U	George Fox University	Newberg, OR	D
George Mason U	George Mason University	Fairfax, VA	D
George Washington U	George Washington University	Washington, D.C.	D
Georgetown C	Georgetown College	Georgetown, KY	M
Georgia Southern U	Georgia Southern University	Statesboro, GA	D
Glendale CC	Glendale Community College	Glendale, CA	A
Glendale CC	Glendale Community College	Glendale, CA	A
Gogebic CC	Gogebic Community College	Ironwood, MI	A
Gonzaga U	Gonzaga University	Spokane, WA	D
Gordon C-GA	Gordon College	Barnesville, GA	A
Gordon-C TheoSem	Gordon-Conwell Theological Seminary	South Hamilton, MA	D
Goucher C	Goucher College	Baltimore, MD	M
Governors ST U	Governors State University	University Park, IL	M
Grambling ST U	Grambling State University	Grambling, LA	D
Grand Rapids CC	Grand Rapids Community College	Grand Rapids, MI	A
Grays Harbor C	Grays Harbor College	Aberdeen, WA	A
Green Mountain C	Green Mountain College	Poultney, VT	B
Greenville C	Greenville College	Greenville, IL	M
Greenville Tech C	Greenville Technical College	Greenville, SC	A
Grinnell C	Grinnell College	Grinnell, IA	B
Grove City C	Grove City College	Grove City, PA	M
Guilford C	Guilford College	Greensboro, NC	B
Guilford Tech CC	Guilford Technical Community College	Jamestown, NC	A
Gwinnett Tech C	Gwinnett Technical College	Lawrenceville, GA	A
H Inst Int Desgn	Harrington Institute of Interior Design	Chicago, IL	B
H LaGrange C	Hannibal-La Grange College	Hannibal, MO	B
Hagerstown Bus C	Hagerstown Business College	Hagerstown, MD	A
Hagerstown CC	Hagerstown Community College	Hagerstown, MD	A
Hamilton C	Hamilton College	Clinton, NY	B
Hampshire C	Hampshire College	Amherst, MA	B
Hanover C	Hanover College	Hanover, IN	B
Harding U Grad Schl Rel	Harding University Graduate School of Religion	Memphis, TN	D
Harding U Main	Harding University Main Campus	Searcy, AR	M
Harrisburg Area C C	Harrisburg Area Community College	Harrisburg, PA	A
Haskell Indian Nations U	Haskell Indian Nations University	Lawrence, KS	B
Haverford C	Haverford College	Haverford, PA	B
Hawkeye CC	Hawkeye Community College	Waterloo, IA	A
Hebrew C	Hebrew College	Newton Center, MA	M
Hebrew U C Jewish Inst	Hebrew Union College - Jewish Institute of Religion Kla	Cincinnati, OH	D

A=Associates   B=Bachelors   M=Masters   D=Doctorate

KEY TO PARTICIPATING INSTITUTIONS

Institution	Full Name of Institution	Location	Carnegie Class
Hebrew U C Jewish Inst	Hebrew Union College-Jewish Institute of Religion (Calif	Los Angeles, CA	D
Heidelberg C	Heidelberg College	Tiffin, OH	M
Henderson CC	Henderson Community College	Henderson, KY	A
Hendrix C	Hendrix College	Conway, AR	B
Henry Ford CC	Henry Ford Community College	Dearborn, MI	A
Highland C C	Highland Community College	Highland, KS	A
Hill C	Hill College	Hillsboro, TX	A
Hillsborough CC	Hillsborough Community College	Tampa, FL	A
Hillsdale Free Will Bap	Hillsdale Free Will Baptist College	Moore, OK	M
Hinds CC	Hinds Community College	Raymond, MS	A
Hiram C	Hiram College	Hiram, OH	B
Hobart &William Smith C	Hobart and William Smith Colleges	Geneva, NY	B
Hocking Tech C	Hocking Technical College	Nelsonville, OH	A
Hofstra U	Hofstra University	Hempstead, NY	D
Holy Apostles C & Sem	Holy Apostles College and Seminary	Cromwell, CT	M
Hood C	Hood College	Frederick, MD	M
Hope C	Hope College	Holland, MI	B
Houghton C	Houghton College	Houghton, NY	B
Houston Acad Med	HAM-TMC Library	Houston, TX	D
Howard C	Howard College	Big Spring, TX	A
Howard CC	Howard Community College	Columbia, MD	A
Howard Payne U	Howard Payne University	Brownwood, TX	B
Humboldt ST U	Humboldt State University	Arcata, CA	M
IL C Optometry	Illinois College of Optometry	Chicago, IL	D
IL E CC Wabash Cntrl C	Illinois Eastern Community Colleges Wabash Valley Colleg	Olney, IL	A
IL Estrn CC-Frontier	Illinois Eastern Community Colleges Frontier Community C	Olney, IL	A
IL Estrn CC-Lincoln Tra	Illinois Eastern Community Colleges (Lincoln Trail Campu	Olney, IL	A
IL Estrn CC-Olney Centr	Illinois Eastern Community Colleges Olney Central Colleg	Olney, IL	A
IL Valley CC	Illinois Valley Community College	Oglesby, IL	A
Iliff Sch Theo	The Iliff School of Theology	Denver, CO	D
Illinois C	Illinois College	Jacksonville, IL	B
IN Purdue U Inpolis	Indiana University-Purdue University Indianapolis	Indianapolis, IN	D
IN U Kokomo	Indiana University Kokomo	Kokomo, IN	M
IN U PA	Indiana University of Pennsylvania	Indiana, PA	D
IN U S Bend	Indiana University South Bend	South Bend, IN	M
IN U-Purdue U Ft Wayne	Indiana University-Purdue University Fort Wayne	Fort Wayne, IN	M
IN Wesleyan U	Indiana Wesleyan University	Marion, IN	M
Independence CC	Independence Community College	Independence, KS	A
Indian Hills CC	Indian Hills Community College	Ottumwa, IA	A
Indiana Inst Technology	Indiana Institute of Technology	Fort Wayne, IN	M
Indiana ST U	Indiana State University	Terre Haute, IN	D

A=Associates   B=Bachelors   M=Masters   D=Doctorate

KEY TO PARTICIPATING INSTITUTIONS

Institution	Full Name of Institution	Location	Carnegie Class
Indiana U	Indiana University	Bloomington, IN	D
Inst Comercial de Puerto Rico Jr C	Instituto Comercial de Puerto Rico Junior College	Arecibo, PR	A
Intl C & Grad School	International College and Graduate School	Honolulu, HI	D
Intl Fine Arts C	Miami International University of Art and Design	Miami, FL	M
Iowa ST U	Iowa State University	Ames, IA	D
J.F. Drake ST Tech C	J.F. Drake State Technical College	Huntsville, AL	A
Jackson ST CC	Jackson State Community College	Jackson, TN	A
Jacksonville C	Jacksonville College	Jacksonville, TX	A
Jacksonville ST U	Jacksonville State University	Jacksonville, AL	M
James Madison U	James Madison University	Harrisonburg, VA	D
Jamestown C	Jamestown College	Jamestown, ND	B
Jamestown CC	Jamestown Community College	Jamestown, NY	A
Jefferson C Health Sciences	Jefferson College of Health Sciences	Roanoke, VA	B
Jefferson CC-NY	Jefferson Community College	Watertown, NY	A
Jefferson C-MO	Jefferson College	Hillsboro, MO	A
Jefferson Davis CC	Jefferson Davis Community College	Brewton, AL	A
Jewish Theol Sem	Jewish Theological Seminary of America	New York, NY	D
John A. Gupton C	John A. Gupton College	Nashville, TN	A
Johnson Bible C	Johnson Bible College	Knoxville, TN	M
Johnson C Smith U	Johnson C. Smith University	Charlotte, NC	B
Jones County Jr C	Jones County Junior College	Ellisville, MS	A
Judson C	Judson College	Elgin, IL	B
Justice Inst BC	Justice Institute of British Columbia	New Westminster, BC	A
Kaplan U	Kaplan University Library	Davenport, IA	A
Kaskaskia C	Kaskaskia College	Centralia, IL	A
Kean U	Kean University	Union, NJ	M
Keene State C	Keene State College	Keene, NH	M
Kent ST U Salem	Kent State University Salem Campus	Salem, OH	B
Kent ST U Stark	Kent State University Stark Campus	Canton, OH	M
Kent ST U Trumbull	Kent State University Trumbull Campus	Warren, OH	B
Kent St U Tuscarawas	Kent State University Tuscarawas Campus	New Philadelphia, O	A
Kent State U	Kent State University	Kent, OH	D
Kentucky Christian C	Kentucky Christian University	Grayson, KY	M
Kentucky ST U	Kentucky State University	Frankfort, KY	M
Kenyon C	Kenyon College	Gambier, OH	B
Kettering C Med Arts	Kettering College of Medical Arts	Kettering, OH	B
Kettering U	Kettering University	Flint, MI	M
Keuka C	Keuka College	Keuka Park, NY	B
Kilgore C	Kilgore College	Kilgore, TX	A
Kilgore C	Kilgore College	Kilgore, TX	A
King's C PA	King's College	Wilkes-Barre, PA	M

A=Associates   B=Bachelors   M=Masters   D=Doctorate

KEY TO PARTICIPATING INSTITUTIONS

Institution	Full Name of Institution	Location	Carnegie Class
Kirtland CC	Kirtland Community College	Roscommon, MI	A
Knox C	Knox College	Galesburg, IL	B
Kwantlen U C	Kwantlen University College	Langley, BC	B
LA Tech U	Louisiana Tech University	Ruston, LA	D
Labette CC	Labette Community College	Parsons, KS	A
Laboure C	Laboure College	Boston, MA	A
LaGrange C	LaGrange College	La Grange, GA	M
Lake City CC	Lake City Community College	Lake City, FL	A
Lakeland Sheboygan	Lakeland College	Sheboygan, WI	M
Lakeview C Nursing	Lakeview College of Nursing	Danville, IL	M
Lambuth U	Lambuth University	Jackson, TN	B
Lancaster Bible C	Lancaster Bible College	Lancaster, PA	M
Lancaster Theo Sem	Lancaster Theological Seminary	Lancaster, PA	D
Lander U	Lander University	Greenwood, SC	M
Landmark C	Landmark College	Putney, VT	A
Lane CC-OR	Lane Community College	Eugene, OR	A
Langara C	Langara College	Vancouver, BC	A
Langston U	Langston University	Langston, OK	M
Lassen CC	Lassen Community College	Susanville, CA	A
Laurentian U JN	Laurentian University	Sudbury, ON	M
Lawrence U	Lawrence University	Appleton, WI	B
Le Moyne C	Noreen Reale Falcone Library, Le Moyne College	Syracuse, NY	M
Lebanon Valley C	Lebanon Valley College	Annville, PA	M
Lehigh U	Lehigh University	Bethlehem, PA	D
Lemoyne-Owen C	Lemoyne-Owen College	Memphis, TN	B
Lesley U	Lesley University	Cambridge, MA	D
Lester B. Pearson C	Lester B. Pearson College of the Pacific	Victoria, BC	B
Lewis U	Lewis University	Romeoville, IL	M
Lewis&Clark C	Lewis and Clark College	Portland, OR	M
Lexington CC	Lexington Community College	Lexington, KY	A
Liberty U	Liberty University	Lynchburg, VA	D
LIFE Bible C	Life Pacific College	San Dimas, CA	B
Lincoln U-MO	Lincoln University	Jefferson City, MO	M
Lindsey Wilson C	Lindsey Wilson College	Columbia, KY	M
Lipscomb U	Lipscomb University	Nashville, TN	M
Lock Haven U PA	Lock Haven University of Pennsylvania	Lock Haven, PA	M
Long Island Business Inst	Long Island Business Institute	Commack, NY	A
Long Island U	Long Island University	Brooklyn, NY	D
Longwood U	Longwood University	Farmville, VA	M
Lord Fairfax CC	Lord Fairfax Community College	Middletown, VA	A
Louisville Pres Theo	Louisville Presbyterian Theological Seminary	Louisville, KY	D

A=Associates   B=Bachelors   M=Masters   D=Doctorate

KEY TO PARTICIPATING INSTITUTIONS

Institution	Full Name of Institution	Location	Ca Cla
Lourdes C	Lourdes College	Sylvania, OH	M
Loyola Marymount U	Loyola Marymount University	Los Angeles, CA	M
Loyola U Chicago	Loyola University of Chicago	Chicago, IL	D
Loyola U New Orleans	Loyola University New Orleans	New Orleans, LA	M
Lubbock Christian U	Lubbock Christian University	Lubbock, TX	M
Luth Theo Sem Philly	Lutheran Theological Seminary at Philadelphia	Philadelphia, PA	M
Luzerne County CC	Luzerne County Community College	Nanticoke, PA	A
Lynchburg C	Lynchburg College	Lynchburg, VA	M
Lyndon State C	Lyndon State College	Lyndonville, VT	B
Lynn U	Lynn University	Boca Raton, FL	D
Lyon C	Lyon College	Batesville, AR	B
Macon State C	Macon State College	Macon, GA	B
Madisonville CC	Madisonville Community College	Madisonville, KY	A
Malone C	Malone College	Canton, OH	M
Manatee CC	Manatee Community College	Bradenton, FL	A
Manchester C	Manchester College	North Manchester, I	M
Manhattan C	Manhattan College	Bronx, NY	M
Maple Woods C C	Maple Woods Community College Library	Kansas City, MO	A
Marist C	Marist College Cannavino Library	Poughkeepsie, NY	M
Marlboro C	Marlboro College	Marlboro, VT	B
Marquette U	Marquette University	Milwaukee, WI	D
Mars Hill C	Mars Hill College	Mars Hill, NC	B
Marshall U	Marshall University	Huntington, WV	D
Martin Luther C	Martin Luther College	New Ulm, MN	B
Mary Baldwin C	Mary Baldwin College	Staunton, VA	M
Mary Washington C	University of Mary Washington [Mary Washington College]	Fredericksburg, VA	M
Marymount C CA	Marymount College	Rancho Palos Verdes	A
Marymount U	Marymount University	Arlington, VA	M
Maryville U St Louis	Maryville University of Saint Louis	Saint Louis, MO	M
Mayo Fndation	Mayo Foundation	Rochester, MN	D
Mayville ST U	Mayville State University	Mayville, ND	B
McDowell Tech CC	McDowell Technical Community College	Marion, NC	A
McKendree C	McKendree College	Lebanon, IL	B
McNeese ST U	McNeese State University	Lake Charles, LA	M
McPherson C	McPherson College	McPherson, KS	B
Medical C Wisconsin	Medical College of Wisconsin	Milwaukee, WI	M
Medicine Hat C	Medicine Hat College	Medicine Hat, AB	A
Mendocino C	Mendocino College	Ukiah, CA	A
Merrimack C	Merrimack College	North Andover, MA	M
Mesa C C	Mesa Community College	Mesa, AZ	A
Methodist C	Methodist College	Fayetteville, NC	B

A=Associates   B=Bachelors   M=Masters   D=Doctorate

264

KEY TO PARTICIPATING INSTITUTIONS

Institution	Full Name of Institution	Location	Carnegie Class
Michigan Tech U	Michigan Technological University	Houghton, MI	D
MidAmer Nazarene U	MidAmerica Nazarene University	Olathe, KS	M
Middle TN ST U	Middle Tennessee State University	Murfreesboro, TN	D
Middlebury C	Middlebury College	Middlebury, VT	D
Middlesex Co C-NJ	Middlesex County College	Edison, NJ	A
Midland C	Midland College	Midland, TX	A
Midland Lutheran C	Midland Lutheran College	Fremont, NE	B
Midwestern U	Midwestern University	Downers Grove, IL	D
Miles CC	Miles Community College	Miles City, MT	A
Millikin U	Millikin University	Decatur, IL	M
Mills C	Mills College	Oakland, CA	D
Millsaps C	Millsaps College	Jackson, MS	M
Milwaukee Inst Art Desi	Milwaukee Institute of Art & Design	Milwaukee, WI	B
Minnesota ST U-Mankato	Minnesota State University, Mankato	Mankato, MN	M
Minot State U	Minot State University	Minot, ND	M
Mississippi County C C	Mississippi County Community College	Blytheville, AR	A
Mississippi Delta C C	Mississippi Delta Community College	Moorhead, MS	A
MO Baptist C	Missouri Baptist College	Saint Louis, MO	B
MO Western ST C	Missouri Western State College	Saint Joseph, MO	B
Monmouth C	Monmouth College	Monmouth, IL	B
Monroe Co CC	Monroe County Community College	Monroe, MI	A
Monterey Inst of Intl Studies	Monterey Institute of International Studies	Monterey, CA	M
Moorpark C	Moorpark College	Moorpark, CA	A
Moravian C	Moravian College	Bethlehem, PA	M
Morehead ST U	Morehead State University	Morehead, KY	M
Morningside C	Morningside College	Sioux City, IA	M
Mount Royal C	Mount Royal College	Calgary, AB	B
Mount Union C	Mount Union College	Alliance, OH	B
Mountain Empire CC	Mountain Empire Community College	Big Stone Gap, VA	A
MS ST U	Mississippi State University	Mississippi State,	D
MS Valley ST U	Mississippi Valley State University	Itta Bena, MS	M
Mt Hood CC	Mt. Hood Community College	Gresham, OR	A
Mt Holyoke C	Mount Holyoke College	South Hadley, MA	M
Mt Holyoke C	Mount Holyoke College	South Hadley, MA	M
Mt Marty C	Mount Marty College	Yankton, SD	M
Mt Mary C-WI	Mount Mary College	Milwaukee, WI	M
MT ST U Northern	Montana State University - Northern	Havre, MT	M
Mt St Vincent U	Mount St Vincent University	Halifax, NS	M
MT Tech U Montana	Montana Tech of The University of Montana	Butte, MT	M
Mt Wachusett CC	Mount Wachusett Community College	Gardner, MA	A
Muhlenberg C	Muhlenberg College	Allentown, PA	B

A=Associates   B=Bachelors   M=Masters   D=Doctorate

KEY TO PARTICIPATING INSTITUTIONS

Institution	Full Name of Institution	Location	Carnegie Class
Multnomah Bible C & Sem	Multnomah Bible College and Biblical Seminary	Portland, OR	S
Murray ST U-KY	Murray State University	Murray, KY	M
Muskingum C	Muskingum College	New Concord, OH	M
Mwest Bap TheoSem	Midwestern Baptist Theological Seminary	Kansas City, MO	D
N Carolina Wesleyan C	North Carolina Wesleyan College	Rocky Mount, NC	B
Natl C Naturopathic Med	National College of Naturopathic Medicine	Portland, OR	M
Natl Defense U	National Defense University	Washington, DC	M
Naval Postgrad Sch	Naval Postgraduate School	Monterey, CA	D
NC A&T ST U	North Carolina Agricultural and Technical State Universi	Greensboro, NC	D
NC Sch Arts	North Carolina School of the Arts	Winston-Salem, NC	M
ND ST C Science	North Dakota State College of Science	Wahpeton, ND	A
ND ST U-Main	North Dakota State University Main Campus	Fargo, ND	D
NE WI Tech C	Northeast Wisconsin Technical College	Green Bay, WI	A
NEastrn IL U	Northeastern Illinois University	Chicago, IL	M
NEastrn U	Northeastern University	Boston, MA	D
New C U South FL	New College of Florida	Sarasota, FL	B
New Eng Cons Music	New England Conservatory of Music	Boston, MA	D
New Hampshire C Tech C	New Hampshire Community Technical College	Berlin, NH	A
New River CC	New River Community College	Dublin, VA	A
NHMCCD-Montgomery C	North Harris Montgomery Community College District-Montg	Conroe, TX	A
Nicolet Area Tech C	Nicolet Area Technical College	Rhinelander, WI	A
Nipissing U	Nipissing University	North Bay, ON	M
NJ City U	New Jersey City University	Jersey City, NJ	M
NJ Inst Tech	New Jersey Institute of Technology	Newark, NJ	D
NM Highlands U	New Mexico Highlands University	Las Vegas, NM	M
NM ST U Alamogordo	New Mexico State University at Alamogordo	Alamogordo, NM	A
NM St U-Carlsbad	New Mexico State University at Carlsbad	Carlsbad, NM	A
North Carolina State U	North Carolina State University	Raleigh, NC	D
North Central C	North Central College	Naperville, IL	M
North Florida C C	North Florida Community College	Madison, FL	A
North Park U	North Park University	Chicago, IL	D
Northeast ST Tech CC	Northeast State Technical Community College	Blountville, TN	A
Northeastern JC	Northeastern Junior College	Sterling, CO	A
Northeastern Ohio U C Med	Northeastern Ohio Universities College of Medicine	Rootstown, OH	D
Northern AZ U	Northern Arizona University	Flagstaff, AZ	D
Northern IL U	Northern Illinois University	De Kalb, IL	D
Northern KY U	Northern Kentucky University	Highland Heights, K	M
Northern ST U	Northern State University	Aberdeen, SD	M
Northwest C	Northwest College	Kirkland, WA	M
Northwestern U	Northwestern University	Evanston, IL	D
Norwich U	Norwich University	Northfield, VT	M

A=Associates   B=Bachelors   M=Masters   D=Doctorate

KEY TO PARTICIPATING INSTITUTIONS

Institution	Full Name of Institution	Location	Carnegie Class
Notre Dame C OH	Notre Dame College	South Euclid, OH	M
Notre Dame Sem	Notre Dame Seminary	New Orleans, LA	M
NW C Chiropractic	Northwestern Health Sciences University	Bloomington, MN	D
NW MO ST U	Northwest Missouri State University	Maryville, MO	M
NW MS CC	Northwest Mississippi Community College	Senatobia, MS	A
Nwestern CT Tech CC	Northwestern Connecticut Community College	Winsted, CT	A
NY Chiropractic C	New York Chiropractic College	Seneca Falls, NY	D
NY Inst Tech Islip	New York Institute of Technology - Central Islip Campus	Central Islip, NY	M
NY Inst Tech Main	New York Institute of Technology Main Campus - Old Westb	Old Westbury, NY	M
Oakland City U	Oakland City University	Oakland City, IN	D
Oakland U	Oakland University	Rochester, MI	D
Oberlin C	Oberlin College	Oberlin, OH	M
Ocean County C	Ocean County College	Toms River, NJ	A
OH Dominican C	Ohio Dominican University	Columbus, OH	B
OH ST U Ag Tech Inst	The Ohio State University Agricultural Technical Institu	Wooster, OH	A
OH U Lancaster	Ohio University Lancaster	Lancaster, OH	M
OH Wesleyan U	Ohio Wesleyan University	Delaware, OH	B
Ohio C Pod Med	Ohio College of Podiatric Medicine	Cleveland, OH	D
Ohio State U	Ohio State University	Columbus, OH	D
OK Panhandle ST U	Oklahoma Panhandle State University	Goodwell, OK	B
Okaloosa-Walton CC	Okaloosa-Walton College	Niceville, FL	A
Olivet Nazarene U	Olivet Nazarene University	Bourbonnais, IL	M
Olympic C	OLYMPIC COLLEGE	Bremerton, WA	A
Olympic C	Olympic College	Bremerton, WA	A
OR Health Sci U	Oregon Health and Science University	Portland, OR	D
OR ST U	Oregon State University	Corvallis, OR	D
Oral Roberts U	Oral Roberts University	Tulsa, OK	D
Orange County CC	Orange County Community College	Middletown, NY	A
Otterbein C	Otterbein College	Westerville, OH	M
PA ST Harrisburg	Penn State Harrisburg Library	Middletown, PA	D
Pace U-NY	Pace University Library	New York, NY	M
Pacific Lutheran U	Pacific Lutheran University	Tacoma, WA	M
Pacific U	Pacific University	Forest Grove, OR	D
Pacific Union C	Pacific Union College	Angwin, CA	M
Paier C Art	Paier College of Art	Hamden, CT	B
Palm Beach Atlantic C	Palm Beach Atlantic College	West Palm Beach, FL	M
Panola C	Panola College	Carthage, TX	A
Parkland C	Parkland College	Champaign, IL	A
Paul D. Camp CC	Paul D. Camp Community College	Suffolk, VA	A
Peace C	Peace College	Raleigh, NC	B
Pellissippi ST Tech CC	Pellissippi State Technical Community College	Knoxville, TN	A

A=Associates   B=Bachelors   M=Masters   D=Doctorate

267

KEY TO PARTICIPATING INSTITUTIONS

Institution	Full Name of Institution	Location	Ca Cla
Pensacola Jr C	Pensacola Junior College	Pensacola, FL	A
Pepperdine	Pepperdine University	Malibu, CA	D
Pfeiffer U	Pfeiffer University	Misenheimer, NC	M
Phila C Osteo Med	Phila College of Osteopathic Medicine	Philadelphia, PA	D
Philadelphia U	Philadelphia University	Philadelphia, PA	M
Phillips Graduate Inst	Phillips Graduate Institute	Encino, CA	D
Piedmont Tech C	Piedmont Technical College	Greenwood, SC	A
Plymouth ST C	Plymouth State University	Plymouth, NH	M
Pont C Josephinum	Pontifical College Josephinum	Columbus, OH	M
Potomac C	Potomac College	Washington, DC	B
Potomac St C-WVU	Potomac State College of West Virginia University	Keyser, WV	A
Prairie ST C	Prairie State College	Chicago Heights, IL	A
Pratt C C	Pratt Community College	Pratt, KS	A
Presb C-Montreal	Presbyterian College of Montreal	Montreal, QC	D
Presbyterian C	Presbyterian College	Clinton, SC	B
Prescott C	Prescott College	Prescott, AZ	M
Princeton TheoSem	Princeton Theological Seminary	Princeton, NJ	D
Princeton U	Princeton University	Princeton, NJ	D
Principia C	Principia College	Elsah, IL	B
Providence C	Providence College	Providence, RI	M
Pueblo C C	Pueblo Community College	Pueblo, CO	A
Pulaski Tech C	Pulaski Technical College	North Little Rock,	A
Purchase C SUNY	Purchase College, State University of New York	Purchase, NY	M
Purdue U	Purdue University	West Lafayette, IN	D
Purdue U Calumet	Purdue University Calumet	Hammond, IN	M
Purdue U North Central Campus	Purdue University North Central Campus	Westville, IN	M
Quincy U	Quincy University	Quincy, IL	M
Quinebaug Vally Comm TC	Quinebaug Valley Community College	Danielson, CT	A
Quinsigamond CC	Quinsigamond Community College	Worcester, MA	A
R Morris C PA	Robert Morris University	Moon Township, PA	D
R.Wesleyan C	Roberts Wesleyan College	Rochester, NY	M
Radford U	Radford University	Radford, VA	M
Ramapo C NJ	Ramapo College of New Jersey	Mahwah, NJ	M
Randolph-Macon C	Randolph-Macon College	Ashland, VA	B
Randolph-Macon WC	Randolph-Macon Woman's College	Lynchburg, VA	B
Recnstrctnst Rabbinical	Reconstructionist Rabbinical College	Wyncote, PA	M
Red Deer C	Red Deer College	Red Deer, AB	A
Redlands CC	Redlands Community College	El Reno, OK	A
Reformed Bible C	Reformed Bible College	Grand Rapids, MI	B
Regent	Regent University	Virginia Beach, VA	D
Regis C	Regis College	Toronto, ON	D

A=Associates   B=Bachelors   M=Masters   D=Doctorate

KEY TO PARTICIPATING INSTITUTIONS

Institution	Full Name of Institution	Location	Carnegie Class
Reinhardt C	Reinhardt College	Waleska, GA	B
Rend Lake C	Rend Lake College	Ina, IL	A
Rensselaer PolyTech	Rensselaer Polytechnic Institute	Troy, NY	D
RI Sch Design	Rhode Island School of Design	Providence, RI	M
Rice U	Rice University	Houston, TX	D
Richmond CC	Richmond Community College	Hamlet, NC	A
Ricks C	BYU-Idaho	Rexburg, ID	B
Ringling Sch Art & Desi	Ringling School of Art and Design	Sarasota, FL	B
Rivier C	Rivier College	Nashua, NH	M
Robeson CC	Robeson Community College	Lumberton, NC	A
Rochester C	Rochester College	Rochester Hills, MI	B
Rochester Comm &Tech C	Rochester Community and Technical College	Rochester, MN	A
Rochester Inst Tech	Rochester Institute of Technology	Rochester, NY	D
Rock Valley C	Rock Valley College	Rockford, IL	A
Rockhurst U	Rockhurst University	Kansas City, MO	M
Rockingham CC	Rockingham Community College	Wentworth, NC	A
Rockland CC	Rockland Community College	Suffern, NY	A
Rocky Mountain C	Rocky Mountain College	Billings, MT	B
Roger Williams U	Roger Williams University	Bristol, RI	M
Rogers ST U	Rogers State University	Claremore, OK	B
Roosevelt U	Roosevelt University	Chicago, IL	M
Rose ST C	Rose State College	Midwest City, OK	A
Rosemont C	Rosemont College	Rosemont, PA	M
Rowan U	Rowan University	Glassboro, NJ	D
Rutgers U	Rutgers University	New Brunswick, NJ	D
S Carolina ST U	South Carolina State University	Orangeburg, SC	D
S.F.Austin ST U	Stephen F. Austin State University	Nacogdoches, TX	D
Salem Teiko U	Salem International University	Salem, WV	M
Salisbury ST U	Salisbury University	Salisbury, MD	M
Salt Lake CC	Salt Lake Community College	Salt Lake City, UT	A
Salve Regina U	Salve Regina University	Newport, RI	D
San Antonio C	San Bernardino Valley College	San Antonio, TX	A
San Fran CC Dst	San Francisco Community College District	San Francisco, CA	A
San Fran ST U	San Francisco State University	San Francisco, CA	D
San Jacinto C South Campus	San Jacinto College South Campus	Houston, TX	A
San Jose ST U	San Jose State University	San Jose, CA	M
San Juan C	San Juan College	Farmington, NM	A
Santa Barbara City C	Santa Barbara City College	Santa Barbara, CA	D
Santa Clara U	Santa Clara University	Santa Clara, CA	D
Savannah ST U	Savannah State University	Savannah, GA	M
Schreiner C	Schreiner University	Kerrville, TX	M

A=Associates   B=Bachelors   M=Masters   D=Doctorate

KEY TO PARTICIPATING INSTITUTIONS

Institution	Full Name of Institution	Location	Ca Cla
Scottsdale CC	Scottsdale Community College	Scottsdale, AZ	A
Scripps C	The Libraries of The Claremont Colleges	Claremont, CA	D
SD Sch Mines & Tech	South Dakota School of Mines and Technology	Rapid City, SD	D
SE C Assemblies God	Southeastern College of the Assemblies of God	Lakeland, FL	B
SE MO ST U	Southeast Missouri State University	Cape Girardeau, MO	M
SE Oklahoma St U	Southeastern Oklahoma State University	Durant, OK	M
Seattle Central CC	Seattle Central Community College	Seattle, WA	D
Seattle Pacific U	Seattle Pacific University	Seattle, WA	D
Seattle U	Seattle University	Seattle, WA	D
Seminole C C	Seminole Community College	Sanford, FL	A
Seton Hill C	Seton Hill College	Greensburg, PA	M
SF Consrv Music	San Francisco Conservatory of Music	San Francisco, CA	M
Shaw U	Shaw University	Raleigh, NC	M
Shawnee ST U	Shawnee State University	Portsmouth, OH	B
Shenandoah U	Shenandoah University	Winchester, VA	D
Shepherd C	Shepherd College	Shepherdstown, WV	B
Shorter C	Shorter College	Rome, GA	M
Siena C	Siena College	Loudonville, NY	B
Silver Lake C	Silver Lake College	Manitowoc, WI	M
Simpson C IA	Dunn Library -- Simpson College	Indianola, IA	B
Sisseton Wahpeton C	Sisseton Wahpeton College	Sisseton, SD	M
Skidmore C	Skidmore College	Saratoga Springs, N	B
Smith C	Smith College	Northampton, MA	D
Snead ST CC	Snead State Community College	Boaz, AL	A
Somerset CC	Somerset Community College	Somerset, KY	A
South Arkansas C C	South Arkansas Community College	El Dorado, AR	A
South C	South University	Savannah, GA	D
South Puget Sound CC	South Puget Sound Community College	Olympia, WA	A
Southeast CC	Southeast Community College	Cumberland, KY	A
Southeastern Louisiana U	Southeastern Louisiana University	Hammond, LA	M
Southern California C of Optometry	Southern California College of Optometry	Fullerton, CA	D
Southern Illinois U	Southern Illinois University	Carbondale, IL	D
Southrn C Opt	Southern College of Optometry	Memphis, TN	M
Southrn IL U Edward	Southern Illinois University at Edwardsville	Edwardsville, IL	M
Southrn Methodist U	Southern Methodist University	Dallas, TX	D
Southrn OR U	Southern Oregon University	Ashland, OR	M
Southrn U A&M Baton	Southern University and Agricultural and Mechanical Coll	Baton Rouge, LA	D
Southrn U-New Orleans	Southern University at New Orleans	New Orleans, LA	A
Southside VA CC	Southside Virginia Community College	Alberta, VA	A
Southwest U	Southwestern University	Georgetown, TX	B
Southwestern C	Southwestern College	Winfield, KS	A

A=Associates   B=Bachelors   M=Masters   D=Doctorate

270

KEY TO PARTICIPATING INSTITUTIONS

Institution	Full Name of Institution	Location	Carnegie Class
Southwestern Oregon C C	Southwestern Oregon Community College	Coos Bay, OR	A
SouthWstrn CC-NC	Southwestern Community College	Sylva, NC	A
Spartan Aero-Flight Sch	Spartan College of Aeronautics Libraries	Tulsa, OK	B
Spartanburg Tech C	Spartanburg Technical College	Spartanburg, SC	A
Spokane C C	Spokane Community College	Spokane, WA	A
Spoon River C	Spoon River College	Canton, IL	A
Spring Hill C	Spring Hill College	Mobile, AL	M
Springfield Tech CC	Springfield Technical Community College	Springfield, MA	A
St Ambrose U	St. Ambrose University	Davenport, IA	M
St Andrews Presby C	St Andrews Presbyterian College	Laurinburg, NC	B
St C.Borromeo Sem	Saint Charles Borromeo Seminary	Wynnewood, PA	M
St Cloud ST U	Saint Cloud State University	Saint Cloud, MN	M
St Francis C PA	Saint Francis University	Loretto, PA	M
St Francis-Xavier U	St Francis Xavier University	Antigonis, NS	M
St John Fisher C	St. John Fisher College	Rochester, NY	M
St John Vianney C Sem	St. John Vianney College Seminary	Miami, FL	B
St John's U NY	St. John's University	Jamaica, NY	D
St Joseph C Suffolk	Saint Joseph's College - Suffolk Campus	Patchogue, NY	M
St Joseph's C IN	Saint Joseph's College	Rensselaer, IN	M
St Joseph's C NY	Saint Joseph's College, New York	Brooklyn, NY	M
St Joseph's Sem	Saint Joseph's Seminary	Yonkers, NY	M
St Louis U	SAINT LOUIS UNIVERSITY	Saint Louis, MO	D
St Martin's C	Saint Martin's College	Lacey, WA	A
St Mary's U TX	Blume Library, St. Mary's University	San Antonio, TX	D
St Mary's U Halifax	Saint Mary's University	Halifax, NS	D
St Meinrad Theo	Saint Meinrad School of Theology	St. Meinrad, IN	M
St Michael's C	Saint Michael's College	Colchester, VT	M
St Norbert C	Saint Norbert College	De Pere, WI	M
St Olaf C	Saint Olaf College	Northfield, MN	B
St Patrick's Sem	Saint Patrick's Seminary	Menlo Park, CA	M
St Peter's Abbey & C	St Peter's Abbey & College	Muenster, SK	M
St Philip's C	St. Philip's College	San Antonio, TX	A
ST U W GA	State University of West Georgia	Carrollton, GA	M
St Vincent Sem	St. Vincent De Paul Regional Seminary	Boynton Beach, FL	M
St Vladimir TheoSem	Saint Vladimir's Orthodox Theological Seminary	Crestwood, NY	D
St. Gregory's U	Saint Gregory's University	Shawnee, OK	B
St. John's C	St. John's College	Annapolis, MD	M
St. Mary's C Maryland	St. Mary's College of Maryland	Saint Mary's City,	B
St. Mary's U Minnesota	Saint Mary's University of Minnesota - Fitzgerald Library	Winona, MN	M
Sterling C-VT	Sterling College	Craftsbury Common,	B
Stetson U	Stetson University	DeLand, FL	M

A=Associates   B=Bachelors   M=Masters   D=Doctorate

KEY TO PARTICIPATING INSTITUTIONS

Institution	Full Name of Institution	Location	Carnegie Class
Stevens Inst Tech	Stevens Institute of Technology	Hoboken, NJ	D
Sthrn Bap Theo Sem	The Southern Baptist Theological Seminary	Louisville, KY	D
Sthrn N.England Sch Law	Southern New England School of Law	N. Dartmouth, MA	S
Sthrn Polytech ST U	Southern Polytechnic State University	Marietta, GA	M
Sthrn U-Shreveport/Boss	Southern University at Shreveport	Shreveport, LA	A
Stillman C	Stillman College	Tuscaloosa, AL	B
Stonehill C	Stonehill College	Easton, MA	M
Sul Ross ST U	Sul Ross State University	Alpine, TX	M
SUNY Albany	State University of New York at Albany	Albany, NY	D
SUNY Binghamton	State University of New York at Binghamton	Binghamton, NY	D
SUNY Brockport	State University of New York College at Brockport	Brockport, NY	M
SUNY Buffalo	State University of New York College at Buffalo	Buffalo, NY	M
SUNY Buffalo	State University of New York at Buffalo	Buffalo, NY	D
SUNY C Enviro Sci & For	State University of New York College of Environmental Sc	Syracuse, NY	D
SUNY C Potsdam	State University of New York College at Potsdam	Potsdam, NY	M
SUNY IT Utica	State University of New York Institute of Technology at	Utica, NY	M
SUNY Oneonta	State University of New York College at Oneonta	Oneonta, NY	M
SUNY Optometry	State University of New York College of Optometry	New York, NY	D
SUNY Oswego	State University of New York College at Oswego	Oswego, NY	M
Surry CC	Surry Community College	Dobson, NC	A
Susquehanna U	Susquehanna University	Selinsgrove, PA	B
SW Baptist Theo Sem	Southwestern Baptist Theological Seminary	Fort Worth, TX	B
SW MO ST U	Southwest Missouri State University	Springfield, MO	M
Swarthmore C	Swarthmore College	Swarthmore, PA	B
Sweet Briar C	Sweet Briar College	Sweet Briar, VA	B
SWstrn Adventist U	Southwestern Adventist University	Keene, TX	M
SWstrn C	Southwestern Community College District	Chula Vista, CA	A
SWstrn OK ST U	Southwestern Oklahoma State University	Weatherford, OK	M
SWstrn U Sch Law	Southwestern University School of Law	Los Angeles, CA	D
Tabor C	Tabor College	Hillsboro, KS	M
Tacoma CC	Tacoma Community College	Tacoma, WA	A
Talladega C	Talladega College	Talladega, AL	B
Tallahassee CC	Tallahassee Community College	Tallahassee, FL	A
Taylor U	Taylor University	Upland, IN	B
Teachers C Columbia	Teachers College, Columbia University	New York, NY	D
Tech C Lowcountry	Technical College of the Lowcountry	Beaufort, SC	A
Teikyo Post U	Post University	Waterbury, CT	B
Temple C	Temple College	Temple, TX	A
Temple U	Temple University	Philadelphia, PA	D
Texas Chiropractic C	Texas Chiropractic College	Pasadena, TX	M
Texas Sthrn U	Texas Southern University	Houston, TX	D

A=Associates B=Bachelors M=Masters D=Doctorate

KEY TO PARTICIPATING INSTITUTIONS

Institution	Full Name of Institution	Location	Carnegie Class
Tiffin U	Tiffin University	Tiffin, OH	M
TM Cooley Law Sch	Thomas M Cooley Law School Library	Lansing, MI	M
TN ST U	Tennessee State University	Nashville, TN	D
TN Tech U	Tennessee Technological University	Cookeville, TN	D
TN Wesleyan C	Merner Pfeiffer Library, Tennessee Wesleyan College	Athens, TN	B
Tompkins Cort CC	Tompkins Cortland Community College	Dryden, NY	A
Towson U	Towson University	Towson, MD	D
Trevecca Nazarene U	Trevecca Nazarene University	Nashville, TN	D
Tri County CC	Tri-County Community College	Murphy, NC	A
Tri ST U	Tri-State University	Angola, IN	B
Trinity C DC	Trinity University	Washington, DC	M
Trinity Christian C	Trinity Christian College	Palos Heights, IL	B
Trinity Luth Sem	Trinity Lutheran Seminary	Columbus, OH	M
Trinity U	Trinity University	San Antonio, TX	M
Trinity Valley CC	Trinity Valley Community College	Athens, TX	A
Trinity West U	Trinity Western University	Langley, BC	B
Trocaire C	Trocaire College	Buffalo, NY	A
Troy ST U	Troy State University	Troy, AL	M
Troy State U Dothan	Troy State University Dothan	Dothan, AL	M
Truett McConnell C	Truett McConnell College	Cleveland, GA	B
Truman ST U	Truman State University	Kirksville, MO	M
Tufts U	Tufts University	Medford, MA	D
TX A&M Comm	Texas A & M University - Commerce	Commerce, TX	D
TX A&M HSC Dentistry	The Texas A & M University System Health Science Center	Dallas, TX	D
TX Christian U	Texas Christian University	Fort Worth, TX	D
TX Lutheran U	Texas Lutheran University	Seguin, TX	B
TX Woman's U	Texas Woman's University	Denton, TX	D
U Alabama	University of Alabama	Tuscaloosa, AL	D
U Alberta	University of Alberta	Edmonton, AL	D
U British Columbia	University of British Columbia	Vancouver, BC	D
U California, Berkeley	University of California, Berkeley	Berkeley, CA	D
U California, Davis	University of California, Davis	Davis, CA	D
U California, Irvine	University of California, Irvine	Irvine, CA	D
U California, Riverside	University of California, Riverside	Riverside, CA	D
U Chicago	University of Chicago	Chicago, IL	D
U Colorado	University of Colorado	Boulder, CO	D
U Connecticut	University of Connecticut	Storrs, CT	D
U Delaware	University of Delaware	Newark, DE	D
U Florida	University of Florida	Gainesville, FL	D
U Houston	University of Houston	Houston, TX	D
U Illinois at Urbana	University of Illinois at Urbana	Urbana, IL	D

A=Associates   B=Bachelors   M=Masters   D=Doctorate

KEY TO PARTICIPATING INSTITUTIONS

Institution	Full Name of Institution	Location	Carnegie Class
U Kansas	University of Kansas	Lawrence, KS	D
U Manitoba	University of Manitoba	Winnipeg, MB	D
U Massachusetts	University of Massachusetts	Amherst, MA	D
U Miami	University of Miami	Coral Gables, FL	D
U Michigan	University of Michigan	Ann Arbor, MI	D
U Montreal	University of Montreal	Montreal, QC	D
U Nebraska-Lincoln	University of Nebraska-Lincoln	Lincoln, NE	D
U New Mexico	University of New Mexico	Albuquerque, NM	D
U Oklahoma	University of Oklahoma	Norman, OK	D
U Oregon	University of Oregon	Eugene, OR	D
U Pittsburgh	University of Pittsburgh	Pittsburgh, PA	D
U Rochester	University of Rochester	Rochester, NY	D
U South Carolina	University of South Carolina	Columbia, SC	D
U Southern California	University of Southern California	Los Angeles, CA	D
U Texas	University of Texas	Austin, TX	D
U Utah	University of Utah	Salt Lake City, UT	D
U Virginia	University of Virginia	Charlottesville, VA	D
U Waterloo	University of Waterloo	Waterloo, ON	D
U Western Ontario	University of Western Ontario	London, ON	D
U Wisconsin	University of Wisconsin	Madison, WI	D
U Akron Wayne C	University of Akron-Wayne College	Orrville, OH	A
U AL Birmingham	University of Alabama at Birmingham	Birmingham, AL	D
U Arts	University of the Arts	Philadelphia, PA	M
U AS for Med Sci	University of Arkansas for Medical Sciences	Little Rock, AR	D
U AS Main Campus	University of Arkansas Main Campus	Fayetteville, AR	D
U AZ	University of Arizona	Tucson, AZ	D
U Baltimore	University of Baltimore	Baltimore, MD	D
U C of Cape Breton	University College of Cape Breton	Sydney, NS	M
U CA Santa Cruz	University of California-Santa Cruz	Santa Cruz, CA	D
U Calgary	University of Calgary	Calgary, AB	D
U Central FL	University of Central Florida	Orlando, FL	D
U Charleston	University of Charleston	Charleston, WV	M
U CO - Colorado Springs	University of Colorado at Colorado Springs	Colorado Springs, CA	D
U CO Denver	University of Colorado at Denver	Denver, CO	D
U CT Health Ctr	University of Connecticut Health Center	Farmington, CT	D
U Dallas	University of Dallas	Irving, TX	D
U Dayton	University of Dayton	Dayton, OH	D
U DC	University of the District of Columbia	Washington, DC	M
U Del Turabo	Universidad Del Turabo	Gurabo, p.r. 00778,	M
U Denver	University of Denver	Denver, CO	D
U Detroit Mercy	University of Detroit Mercy	Detroit, MI	D

A=Associates   B=Bachelors   M=Masters   D=Doctorate

KEY TO PARTICIPATING INSTITUTIONS

Institution	Full Name of Institution	Location	Carnegie Class
U Findlay	The University of Findlay	Findlay, OH	M
U Hawaii-Hilo	University of Hawaii at Hilo	Hilo, HI	M
U HI-Kapiolani CC	University of Hawaii Kapiolani Community College	Honolulu, HI	A
U HI-Kauai CC	University of Hawaii Kauai Community College	Lihue, HI	M
U HI-Leeward CC	University of Hawaii, Leeward Community College	Pearl City, HI	A
U HI-Maui CC	University of Hawaii Maui Community College	Kahului, HI	A
U HI-Windward CC	University of Hawaii Windward Community College	Kaneohe, HI	A
U Houston	University of Houston - Clear Lake	Houston, TX	M
U Incarnate Word	University of the Incarnate Word	San Antonio, TX	D
U LA Lafayette	University of Louisiana at Lafayette	Lafayette, LA	D
U LaVerne	University of LaVerne	La Verne, CA	D
U Lethbridge	University of Lethbridge	Lethbridge, AB	D
U Maine	University of Maine	Orono, ME	D
U Maine - Machias	University of Maine at Machias	Machias, ME	B
U Mary	University of Mary	Bismarck, ND	M
U Mass Lowell	University of Massachusetts Lowell	Lowell, MA	D
U MD Baltimore Co	University of Maryland Baltimore County	Baltimore, MD	D
U MD U C	University of Maryland University College	Adelphi, MD	D
U ME Fort Kent	University of Maine at Fort Kent	Fort Kent, ME	B
U Med & Dentistry NJ	University of Medicine and Dentistry of New Jersey	Newark, NJ	D
U Memphis	The University of Memphis	Memphis, TN	D
U MI Dearborn	University of Michigan-Dearborn	Dearborn, MI	M
U MO Columbia	University of Missouri - Columbia	Columbia, MO	D
U MO KS City	University of Missouri-Kansas City	Kansas City, MO	D
U MO St Louis	University of Missouri-Saint Louis	Saint Louis, MO	D
U Mobile	University of Mobile	Mobile, AL	M
U N Iowa	University of Northern Iowa	Cedar Falls, IA	D
U ND Main	University of North Dakota Main Campus	Grand Forks, ND	D
U NE Kearney	University of Nebraska at Kearney	Kearney, NE	M
U NE-Omaha	University of Nebraska at Omaha	Omaha, NE	D
U New Mexico-Taos	University of New Mexico-Taos	Taos, NM	A
U New Orleans	University of New Orleans	New Orleans, LA	D
U NH	University of New Hampshire	Durham, NH	D
U NM Gallup Branch	University of New Mexico Gallup Branch	Gallup, NM	A
U North FL	University of North Florida	Jacksonville, FL	D
U Northern CO	University of Northern Colorado	Greeley, CO	D
U NV Las Vegas	University of Nevada-Las Vegas	Las Vegas, NV	D
U of Idaho	University of Idaho	Moscow, ID	D
U of Rhode Island	University of Rhode Island	Kingston, RI	D
U of St. Mary	University of Saint Mary	Leavenworth, KS	D
U of Texas El Paso	University of Texas at El Paso	El Paso, TX	D

A=Associates   B=Bachelors   M=Masters   D=Doctorate

KEY TO PARTICIPATING INSTITUTIONS

Institution	Full Name of Institution	Location	Carnegie Class
U of Wisconsin	University of Wisconsin - Milwaukee	Milwaukee, WI	D
U Ottawa	Universite d'Ottawa	Ottawa, ON	D
U Ozarks	University of the Ozarks	Clarksville, AR	B
U Pacific	University of the Pacific	Stockton, CA	D
U Pitt Titusville	University of Pittsburgh at Titusville	Titusville, PA	A
U Portland	University of Portland	Portland, OR	M
U PQ Ecole tech	École de Technologie Supérieure	Montreal, QC	D
U PR Mayaguez	University of Puerto Rico Mayaguez Campus	Mayaguez, PR	D
U Quebec	Tele-universite	Quebec, QC	D
U Regina	University of Regina	Regina, SK	D
U Richmond	University of Richmond	Richmond, VA	M
U Rio Grande	University of Rio Grande	Rio Grande, OH	M
U S Dakota	University of South Dakota	Vermillion, SD	D
U San Diego	University of San Diego	San Diego, CA	D
U San Fran	University of San Francisco	San Francisco, CA	D
U Sciences Phila	University of the Sciences in Philadelphia	Philadelphia, PA	D
U Scranton	The University of Scranton	Scranton, PA	M
U South FL	University of South Florida	Tampa, FL	D
U Sthn IN	University of Southern Indiana	Evansville, IN	M
U Sthrn Maine	University of Southern Maine	Portland, ME	D
U Sthrn Mississippi	University of Southern Mississippi	Hattiesburg, MS	D
U Tampa	University of Tampa	Tampa, FL	M
U Theo Sem Presb	Union Theological Seminary and Presbyterian School of Ch	Richmond, VA	D
U TN Chatt	University of Tennessee at Chattanooga	Chattanooga, TN	M
U TN Martin	University of Tennessee at Martin	Martin, TN	M
U Toledo	The University of Toledo	Toledo, OH	D
U TX Arlington	University of Texas at Arlington	Arlington, TX	D
U TX Dallas	University of Texas at Dallas	Richardson, TX	D
U TX Hlth Sci Ctr S.Ant	University of Texas Health Science Center at San Antonio	San Antonio, TX	D
U TX Tyler	University of Texas at Tyler	Tyler, TX	M
U VA C Wise	The University of Virginia's College at Wise	Wise, VA	B
U Victoria	University of Victoria	Victoria, BC	D
U West AL	The University of West Alabama	Livingston, AL	M
U West FL	University of West Florida	Pensacola, FL	D
U WI E Claire	University of Wisconsin-Eau Claire	Eau Claire, WI	M
U WI La Crosse	University of Wisconsin-La Crosse	La Crosse, WI	M
U WI Platteville	University of Wisconsin-Platteville	Platteville, WI	M
U Windsor	University of Windsor	Windsor, ON	D
U Winnipeg	University of Winnipeg	Winnipeg, MB	M
U Wyoming	University of Wyoming	Laramie, WY	D
UNC Asheville	University of North Carolina at Asheville	Asheville, NC	M

A=Associates   B=Bachelors   M=Masters   D=Doctorate

KEY TO PARTICIPATING INSTITUTIONS

Institution	Full Name of Institution	Location	Carnegie Class
UNC Charlotte	University of North Carolina at Charlotte	Charlotte, NC	D
UNC Greensboro	University of North Carolina at Greensboro	Greensboro, NC	D
UNC Pembroke	University of North Carolina at Pembroke	Pembroke, NC	M
UNC Wilmington	University of North Carolina at Wilmington	Wilmington, NC	D
Unification Theo Sem	Unification Theological Seminary	Barrytown, NY	D
Union C	Union College	Lincoln, NE	B
Union C-NY	Union College	Schenectady, NY	M
United Theo Sem-Twin Ci	United Theological Seminary of the Twin Cities	New Brighton, MN	D
Université Laval	Université Laval	Sainte-Foy, QC	D
UNT HSC Ft Worth	University of North Texas Health Science Center at Fort	Fort Worth, TX	D
US C Guard Acad	United States Coast Guard Academy	New London, CT	B
US Merchant Marine Acad	United States Merchant Marine Academy	Kings Point, NY	B
US Mil Acad	United States Military Academy	West Point, NY	B
US Naval Acad	U. S. Naval Academy	Annapolis, MD	B
UT Valley ST C	Utah Valley State College	Orem, UT	B
VA Union U	Virginia Union University	Richmond, VA	D
VA Wesleyan C	Virginia Wesleyan College	Norfolk, VA	B
VA Western CC	Virginia Western Community College	Roanoke, VA	A
Valdosta ST U	Valdosta State University	Valdosta, GA	D
Valparaiso U	Valparaiso University Christopher Center for Library & I	Valparaiso, IN	M
Vanderbilt U	Vanderbilt University	Nashville, TN	D
Vassar C	Vassar College	Poughkeepsie, NY	B
VCU	Virginia Commonwealth University	Richmond, VA	D
Victoria U	Victoria University	Toronto, ON	D
Villa Julie C	Villa Julie College	Stevenson, MD	M
Villanova U	Villanova University	Villanova, PA	D
Virginia Polytechnic Institute & Stat	Virginia Polytechnic Institute & State University	Blacksburg, VA	D
Virginia ST U	Virginia State University	Petersburg, VA	D
VMI	Virginia Military Institute Preston Library	Lexington, VA	B
VT Law School	Vermont Law School	South Royalton, VT	D
W.Carey College	William Carey College	Hattiesburg, MS	M
W.Mitchell C Law	William Mitchell College of Law	Saint Paul, MN	M
W.Rainey Harper C	William Rainey Harper College	Palatine, IL	A
Wabash C	Wabash College	Crawfordsville, IN	B
Wake Forest U	Wake Forest University	Winston-Salem, NC	D
Walla Walla C	Walla Walla College	College Place, WA	M
Walsh C Acct Bus Admin	Walsh College of Accountancy and Business Administration	Troy, MI	M
Warner Sthrn C	Warner Southern College	Lake Wales, FL	B
Warren Wilson C	Warren Wilson College	Asheville, NC	B
Wartburg Theo Sem	Wartburg Theological Seminary	Dubuque, IA	M
Washburn U Topeka	Washburn University of Topeka	Topeka, KS	M

A=Associates   B=Bachelors   M=Masters   D=Doctorate

KEY TO PARTICIPATING INSTITUTIONS

Institution	Full Name of Institution	Location	Carnegie Class
Washington C	Washington College	Chestertown, MD	M
Washington State U	Washington State University	Pullman, WA	D
Washington Theo Union	Washington Theological Union	Washington, DC	M
Washington U	Washington University in St. Louis	Saint Louis, MO	D
Waycross C	Waycross College	Waycross, GA	A
Wayland Baptist U	Wayland Baptist University	Plainview, TX	M
Wayne ST C	Wayne State College, Conn Library	Wayne, NE	M
Wayne State U	Wayne State University	Detroit, MI	D
Weatherford C	Weatherford College	Weatherford, TX	A
Webber Intl U	Webber International University	Babson Park, FL	M
Wells C	Wells College	Aurora, NY	B
Wentworth Mil Acad & Jr	Wentworth Military Academy and Junior College	Lexington, MO	A
Wesley C	Wesley College	Dover, DE	M
Wesley Theo Sem	Wesley Theological Seminary	Washington, DC	D
West Chester U PA	West Chester University of Pennsylvania	West Chester, PA	M
West TX A & M U	West Texas A&M University	Canyon, TX	M
West VA U	West Virginia University	Morgantown, WV	D
West VA Wesleyan C	West Virginia Wesleyan College	Buckhannon, WV	M
West Valley C	West Valley College	Saratoga, CA	A
Western IA Tech CC	Western Iowa Tech Community College	Sioux City, IA	A
Western MD C	McDaniel College	Westminster, MD	M
Western MI U	Western Michigan University	Kalamazoo, MI	D
Western OR U	Western Oregon University - Wayne and Lynn Hamersly Libr	Monmouth, OR	M
Western Sem	Western Seminary	Portland, OR	M
Western ST C	Western State College	Gunnison, CO	B
Western WA U	Western Washington University	Bellingham, WA	M
Westfield ST C	Westfield State College	Westfield, MA	M
Westminster C	Westminster College	Salt Lake City, UT	M
Westmnster Theo Sem-PA	Westminster Theological Seminary	Philadelphia, PA	D
Westmont C	Westmont College	Santa Barbara, CA	B
Wharton Co Jr C	Wharton County Junior College	Wharton, TX	A
Wheaton C	Wheaton College	Wheaton, IL	D
Wheeling Jesuit U	Wheeling Jesuit University	Wheeling, WV	M
Whitman C	Whitman College	Walla Walla, WA	B
Whitworth C	Whitworth College	Spokane, WA	M
Wichita State U	Wichita State University	Wichita, KS	D
Widener U	Widener University	Chester, PA	D
Wiley C	Wiley College	Marshall, TX	B
Wilfrid Laurier U	Wilfrid Laurier University Library	Waterloo, ON	D
Wilkes C C	Wilkes Community College	Wilkesboro, NC	A
Wilkes U	Willamette University	Salem, OR	M

A=Associates   B=Bachelors   M=Masters   D=Doctorate

278

KEY TO PARTICIPATING INSTITUTIONS

Institution	Full Name of Institution	Location	Carnegie Class
William Woods U	William Woods University	Fulton, MO	M
Williams C	Williams College	Williamstown, MA	M
Winston-Salem ST U	Winston-Salem State University	Winston-Salem, NC	B
Wofford C	Wofford College	Spartanburg, SC	B
Worchester PTech Inst	Worcester Polytechnic Institute	Worcester, MA	D
Wright Institute	The Wright Institute	Berkeley, CA	D
Wright ST U-Main	Wright State University Main Campus	Dayton, OH	D
Wstrn IL U	Western Illinois University	Macomb, IL	M
Wstrn Piedmont CC	Western Piedmont Community College	Morganton, NC	A
Wstrn Theo Sem	Western Theological Seminary	Holland, MI	M
Xavier U	Xavier University	Cincinnati, OH	D
Xavier U LA	Xavier University of Louisiana	New Orleans, LA	M
Yakima Valley CC	Yakima Valley Community College	Yakima, WA	A
Yale U	Yale University	New Haven, CT	D
Yeshiva U	Yeshiva University	New York, NY	D
York C	York College	York, NE	B
Young Harris C	Young Harris College	Young Harris, GA	A
Yuba C	Yuba Community College District	Marysville, CA	A

A=Associates   B=Bachelors   M=Masters   D=Doctorate

ACRL STATISTICS QUESTIONNAIRE, 2003-04

Please do not leave any lines blank. If an exact figure is unavailable, use "-1" (that is, "U/A"). If the appropriate answer is zero or none, use "0." For non-university libraries, if a question is not applicable in your library, use "-2" (that is, "N/A"). University libraries should not use –2. Definitions of statistical categories can be found in NISO Z39.7-200X, *Draft Information Services and Use: Metrics & statistics for libraries and information providers--Data Dictionary* <http://www.niso.org/emetrics/current/index.html >. ARL has gradually modified the interpretation of the standard definitions to accommodate electronic resources based on conventions described in the *ARL Statistics Q&A*. These conventions have been established through discussions within the ARL Statistics and Measurement Committee and with the ARL Survey Coordinators who fill in these surveys on an annual basis.

Reporting Institution _____

Date Returned to ARL _____

Report Prepared by (name) _____

Title _____

Email address _____ Phone number _____

Contact person (if different) _____

Title _____

Email address_____ Phone number _____

VOLUMES
(See instructions, Q1-4.)
1a. Volumes held June 30, 2003.
(Exclude microforms, uncataloged govt. docs., maps, a/v material.
Record figure reported last year or footnote adjusted figure on p. 4.)   _____

2. Volumes added during year -- Gross. *(See instructions, Q2.*
Exclude microforms, uncataloged govt. docs., maps, a/v material.)   _____

2a. Volumes withdrawn during year.
(Exclude microforms, uncataloged govt. docs., maps, a/v material.)   _____

3. Volumes added during year -- Net. *(Subtract line 2a from line 2.)*   _____

1. Volumes held June 30, 2004. *(Add line 1a to line 3.)*   _____

4. Number of monographic volumes purchased. *(See instruction Q4.*
Volumes for which expenditures are reported on line 16. Footnote if titles.)   _____

OTHER COLLECTIONS
Serials: *(See instruction Q5-7.)*
5. Number of current serials, including periodicals, purchased.   _____

6. Number of current serials, including periodicals, received but not purchased.   _____
(Exchanges, gifts, deposits, etc. See instruction Q6.)

7. Total number of current serials received. *(Add line 5 to line 6.)* _____

Other Library Materials: *(Record total number of pieces held June 30, 2004.)*

8. Microform units. *(See instruction Q8.)* _____

9. Government documents not counted elsewhere. *(See instruction Q9.)* _____

10. Computer files. *(See instruction Q10.)* _____

11. Manuscripts and archives. (linear ft.) *(See instruction Q11.)* _____

Audiovisual materials:

12. Cartographic. *(See instruction Q12.)* _____

13. Graphic. *(See instruction Q13.)* _____

14. Audio. *(See instruction Q14.)* _____

15. Film and Video. *(See instruction Q15.)* _____

EXPENDITURES *(See instruction Q16-27.)*
Are the below figures reported in Canadian dollars? _____Yes _____No

Library Materials:
16. Monographs. *(Expenditures for volumes reported on line 4. See instruction Q16.)* _____

17. Current serials including periodicals. *(See instruction Q17.)* _____

18. Other library materials *(e.g., microforms, a/v, etc. See instruction Q18.)* _____

19. Miscellaneous.
(All materials fund expenditures not included above. See instruction Q19.) _____

20. Total library materials *(Add lines 16, 17, 18, 19.)* _____

21. **Contract binding:**
(See instruction Q21; also report figure on 2003-04 ARL Preservation Survey) _____

Salaries and Wages: *(See instruction Q22-25.)*
22. Professional staff. _____

23. Support staff. _____

24. Student assistants. *(See instruction Q24-25.)* _____

25. Total salaries and wages. *(Add lines 22, 23, 24.)* _____

26. **Other operating expenditures:** *(See instruction Q26.)* _____

27. **Total library expenditures:** *(Add lines 20, 21, 25, 26.)* _____

Electronic Materials Expenditures: *(See instructions, Q28-Q32)*
28. Computer files *(One-time/monographic purchases. See instructions, Q28.)*   _____

29. Electronic serials. *(See instructions, Q29.)*   _____

30. Bibliograhpic Utilities, Networks, and Consortia. *(See instructions, Q30.)*   _____

30a. From internal library sources.   _____

30b. From external sources.   _____

31. Computer hardware and software. *(See instructions, Q31.)*   _____

32. Document Delivery/Interlibrary Loan. *(See instructions, Q32.)*   _____

PERSONNEL AND PUBLIC SERVICES

Personnel: *(See instructions, Q33-36. Round figures to nearest whole number.)*
33. Professional staff, FTE. *(See instruction Q33.)*   _____

34. Support staff, FTE.   _____

35. Student assistants, FTE. *(See instruction Q35.)*   _____

36. Total FTE staff. *(Add lines 33, 34, 35.)*   _____

Staffed Service Points and Hours:
37. Number of staffed library service points. *(See instructions, Q37.)*   _____

38. Number of weekly public service hours. *(See instructions, Q38.)*   _____

Instruction: *(See instructions, Q39-40.)*
39. Number of library presentations to groups *(See instructions, Q39.)*   _____

39a. Figure based on sampling? _____Yes _____No

40. Number of total participants in group presentations reported on line 39.   _____
(See instructions, Q40.)

40a. Figure based on sampling? _____Yes _____No

Reference: *(See instructions, Q41.)*
41. Number of reference transactions   _____

41a. Figure based on sampling? _____Yes _____No

Circulation: *(See instructions, Q42-43.)*
42. Number of initial circulations (excluding reserves).   _____

43. Total circulations (initial and renewals, excluding reserves).   _____

Interlibrary Loans: *(See instructions, Q44-45.)*
44. Total number of filled requests for materials **provided** to other libraries.   _____

45. Total number of filled requests for materials **received** from
other libraries or providers.   _____

LOCAL CHARACTERISTICS
Ph.D. Degrees and Faculty:
46. Number of Ph.D.s awarded in FY2003-04. *(See instructions, Q46.)*   _____

47. Number of fields in which Ph.D.s can be awarded. *(See instructions, Q47.)*   _____

48. Number of full-time instructional faculty in FY2003-04. *(See instructions, Q48.)* _____

Enrollment -- Fall 2003 (totals): *(See instructions, Q49-52;*
line numbers refer to IPEDS survey form.)
49. Full-time students, undergraduate and graduate.   _____
(Add line 8, columns 15 & 16, and line 14, columns 15 & 16.)

50. Part-time students, undergraduate and graduate.   _____
(Add line 22, columns 15 & 16, and line 28, columns 15 & 16.)

51. Full-time graduate students. *(Line 14, columns 15 & 16.)*   _____

52. Part-time graduate students. *(Line 28, columns 15 & 16.)*   _____

Attributes:
53. Basis of volume count is: _____ Physical. _____ Bibliographic. *(See instructions, Q53.)*

54. Government documents are included in count of Current Serials. _____ Yes. _____ No.

55. Fringe benefits are included in expenditures for salaries and wages. _____ Yes. _____ No.

56. Law Library statistics are included. _____ Yes. _____ No. _____ We do not have a Law Library.

57. Medical Library statistics are included. _____ Yes. _____ No. _____ We do not have a Medical
Library.

58. Other main campus libraries included: [list in "Footnotes"]

59. Branch Campus Libraries. *(See paragraph six of the General Instructions.)*
Figures include branch CAMPUS libraries:
_____ Yes. _____ No. _____ We have only one campus.
If branch campus libraries are included, please specify which campuses in "Footnotes."
If branch campus libraries are not included, please specify which campuses in "Footnotes."

FOOTNOTES *(See instructions, Q60.)*
60. A copy of your library's footnotes as they appeared in the published *ARL Statistics 2002-03* appears on
your library's survey form on the World Wide Web at <http://lrc.lis.uiuc.edu/ARL/survey.cgi/>. Please
make revisions, additions, and deletions as appropriate. If any footnotes published last year are unchanged,
please leave them unchanged to indicate that they are still valid. Please note that no footnotes will be shown
for those questions that previously appeared in the *ARL Supplementary Statistics 2002-03*; those will need
to be re-typed from scratch.

ACRL STATISTICS QUESTIONNAIRE, 2003-04
INSTRUCTIONS FOR COMPLETING THE QUESTIONNAIRE
General Instructions

Definitions of statistical categories can be found in NISO Z39.7-200X, *Draft Information Services and Use: Metrics &statistics for libraries and information providers--Data Dictionary* <http://www.niso.org/emetrics/current/index.html >. ARL has gradually modified the interpretation of the standard definitions to accommodate electronic resources based on conventions described in the *ARL Statistics Q&A*. These conventions have been established through discussions within the ARL Statistics and Measurement Committee and with the ARL Survey Coordinators who fill in these surveys on an annual basis. For example, for definitions relating to electronic serials, see a discussion document prepared by Julia Blixrud <http://www.arl.org/stats/counting.html>.

The questionnaire assumes a fiscal year ending **June 30, 2004**. If your fiscal year is different, please provide a footnote in the "Footnotes" section of the questionnaire.

Please do not use decimals. All figures should be rounded to the nearest whole number.

Please do not leave any lines blank. If an exact figure is unavailable, use **-1**, i.e., "U/A." If the appropriate answer is zero or none, use **0**. For non-university libraries, if a question is not applicable to your library, use **-2**, i.e., "N/A." (**Academic libraries should *never* use –2 or N/A.**)

In a university that includes both main and branch campuses, an effort should be made to report figures for the main campus only. (The U.S. National Center for Education Statistics, Integrated Postsecondary Education Data System (IPEDS) defines a **branch institution** as "a campus or site of an educational institution that is not temporary, is located in a community beyond a reasonable commuting distance from its parent institution, and offers organized programs of study, not just courses.") If figures for libraries located at branch campuses are reported, please provide an explanation in the "Footnotes" section of the questionnaire.

A **branch library** is defined as an auxiliary library service outlet with quarters separate from the central library of an institution, which has a basic collection of books and other materials, a regular staffing level, and an established schedule. A branch library is administered either by the central library or (as in the case of some law and medical libraries) through the administrative structure of other units within the university. Departmental study/reading rooms are not included.

Specific Instructions
Questions 1-4. Volumes in Library. Use the ANSI/NISO Z39.7-1995 definition for **volume** as follows:

> *a single physical unit of any printed, typewritten, handwritten, mimeographed, or processed work, distinguished from other units by a separate binding, encasement, portfolio, or other clear distinction, which has been cataloged, classified, and made ready for use, and which is typically the unit used to charge circulation transactions.*

Include duplicates and bound volumes of periodicals. For purposes of this questionnaire, unclassified bound serials arranged in alphabetical order are considered classified. Exclude microforms, maps, nonprint materials, and uncataloged items. If any of these items cannot be excluded, please provide an explanatory footnote in the "Footnotes" section of the questionnaire.

Include government document volumes that are accessible through the library's catalogs regardless of whether they are separately shelved. "Classified" includes documents arranged by Superintendent of Documents, CODOC, or similar numbers. "Cataloged" includes documents for which records are provided by the library or downloaded from other sources into the library's card or online catalogs. Documents should, to the extent possible, be counted as they would if they were in bound volumes (e.g., 12 issues of an annual serial would be one or two volumes). Title and piece counts should not be considered the same as volume counts. If a volume count has not been kept, it may be estimated through sampling a representative group of title records and determining the corresponding number of volumes, then extrapolating to the rest of the collection. As an alternative, an estimate may be made using the following formulae:

52 documents pieces per foot

10 "traditional" volumes per foot

5.2 documents pieces per volume

If either formulas or sampling are used for deriving your count, please indicate in a footnote.

Question 2. Volumes Added. Include only volumes cataloged, classified, and made ready for use. Include government documents if they have been included in the count of volumes on line 1a. Do not include as part of Volumes Added Gross any government documents or other collections (such as large gift collections) that were added to the collection as the result of a one time download or addition to the OPAC. Include these items in Volumes Held of the previous year (Line 1a) and provide a footnote explaining the revision of Line 1a.

Question 4. Monographic Volumes Purchased. Report number of volumes purchased. Include all volumes for which an expenditure was made during 2003-04, including volumes paid for in advance but not received during the fiscal year.

Include monographs in series and continuations. If only number of titles purchased can be reported, please report the data and provide an explanatory footnote in the "Footnotes" section of the questionnaire. **Note:** This question is concerned with volumes purchased rather than volumes received or cataloged. Question 16 requests the expenditure for the volumes counted here.

Questions 5-7. Serials. Report the total number of subscriptions, not titles. Include duplicate subscriptions and, to the extent possible, all government document serials even if housed in a separate documents collection. Verify the inclusion or exclusion of document serials in Question 54 of the questionnaire. Exclude unnumbered monographic and publishers' series.

Electronic serials acquired as part of an aggregated package (e.g., Project MUSE, Academic IDEAL) should be counted by title. A **serial** is

a publication in any medium issued in successive parts bearing numerical or chronological designations and intended to be continued indefinitely. This definition includes periodicals, newspapers, and annuals (reports, yearbooks, etc.); the journals, memoirs, proceedings, transactions, etc. of societies; and numbered monographic series.

Question 6. Serials: Not Purchased. If separate counts of nonpurchased and purchased serials are not available, report only the total number of current serials received on line 7, and report **-1**, i.e., "U/A," for lines 5 and 6.

Question 8. Microforms. Report the total number of physical units: reels of microfilm, microcards, and microprint and microfiche sheets. Include all government documents in microform; provide a footnote in the "Footnotes" section of the questionnaire if documents are excluded.

Question 9. Government documents. Report the total number of physical units (pieces) of government documents in paper format that have not been counted elsewhere. Include local, state, national, and international documents; include documents purchased from a commercial source if shelved with separate documents collections and not counted above.

Include serials and monographs. To estimate pieces from a measurement of linear feet, use the formula

1 foot = 52 pieces

and indicate in a footnote that the count is based on this estimate. Exclude microforms and nonprint formats such as maps or CD-ROMs. Adjust line 1a, i.e., last year's Volumes Held, and provide a footnote if you are adding records to the OPAC for government documents previously held but not counted as part of Volumes Held (line 1a).

Question 10. Computer files. Include the number of pieces of computer-readable disks, tapes, CD-ROMs, and similar machine-readable files comprising data or programs that are **locally held as part of the library's collections** available to library clients. Examples are U.S. Census data tapes, sample research software, locally-mounted databases, and reference tools on CD-ROM, tape or disk. Exclude bibliographic records used to manage the collection (i.e., the library's own catalog in machine-readable form), library system software, and microcomputer software used only by the library staff.

Question 11. Manuscripts and archives. Include both manuscripts and archives measured in linear feet.

Question 12. Cartographic materials. Include the numbers of pieces of two- and three-dimensional maps and globes. Include satellite and aerial photographs and images.

Question 13. Graphic materials. Include the number of pieces of prints, pictures, photographs, postcards, slides, transparencies, film strips, and the like.

Question 14. Audio materials. Include the number of pieces of audiocassettes, phonodiscs, audio compact discs, reel-to-reel tapes, and other sound recordings.

Question 15. Film and video materials. Include the number of pieces of motion pictures, videocassettes, video laser discs, and similar visual materials.

Questions 16-27. Expenditures. Report all expenditures of funds that come to the library from the regular institutional budget, and from sources such as research grants, special projects, gifts and endowments, and fees for service. (For question 25, include non-library funds; see instruction Q24-25.) Do not report encumbrances of funds that have not yet been expended. **Canadian libraries should report expenditures in Canadian dollars.** (To determine figures in U.S. dollars, divide Canadian dollar amounts by 1.34328, the average monthly noon exchange rate published in the Bank of Canada *Review* for the period July 2003-June 2004.) **Please round figures to the nearest dollar.**

Question 16. Monographs. Report expenditures for volumes counted on line 4.

Question 17. Current Serials. Report expenditures for serials counted on line 5. Exclude unnumbered monographic and publishers' series, and encumbrances.

Question 18. Other library materials. Include expenditures for all materials not reported in Questions 16 and 17, e.g., backfiles of serials, charts and maps, audiovisual materials, manuscripts, etc. If expenditures for these materials are included in lines 16 and/or 17 and cannot be disaggregated, please report **-1**, i.e., "U/A," and provide a footnote in the "Footnotes" section of the questionnaire. Do not include encumbrances.

Question 19. Miscellaneous expenditures. Include any other **materials funds expenditures** not included in questions 16-18, e.g., expenditures for bibliographic utilities, literature searching, security devices, memberships for the purposes of publications, etc. Please list categories, with amounts, in a footnote in the "Footnotes" section of the questionnaire. **Note:** If your library does not use materials funds for non-materials expenditures—i.e., such expenditures are included in "Other Operating Expenditures"—**report 0, not -1, i.e., "U/A,"** on line 19.

Question 21. Contract Binding. Include only contract expenditures for binding done outside the library. If all binding is done in-house, state this fact and give in-house expenditures in a footnote in the "Footnotes" section of the questionnaire; do not include personnel expenditures. (This figure should also be reported in the 2003-04 ARL Preservation Survey, question 7b.)

Questions 22-25. Salaries and wages. Exclude fringe benefits. If professional and support staff salaries cannot be separated, enter **-1**, i.e., "U/A," on lines 22 and 23 and enter total staff on line 25.

Question 24. Salaries and wages: Student Assistants. Report 100% of student wages regardless of budgetary source of funds. Include federal and local funds for work study students.

Question 26. Other operating expenditures. Exclude expenditures for buildings, maintenance, and fringe benefits.

Questions 28-32. Electronic materials expenditures. These items are intended to indicate what portion of your institution's total library expenditures are dedicated to electronic resources and services. Please use the Footnotes to indicate any electronic materials expenditures you believe not to be covered by these questions. **All expenditures recorded in these questions should have been included in Question 27, total library expenditures.**

Question 28. Computer files. Report expenditures that are not current serials (i.e. are non-subscription, one-time, or monographic in nature) for software and machine-readable materials considered part of the collections. Examples include periodical backfiles, literature collections, one-time costs for JSTOR membership, etc. Expenditures reported here may be derived from any of the following categories: Monographs (Q16), Other Library Materials (Q18), Miscellaneous (Q19), or Other Operating Expenditures (Q26).

Question 29. Electronic Serials. Report subscription expenditures (or those which are expected to be ongoing commitments) for serial publications whose primary format is electronic and for online searches of remote databases such as OCLC FirstSearch, DIALOG, Lexis-Nexis, etc. Examples include paid subscriptions for electronic journals and indexes/abstracts available via the Internet, CD-ROM serials, and annual access fees for resources purchased on a "one-time" basis, such as literature collections, JSTOR membership, etc. Not all items whose expenditures are counted here will be included in Total Current Serials (Questions 5-7) or Current Serial Expenditures (Question 17).

Q30a-b. Bibliographic Utilities, Networks, and Consortia. Because it is increasingly common for ARL Libraries to enter into consortial arrangements to purchase access to electronic resources, both "Library" and "External" expenditure blanks and instructions are provided. Please use the Footnotes to describe expenditures that you believe are not covered by the question, or situations that do not seem to fit the instructions.

Q30a. From internal library sources. Report expenditures paid by the Library for services provided by national, regional, and local bibliographic utilities, networks, and consortia, such as OCLC and RLG, unless for user database access and subscriptions, which should be reported in Questions 1 or 2. Include only expenditures that are part of Other Operating Expenditures (Q26).

Q30b. From external sources. If your library receives access to computer files, electronic serials or search services through one or more centrally-funded system or consortial arrangements for which it does not pay fully and/or directly (for example, funding is provided by the state on behalf of all members), enter the amount paid by external bodies on its behalf. If the specific dollar amount is not known, but the total student FTE for the consortium and amount spent for the academic members are known, divide the overall amount spent by your institution's share of the total student FTE.

Q31. Computer hardware and software. Report expenditures from the library budget for computer hardware and software used to support library operations, whether purchased or leased, mainframe or microcomputer, and whether for staff or public use. Include expenditures for: maintenance; equipment used to run information service products when those expenditures can be separated from the price of the product; telecommunications infrastructure costs, such as wiring, hubs, routers, etc. Include only expenditures that are part of Other Operating Expenditures (Q26).

Q32. Document Delivery/Interlibrary Loan. Report expenditures for document delivery and interlibrary loan services (both borrowing and lending). Include fees paid for photocopies, costs of telefacsimile transmission, royalties and access fees paid to provide document delivery or interlibrary loan. Include fees paid to bibliographic utilities if the portion paid for interlibrary loan can be separately counted. Include only expenditures that are part of Miscellaneous Materials Expenditures (Q19) or Other Operating Expenditures (Q26), and only for those ILL/DD programs with data recorded in Questions 44-45.

Questions 33-36. Personnel. Report the number of staff in filled positions, or positions that are only temporarily vacant. ARL defines temporarily vacant positions as positions that were vacated during the fiscal year for which ARL data were submitted, for which there is a firm intent to refill, and for which there are expenditures for salaries reported on lines 22-25.

Include cost recovery positions and staff hired for special projects and grants, but provide an explanatory footnote indicating the number of such staff. If such staff cannot be included, provide a footnote in the "Footnotes" section of the questionnaire. To compute full-time equivalents of part-time employees and student assistants, take the total number of hours per week (or year) worked by part-time employees in each category and divide it by the number of hours considered by the reporting library to be a full-time work week (or year). **Round figures to the nearest whole numbers.**

Question 33. Professional Staff. Since the criteria for determining professional status vary among libraries, there is no attempt to define the term "professional." Each library should report those staff members it considers professional, including, when appropriate, staff who are not librarians in the strict sense of the term, for example computer experts, systems analysts, or budget officers.

Question 35. Student Assistants. Report the total FTE (see instruction Q33-36) of student assistants employed on an hourly basis whose wages are paid from funds under library control or from a budget other than the library's, including federal work-study programs. Exclude maintenance and custodial staff.

Question 37. Number of staffed library service points. Count the number of staffed public service points in the main library and in all branch libraries reported in this inventory, including reference desks, information desks, circulation, current periodicals, reserve rooms, reprographic services (if staffed as a public facility), etc. Report the number of designated locations, not the number of staff.

Question 38. Number of weekly public service hours. Report an unduplicated count of the total public service hours per typical full-service week (i.e., no holidays or other special accommodations) across both main library and branches using the following method (corresponds to IPEDS): If a library is open from 9:00 a.m. to 5:00 p.m. Monday through Friday, it should report 40 hours per week. If several of its branches are also open during these hours, the figure remains 40 hours per week. Should Branch A also be open one evening from 7:00 p.m. to 9:00 p.m., the total hours during which users can find service somewhere within the system becomes 42 hours per week. If Branch B is open the same hours on the same evening, the count is still 42, but if Branch B is open two hours on another evening, or remains open two hours later, the total is then 44 hours per week. **Exclude 24-hour unstaffed reserve or similar reading rooms.** The maximum total is 168 (i.e., a staffed reading room open 7 days per week, 24 hours per day).

Questions 39-40. Instruction. Sampling based on a typical week may be used to extrapolate TO A FULL YEAR for Questions 39 and 40. Please indicate if responses are based on sampling.

Question 39. Presentations to Groups. Report the total number of sessions during the year of presentations made as part of formal bibliographic instruction programs and through other planned class presentations, orientation sessions, and tours. If the library sponsors multi-session or credit courses that meet several times over the course of a semester, each session should be counted. Presentations to groups may be for either bibliographic instruction, cultural, recreational, or educational purposes. Presentations both on and off the premises should be included as long as they are sponsored by the library. Do not include meetings sponsored by other groups using library meeting rooms. Please indicate if the figure is based on sampling.

Question 40. Participants in Group Presentations. Report the total number of participants in the presentations reported on line 39. For multi-session classes with a constant enrollment, count each person only once. Personal, one-to-one instruction in the use of sources should be counted as reference transactions on line 41. Please indicate if the figure is based on sampling. Use the "Footnotes" section to describe any special situations.

Question 41. Reference Transactions. Report the total number of reference transactions. A **reference transaction** is

> *an information contact that involves the knowledge, use, recommendations, interpretation, or instruction in the use of one or more information sources by a member of the library staff. The term includes information and referral service. Information sources include (a) printed and nonprinted material; (b) machine-readable databases (including computer-assisted instruction); (c) the library's own catalogs and other holdings records; (d) other libraries and institutions through communication or referral; and (e) persons both inside and outside the library. When a staff member uses information gained from previous use of information sources to answer a question, the transaction is reported as a reference transaction even if the source is not consulted again.*

If a contact includes both reference and directional services, it should be reported as one reference transaction. Duration should not be an element in determining whether a transaction is a reference transaction. Sampling based on a typical week may be used to extrapolate TO A FULL YEAR for Question 41. Please indicate if the figure is based on sampling. EXCLUDE SIMPLE DIRECTIONAL QUESTIONS. A directional transaction is an information contact that facilitates the logistical use of the library and that does not involve the knowledge, use, recommendations, interpretation, or instruction in the use of any information sources other than those that describe the library, such as schedules, floor plans, and handbooks.

Questions 42-43. Circulation. For Question 42, count the number of initial circulations during the fiscal year from the general collection for use usually (although not always) outside the library. Do not count renewals. Include circulations to and from remote storage facilities for library users (i.e., do not include transactions reflecting transfers or stages of technical processing). Count the total number of items lent, not the number of borrowers. For Question 43, report total circulation for the fiscal year including initial transactions reported on line 42 and renewal transactions. Exclude reserve circulations; these are no longer reported.

Questions 44-45. Interlibrary Loans. Report the number of requests for material (both returnables and non-returnables) provided to other libraries on line 44 and the number of filled requests for material received from libraries or other providers on line 45. On both lines, include originals, photocopies, and materials sent by telefacsimile or other forms of electronic transmission. Include patron-initiated transactions. Do not include transactions between libraries covered by this questionnaire.

Questions 46. Ph.D. Degrees. Report the number awarded during the 2003-04 fiscal year. Please note that only the number of Ph.D. degrees are to be counted. Statistics on all other advanced degrees (e.g., D.Ed., D.P.A., M.D., J.D.) should not be reported in this survey. If you are unable to provide a figure for Ph.D.s only, please add a footnote in the "Footnotes" section of the questionnaire.

Question 47. Ph.D. Fields. For the purposes of this report, Ph.D. fields are defined as the specific discipline specialties enumerated in the U.S. Department of Education's Integrated Postsecondary Education Data System (IPEDS) "Completions" Survey. Although the IPEDS form requests figures for all doctoral degrees, only fields in which Ph.D.s are awarded should be reported on the ARL questionnaire. Any exceptions should be footnoted in the "Footnotes" section of the questionnaire.

Question 48. Instructional Faculty. Instructional faculty are defined by the U.S. Dept. of Education as

> *members of the instruction/research staff who are employed full-time as defined by the institution, including faculty with released time for research and faculty on sabbatical leave.*

Full-time counts generally exclude faculty who are employed to teach fewer than two semesters, three quarters, two trimesters, or two four-month sessions; replacements for faculty on sabbatical leave or leave without pay; faculty for preclinical and clinical medicine; faculty who are donating their services; faculty who are members of military organizations and paid on a different pay scale from civilian employees; academic officers, whose primary duties are administrative; and graduate students who assist in the instruction of courses. Please be sure the number reported, and the basis for counting, are consistent with those for 2002-03 (unless in previous years faculty were counted who should have been excluded according to the above definition). Please footnote any discrepancies.

Questions 49-52. Enrollment. U.S. libraries should use the Fall 2003 enrollment figures reported to the Department of Education on the form entitled "Integrated Postsecondary Education Data System, Fall Enrollment 2003." The line and column numbers on the IPEDS form for each category are noted on the questionnaire. Please check these figures against the enrollment figures reported to ARL last year to ensure consistency and accuracy. **Note:** In the past, the number of part-time students reported was FTE; the number now reported to IPEDS is a head count of part-time students. Canadian libraries should note that the category "graduate students" as reported here includes all post-baccalaureate students.

Question 53: Basis of Volume Count. A physical count is a piece count; a bibliographic count is a catalog record count.

Question 60. Footnotes. Explanatory footnotes will be included with the published statistics. Reporting libraries are urged to record in the footnote section any information that would clarify the figures submitted, e.g., the inclusion of branch campus libraries (see paragraph six of the "General Instructions" for definition of branch campus libraries). For the first time, the footnotes from the previous year will be presented in the web form. Please update, delete, or leave them unchanged if they remain valid. Note that the number in parentheses refers to the appropriate column on the Library Data Tables in the published *ARL Statistics*, as well as to the corresponding line number on the questionnaire. Please make an effort to word your footnotes in a manner consistent with notes appearing in the published report, so that the ARL Office can interpret your footnotes correctly.

ACRL SUPPLEMENTARY STATISTICS 2003-04

Definitions of the statistical categories used in this questionnaire can be found in *Information Services and Use: Metrics & statistics for libraries and information providers--Data Dictionary*, NISO Z39.7- 200X Draft (http://www.niso.org/emetrics/current/index.html). ARL has gradually modified the interpretation of the standard definitions to accommodate electronic resources based on conventions, which will be described in an E-Metrics Q&A. These conventions have been established through discussions within the ARL Statistics and Measurement Committee and with the ARL Survey Coordinators who fill in those surveys on an annual basis.

Please read all instructions carefully before you answer the questionnaire. Make sure your responses are as complete and accurate as possible. Give estimates when you must, but please do not make wild guesses. Use the FOOTNOTES section to expand upon or clarify your responses.

All questions assume a *fiscal year ending June 30, 2004*. If your library's fiscal year is different, please use the FOOTNOTES section to explain.

Please complete all entries. If your library does not perform a given function or had no activity for this function or if the appropriate answer is zero or none, use **0**. If an exact figure is unavailable, use **–1**, i.e., "U/A." **Please do not leave any lines blank**.

Please do not use decimals. All figures should be rounded to the nearest whole number. In a university that includes both main and branch campuses, an effort should be made to report figures for the main campus only. (The U.S. National Center for Education Statistics, Integrated Postsecondary Education Data System (IPEDS) defines a **branch institution** as "a campus or site of an educational institution that is not temporary, is located in a community beyond a reasonable commuting distance from its parent institution, and offers organized programs of study, not just courses.") If figures for libraries located at branch campuses are reported, please provide an explanation in the FOOTNOTES section of the questionnaire.

A **branch library** is defined as an auxiliary library service outlet with quarters separate from the central library of an institution, which has a basic collection of books and other materials, a regular staffing level, and an established schedule. A branch library is administered either by the central library or (as in the case of some law and medical libraries) through administrative structure of other units within the university. Departmental study/reading rooms are not included. If figures for branch libraries are reported, please provide an explanation in the FOOTNOTES section of the questionnaire.

Number of Networked Electronic Resources
1. Number of electronic journals purchased. _____

> Number of electronic journal subscriptions that the library provides to users and for which the library pays some fee for access either through an individual institutional licensing contract with the provider of journals or through other arrangements (e.g., library-funded consortia, centrally-funded consortia or through state or national purchasing plans).
> Include electronic journals offered by established scholarly journal publishing houses (e.g., Elsevier's ScienceDirect); scholarly societies (e.g., American Chemical Society journals and American Institute of Physics Online); services that aggregate journal content (e.g., Expanded Academic ASAP or Lexis/Nexis); and, from those publishers using an external delivery platform (BioOne, EbscoOnline, Highwire, and OCLC ECO). The number of electronic journals purchased reported here could include journals for which you may have reported expenditures in the *ARL Statistics*.

2. Number of electronic "full-text" journals purchased.
_____

This is a subset of #1, *Number of electronic journals purchased.* "Full-text" journals, such as those from Elsevier's Science Direct or Kluwer Online Journals, should contain the journals' complete contents. Include electronic full-text journals from the sources described above. Exclude services that aggregate or provide only partial coverage of journal content (e.g., Expanded Academic ASAP or Lexis/Nexis).

3. Number of electronic journals not purchased.
_____

Number of unique electronic journals for which the library pays no fee and for which the library has taken responsibility for providing access either through cataloging in its OPAC or other forms of local organization (web site, databases, etc.). Include journals that are free through centrally-funded consortia. Include government documents.

4. Number of electronic reference sources.
_____

This includes licensed citation indexes and abstracts; full-text reference sources (e.g. encyclopedias, almanacs, biographical and statistical sources, and other quick fact-finding sources); full-text journal and periodical article collection services (e.g., EBSCOhost, ProQuest, Academic Universe, and INFOTRAC OneFile); dissertation and conference proceedings databases; and, those databases that institutions mount locally. Include databases that contain journals reported in #1. Please describe in the Footnotes, if ebooks are included in this count.

5. Number of electronic books.
_____

Number of electronic full-text monographs that the library offers to its users and for which the library pays some fee for access either through an individual institutional licensing contract with the provider of journals or through other arrangements (e.g., library-funded consortia, centrally-funded consortia or through state or national purchasing plans). This includes electronic books purchased through vendors, such as netLibrary and Books24x7, and electronic books that come as part of aggregate services. Include individual volumes of ebook sets that are counted as individual reference sources reported in #4. Exclude locally digitized electronic books, electronic theses and dissertations, locally created digital archival collections, and other special collections. Do not include machine-readable books distributed on CD-ROM, or accompanied by print books.

Expenditures for Networked Electronic Resources

Are the below figures reported in Canadian dollars? _____Yes _____No

6. Expenditures for current electronic journals purchased.
_____

Include membership fees (such as JSTOR) as well as annual access and service fees paid directly or through consortia arrangements. Include initial purchase cost only for items purchased this fiscal year. Expenditures reported here are for journals reported in #1.

7. Expenditures for electronic "full-text" journals.
_____

Include membership fees (such as JSTOR) as well as annual access and service fees paid directly or through consortia arrangements. Include initial purchase cost only for items purchased this fiscal year. Expenditures here are for journals reported in #2.

8. Expenditures for electronic reference sources. _____

Include annual access and service fees paid directly or through consortia arrangements. Include initial purchase cost only for items purchased this fiscal year. Expenditures here are for the reference sources reported in #4.

9. Expenditures for electronic books. _____

Include annual access and service fees paid directly or through consortia arrangements. Include initial purchase cost only for items purchased this fiscal year. Expenditures here are for the electronic books report in #5.

Use of Networked Electronic Resources and Services
10. Number of virtual reference transactions. _____

Virtual reference transactions are conducted via email, a library's website, or other network communications mechanisms designed to support electronic reference. A virtual reference transaction _must_ include a question _either_ received electronically (e.g., via e-mail, WWW form, etc.) _or_ responded to electronically. A transactions that is both received and responded to electronically is counted as _one_ transaction. Exclude phone and fax traffic unless either the question or answer transaction occurs via the manner described above. Include counts accrued from participation in any local and national projects, such as DigiRef and the Library of Congress's CDRS (Collaborative Digital Reference Service). A reference transaction is an information contact, which involves the knowledge, use, recommendations, interpretation, or instruction in the use of one or more information sources by any member of the library staff (e.g., circulation, technical or reference services).

11. Does your library offer federated searching across networked electronic resources?   Yes / No

Networked electronic resources may include any information resource, such as databases, journals, ebooks, reference materials, and non-textual resources that are provided to the library's users through licensing and contractual agreements. Include electronic resources that institutions mount locally.

12. Number of logins (sessions) to networked electronic resources. _____

12a. Number of resources for which you are reporting. _____

A session or login is one cycle of user activities that typically starts when a user connects to an electronic resource and ends with explicit termination of activities (by leaving through logout or exit) or implicit termination (time out due to user inactivity). In a footnote, please include the types of resources reported in 12a.

13. Number of queries (searches) in networked electronic resources. _____

13a. Number of resources for which you are reporting. _____

A search is intended to represent a unique intellectual inquiry. Typically, a search is recorded each time a search request is sent/submitted to the server. In a footnote, please include the types of resources reported in 13a.

14. Number of items requested in networked electronic resources. _____

14a. Number of resources for which you are reporting. _____

Items reported can include citations, abstracts, tables of contents, full-text articles, images and sound files. Requests may include viewing, downloading, emailing, and printing to the extent the activity can be recorded and controlled by the server rather than browser. In a footnote, please include the types of resources reported in 14a.

15. Number of virtual visits.

15a. Number of virtual visits to library's website. _____

15b. Number of virtual visits to library's catalog. _____

15c. Excludes virtual visits from inside the library?   Yes / No

Virtual visits include a user's request of the library web site or catalog from outside the library building excluding the number of pages or gratuitous elements (images, style sheets) viewed. Exclude, if possible, virtual visits from within the library, from robot or spider crawls and from page reloads. A visit is usually determined by a user's IP address, which can be misleading due to Internet Service Providers (ISPs) and Firewalls or Proxy Servers. Thus, this measure is actually an estimate of the visits.

Library Digitization Activities
16. Number and Size of Library Digital Collections.

16a. Number of Collections. _____

16b. Size (in megabytes). _____

16c. Items. _____

Library digital collections can include born digital materials or those created in or converted from different formats (e.g., paper, microfilm, tapes, etc.) by the library and made available to users electronically. This includes locally held digital materials that are not purchased or acquired through other arrangements (e.g., vendor, individual or consortia licensing agreements). Born digital collections can include materials self-archived in an institutional repository. Created or converted digital collections can include electronic theses and dissertations (ETDs); special collections materials; maps; sound recordings; and, films. For each type of collection (e.g., text, image, multimedia), include the size (in megabytes) and, if possible, the number of items (e.g. unique files) in each collection. Exclude back up copies or mirror sites since items should be counted only once. Exclude e-reserves and ETDs provided by ProQuest or other vendors. In the footnote, provide a paragraph describing the general nature of library digital collections and, if possible, provide the URL where collections are listed.

17. Use of Library Digital Collections.

17a. Number of times items accessed. _____

17b. Number of queries conducted. _____

Number of times library digital collection items (unique files) were accessed and the number of searches (queries) conducted (if there is such a capability) during the reporting period. Please explain in a footnote how library digital collections are accessed, and if possible, list the URLs of those collections.

18. Direct cost of digital collections construction and management.

18a. Direct cost of personnel _____

18b. Direct cost of equipment, software or contracted services. _____

Annual direct costs (personnel, equipment, software, contracted services and similar items) spent to create digital materials (texts, images, and multimedia) or to convert existing materials into digital form for the purpose of making them electronically available to users. Include expenditures related to digitization, OCR, editorial, creation of markup texts, and preparation of metadata for access to digitized materials, data storage, and copyright clearance. Exclude expenditures for information resources purchased or acquired from outside the institution through individual or consortia licensing agreements. In the footnote, please describe any additional funding (university, state, private grants, etc.) provided specifically for the library's digitization activities.

19. Volumes Held Collectively _____

The defining criterion is that the library has devoted financial resources for the purchase of these items and is taking responsibility for their availability through participation in a cooperative that supports shared ownership. The library demonstrates commitment to the shared storage facility by supporting the consortium financially through a legally binding arrangement. Include here volumes originally held and now withdrawn from the local collection because they are held in a "shared" remote storage facility starting with volumes that have been transferred during fiscal year 2003-04. Exclude volumes held collectively because they are held by other organizations such as the Center of Research Libraries (CRL) that are supported by membership dues and determination on whether to maintain membership may vary from year to year.

Footnotes:

Printed in the United States
33043LVS00001B/79-252